Implementing
Oracle Financial Analyzer

Implementing
Oracle Financial
Analyzer

Delivering value-added business processes with
Oracle Analytic Solutions

John Cunningham ■ Fred Dean ■ Guy Stevens

▲▼ Addison-Wesley
an imprint of **Pearson Education**

Harlow, England ■ London ■ New York ■ Reading, Massachusetts ■ San Francisco
Toronto ■ Don Mills, Ontario ■ Sydney ■ Tokyo ■ Singapore ■ Hong Kong ■ Seoul
Taipei ■ Cape Town ■ Madrid ■ Mexico City ■ Amsterdam ■ Munich ■ Paris ■ Milan

PEARSON EDUCATION LIMITED

Head Office:
Edinburgh Gate
Harlow CM20 2JE
Tel: +44 (0)1279 623623
Fax: +44 (0)1279 431059

London Office:
128 Long Acre
London WC2E 9AN
Tel: +44 (0)20 7447 2000
Fax: +44 (0)20 7240 5771
Website: www.aw.com/cseng/

First published in Great Britain in 2001

© Pearson Education Ltd 2001

The rights of John Cunningham, Fred Dean and Guy Stevens to be identified as the Authors of this Work
have been asserted by them in accordance with the Copyright, Designs and Patents Act 1988.

ISBN 0-201-67527-7

British Library Cataloguing in Publication Data
A CIP catalogue record for this book can be obtained from the British Library.

Library of Congress Cataloging in Publication Data
Applied for.

The programs in this book have been included for their instructional value. The publisher does not
offer any warranties or representations in respect of their fitness for a particular purpose,
nor does the publisher accept any liability for any loss or damage arising from their use.

Many of the designations used by manufacturers and sellers to distinguish their
products are claimed as trademarks. Pearson Education Limited has made every
attempt to supply trademark information about manufacturers and their products mentioned
in this book. A list of trademark designations and their owners appears on page xii.

Pearson Education has made every effort to seek permission
to reproduce the screenshots used in this book.

10 9 8 7 6 5 4 3 2 1

Typeset by Pantek Arts Ltd, Maidstone, Kent.
Printed and bound in the USA.

The Publishers' policy is to use paper manufactured from sustainable forests.

Contents

Preface

In Chapter 1, we state that one of the reasons for writing this book is to place in the public domain the general project principles specific to an OFA project implementation. This is achieved by abstracting knowledge from many OFA projects, rather than any particular one. Project success, whether it be the first OFA project or the extension of an existing one, is more likely where common knowledge accruing from many projects is shared. We write this book in the common interest of all OFA users and the long-term future of OFA.

Everyone involved in an OFA project will have a different view of the correct way to implement the product. We have attempted to abstract enduring project principles from project documentation, interviews with those involved and personal experience. The principles do not cover every project eventuality, but we hope our attempts in this book are at least a credible first pass.

We have also sought to provide a road map on the technical architectural issues which touch OFA implementations. We argue the case as to why OFA, as an application development framework rather than a package, offers a more technically correct approach to delivering a number of cognate business processes.

From the foregoing, it is clear that some balance had to be found between communicating best practice and polemic. Readers will no doubt make their own judgement as to whether the balance is right, based on their own individual perspective. For those who remember Express before OFA, we would beg indulgence if we cover some ground too lightly. For those who know nothing of Express or indeed OFA, we hope enough is communicated to be interesting, and perhaps useful.

John Cunningham
Fred Dean
Guy Stevens

November 2000

Acknowledgements

It is hard to pick out from the many conversations and joint professional experiences that lead to a book of this kind the names of those who merit specific acknowledgement. However, our greatest thanks must go to the reviewers, Alan Nevill, David McNeight and Matthew Shaw. Without their input to this first attempt to place the principles of implementing OFA into a book format, the results would have been less than you see now.

Thanks go to all the members of the Oracle UK Business Intelligence Competency Centre, and especially JKC's team members, past and present, for the challenges they offered to his ideas. To Andy Gale, Senior Sales Consulting Manager, UK Business Intelligence and Warehousing Competency Centre, Steve Hurrell, Senior Product Director, Analytic Solutions, and Marianne Slight, Senior Product Manager, much thanks for their support throughout the process to publication.

We would also like to thank Antony Macrae of marchFIRST and Rob Taylor of DHL for their input and wise words.

Conventions

The following conventions are used in this book:

In referring to OFA menu choices, upper case is used on the first letter, thus:
    File (Open, Save etc.), Tools, Solve, Group Solve etc. Etc.

In describing paths through menus, dashes are used, as below
    File – Open – New – Graph

Types of OFA Client are expressed as follows:
    Budget Workstation, Data Entry Form, Data Capture Tool kit, Analyst Workstation

Tiered Architecture, as per User Manual, so:
    Super Administrator (or SuperDBA), Administrator (or SubDBA), Task Processor, Super Shared Database, Sub Shared Database

Where dimensionality is being indicated, brackets are used as below:
    <Account Organization Time>

Since 'cube' is short and meaningful when discussing Financial Data Items, cube is used throughout, thus:
    Express cube, inter-cube arithmetic etc.

When referring to data, upper case first letter is used, thus:
    Actuals, Forecast, Budget Version

When referring specifically to OFA structures and function names, upper case first letter is used, thus:
    Financial Data Item
    Dimension Value
    Hierarchy
    Attribute
    Model
    Report
    Graph
    Worksheet
    Submit
    Express Stored Procedure Language (Express SPL programs hereafter) programs
    Solve Definitions
    GL Link
    Formula
    OFA front end, not GUI (graphical user interface)

Trademark notice

Acknowledgement

Material taken from Kimball, R., 1996, *The Data Warehouse Toolkit, Practical Techniques for Building Dimensional Data Warehouses* has been reprinted by permission of Jossey-Bass, Inc., a subsidiary of John Wiley & Sons, Inc.

1 Introduction

OVERVIEW OF ORACLE FINANCIAL ANALYZER

Oracle Financial Analyzer was developed to provide an application development framework, or toolkit, to deliver certain business processes. The processes envisaged were primarily the following:

- financial, management and regulatory reporting, including KPI measurement of enterprise performance;

- sales and financial planning, budgeting and forecasting;

- traditional costing and activity-based cost management – enabling, for example, product and channel profitability analysis;

- decision support in investment/disinvestment modelling and maximization of shareholder value.

Processes such as these often involve many sources of information. Some of these sources come from existing production systems and some are gathered from OFA users. OFA allows an enterprise view to be taken of all types of data, and calculations to be done on the data within a controlled environment, before reporting the results across the enterprise. The generic OFA process model is set out in Figure 1.1.

1.1.1 Production data

Production data may be captured by enterprise production systems such as the General Ledger, Purchasing, Sales, Manufacturing, Call Centre. They are all characterized by the execution of a 'transaction' in the normal course of operating the business. A transaction in this sense might be an order placed, an invoice rendered, a stock call-off or a call to the Call Centre.

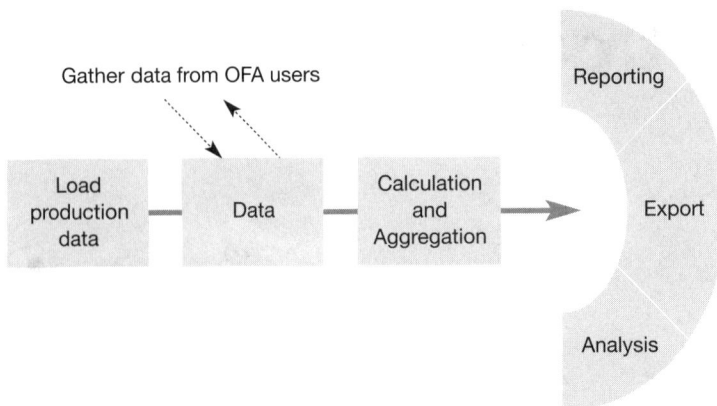

FIG 1.1   **The generic OFA process model**

1.1.2 Data gathered from OFA users

Data gathered from OFA users does not arise as a result of a transaction. It has to be requested from them. Examples are a forecast plan, a budget, a time allocation, a foreign exchange forecast, a customer satisfaction 'view', a late adjustment to a report which was run before an important transaction was processed. None of this data will necessarily end up in production systems. As we shall note later, much of the success of Oracle Financial Analyzer can be traced to an early design decision, to provide an 'out-of-the-box' iterative request and submission process, represented in the 'Gather data from OFA users' part of Figure 1.1.

1.1.3 The data

The OFA data is held in a multidimensional database called Express. Express is a multidimensional online analytical processing (MOLAP) database, structured to provide fast response to user queries. In contrast, a relational database is designed to hold and efficiently process transactions.

1.1.4 Calculations and aggregations

Express has a richly functional stored procedure language (Express SPL hereafter), which allows the functionality delivered in the OFA front end to be supplemented by custom programs written in Express SPL and called by the OFA front end to conceal complexity from the user. The history of OFA has been a continuous process of providing more functionality in the front end, so reducing the need for custom programming in Express SPL, while harnessing the increasing power of the underlying Express multidimensional database. The continuous development of Express is a key factor in being able to deliver performance for large and complex calculations and aggregations.

1.1.5 Reporting and analysis

The OFA front end harnesses the underlying multidimensional Express data model to provide easy-to-use facilities for the user to manipulate the data or perform complex analysis. OFA maintains a 'one view of the truth' methodology, providing an 'out-of-the-box' control process which can be used to maintain integrity of the database, whilst providing local flexibility to users. The progressive replacement of the Visual Basic front end by Java applets provides these benefits to potentially very large populations of users via the Internet.

OFA is only one of the clients to the Express multidimensional database. Other Express clients are covered in Section 3.3.

1.1.6 Export

Express and OFA provide several mechanisms for exporting data for use as inputs to other systems.

1.2 OBJECTIVES OF THIS BOOK

1. *To assist the business analyst in mapping requirements to OFA functionality*

   The OFA toolkit can be applied to many business processes. No matter what the process, our aim is to help the analyst ensure that the mapping is as close as possible.

2. *To explain the general principles regarding project implementation*

   OFA can be implemented on a small scale or to deliver major enterprise systems. However it is used, OFA projects have shared characteristics. One reason for writing this book is to place in the public domain such general principles as can be abstracted from study of many projects, rather than any particular project. Project success, whether a first project or the extension of an existing one, is more likely where common knowledge, accruing from many projects, is harnessed.

3. *To demonstrate why OFA offers a technically correct approach to delivering a number of cognate business processes*

    The data warehouse phenomenon has challenged the IT community to provide 'one view of the truth' regarding the corporate data which underpins all business processes. But how is non-production data – data gathered from people in an interactive manner during business processes such as planning, forecasting, budgeting, activity-based and value-based management – to be managed in a robust, enterprise way? The data warehousing literature suggests that the extraction, transformation and loading process adequately covers all data gathering requirements. It manifestly does not; after five years of experience since the publication of a number of influential books on data warehousing, these business processes are often still conducted within their own islands of data and are not integrated into an enterprise technical architecture.

| 1.3 | | **ROAD MAP FOR THE BOOK** |

The path taken through this book will differ depending on the reader.

1.3.1 Those who are not familiar with OFA

For those who are not familiar with OFA, following the order of the chapters is the correct approach. On reaching Chapter 5, and Section 5.5 in particular, newcomers may find that they can ignore areas where deep OFA or Express knowledge is required. They can then move to the Cases to reinforce what they have picked up earlier.

1.3.2 Those already familiar with OFA and Express

Those already familiar with OFA and Express may be more selective. Each chapter has its own road map. While the road maps are designed to assist all kinds of reader to get a structure in place before reading the detail, they may also be useful in assisting the experienced reader to decide what to read and what to leave out.

1.3.3 The order of chapters

The order of chapters is designed to take the reader initially from overview to project scoping for Oracle Financial Analyzer and then to Oracle Financial Analyzer key features. This may be sufficient to meet the requirements of **business analysts**, interested primarily in mapping OFA to business requirements.

However, **technical architects** may be mainly interested in how OFA fits with the ERP or data warehouse, and may therefore pass quickly to Chapter 4. **Project**

managers may also pass quickly through preceding chapters to Chapter 5. There they will find that all of the phases of an OFA project are discussed and can concentrate on those that meet their particular interest.

This book does not seek to replace Oracle's own methods and documentation in support of OFA. Neither does it attempt to provide Express programming training. Rather, it seeks to add insights gained from the experience of a number of OFA projects. Therefore, both **experienced and inexperienced OFA implementers** will find that Chapter 5 confirms and adds these insights to their own existing knowledge. In this sense, Chapter 5 is probably the core chapter of the book.

Review of the Case Studies should be valuable for all readers, as the nine sections of Chapter 5 are all addressed to some degree in each of the cases.

1.3.4 The Appendices

The first three Appendices, Express Tuning for OFA, Data Loading and the GL Link will be of interest to the more technical reader, who may already be familiar with Oracle documents on these subjects. Here our intention is to add to the material already in the public domain. The Appendix on history, future developments and their potential impact will allow all readers to share our view on the perennial problem of software, i.e. how to assess the implications of new functionality for systems being delivered now.

1.3.5 The CD

Finally, the CD prompts the new OFA user to model a regional organization with Sales, Finance and Board requirements, and all client types including a Web interface. The script explains the structure of the organization, and prompts the user to perform some of the tasks required to operate a tiered OFA system. This will enable new OFA Administrators to validate their progress in understanding how a complete OFA architecture is deployed.

2 Project scoping for Oracle Financial Analyzer

ROAD MAP

This chapter sets out to assist the reader to scope an OFA project. It identifies the business processes to which OFA should and should not be applied. We step though the issues as below:

2.1 Identifying the business processes to which OFA can be applied

- The value propositions which support the use of OFA
- The generic OFA process model
- The business processes to which the OFA generic process model is commonly applied
- Questions the analyst needs to ask to identify if OFA can meet specific business requirements

2.2 Package solutions as part of the solution architecture

The business requirements may be better met in part by a package, rather than OFA on its own, so we consider the issues, covering:

- use of spreadsheets within an OFA solution architecture; and
- use of single business process packages (such as balanced scorecard software) within an OFA solution architecture.

2.3   Common data sources and business processes

Finally, unlike single business process packages, the OFA application development framework can be used to implement more than one business process. These processes often use the same data and also the same structures used to order the data – the metadata. We consider how OFA can be used to support many business processes by simply managing the data and the metadata required to deliver these processes.

2.1   IDENTIFYING THE BUSINESS PROCESSES TO WHICH OFA CAN BE APPLIED

2.1.1 The value propositions which have supported use of OFA

As an application development framework, OFA can be used for many business processes. The analyst must study the desired business processes to establish whether the requirements can be met by OFA functionality which comes 'out of the box', as supplemented by programs written in the Express SPL language. This establishes if 'it can be done'. However, all projects take time to implement, and deciding 'if it should be done' requires estimating project duration/cost and balancing cost against benefits. This is the value proposition – 'why it should be done'. With OFA the value proposition has been based on issues such as:

- reducing the time taken to consolidate management reports of reporting units;
- reducing the time taken in the budget data collection process;
- handling changes in workload or organizational structures;
- enabling fast recalculation and consolidation of the monthly re-forecast;
- reversing the 80/20 relationship; data preparation vs. analysis and control;
- forecasting more often, with more accuracy and in more detail;
- uncovering the real cost of service for product/customer/channel;
- scenario modelling in high-level planning;
- modelling the ultimate impact on shareholder value.

Sometimes the benefits are measurable, sometimes they are intangible. The analyst must still make a value proposition. As we will see later, the benefits of using OFA sometimes arose from impact on processes which were not considered in the value proposition.

2.1.2 The generic OFA process model

OFA is normally applicable where there is a need to:

- load and analyze production data;
- gather further data from OFA users;
- perform calculations and aggregations;
- provide the results to users for reporting and analysis purposes;
- or simply export the results for use in another application.

The data does not need to be financial in nature. If the business problem reveals a requirement for the generic processes as above, it does not matter whether the data handled is financial or not. OFA has been used to gather, analyze and report on data as diverse as crime statistics and metrics that monitor the performance of sales forces.

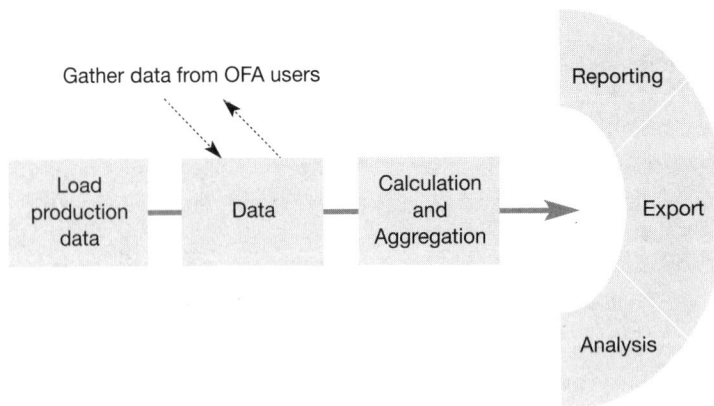

FIG 2.1   The generic OFA process model

Load production data

The sources of production data are normally tightly controlled production systems, where the data is subjected to validation prior to acceptance. Typically the data is transactional. These transactions are validated as each field is entered by the user. Production data may be subject, in some cases, to workflow, whereby each stage in the underlying business process is subject to sequential programmatic control, with the system issuing alerts as the business rules are triggered. For example, update of the GL is run automatically when the sub-ledger routines have all run successfully and reasonableness checks have been performed programmatically. Alerts are issued if either of the steps has failed.

During the load process into OFA, there may need to be further validation, but the emphasis then is on ensuring that the data is loaded successfully. While the data may be aggregated during the load process, it will not normally be subjected to review and possible change.

Gathering data from OFA users

Is there a process of gathering data from people?

One means of confirming the choice of OFA for a business process is to ask if there is a process of gathering data from people. If so, it is necessary to analyze the precise nature of the processes by decomposing them further into the detailed tasks involved. If OFA is appropriate, the data process will decompose into tasks which, as reflected by the arrows in Figure 2.1, go both ways:

1. ask user for data;

2. user performs data entry;

3. calculations are performed by user;

4. data is passed up the organization into the data store kept at that level;

5. the data is reviewed and may be changed by this higher-level management;

and, in a tiered management structure:

6. ask users at that level for data;

7. users perform data entry;

8. calculations are performed by users;

9. data is passed further up the organization and so on.

Consider a situation where data has to be gathered from people at the leaf level in the organizational hierarchy for Head Office purposes. An example of this process is where a multinational company delegates budget responsibility to individual countries. Each country would prepare its budget in local currency and conduct 'what-if' modelling on the budget for different exchange rates and investment priorities before finally submitting the budget to Head Office. Head Office may take a different view on exchange rates and recalculate the country budgets before consolidating the corporate view.

But the process should not simply require a data entry application

The fit of OFA to the business problem is dependent on the underlying business process being one of asking the user to enter data, the user entering data, and the data being recalculated, reviewed and potential changes made, as data is captured and passed upwards from individual to Head Office. If this is not the case, then the process might simply require a data entry application, not OFA. A data entry application will involve:

- validation as data is entered in each field,
- transactional level of granularity and, critically,
- not involving any request or review process, other than field-by-field validation.

OFA does not naturally support data capture in this sense. The fit of OFA is therefore dependent on the analyst performing detailed analysis on any requirement to gather data. Without it, there is a material risk of the wrong technology being applied.

It can be applied to both financial and non-financial data

If the business process reveals an OFA-type data gathering/review/amend process, it does not matter whether the data handled is financial or not. For example, the implementation problem in human resource planning is the capture of data such as forecast headcount, grade required, etc. in addition to financial data such as local payroll burden, taxes, etc. An OFA architecture simply to gather the data in a robust, controlled way will make a great contribution to project success, even if, as discussed further in Section 2.2, packaged solutions are used in the solution architecture to perform calculation, reporting and analysis.

There are substantial volumes of data to be gathered from people and/or there is a large user community

Gathering data from people is clearly a non-trivial issue where large enterprises are concerned. OFA offers an approach to achieving a degree of control where there are substantial volumes of data, and/or there is a large user community involved in the data gathering process and that user community is geographically dispersed.

Perform calculations and aggregations on the data

OFA is often deployed where the use of spreadsheets, or other personal productivity tools, for enterprise processes has resulted in lack of robustness as limits are reached in data volumes and integrity. While lack of robustness is important, a serious threat to the business exists where calculations and aggregations used to transform the data collected are enterprise rules, and constitute part of the key business knowledge of the enterprise. Risk of loss of this knowledge arising from staff leaving should be mitigated by capturing the knowledge in OFA. Staff may argue that their knowledge is heuristic, not capable of being captured. A good example is a heuristic rule applied by an experienced planning manager, who will override the results of, say, a Holt Winters-based forecast because he 'knows' that one of the predicted figures is too high. If he is prepared to convert his heuristic rule into a programmatic rule – 'remove 10 per cent of the predicted Q4 figure if it is 175 per cent of Q4 last year', for example, it then potentially becomes an enterprise business rule, and should be captured on the grounds of efficiency and knowledge management.

Provide reporting and analysis facilities on the calculated and aggregated data

By reporting, we mean deliver the calculated and aggregated data in a flexible reporting environment which allows the user to take different views of the data. By analysis, we mean model structures and data to provide 'what-if' functionality.

Export the calculated and aggregated data to other applications

The calculated and aggregated data might simply be made available to other applications.

2.1.3 The business processes to which the OFA generic process model is commonly applied

Typical common business processes to which OFA has been applied are listed below:

- *General ledger (GL): financial management reporting and analysis*
  This includes all forms of management reporting on financial data, and the role of financial data in the performance monitoring process. That process involves comparison of actuals with some form of financial target, such as plan, budget or commitment. It will cover exception reporting and variance analysis. The level of analysis is that which can be supported by the GL Chart of Accounts. It does not cover the preparation of the targets.

- *Planning, budgeting and forecasting*
  This covers the preparation of all forms of target, be they plans, budgets or forecasts. The performance monitoring process will of course use the results of this process, as in the General Ledger and management reporting process above. The following sub-processes in the planning, budgeting and forecasting cycle are included:

    Sales targets

    Cost targets:
       Direct input costs
       Direct payroll costs

    Contribution targets
       Indirect costs

    Target profit before fixed overheads
       Fixed overheads (including financing)

    Target net profit before tax
       Corporate taxation

    Target profits after tax available for distribution to the shareholders

    Capital budgeting and investment analysis

    Cash flow planning

■ *More granular reporting and analysis, requiring more sophisticated modelling*
The first two processes can be conducted at an aggregate level, with the level of analysis being at GL Chart of Accounts level. More granular reporting and analysis means when they are conducted at a more detailed level such as by Product and/or Customer and/or Project and/or Channel, etc. This will require more sophisticated modelling than at the Chart of Accounts level. It will cover cost allocation, which may be of the cascade type.

■ *Activity-based cost management, where the focus is on process efficiency, as well as profitability*
Driving the cost of resources to activities, which are then traced to outputs, such as Product and/or Customer and/or Project and/or Channel, is the focus. Again this will require more sophisticated modelling than at the Chart of Accounts level. It will cover cost allocation of the iterative, as well as the cascade type.

■ *Value-based management, where the focus is on managing the impact of decisions on total shareholder return*
Decision support in investment or disinvestment decisions and financial management of the balance sheet, leading to maximization of shareholder value, is the focus. Sophisticated modelling is required.

Three important further issues need to be considered in the application of OFA to the processes set out above. Taking them one by one:

1. *Are any of the groups of users involved in data gathering, reporting or analysis processes in a tiered organizational structure?*
Tiered organizational structures, as represented by the Business Unit 1 and Business Unit 2 layer in Figure 2.2, present opportunities for the use of Oracle Financial Analyzer to provide business units with their own views of data, while enabling rapid consolidation to a consistent company, division or group level.

2. *Is there a need to provide a group of users with autonomy to determine their own structures and data, albeit within a higher-level consistent corporate standard?*
There may be a need to set standards, in terms of structures, for preparing plans, budgets and forecasts centrally, but also to provide flexible templates to accommodate detailed differences at local level. OFA can facilitate good management practice in empowering business units and individuals in the way it allows for distribution and retrieval of data and the structures that manipulate it. This makes it possible to strike a balance between centralized control and devolved responsibility.

3. *Are any of the groups of users geographically distributed?*
This may not be an issue as business unit databases can exist on the same physical machine even if the user communities are geographically diverse. However, if there are issues with network performance, OFA can be deployed over local machines, as discussed further in Section 5.6.

Seeking answers to these three questions is crucial to determining whether OFA is appropriate to a business process. Also, as we shall see later in Chapter 5, they are also critical to the design of the OFA application architecture, and to the design of the technical infrastructure which supports the OFA application. Figure 2.2 summarizes an OFA concept central to the foregoing, that of the distributed architecture.

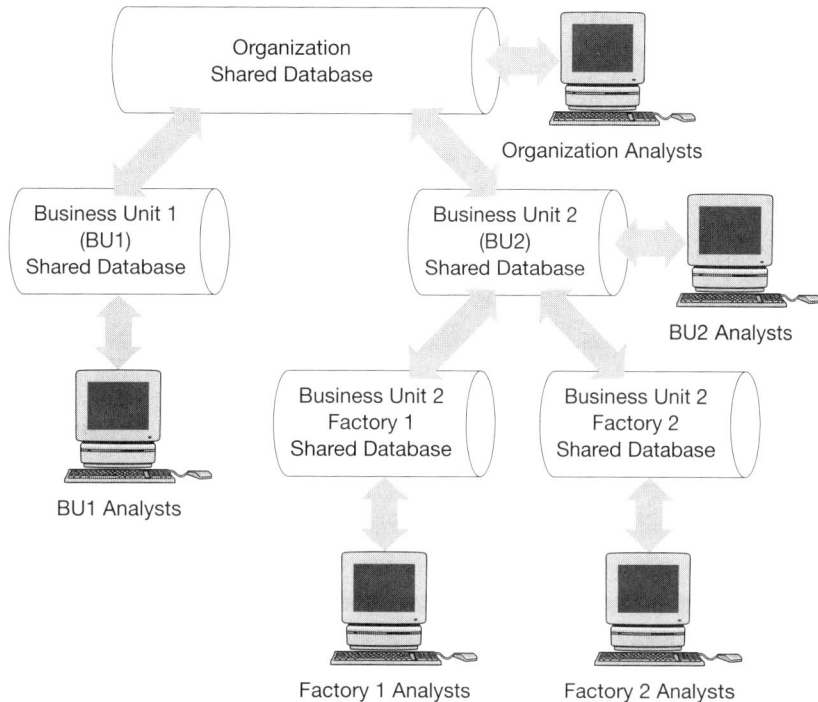

FIG 2.2   **The OFA distributed architecture**

OFA is an application development framework – a toolkit – designed to enable a potentially large distributed group of people to participate in certain business processes which have common features. OFA's distributed architecture is crucial in this and is discussed in detail in Chapter 3. For now, it is sufficient to consider that each user of OFA has access to his or her own subset of the same shared data and structures, ensuring consistency of reporting and analysis against 'one view of the truth'. Hence, for example, when performance measures are discussed in a management meeting everyone can be confident that they have been calculated from the same data source using standard structures, be they accounting roll-ups, product hierarchies or organization hierarchies.

Data volumes and user population size; what is their impact on the choice of OFA to deliver a business process?

An analysis of 10 implementations in place in 1999 gave the following statistics:

Database size   2–20 Gb
User population   50–740

So do data volumes and user population size impact on the fit of OFA to a particular requirement?

There are no simple generalizations which can be made in this area. It is true that the OFA development path has emphasized that a key objective is the efficient administration of large user populations. In parallel with this, OFA inherits benefits from the underlying database development program which has delivered very substantial gains in terms of scalability and performance. Web data capture can be expected to result in user populations of thousands, not just the high hundreds, with global roll-outs made more possible with the Internet delivery platform.

However, it is possible to apply OFA to processes where data volumes are modest and the user population is small and centralized, described as niche business processes below. In addition to these niche applications, there may be special situations such as:

- a 'quick win' project to get flexible reporting out of the GL for a small group of Head Office users;
- an existing OFA implementation which can be extended. Since OFA is an application development framework which can support many processes from common data, the cost of implementating and rolling out a further process can be reduced through minimization of learning costs.

Niche business processes

There are many niche applications which harness some of the generic processes represented in Figure 2.1, but not necessarily all of them, or perhaps not yet. For example, use is made in the capital markets of the calculation and aggregation facilities alone to model sophisticated financial instruments, such as futures and swaps. The results are exported to another reporting and analysis application. No use is made of OFA to gather data from people, or of the reporting and analysis facilities. Hence the process model looks more like Figure 2.3.

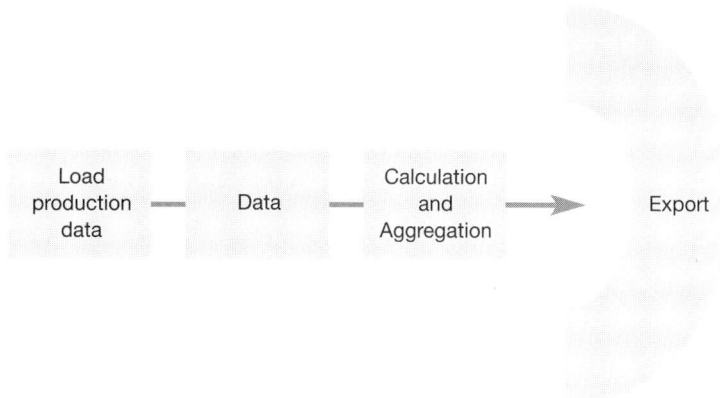

```
   Load
production  ───  Data  ───  Calculation  ══════▶  Export
   data                      and
                         Aggregation
```

FIG 2.3   **A reduced generic OFA process model**

2.1.4 Questions the analyst needs to ask to identify whether OFA can meet specific business requirements

To understand the scope of a potential project it may be useful to ask a series of questions, following the processes and issues set out above.

Is there a problem with GL and management reporting?

Many companies reload data from general ledgers into spreadsheets, or export data to systems capable of multidimensional analysis for management reporting. One of the reasons often quoted is that the current GL cannot provide the type and quality of reports required. Certainly if the general ledger is difficult to change, or does not provide flexible reporting and analysis, use of OFA can address these shortcomings. Oracle Financial Analyzer can load actuals data, merge it with other data gathered from outside the production system and facilitate regular reporting, or ad-hoc reporting, for management purposes. Users have access to a flexible report writer for analysis or can even access the data held in Express via Excel. Indeed, if the GL is Oracle, the manager can drill back to detailed information (provided it was created in the GL) to follow a line of enquiry.

OFA is optimized to deliver performance when conducting reporting or analysis on aggregate data held in a multidimensional data structure. It is not an ad-hoc query tool designed to retrieve highly granular information from relational databases or conduct multidimensional analysis on highly attributed granular data held in a star or snowflake schema. The reporting facilities of the GL or supporting sub-ledgers should be able to produce highly granular reports such as expense reports by individual, invoices received from one supplier, and the like. If such facilities are inadequate, there are many products which can query the data through an easy-to-use front end to conduct multidimensional queries on relational schemas of various kinds. Oracle's Discover is one of a number of products in this area, another is Business Objects. Note that these products are read-only; there are no facilities to gather data to supplement production data or to conduct calculations and aggregations. There may be performance implications when using such tools to look at aggregate views calculated on the fly. If so, the OFA options of pre-summarization and batch load into an off-line database are appropriate.

Is there a need to improve planning, budgeting or forecasting processes?

Many organizations prepare a three- or five-year (rolling) strategic plan, but budget on an annual basis, conducting a re-forecasting process for the four to eight quarters ahead, updated monthly or quarterly. The planning process produces baseline assumptions, such as market share, sector growth, economic growth, input price inflation, and so on, which are handed down to the business units. Budget proposals are prepared within those assumptions on a bottom-up basis from the business units, after which there may be iterations to reconcile business unit and Head Office views. This process provides a target thereafter so that management can monitor the financial performance of the organization and its business units by comparison of actual results against the budget/re-forecast.

Successive surveys have revealed that organizations typically devolve responsibility for such planning, budgeting and forecasting to business unit management, supported by accountants. However, the majority of respondents rely on spreadsheets to prepare plans – a tool not designed to support a distributed process of this nature. Furthermore, unless there is a fully developed enterprise resource planning (ERP) system, the source of the actuals data may be from general ledger and many other types of operational systems which are not usually integrated (Figure 2.4). Transferring and often rekeying both actuals and planning, budget and forecast data into spreadsheet models has been the only available way of pulling information together. This 'islands of data' problem can result in much of a finance manager's time being spent collecting and preparing data, rather than being available for modelling, analysis and control.

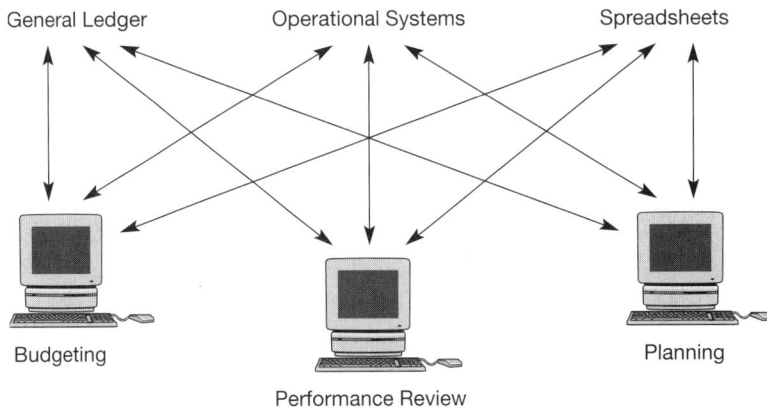

General Ledger   Operational Systems   Spreadsheets

Budgeting   Performance Review   Planning

FIG 2.4   **Fragmented financial information**

To replace this approach, Oracle Financial Analyzer provides facilities to populate an underlying Express multidimensional database from many sources to create an integrated, enterprise-wide database from which reports can be drawn for review (Figure 2.5).

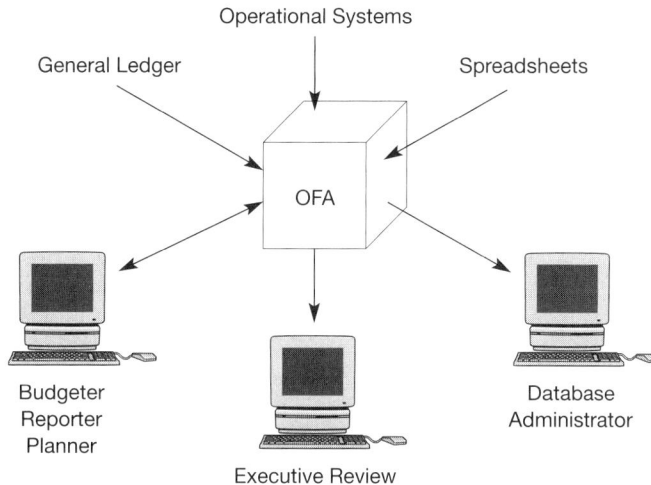

FIG 2.5   An integrated enterprise-wide database

It also provides the required infrastructure for modelling the plans, budgets and forecasts and ultimately for communicating data to the users. Both financial analysts and operational managers can exploit Oracle Financial Analyzer functions to conduct repetitive analysis through exception reporting, while permitting exploratory activity such as 'slice and dice' and drill down product, account and organization hierarchies.

Oracle's internal use of the product is a typical example. OFA is used to deliver the budgeting, forecasting and monitoring for Oracle worldwide. With over 640 users, the group that maintains the system has followed the self-service model in providing a Web site where their users can download installations, patches, documentation, answers to support questions, etc. The forecasting process gives insight into how the system operates in managing data across what is a large enterprise trading in 130 countries in multiple currencies. Each month the 130 countries provide a re-forecast for the next quarter which is passed up through the four regions, reviewed and presented with Actuals and Budget for the period to central management.

Is there a need for more granular reporting and analysis, requiring more sophisticated modelling?

Analysis of information at an aggregate level, such as at GL Chart of Accounts level, may be sufficient in some circumstances, such as in the public sector where the crucial issue may be whether or not a particular item is nearing the voted budget provision. The OFA exception report will draw attention to the need to avoid overspend or seek virement from an underspent budget line. In contrast, key indicators of the need for more granular reporting and analysis, requiring more sophisticated modelling, will be when answers to the following questions are important:

- Which brands are profitable?
- Which products are profitable?
- Which customers or channels are profitable?
- What drives profitability?

Profit is the primary indicator of performance, but there is a range of approaches to measuring profit, from highly aggregate views to highly detailed. Indeed, there are many other objectives besides profit improvement – satisfying the needs of customers, suppliers and employees as well as shareholders, as reflected in the Balanced Scorecard performance measurement approach. However, the profit measure can simply be contribution, which focuses on price less direct cost. Using contribution as a measure of profitability is extremely useful in reporting and analysis, including 'what-if' modelling:

Sales	xxxxx
less direct costs:	
Direct input costs	xxxxx
Direct payroll costs	xxxxx
Other direct costs	xxxxx
	———
Contribution	xxxxx
	———

With buyers using the Web as a source of immediate price information and as the choice of products or services becomes much wider, there is a challenge to price the product or service correctly to achieve a positive contribution. Direct product or service costs may be relatively easy to model. For example, product P has a buy-in cost of X, a packaging cost of Y and a delivery cost of Z. Modelling contribution allows the effect of changing price or direct cost to be clearly seen. Let us ignore for now the need to model the absorption and allocation of overheads such as corporate marketing costs to products, brands, channels, etc.

For reporting purposes, more granular reporting and analysis means providing information at a more detailed level to support each measure. Thus, the sales number will be broken down by product group and/or customer and/or channel, with the direct cost number similarly analyzed. OFA can provide modelling to support this requirement. At one end of the spectrum, the user can see the effect of simply rolling up a product, customer, account or project hierarchy in a different way, perhaps to see the effects of restructuring the business and have the changes automatically reflected in reports. At the other end, OFA allows the user to manipulate the data within the Express multidimensional database by making changes to data and structures. Examples of both can be seen in the following:

- providing different views of the same data – a national account manager will have access only to his or her particular customers whereas a regional manager will have access to all of the accounts in his or her territory;

- providing a standard approach to review all product groups, efficient in terms of management time absorbed in the process, while still offering flexibility in reporting data – either at the corporate level or to an individual brand manager;

- modelling material, conversion, distribution costs explicitly, with sub-models for each cost type consolidating into one cost model;

- modelling different price, discounts and margin options by changing both model and data.

Cost allocation and profitability

Ultimately all efforts to understand cost are really about understanding and influencing profit at the business segment level, e.g. at the channel, customer, product, service level. It is relatively easy to measure profit at the total business level (although even here we have the different treatments of capital expenditure, etc., to contend with), but measuring profit at a detailed level requires cost allocation on some basis. It could mean performing top-down allocations or modelling alternative cost allocation methods. However, cost allocations of varying degrees of sophistication may be required. OFA offers facilities to provide many cost allocation alternatives, certainly as wide as is normally attempted in spreadsheets or fourth-generation programming languages (4GLs).

Examples are where indirect costs may be incurred at a corporate level, but contribute to some or all products in the product hierarchy. If sales are to be analysed by drilling down on the product hierarchy, say:

All products
 Product categories
  Product groups
   Products at stock-keeping unit (SKU) level

then the true costs picture at each level may need to reflect not just direct cost, but an appropriate allocation of indirect costs. The allocation may also need to consider products delivered through different channels to different customer types, and hence the allocation is down a multidimensional structure. OFA can handle such allocations, because it uses a multidimensional database to hold and manipulate the data.

Is there a need for activity-based cost management, where the focus is on process efficiency, as well as profitability?

For many types of business, and particularly businesses that provide intangible products, the need for process efficiency analysis as well as profitability analysis means activity-based management and the methodologies of activity-based costing (ABC). The cost allocation processes discussed in the previous section are not activity-based cost management, but represent one end of the spectrum of cost allocation in simply spreading aggregate costs based on, say, sales volumes by product. At the other end of the spectrum is full activity-based costing of the full demand and supply chain to arrive at product, customer or customer segment and channel profitability.

Costs are *not* allocated to product, brand, region, customer, project etc. directly. Instead the activity-based management (ABM) process allocates costs firstly to the activities which support the demand and supply chain. This provides the costs of activities to enable review of the cost of business processes (which may then be changed as a result of decisions made based on the review). Thereafter the unit costs of providing the activities are applied to output volumes to arrive at the real cost of what is being sold.

Oracle Financial Analyzer has been used both:

- as a prototyping tool to evaluate activity-based approaches to costing, and

- as a comprehensive architecture for delivering operational ABM.

There may in fact be a need to support immediately the more traditional cost allocation approaches such as standard costing. Oracle Financial Analyzer can initially provide the framework for this, but allowing a transition to full activity-based management approaches in due course. This should minimize risk, since the critical success factors for a successful transition from traditional costing to the desired activity-based state are:

- integrating an activity-based approach with existing financial processes by using common systems, data and reports;

- ability to evolve an ABC model that reflects the unique characteristics of the business;

- ensure that early benefits are visible and can be delivered quickly;

- enhance credibility of new measures by providing comparatives with previous methodology, thereby avoiding a big-bang switch to an unfamiliar and untrusted new measurement method.

Niche applications

Is there a need for unit costing calculations in support of pricing decisions?

OFA can be used to provide unit cost calculations in support of pricing decisions, both internal and external. The focus is not process efficiency, where the classical ABM model can allow management to understand how products consume the activities which are provided by resources. Instead the focus is to allow pricing to the customer or as internal transfer charges between business units. Unit costs are key to the calculations; e.g. in the financial services sector, the cost of an automated teller machine (ATM) transaction, of providing a customer with travellers' cheques across a counter, of setting up a unitized fund for a policy holder. The transaction volumes upon which the unit costs are based are typically captured in a data warehouse or data mart which can be an Express database or a relational database management system (RDBMS). The costs themselves will be loaded into OFA from the GL, typically using the Chart of Accounts segments of cost centre, account and time. Aggregations on the cost centre hierarchy provide cost pools which, after allocation of support to direct cost pools, provide costs which share a transaction volume driver. Dividing the cost pools by transaction driver volumes provides unit costs to be used in pricing decisions and profitability analysis, by merging income information with the cost data.

The focus of interest might be profitability of:

a) individual channels to market;

b) product or product group profitability;

c) customer or customer group profitability.

These are listed in order of increasing granularity. Thus a bank or insurance company might have 10 channels to market, hundreds of products (organized into a few product groups), but millions of customers. Certain functions of OFA may not perform adequately with customer or product numbers exceeding 100,000. By segmenting the customers into smaller groups by demographics, say, age ranges 28–35, 36–42 etc., the volumetrics on this part of the calculation may be relatively modest; at the leaf level:

Accounts	2,000
Cost centres	1,500
Transactions to be costed	400

A large element of costs is payroll costs, which should be at an aggregate salary grade level, rather than the individual employee level, for volumetric constraint reasons discussed above. The allocation processes from support cost pools to direct cost pools will be 'simple', not cascade or iterative; the expression 'simple cost allocations' is commonly used to distinguish such cost allocation processes from 'complex cost allocations', which include ABC.

The transaction volumes will be large and typically loaded from production systems, rather than gathered from OFA users. The allocation bases are typically static and the result of studies performed from time to time by cost analysts. Mapped against the generic OFA process model, such requirements look as shown in Figure 2.6.

As discussed above, if the volumetrics are modest, there will be a potential mapping of OFA to solving the business problem. However, volumetrics and some other related considerations need to be kept in mind and are discussed next.

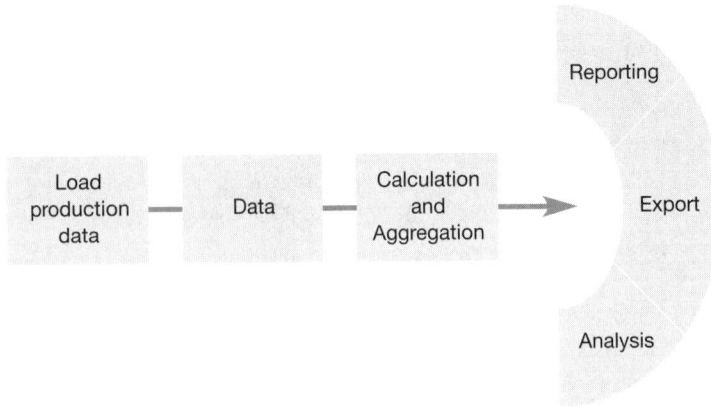

FIG 2.6   A reduced generic OFA process model

Is there a need for static, high volume, 'black box' cost allocation business processes?

Examples of what is meant by static, high volume cost allocation processes exist in many industries. We consider an example from the financial services industry. A product provider in this industry commonly sells products – a personal pension, an investment bond or an endowment policy – and the products are backed by a number of funds into which the customers' contributions/investments or regular premiums are paid. Costs are incurred by the product provider, for example in providing common services to support the funds. Such costs are accumulated in the GL in account balances which may need to be split over a number of funds and allocated to individual customers' shares in the funds.

The rules by which these de-facto cost pools may be split are highly static; for example, by the number of policies in force at a specific date, as specified in the accounting rules set by the regulatory authority or as in the Trust Deed which creates a fund. These rules do not change often and hence may be coded into the system which can most easily hold *all* the required 'production' data, costs and drivers and perform the allocations.

The GL typically has the ability to do allocations of this static nature (Oracle's Mass Allocations functionality, for example) and may be fed with driver data from, say, the policy administration system. Where the GL does not have facilities to hold statistical data and apply it to cost balances, external packages may be used, but they are essentially black box calculation engines, designed to process high volume transactions. Oracle itself provides a module within the Oracle Financial Services suite called Performance Analyzer, originally developed to address the requirements of the banking industry, where such processes are common.

Even if OFA could be used to process efficiently the volumes of data required, there is no requirement for OFA's generic processes, such as flexible reporting and analysis facilities, the ability to conduct 'what-if' analyses by re-mapping resources to activities to cost objects, gathering activity-level information to enable review of business processes, etc. The static, high volume, 'black box' cost allocation business process is more like Figure 2.7.

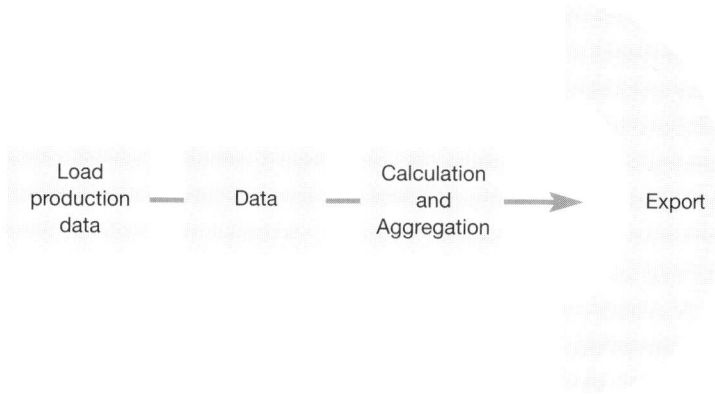

Load production data — Data — Calculation and Aggregation ⟶ Export

FIG 2.7　　**A reduced generic OFA process model**

While OFA potentially could be used for this type of process, the data volumes being handled may result in poor performance, and the business case will not be as strong as in situations where more of the OFA generic processes are utilized. This leads naturally to consideration of the use of packages in conjunction with an OFA-based solution.

Use of packages within an OFA-based solution

Packages exist which address single business processes such as planning/budgeting/ forecasting, activity-based management, etc. They can certainly meet the requirements of a department or small business unit for a solution to the single business process at issue, with modest inputs of both package supplier and customer time in the implementation process. There are many opportunities to harness point solution packages within an OFA architecture, as considered later.

Do the business processes go beyond financial numbers?

Oracle Financial Analyzer can be used to handle both financial and non-financial data such as:

- product volumes;
- customer numbers or number of customer accounts;
- branches/outlet performance metrics.

The data management capabilities enable large volumes of data to be handled effectively, while minimizing the time spent pulling the data together. A distributed architecture ensures that a wide range of users have immediate access to that data, enabling the enterprise to:

- integrate data from sales, manufacturing and planning into a central database;
- share consistent data and standardize reporting across business groups;
- make considerable time savings in reporting and forecasting;
- reduce rekeying errors by reading data automatically.

Is there a need for technical financial consolidation?

There is often confusion between the process of calculating and aggregating numbers to provide management information and technical financial consolidation. What is meant by technical financial consolidation?

Technical financial consolidation is relevant only when a company holds shares in other companies. The holding company is required to prepare statutory accounts to show group financial information under the accounting rules of the country in which the holding company is domiciled. For example, a UK-based holding company reports under the UK Companies Act in respect of operations conducted by business units which operate worldwide. There is a local currency for each business unit, but the holding company is required to report in the currency of the country of its domicile, i.e. UK GBP.

The following issues arise:

1. Statutory reporting rarely follows the format used for internal management reporting.

2. Inter-company trading between subsidiaries needs to be eliminated when consolidating the group Profit and Loss account.

3. Foreign currency conversion is required when consolidating the group Profit and Loss or Balance Sheet in the group reporting currency from subsidiary companies which trade in local currency.

4. Minority shareholders' interests need to be calculated when consolidating the group Profit and Loss or Balance Sheet.

5. The same issues as in 2, 3 and 4 above when dealing with companies which are not subsidiaries, but where the shareholding of the holding company is significant, say between 25 and 50 per cent. These are known as associated companies in UK company law.

6. There needs to be a full debit and credit audit trail on all of the financial processes as above.

If issue 1 and any one of the other issues above exist, then there is probably a need for technical financial consolidation as opposed to the simple currency conversion, calculation and aggregation processes which are performed during the preparation of management accounts.

How are statutory accounts typically prepared?

Generally speaking, the GL provides the transactional information, summarized by a detailed chart of accounts which is then adjusted outside the GL to comply with statutory reporting rules, although it is the goal of most finance managers that such adjustments are made within the GL. OFA has been used to support the process of adjustment between the GL and the final draft statutory accounts. The Express-based FCRS – the Financial Consolidation and Reporting System – was available as a package in this marketplace, until it was withdrawn in 1997. There are a number of packages currently marketed designed to fulfil specific consolidation requirements. There is no underlying technology reason why OFA could not be used for both management reporting and technical financial consolidation; FCRS clearly met the technical financial consolidation requirement in the past. However, providing all the functionality referred to in the issues listed above is challenging. In particular, the provision of audit trails would require customization as OFA does not support DR/CR journals as a means of adjusting balances 'out of the box'. Finally, since it would be a highly customized application, upgrades may present challenges.

When to consider an OFA approach to technical financial consolidation?

Since it can be done, a decision to do it will have to made on cost/benefit criteria. Since the required functionality will have to be built, there is the cost of what is essentially a software development life cycle. If there are existing OFA skills in the organization concerned and an existing OFA management reporting system, then costs may be less and benefits greater in terms of integration than where there is no such existing OFA/Express expertise.

Is there a need for value-based management, where the focus is on managing the impact of decisions on total shareholder return?

If all decisions made by management, whether at the enterprise, business unit or product management level, were measured by their impact on the share price plus distributed dividends, a company would have fully embraced what has become known as value-based management (VBM). Note the concept of total return:

Total return to shareholders = rise in share price + dividends paid

Some very successful companies have never paid a dividend, but the total return has been high as the share price has risen.

Performance measures used in VBM fall into two groups:

- Non-copyright approaches drawn from financial management research such as

  Return on net assets
  Return on capital employed
  Risk Adjusted Return on Capital

  where return is defined in a range of ways, such as net operating profit after tax (NOPAT), and capital employed by some form of restated value of assets or of funds invested in the business.

- The copyright approaches, such as EVA (Economic Value Added), marketed by specialist consultancies, such as the firm which produced EVA, Stern Stewart, which typically use an adjusted version of NOPAT and particular definitions of the cost of the capital invested in the business.

The overall objective is to measure performance internally in a way that will encourage management at all levels to take decisions that balance return with the investment generating the return. However, there must be no encouragement to minimize investment to enhance short-term returns.

OFA is clearly capable of providing a means of forecasting earnings and aggregating the results up a 'product to business unit to group hierarchy'. In one example where OFA is being used for managerial accounting, the measures include a calculation of EVA and other VBM-related measures, as well as traditional financial key performance indicators (KPIs).

Tax planning: a crucial component of calculating NOPAT

Managing corporate tax liability is critical to maximizing NOPAT, which is often used in value-based management models. However, managing corporate tax exposure is often a major contributor to the 'spreadsheet factory'.

In Figure 2.8, to report on the ledger, say, for statutory reporting purposes, the GL's report and query features may be used, providing one audited view of the truth. However, in preparing the corporate tax calculations, the tax department is often forced to use retyped data from disparate sources – GL, Fixed Assets – with error and inefficiency as an underlying but real cost. Even if the data is successfully entered into the tax department's spreadsheets, the problems of using a personal productivity tool for enterprise purposes is likely to emerge:

Who has got the correct version?

Quality:

- Did we all use the correct capital allowance rates?
- Are we reasonably sure that the taxable profits are correctly assembled from all the potential sources of income/capital gains?
- Did we have enough time to review the results before submission to the authorities, or were we too busy working the numbers?

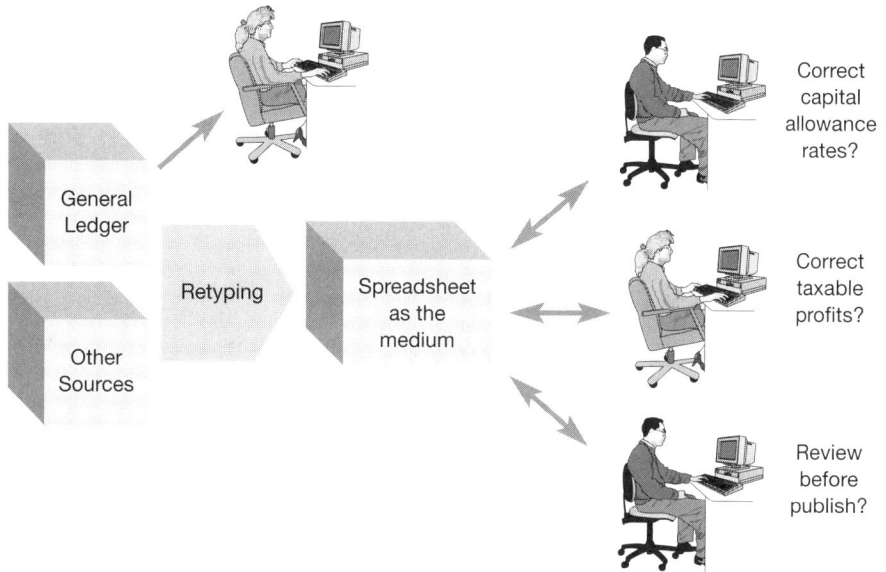

FIG 2.8   Managing corporate tax exposure

This problem is exacerbated if the tax department is responsible for geographically dispersed businesses each using its own disparate legacy fixed asset system.

It is obvious that the business process is supported by the generic processes supported by Oracle Financial Analyzer (Figure 2.9).

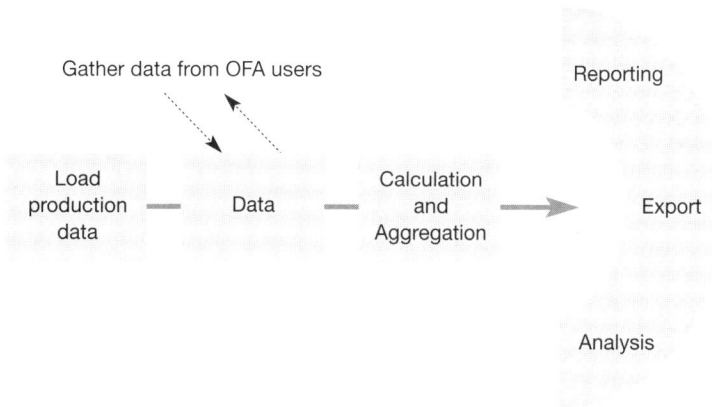

FIG 2.9   The generic OFA process model

Consider the UK's corporate tax (CT) regime, which has substantial similarities with the tax regimes of other countries, particularly those of Australia, France, Germany and the US. The UK CT regime requires looking back at the actual results, but also requires estimating future profits and capital expenditure at the half-year point to predict the total liability for the current year. Having loaded the year-to-date production Actuals, the steps are to:

- estimate profits for the remainder of the year, including an estimate of capital allowances;
- compute tax liability for the year;
- remit $\frac{1}{4}$ of the full bill after the half year, remit the next payment in month 10, and so on.

These steps are just those supporting the planning, budgeting and forecasting process. The planning assumptions include possible changes to the tax rules, easily modelled in OFA, while different business units can be invited through an OFA Worksheet or Data Entry Form to cooperate in a series of iterations, until all parties have had their say. When each forecast item is finalized, it can be submitted back to the Shared database to be shared with all Financial Analyzer users involved in the tax compliance and planning process.

Performing the calculations

Performing the sequence of calculations in the correct order is vital; failure, for example, to eliminate the cost of disposals from the depreciation calculations will require many of the calculations to be repeated. Run as a single OFA process, the complete sequence can commence after loading actuals and making forecasts or changes in an OFA Worksheet to get the tax bill for the year. Reports can be defined to reflect the tax return of each relevant country. We can now do some 'what-if' on the process, perhaps by:

- changing profits, allowing the business OFA users to input possible outcomes;
- examining the effect of accelerating or deferring capital expenditure;
- changing future tax rates, allowing the tax department to exercise their expertise in a proactive way rather than just being focused on compliance.

2.2   PACKAGED SOLUTIONS AS PART OF THE SOLUTION ARCHITECTURE

2.2.1 OFA and the spreadsheet

The introduction of the spreadsheet in the 1980s provided a flexible personal productivity tool with an attractive user interface which was cheap and hence could be purchased at the departmental level. The spreadsheet enabled business users to work around some of the constraints of enterprise systems, for instance to produce reports or prepare plans, budgets and ad-hoc revenue or cost models. However, as personal productivity tools, they were never designed to operate within enterprise-wide systems for the gathering and distribution of information.

Some consequences become immediately obvious to the user, for instance when large volumes of data are involved. The individual rapidly experiences the consequences of using a personal productivity tool for enterprise purposes as, for example, when a volume limit is encountered during use of a spreadsheet.

Some of the major consequences are experienced only at the organizational level, without being measurable at the individual level. For instance, if a spreadsheet becomes a significant part of the data gathering chain, the user may appear to be busy, but may in fact be reworking a fragile and highly inefficient de-facto program or repeating a file transfer process which has become disorderly. The organization bears the heavy and unmeasurable cost of rekeying and data integrity issues, but few metrics exist to assess the efficiency of the spreadsheet user. Not surprisingly, those who operate with spreadsheets often resist their replacement with enterprise systems, on the grounds that the enterprise system is not 'user-friendly', when the reality is that management is seeking to impose control and efficiency, which represents erosion of their freedom.

In many OFA implementations, there is often a role for the spreadsheet as a personal productivity tool:

- There may be existing spreadsheets at a level of detail unnecessary within the OFA implementation which can be cut and pasted into an OFA Worksheet or Data Entry Form for onward transmission into OFA as an enterprise data capture system.

- It may be productive for the user to experiment with different structures and data within the spreadsheet prior to creating the appropriate structures in an OFA Budget Workstation or simply cutting and pasting data into an OFA Worksheet or Data Entry Form.

- It may be used as a means of continuing non-enterprise modelling in a client/server environment, prior to cutting and pasting into the OFA Data Entry Form which provides a Web-enabled data capture system. This will be true for as long as the spreadsheet is delivered in a client/server architecture, rather than the Internet delivery model.

For the reasons discussed earlier, the spreadsheet should not be used as an output device, unless simply to format the contents in a more appealing way than is possible within OFA. The 'one view of the truth' should not be tampered with. Likewise, it should not be used to aggregate production data and data gathered from people, since the control of what we shall see is called the Task Processor will be lost.

2.2.2 Packages for individual business processes

Ironically, as the concept of workflow permeated mainstream software design philosophy (particularly in the ERP area), in response to the business process re-engineering development of the mid-1990s, no strong process-flow model emerged to challenge the 'spreadsheet factory' other than the emergence of packaged budgeting systems. These packages may encourage the development of 'islands of data' as discussed earlier. However, recognition that packaged software effectively shares the cost of ownership for all users provides an argument for using packages to address common business processes such as:

- multidimensional analysis and reporting;
- financial planning and budgeting;
- balanced scorecard;
- activity-based methods;
- modelling of shareholder value.

At an information strategy level, there are two problems:

a) The need to create and maintain separate interfaces from source systems between many point solutions imposes costs, when much of the data is common across the packages, as discussed later.

b) Separate packages have to be learnt, used and maintained, and supplier relationships managed, all of which attracts costs.

Business literature is starting to recognize these realities, as exemplified in this quote from *Accountancy* on Balanced Scorecard software: 'You need software that's not wedded solely to the corporate scorecard approach ...' (Hurren, 1998). But the option of using a package within an OFA-based solution should be considered in certain circumstances.

2.2.3 The option of using packages within an OFA-based solution architecture

If there is a requirement for calculation rules which map easily into an existing package, perhaps one already in use, the option should be contemplated, subject to the following considerations:

- The actuals should be imported from OFA, not directly from the production source, since this creates the possibility of inconsistency.
- The process of import should be efficient and maintainable.
- Production data, data gathered from OFA users into OFA or structures (product hierarchies etc.) can be exported to the package, but only data should come back into OFA.

The strategy should be to use the package as a calculation engine, fed by OFA's data, which then feeds OFA for reporting, analysis and export. The amended generic process diagram will look like Figure 2.10.

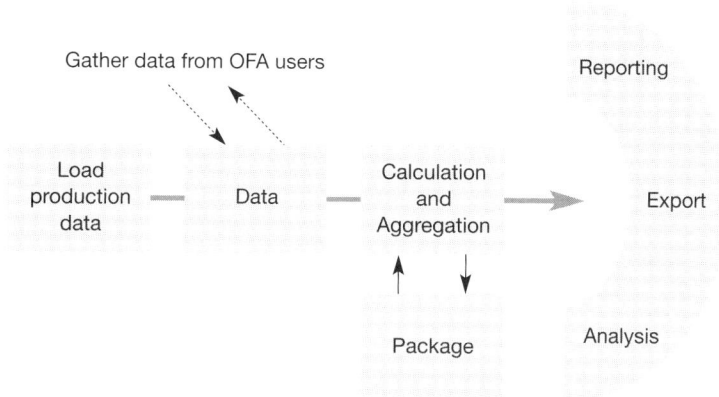

FIG 2.10   Integrating the packaged approach with OFA

Advantages of integrating the packaged approach with OFA include the following:

1. *Inheriting the business rules of niche applications without development overhead*
   Consider a production planning application, which optimizes the supply chain by evaluating production plans against constraints. OFA is interested in the results, typically the final output plan data. Capturing the business rules into OFA would simply be a project overhead.

2. *Highly granular calculations*
   If the business requirement is to manipulate highly granular data (the run-off of balances from a bank's deposits and loan book for instance), the data volumes may explode within the multidimensional database Express model. Many packages which handle highly granular data use RDBMS, often Oracle 8, as the hosting database, and hence inherit scalability; therefore, for highly granular applications, there are some advantages to simply using an existing package.

3. *Situations where packaged solutions have* already been *implemented*
   Where packaged solutions have *already been* implemented, perhaps only at the departmental level, a compromise is possible by using OFA's common application development and delivery framework to set up an enterprise solution architecture, within which the existing package is accommodated. This approach has been used at a bank which had implemented activity-based costing using a popular ABC package within the strategic cost management group, before implementing an OFA-based financial data mart (FDM) for the enterprise. The situation is represented in Figure 2.11.

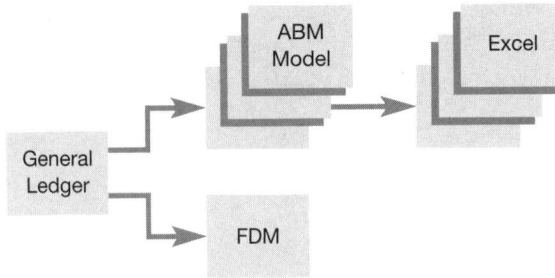

FIG 2.11   **The processes before integrating the packaged approach with OFA**

There were a number of issues:

- many broadly identical data flows from the GL to the ABM models and Financial Analyzer;
- unwieldy ABM reporting via Excel;
- high administrative overhead to populate Excel for ABM reporting;
- difficulty in controlling 'enterprise' definitions, i.e. Activities;
- difficulty in consolidating local ABM models to provide an enterprise view;
- duplication of data in the ABM models and FDM requires reconciliation between the two environments to ensure consistency.

There were two potential solutions: replacement with an OFA-based activity-based management solution or combining the third-party activity-based management within the OFA-based financial data mart, as the data gathering and reporting solution, as shown in Figure 2.12. The second was chosen. Note that the need for 'local' businesses to adopt a self-sufficient approach to their ABM modelling is sustained.

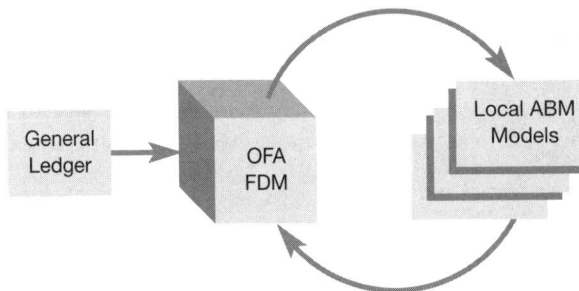

FIG 2.12   **The processes after integrating the packaged approach with OFA**

COMMON DATA SOURCES AND BUSINESS PROCESSES

As discussed earlier, OFA is applicable to more than one business process and can utilize single process packages within an OFA solution architecture (Figure 2.13).

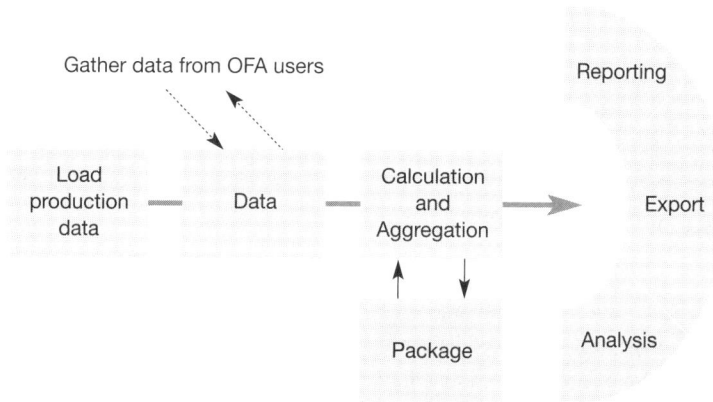

FIG 2.13 **Integrating the packaged approach with OFA**

The business processes have data gathering from OFA users as a critical phase. Much of the implementation challenge is simply to set up processes by which the data will be gathered in a robust and repeatable way, for example in a payroll budgeting project to capture data such as headcount. An OFA architecture simply to gather the data in a robust, controlled way will make a great contribution to a project's success, even if, as discussed earlier, packaged solutions are used in the solution architecture.

2.3.1 Sourcing the data, and commonality of data across business processes

The business processes to which OFA is applied tend to have degrees of commonality in regard to the data they process. Budgeting involves gathering headcount and grade numbers, and management reporting uses these in comparing Actuals with Budget; sales forecasts by Product and Channel are used in planning, but the numbers might be used to cascade marketing costs for profitability analysis.

Consider the example shown in Figure 2.14, in which an activity-based cost allocation of the GL balance of £498,000 required the gathering of driver data, in this case time allocations (70, 80, 63, 36 person-weeks) against the four activities shown. As we shall see, for Balanced Scorecard purposes, the time allocations are performance measures, the Actuals against which planned time might have been compared. This leads to the unsurprising conclusion that the data supports more than one business process and hence is common data.

			Actual	**Budget**
Activity 1	70	Docking Late	140,000	
Activity 2	80	Eqpt Unavailable	160,000	
Activity 3	63	Rework	126,000	
Activity 4	36	Planned Work	72,000	
	Cost of Refit		**498,000**	**500,000**

FIG 2.14   Activity-based costing report

Looking at the example in detail, the cost of refit has been obtained from the ledger in the sum of £498,000. The budget is £500,000 and all appears to be well. Activity-based analysis reveals that, in the period concerned, of the 249 person-weeks that have been used for the refit, only 36 were allocated to planned maintenance; 70 were lost due to docking late, 80 due to lost time waiting for equipment to be made available and 63 used in reworking previous jobs.

Activity-based costing allocates the £498,000 of cost against the activities as follows:

A1	70	140,000
A2	80	160,000
A3	63	126,000
A4	36	72,000
	249	498,000

(In OFA, we would typically use an Express SPL program to allocate the costs of £498,000, based upon the series of numbers, 70 80 63 36 totalling 249. We address this in more detail later.) The activity-based cost analyst might bring to the attention of the appropriate managers the cost of each activity and invite explanation/action. Each manager is essentially asked to review the business processes from the point of view of the cost of value-added activity versus costs of non-value-added activity.

Meanwhile, the performance measurement group are preparing the corporate Balanced Scorecard data for the period. The classic four-quadrant Balanced Scorecard model looks like Figure 2.15.

Finance	Internal Process
People	Customers

FIG 2.15   **The Balanced Scorecard**

To populate the Internal Process and People quadrants, the performance management group will have asked process managers to set targets for the period, to be ultimately compared with the Actuals, say:

Refit Programme	*Performance Target (person-weeks)*
Time lost due to docking	55
Time lost re equipment	90
Rework	60
Planned effort	40

The Balanced Scorecard will gather Actuals to compare with the targets previously agreed. These Actuals are of course the same numbers used to allocate cost by the cost analyst group:

	Actual	*Target*
A1	70	55
A2	80	90
A3	63	60
A4	36	40

It would be inefficient if the performance management group were to send out an enquiry to the same process managers from whom identical information has been already collected by the cost analysts.

We can conclude from the example that much of the data for the Balanced Scorecard would have already been gathered from production systems and people directly for other purposes. The use of OFA to create a data mart of common data for a number of business processes seems to make sense. In using the functionality represented in our familiar diagram (Figure 2.16), production data may be loaded from systems containing production data, while data, including text, is gathered from OFA users, and then made available for display in a separate Balanced Scorecard application.

The Balanced Scorecard application is fed from an OFA export, while the requirements for planning, budgeting, cost allocations of all types, reporting and analysis are all delivered from 'one view of the truth'.

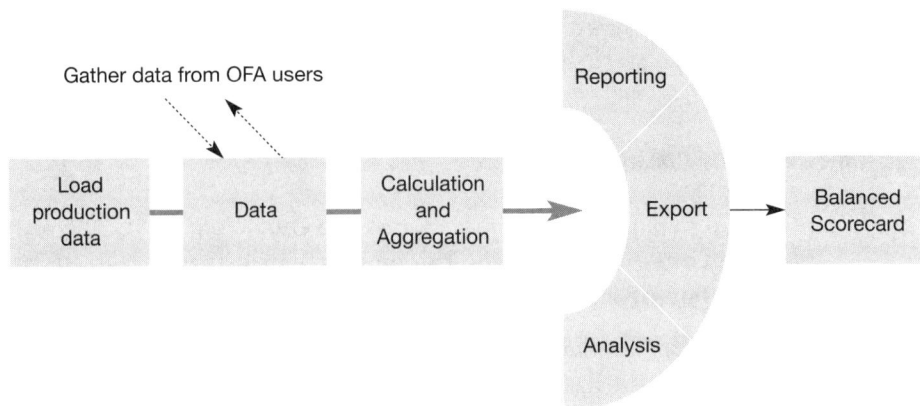

FIG 2.16   **A solution architecture using OFA to feed the Balanced Scorecard**

2.3.2 Sourcing the metadata, and commonality of metadata across business processes

Metadata is 'data about data', and can be thought of in the OFA sense as the structures which exist independently of the data they manipulate or display. Metadata can be a product hierarchy, a chart of accounts roll-up or an attribute of data, such as 'product 4 is a category A product, products 1, 2 and 3 are category B products'. OFA understands the difference between structures and data because of the fundamental design decision taken to separate structures from the data, reflected in the functionality of the Manage menu, as in the screen shot shown in Figure 2.17, which will be discussed later in more detail.

Distributing the data and the metadata

The numerical example considered earlier concentrated on data, not the structures which manage the data. The screen shot shown in Figure 2.18 shows the process by which OFA distributes metadata to the user, examples of metadata being an Attribute and a Hierarchy, as well as a Report and a Worksheet, which are more correctly described as templates. The Distribute Structures menu option shows the structures and templates being distributed. The data is distributed separately, as we shall see later. This is logical, since it is the structures – the metadata – that manage the data; without the metadata, the data is itself meaningless.

Sourcing the metadata

A project may involve use of tools which execute SQL against the tables of a relational database, such as Oracle Discoverer or Oracle Reports, as well as OFA which manipulates data in Express. There is an obvious need to 'share' metadata, so that,

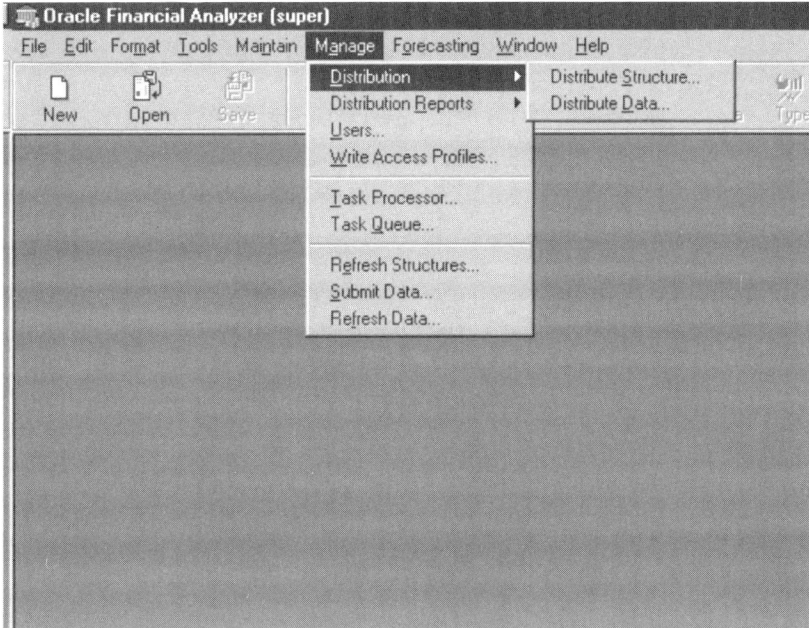

FIG 2.17   Distribute structures and data separately

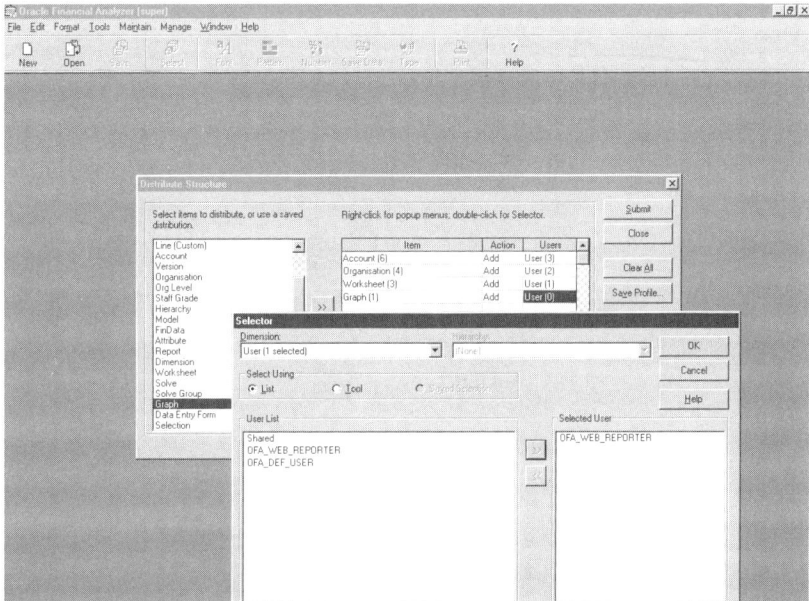

FIG 2.18   Distributing structures

regardless of the product being used, reporting, ad-hoc queries and more complex modelling and analysis can be conducted without the user having to understand new structures every time he or she moves from one application to the other. A product hierarchy and the product names in the hierarchy should be the same, regardless of the application.

The problem of sourcing of the metadata arises. From the foregoing, it should be clear that there are good facilities for controlling the distribution of structures and data *once they are in OFA*. The issue of where both structures and data *come from* is tied up with the issue of the data warehouse, and the related enterprise resource planning system issue. These issues are dealt with in Chapter 4.

Clearly, with production data and corporate metadata for many business processes sourced from one place, OFA can then be used to gather data once only from OFA users, and merge it with production data and metadata so that 'one view of the truth' is available for many cognate business processes. Duplication of data, metadata and data capture processes across many single-function packages does not make sense.

3 Oracle Financial Analyzer key features

ROAD MAP

This chapter commences with a summary of the functionality within OFA. It does not assume that the reader has attended the introductory courses run by Oracle or has access to the User Guide. Hence it can provide an overview for such readers. For those already familiar with OFA, this chapter can be skipped, but some of the issues raised may offer an alternative slant to the reader's previous experience and hence prove useful. After reading this chapter, the reader will appreciate that OFA is an application development framework and be aware of:

3.1   OFA key features and functions

3.2   How OFA provides controlled flow of structures and data – not files

3.3   The different types of OFA client and hence the options available to the OFA system designer.

3.1 OFA KEY FEATURES AND FUNCTIONS

In this section, we highlight the individual features and functions of Oracle Financial Analyzer, how the distributed architecture works, the client types available, and discuss how these features, functions and client types can be exploited to address business processes.

3.1.1 OFA: not a package, but an application development framework

It is best to think of OFA as an application development framework, which contemplates certain business processes. A package delivers a set of functions, say budgeting, activity-based costing, reporting, balanced scorecard. These packages can be used to deliver single business processes, but may result in 'islands of data'. OFA can be used to deliver many business processes, while allowing the sharing of data, providing 'one view of the truth'.

3.1.2 What is the OFA distributed architecture?

The ability to deliver a tiered distributed architecture was key to the success of Oracle Financial Analyzer. It is absolutely critical to all involved in implementing OFA to have a clear understanding of what is possible. Figure 3.1 summarizes the key features of a tiered distributed architecture.

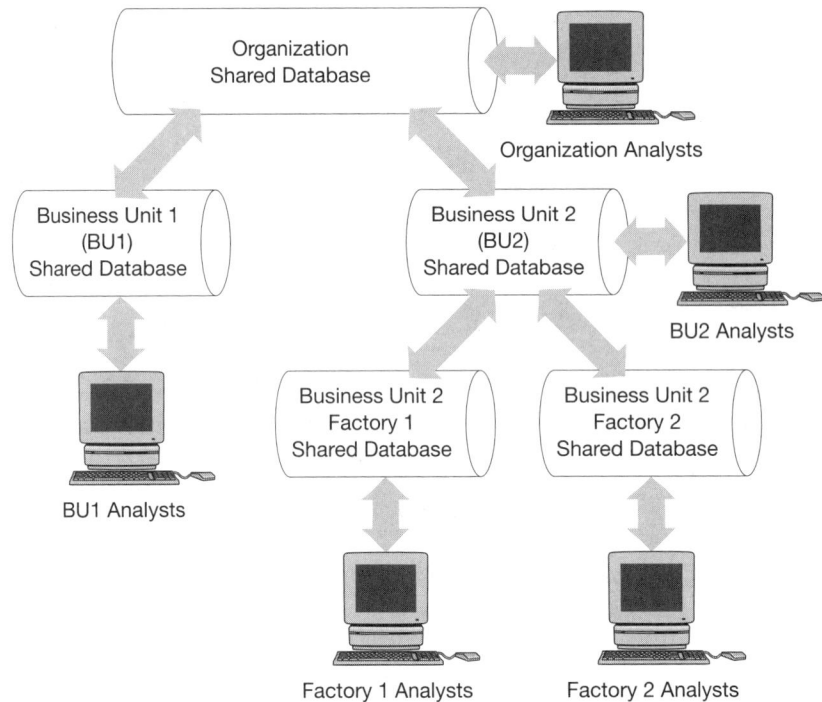

FIG 3.1   **A tiered distributed OFA architecture**

An **Administrator** defines and maintains standard structures, such as Dimensions, Hierarchies, Attributes, Models, Reports, Graphs, and determines what is available to each user on a read-only or read write basis. He or she also controls the collection, consolidation and distribution of this information throughout the organisation. A hierarchy of these database administrators, controlled by a Super Administrator, can effectively support a tiered, shared information environment.

Administrators can create **Sub Administrators**, who can, in turn, create other Sub Administrators. The ability to design and build a tiered distributed architecture reduces the size and complexity of the top-level structures in Oracle Financial Analyzer and permits greater autonomy and control at lower levels and remote sites. Large, complex and frequently changing structures can be managed effectively. Diverse organizations with many business streams, each having different structures and processes, can be supported efficiently in this way.

3.1.3 OFA workstations?

Oracle Financial Analyzer works from the premise that different users require different perspectives of the same data, and different functionality to analyze and process that data. As we shall see later, Oracle Financial Analyzer offers a series of workstation types tailored to the needs of the budgeter, analyst, reporter and administrator. Users are associated with a single Shared Database and are assigned a workstation in line with their role. A **Budget Workstation** allows the user to copy or download data from the Shared Database to a local Workstation, report, analyze, create and modify data – perhaps prepare the latest forecast or next budget – and export the revised data back to the Shared Database, as required. Such users may often see more than they can change by having access to data on areas of related responsibility, but they are only able to Submit changes to figures for which they have appropriate authorization. A Budget Workstation provides specific facilities to model and modify data locally. Since these Workstations hold data locally, they can typically hold 10 per cent of the data held centrally. This is an important issue to consider when estimating disk size requirements, as discussed in Sections 5.5 and 5.6. Another type of Workstation is the **Analyst Workstation** which provides read-only access to the larger Shared Database held on the server, but can Save an OFA Worksheet to send data to the Shared Database. By storing only the menus and personal report templates in the Analyst's personal database, there is little impact on overall database size.

3.1.4 What does OFA use as the underlying database?

Oracle Financial Analyzer uses Oracle Express Server as its underpinning database. This is a multidimensional database technology, rather than Oracle's RDBMS technology. Oracle Express Server is optimized for the query and analysis of corporate data. Such analysis is often called Business Intelligence. Historically, Oracle Express Server was one of the first online analytical processing (OLAP) servers to use a multidimensional data model. The model is complementary to relational systems used for online transaction processing (OLTP).

3.1.5 What are the key features and benefits of Express-based functionality?

- Multidimensional data structures ('cubes') to support analysis that is natural for end users, who, when thinking of measures such as Sales, tend to think about the dimensions of their world, such as Product, Market and Time.

- Multiple cubes to support different data requirements across corporate departments. Hence Oracle Express supports measures of different dimensionality in one database. For example, the data item Unit Cost, which is dimensioned only by Product and Time, can coexist with Sales, which is dimensioned by Market, Product and Time. Only if unit costs vary across markets will they be included in the same data item as sales.

- Express also includes a fourth-generation language, which provides a function library supporting modelling, forecasting, simulation and what-if analysis. The function library has over 500 functions. Since time is an important dimension in all applications, the following time-series functions are provided:

> LAG Function
>
> LAGABSPCT Function
>
> LAGDIF Function
>
> LAGPCT Function
>
> LEAD Function
>
> MOVINGAVERAGE Function
>
> MOVINGMAX Function
>
> MOVINGMIN Function
>
> MOVINGTOTAL Function

and since Finance is a common application, the following for Financial Operations:

> DEPRDECL Function
>
> DEPRDECLSW Function
>
> DEPRSL Function
>
> DEPRSOYD Function
>
> FINTSCHED Function
>
> FPMTSCHED Function
>
> GROWRATE Function
>
> IRR Function

  NPV Function

  VINTSCHED Function

  VPMTSCHED Function

OFA is often used in situations where there are non-financial numbers, such as in Sales forecasting, and hence the function library includes Forecasts and Regression functions:

  FORECAST Command – straight-line trend, exponential growth, or Holt-Winters extrapolation

  REGRESS Command – multiple linear regression

3.1.6 A closer look at multidimensional data management with Express

Consider the area of management reporting. This typically includes monthly updated profit and loss items, summary balance sheet data, key performance ratios and indicators, cash flow forecasts and stock and production information. This data is **multidimensional** and contains financial and non-financial numbers. One view of the data could be as follows:

  An Account dimension covering such items as income and costs. The data is by period and totalled over time (quarters and years), hence a Time dimension. The data is aggregated by levels in the organization (divisions and branches), hence an Organization or Cost Centre dimension.

  and

  the data is held as actual, budget and forecast (scenarios). Other scenarios, such as variance between scenarios, can be calculated. Through Express, Oracle Financial Analyzer creates Actuals cubes, Budget cubes and Forecast cubes. These data items share dimensionality and can be visualized as shown in Figure 3.2.

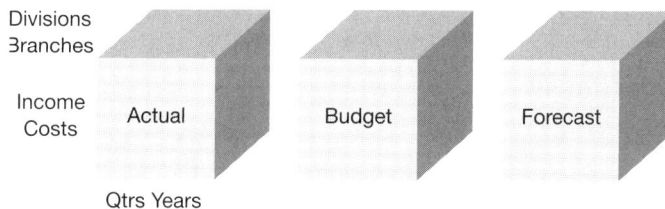

FIG 3.2   **A three-dimensional view of the data**

This represents just one three-dimensional view of the data. This may be sufficient for standard reporting to corporate level, but management at the divisional level often require further perspectives on the data. Instead of forcing one structure on the data, **Oracle Financial Analyzer allows the definition of any number of dimensions**, and any number of differently dimensioned pieces of information, or Financial Data Items. For example, data may also be held as follows:

Budget sales data FDI,

with the following dimensions (Figure 3.3):

Time
Line Item covering unit sales volumes, price, gross sales value
Product aggregated from individual product into category
Organization allowing analysis of budget sales by department and division

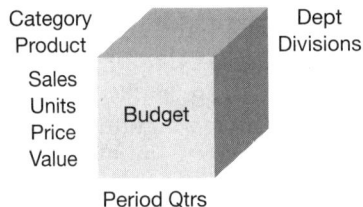

FIG 3.3   **A four-dimensional view of the data**

Another view could be personnel data organized by <Job classification, Organization and Time>. We shall see more of this in the Case Studies. Oracle Financial Analyzer allows as many cubes to be defined as are required. Later we shall see how these cubes can be manipulated to **easily restructure**, **combine**, **model**, **aggregate** and **compare** the differently structured data. The flexibility of Oracle Financial Analyzer as an application development framework owes much to the multi-cube capabilities of Express. This flexibility provides capabilities to handle at a local and Head Office level the complex needs of organizations with diverse business units.

3.1.7 Transparency of the cube diagram as a system specification document

We shall look later at the use of cube diagrams as a design document for the system. The transparency of the cube diagram enables the business person to understand what is being designed and hence there is less danger of confusion between the system designer and the user. Figure 3.4 shows how a cube diagram makes explicit a simple calculation.

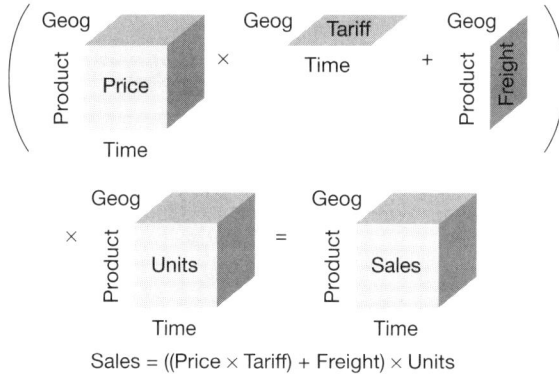

Sales = ((Price × Tariff) + Freight) × Units

FIG 3.4   A cube diagram for a simple calculation

The calculation identifies the sales value by:

- multiplying the base price of each product by the tariff, an uplift based upon where it will be sold;

- then adding the cost of freight for that product, which itself depends upon where it will be delivered;

- then multiplying the price so calculated by the number of units sold into that geography.

Instead of a low-level program or a set of SQL statements, which are likely to be incomprehensible to the business user, the meaning of the diagram is transparent. In general, the OFA structures provide a highly transparent view of the system requirement, to which the system builder can refer the business user to clarify the detailed requirements during the system build. This is why documentation of the required OFA structures and the process flows which perform calculation and aggregation is often done incrementally, particularly when prototyping and conference room pilots are being used to gain user commitment during implementation.

3.1.8 OFA and Express

The current architecture of the OFA application development framework is summarized in Figure 3.5. A more detailed view can be found in Appendix D, Figure D.1.

HTML/Java provides client-side functionality connecting to the Express Shared multidimensional database through HTTP via Web Agent. Windows clients, written in Visual Basic, access the Shared Database through SNAPI (Structured N-dimensional Application Program Interface) or XCA (Express Communications Architecture) in thick client mode. Excel also accesses the Express Shared database through SNAPI. The Shared Database contains structures and data. A separate Express database, the Super Database, maintains the structures – the metadata – updating the Shared Database when appropriate.

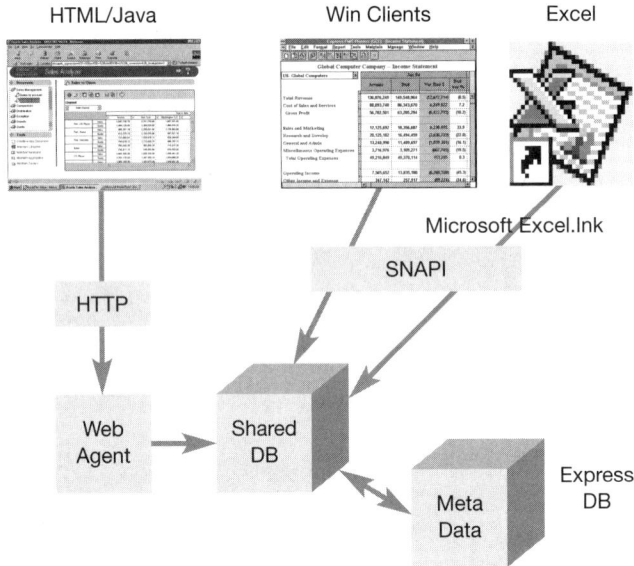

FIG 3.5
The current architecture of OFA

The OFA client-side functionality implemented in Visual Basic is a set of WBX, DLL and EXE files. The end user, whether as Administrator or ultimate end user, will normally operate through this 'front end'.

The 'back end' is the Express database, a set of Express DB files. As noted earlier, Express has a richly functional Stored Procedure Language (the Express SPL hereafter). The 'front end' allows the user to use the Express SPL, but without needing to know the Express SPL syntax.

3.1.9 OFA and Express catalogs

A catalog is an Express cube, holding information about the OFA implementation. It is usually a two-dimensional text variable. The internal working of OFA uses catalogs extensively to record information about user-created structures. Catalogs are normally populated at implementation time when the front-end GUI (graphical user interface) is used. Consider, for example, the USER.CATALOG, which is populated when creating new OFA users. The Express cube has two dimensions, USER.ENTRY and USER.PROP (Figure 3.6).

When the OFA front end is used, the USER.ENTRY dimension values will be increased (or decreased). For example, the USER.CATALOG shown in Figure 3.7 has three values for the USER.ENTRY dimension, SHARED, AA and FO, reflecting the fact that, in addition to the Shared, there are two OFA users in this OFA implementation, AA and FO1234. (Note that AA is always used as the code for the Super Administrator user. The codes used for all other users are alpha-numerics, randomly

USER.ENTRY

USER.PROP

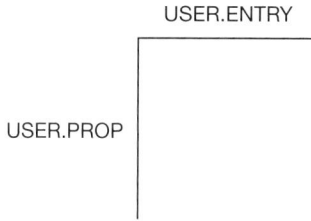

FIG 3.6   **The user catalog**

generated by OFA. They have no significance to the front end, and are not seen by the user, but provide OFA with a unique reference by which each user is stored.) The users must have a DESCRIPTION, a TYPE and a USER.ID, assigned during the set-up process in the GUI.

| | **USER.ENTRY** | | |
USER.PROPERTY	SHARED	AA	FO1234
DESCRIPTION	Shared	SuperDBA	BWI
TYPE	SHARED	DBA	BUDGET
USER ID		JKC	BUDI

FIG 3.7   **The user catalog populated**

On implementation, many entries will be made in many catalogs to reflect the structures and data in the implementation. Catalogs maintained in OFA are sometimes published by Oracle, but this is not true of every OFA version.

3.1.10 Custom programs in Express SPL

The GUI allows a working OFA environment to be created. In addition, Express SPL custom routines can be created to supplement functionality not available in the GUI. These routines can be included in the 'ADD-IN' menus, to provide functions such as:

- maintenance of dimension values from other dimensions;
- sorting of dimension values;
- building hierarchies from attributes;
- automatic distributions.

This list just gives examples of the way the existing functionality can be enhanced. Each implementation will have its own potential for these types of enhancement.

3.1.11 Time intelligence

Oracle Financial Analyzer understands time when aggregating to more aggregate time periods. Using aggregation of months into quarters as an example, the standard time aggregation rules are:

add months into quarters (typically for revenue and expense lines)

    e.g.   qtr1 = jan+feb+mar

opening balances (typically for balance sheet or cash flow items)

    e.g.   qtr1 = jan

closing or end of period balances

    e.g.   qtr1 = mar

average the month figures into quarters

    e.g.   items such as headcount

recalculate quarters

    e.g.   profit margin ratio

The default Oracle Financial Analyzer Time dimension has 12 periods, 4 quarters and a year total. It can be replaced by an alternative time dimension to reflect the user's business, e.g. 13 periods can be specified instead of the standard 12, or half-years can be added.

3.1.12 Hierarchies

Oracle Financial Analyzer can provide an unlimited number of tree hierarchies on any dimension to provide multiple aggregated views of the data. It also enables 'what-if' questions to be asked, such as the effect on profitability of:

- rationalizing the regional reporting structure;
- introducing a new product range under our leading brand;
- moving production from one plant to another.

Questions like these can be answered quickly by using dynamic point and click tools to modify existing hierarchies or create new ones. An example of a hierarchy may be a Sales division that has three three regions and four or five branches in each region.

In the example shown in Figure 3.8, to add the Western region to the hierarchy defined on the right, the user can drag it from the list of available organizations on the left, and drop it on the 'appropriate' organization on the right. The value will be inserted into the hierarchy using the rule chosen. It will be inserted either as a:

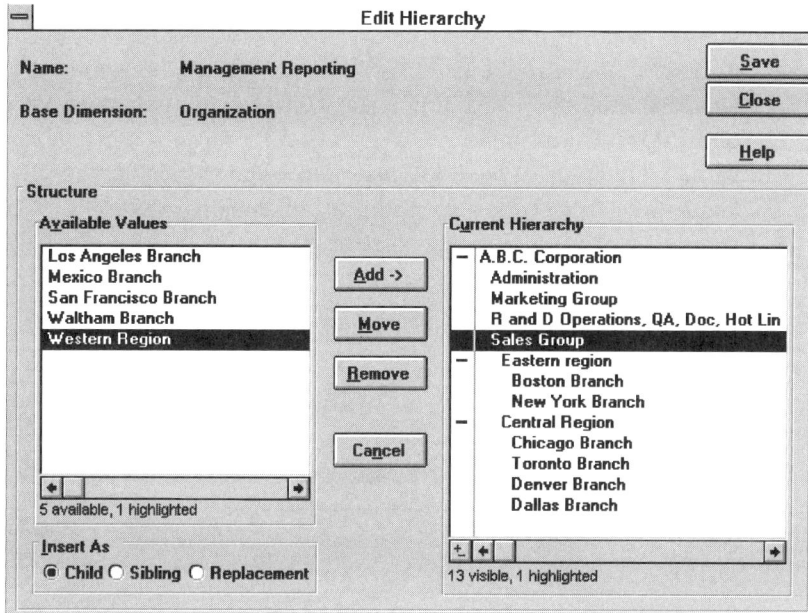

FIG 3.8   Maintaining an organizational hierarchy

■ child, Western Region will report to the Sales Group;

■ sibling, Western Region will report to ABC Corp, alongside Sales Group; or

■ replacement, Western Region will replace the Sales Group.

The diagram shows the tree-like nature of a hierarchy. In this case ABC Corp. is the root of the hierarchy, the regions are branches and the depots are the leaves.

To manage large hierarchies, further drill-up and drill-down facilities are provided to expand or contract the list to the levels in the hierarchies required.

There are, however, some constraints on usability when dealing with very large hierarchies:

■ Long lists of dimension values make drag and drop maintenance unwieldy.

■ There are no facilities to sort the dimension values to facilitate drag and drop.

This means that the hierarchies need to be maintained externally from the OFA GUI, perhaps by sorting them in a spreadsheet and reloading.

(Note: Hierarchies manage dimension values in a tree, calculating and storing results for each level of the tree. This has implications for database size. In contrast, some data items do not need to be stored, since they are only used at reporting time. Formulae can be used to calculate such values, e.g. variance between actual and budget. Financial Analyzer does not store these values but calculates them when required, e.g. when a report is opened.)

3.1.13 Attributes

Attributes behave very much like 'keywords' for searching and extracting data. Oracle Financial Analyzer can use these keywords to build relationships between different dimensions. For example, the members of the organization dimension can be referenced by the type of organizational unit – branch, region and division, as shown in Figure 3.9. This type of grouping of dimension values allows quick selection of common groups for reporting purposes.

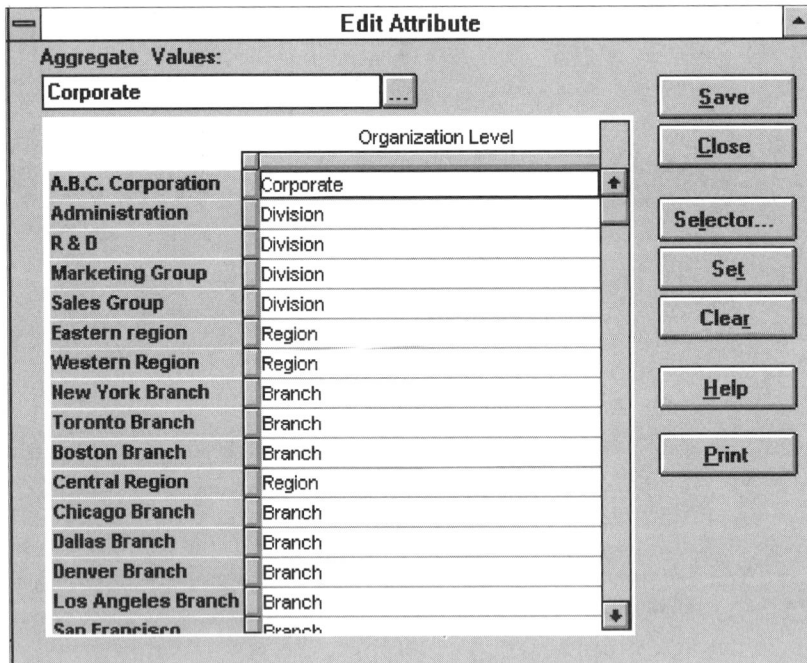

Edit Attribute

Aggregate Values:

Corporate   [...]

	Organization Level
A.B.C. Corporation	Corporate
Administration	Division
R & D	Division
Marketing Group	Division
Sales Group	Division
Eastern region	Region
Western Region	Region
New York Branch	Branch
Toronto Branch	Branch
Boston Branch	Branch
Central Region	Region
Chicago Branch	Branch
Dallas Branch	Branch
Denver Branch	Branch
Los Angeles Branch	Branch
San Francisco	Branch

Save | Close | Selector... | Set | Clear | Help | Print

FIG 3.9   Maintaining an organization-level Attribute

Attributes can allow the user to report on aggregate common dimension values 'on the fly', since the Branch view in the example above is not pre-calculated and hence is not a stored data item. This 'on-the-fly' aggregation is not a facility provided by OFA but can be built using the Express SPL. The use of Attributes in this way can be extremely efficient in terms of database sizing.

As the screen shot shows, Attributes are easy to maintain. They allow considerable flexibility in analysis and reporting, and are also extremely useful in referencing data within Express SPL programs, as we will see in more detail in subsequent chapters.

3.1.14 Models

Models are equations built on a single dimension. Most budgeting Models are developed across the Account dimension since many of the dimension values on that dimension are typically calculated from input dimension values, e.g. profit = revenue – expenses. Models to calculate actuals can be different from the Models for calculating the budget. The Actuals Model may recognize that the majority of data will be imported from external systems such as the General Ledger, whereas Budget Models may define parameter-based formulae using business drivers such as headcount to drive salary costs.

Models can vary by organizational unit; for example, business units engaging in fundamentally different types of activity may well treat overhead allocations differently and so will utilize different allocation Models.

Models are defined through prompted definition of equations (Figure 3.10). Equations use standard arithmetical operators as well as time-series functions such as Lag (used, for example, to model current values using prior year figures as a basis). OFA's understanding of time can enhance the modelling process.

The Oracle Financial Analyzer Model provides access to the full Express function library. The user uses Express SPL syntax to build the Model. Simple functions are provided using a point and click approach (Figure 3.11), but the user can enter more complex calculations directly.

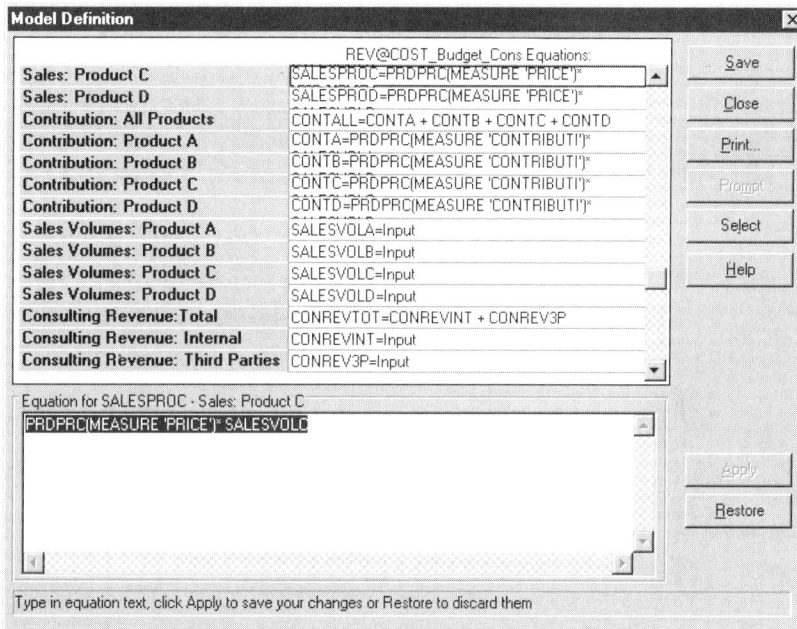

FIG 3.10   An OFA Model on the Account dimension

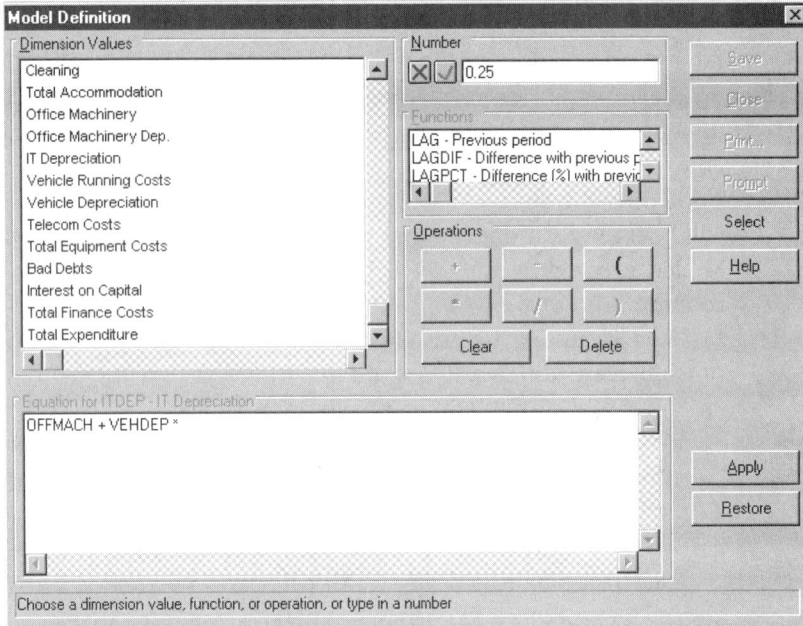

FIG 3.11   **Point and click prompted Model definition**

Unlike a spreadsheet where data and logic are stored together, Oracle Financial Analyzer Models store data separately from the Model rules. The benefits of independence of logic and data can be seen on many business processes. For example, alternative cost allocation Models can be evaluated without duplicating data; it is only the new Model that needs to be stored.

The Administrator will create Models which meet corporate or business unit standards. Users can create their own, more detailed models as required. By adding more detail than the standard system, by defining further line items and calculations, perhaps to derive costs at a specific operational level, users can prepare their budgets and forecasts at the appropriate level of detail. They can then submit the aggregate data to the centre.

In this way the corporate-level database structures are controlled at the centre, whilst autonomy and independence are retained by user departments. This controlled independence of budgetary models enables different what-if analysis for different organizations and budget versions, whilst ensuring consistent calculations for universal or consolidated items.

3.1.15 Solve Definitions

Recalculation of Models and aggregation of the resulting data up Hierarchies is required after data is changed and/or Hierarchies are amended. When it is appropri-

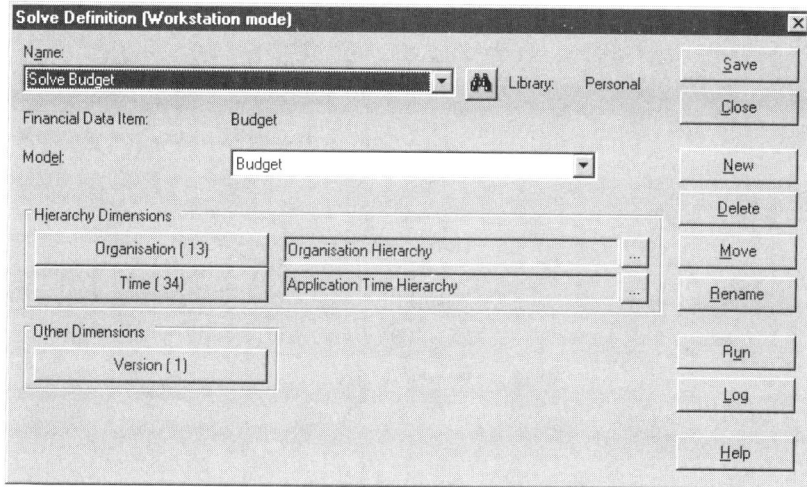

FIG 3.12   The Solve Definition maintenance screen

ate to calculate new values for Financial Data Items for use in Reports, Graphs and Worksheets, it is necessary to run a Solve Definition. A Solve Definition typically contains information about which Financial Data Item is to be calculated or recalculated, which Model is to be used in the calculation, which Dimension values are to be applied, and which Hierarchies are involved, and any Express SPL programs which need to be executed during the Solve (Figure 3.12).

3.1.16 The Worksheet

The OFA Worksheet allows:

- data to be manually input to Oracle Financial Analyzer. The submission of the data to the centre is under the control of the Task Processor, as we will see later;
- data to be retrieved from the Shared Database;
- the use of tools to spread, copy and grow the data in the Worksheet;
- alternative OFA Models and aggregation Hierarchies to be applied to the data *in the Worksheet* to calculate and aggregate results.

An OFA Worksheet is defined in exactly the same way as an OFA Report, Graph or Data Entry Form. Using Selector scripts, all OFA clients can automatically reflect changes to business structures or be dynamically linked to the data.

'Increase' functions within the Worksheet

Values in a range of selected cells may be increased (or decreased by prefixing the minus sign) by an amount or percentage (Figure 3.13).

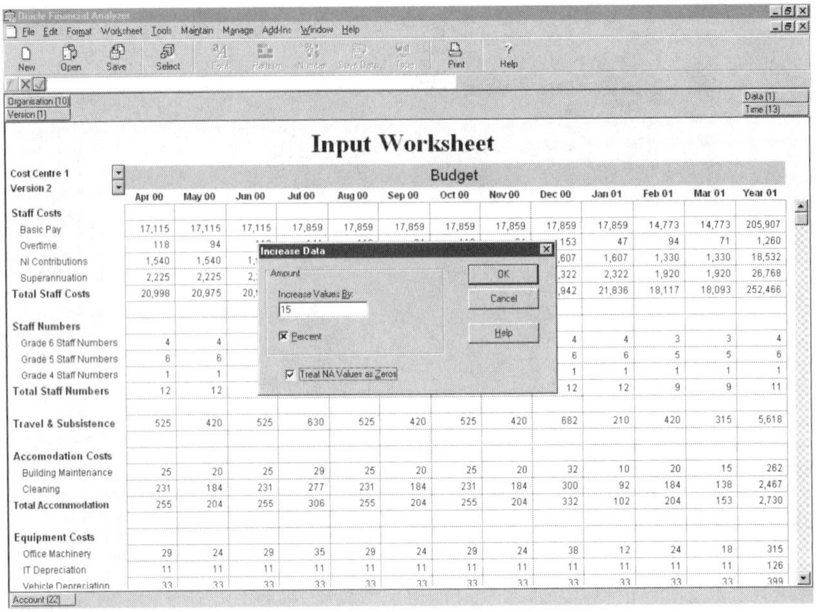

FIG 3.13 'Increase' functions within the Worksheet

'Spread' functions within the Worksheet

Spread functions are provided in the Worksheet to help business processes such as the preparation of phased budgets, top-down budget and cost allocations in which aggregate-level data has to be reallocated. For example:

- annual or quarterly data can be phased to individual time periods;
- aggregate data for an organization can be spread to its reporting units;
- total costs for a brand can be allocated to its family's products.

Oracle Financial Analyzer gives the user several methods to spread the data in the Worksheet, as shown in Figure 3.14:

- spread evenly;
- spread with the same distribution profile, perhaps previously created using the 'Increase' facilities;
- spread with the same profile as another account line, organization etc.

And the allocation can be made to:

- just children of the selected parent(s);
- all descendants, i.e. to the lowest level in the hierarchy selected;
- or just to the reporting elements included in the worksheet.

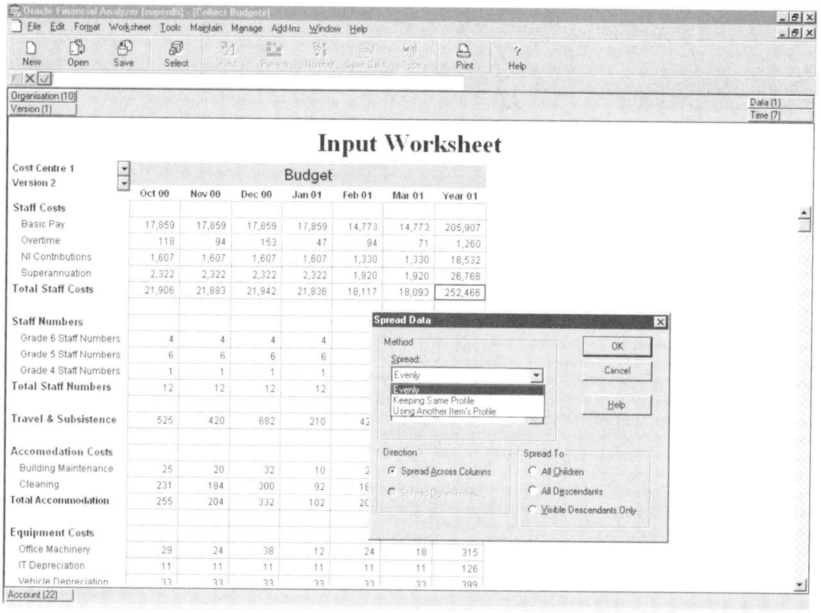

FIG 3.14   'Spread' functions within the Worksheet

Allocations can be automated by associating an OFA Model with the Worksheet, allowing predefined allocation rules to be set up and run whenever the data changes. It is important to keep in mind that the spread applies only to the data in the Worksheet; no change is made to the data held in the Shared Database. Furthermore, the data is spread across only one dimension at a time. This means that if the data is dimensioned by, say, <Product Organization Customer Time>, we can only spread by Product or Organization or Customer, one at a time. (Custom spread methods can be hooked into a Worksheet, if required, by use of an Express SPL program.)

The Worksheet and multidimensional modelling

The Worksheet provides a multidimensional modelling environment, allowing 'drag, and drop' reorientation to allow the user to work on the appropriate parts of a budget or forecast, with the appropriate point of view. The Worksheet above had the Account dimension in the rows, with the Organization, Version and Time dimensions into the page. The user reorientates the view with Organization now down the page; it has been reorientated by dragging and dropping dimension tiles so that line items are displayed into the Worksheet with selected Organizations as rows (Figure 3.15).

The user can now 'page' through the Worksheet to see all different expenses by cost centre for all time periods.

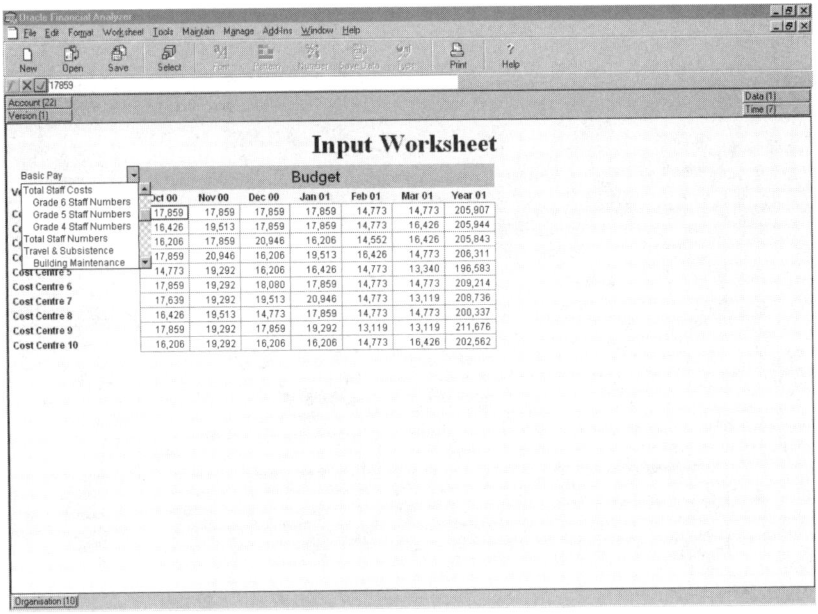

FIG 3.15 Multidimensional Worksheet modelling – change the view

Like a spreadsheet, the data in the Worksheet can be recalculated by applying the selected Model together with the appropriate Hierarchy for aggregation purposes.

Typical recalculation options in a worksheet

Recalculating a Worksheet has an effect only on the data in the Worksheet, not on the central Shared Database, as we shall see later, when we return to discussion of the Solve Definition. As noted earlier, when it is appropriate to calculate new values of Financial Data Items for the central Shared Database, so that they can be used in all reports, graphs and worksheets, it is necessary to run a Solve Definition. Solve Definitions can be associated with the OFA Worksheet, but are much more important in the context of the distributed architecture of OFA, which will be dealt with later.

3.1.17 Oracle Financial Analyzer and spreadsheets

Copy and Paste to and from Excel

Recognizing that most enterprises have made considerable intentional, or unintentional, investments in spreadsheet technology, OFA offers the opportunity to avoid rekeying data by transferring data to and from spreadsheets to OFA Worksheets using Copy and Paste or by exporting files. As noted in Chapter 2, however, the intent should be to avoid having hundreds of spreadsheet files to manage. Oracle

Financial Analyzer allows the spreadsheet to be exploited as the personal tool it was designed to be, in permitting personal calculations, while being able to take the results into OFA for enterprise use.

The Spreadsheet Add-In

An Add-In to MS-Excel is provided to allow Excel users to query and report on Express databases maintained by Oracle Financial Analyzer data in Excel itself (Figure 3.16) and also Express databases created by other client software, such as Web Publisher. This Add-In also provides access to the Selector (which we will cover later) to provide querying capabilities directly from Excel. Drilldown and rotation are also available through the use of the Excel Add-In. In this way, Oracle Financial Analyzer aims to provide the spreadsheet user with easy access to the definitive 'one view of the truth'. (As this data access tool can operate in both read and write modes and does not use the OFA client front end, security is an issue which must be addressed carefully when deploying this tool, otherwise the 'one view of the truth' may be endangered.)

In summary, Oracle Financial Analyzer combines both spreadsheet and database/modelling technologies. This provides flexibility and control, but in a corporate-wide application. Appropriate functions also exist to enable data held in the Shared Database to be integrated with existing analytical models and other personal tools, such as the word processor for report production. The challenge is to move people away from the 'hundreds of spreadsheets' mountain.

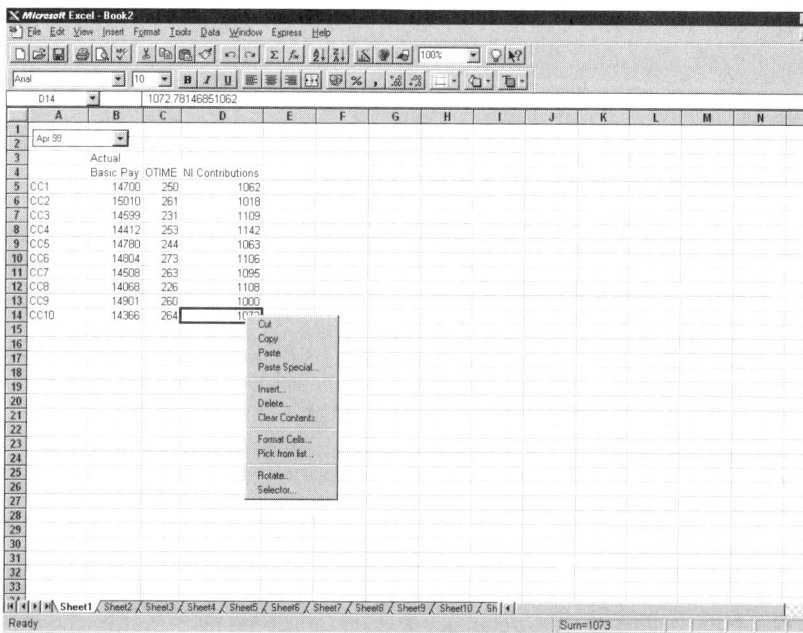

FIG 3.16 The Spreadsheet Add-In

3.1.18 Reporting and analysis

Central to reporting and analysis is the multidimensional cube idiom, which in the Express multidimensional database is a 'variable' and in OFA the 'Financial Data Item' or FDI. There are many products which have harnessed the cube idiom in the marketplace, for the simple reason that its use makes report generation and manipulation essentially What You See Is What You Get (WYSIWYG) for the end user. It has become known as 'slice and dice', with the usual facilities for formatting, fonts, boxing and shading. OFA inherits these facilities from Express, but also provides a means of distribution of standard reports from the Shared Database. There is no need for IT to configure reports for the user, and hence OFA provides self-service reporting.

Self-service and pre-built reports distributed from the Shared Database

Self-service is good but there is no need for users to have to create all the reports they need. For example, a summary P&L report produced for the current quarter, comparing actual with budget and calculating the variance for a selection of organizations, can be produced as a standard shared report – perhaps to be included in a monthly reporting pack. Such shared reports cannot be modified by users directly. If a standard report doesn't meet a user's specific requirements – the user is interested in just two or three P&L items, total revenue and gross profit, and would like to compare them for a selection of organizations – he or she can easily copy and modify the report to achieve this. Or, by changing the dimensionality of the report, organizations can appear down the page, with the selected line items inserted, as we have seen earlier with the Worksheet, as shown in Figure 3.17.

The Selector

The content and scope of a report is defined using a powerful tool called the **Selector**. This tool is common to all Oracle Analytic Solutions software applications. The Selector is a data navigation tool which prompts the user through a variety of options in order to select the dimension values to display. In the example shown in Figure 3.18, reports for ABC Corp. and its cost centres are no longer required; they have been removed from the selected list by highlighting them in the Selected Organizations box on the right and choosing Remove. The report is now restricted to the Sales Group and its regions.

In exactly the same way, the original summary P&L has been reduced to just two lines, Revenue and Profit, this time selecting values from the line item dimension (Figure 3.19).

The left-hand box provides the list of values available for reporting. A user will typically have restricted access to a subset of the values in the Shared Database. Any number of hierarchies can be defined to provide different aggregations, views and

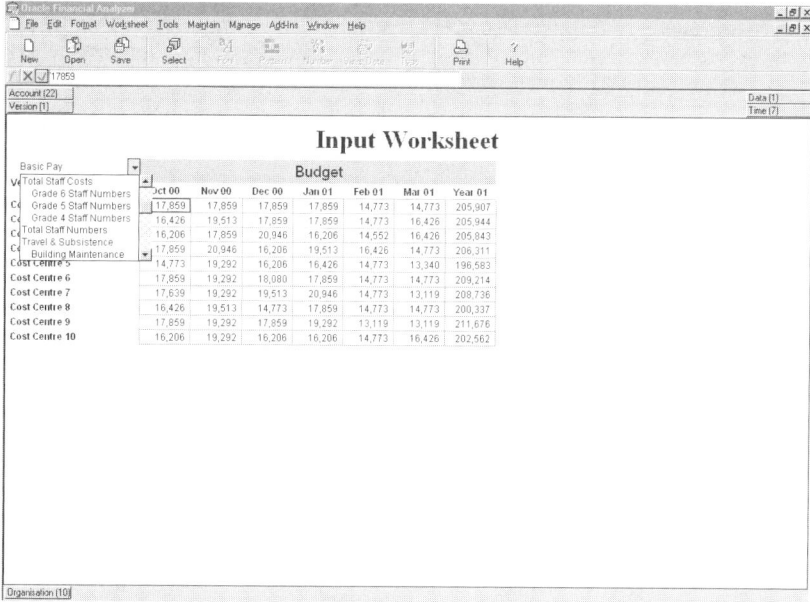

FIG 3.17   Changing the view

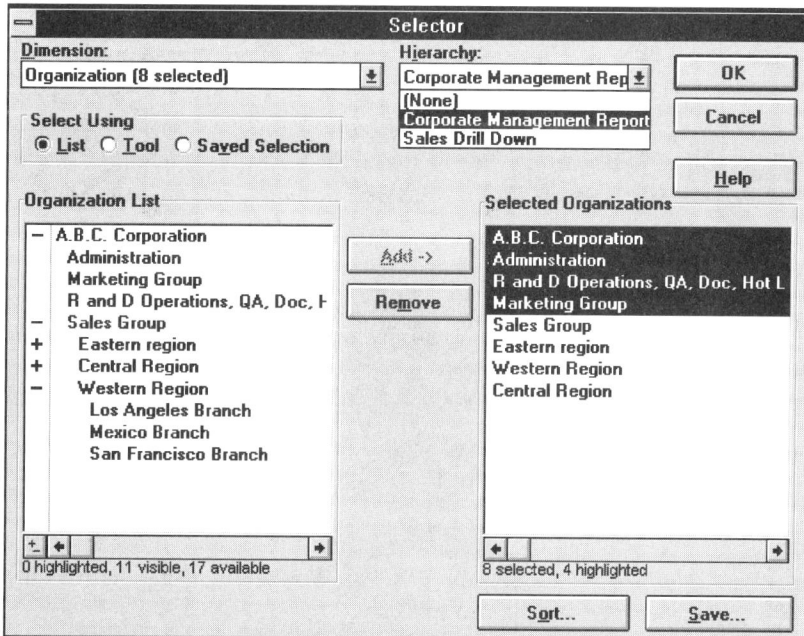

FIG 3.18   Selecting report content – end-user functionality

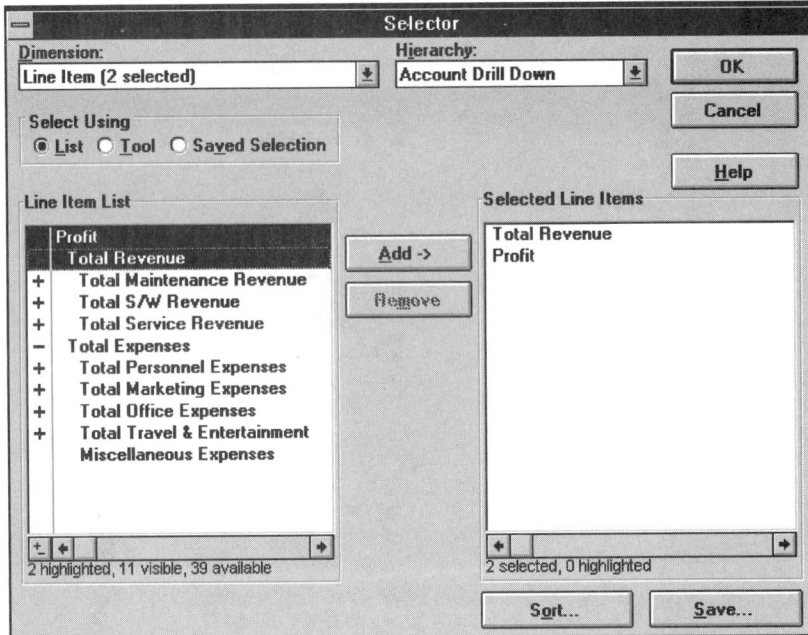

FIG 3.19   Selecting account lines

drill-down paths for analysis and modelling purposes. The user can navigate through and select from many thousands of values using the drill-down (signified by a +) or drill-up (–) facilities. Highlighting the series of values required and then choosing the ADD button will include them in the report. The values highlighted will be added to the list on the right. In this example the user highlights Profit and Total Revenue, shown in the box on the left, and chooses ADD.

Selector tools

Selecting from a list of dimension values may be sufficient; however, with potentially thousands of products, organizations or account lines to choose from, a number of Selector **tools** are provided to assist the user to identify the values they want to see in a Report, Graph, Worksheet or Data Entry Form. These tools can be combined using the operators Select, Add, Keep and Remove to create and save a script of sequenced actions, to be shared across any number of these documents (Figure 3.20).

Select by user-defined Attribute

Dimension values can be selected by attribute, a powerful implementation of the 'keyword' principle. Examples are:

■ the selecting of organizations based on their type – attributes in the example shown in Figures 3.21 and 3.22 are division, branch, region, department.

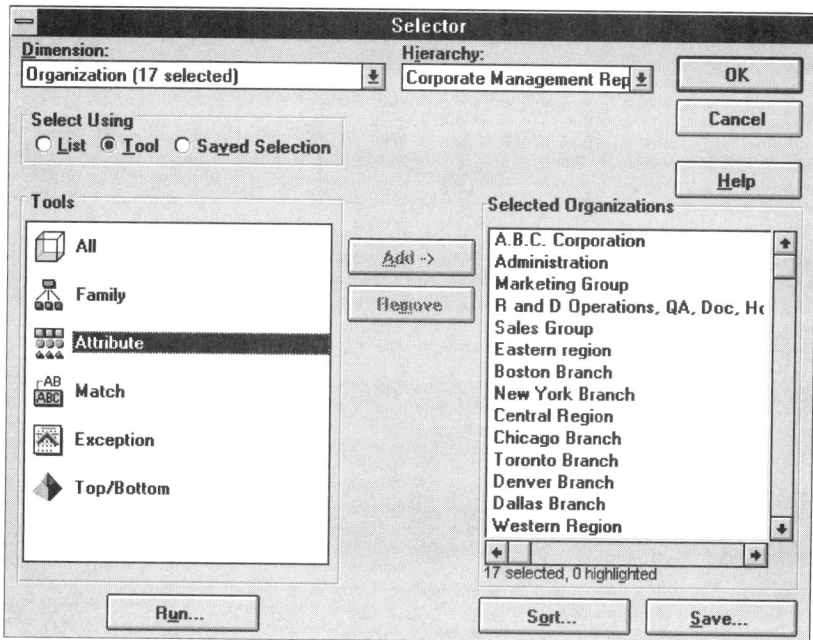

FIG 3.20   The Selector tools

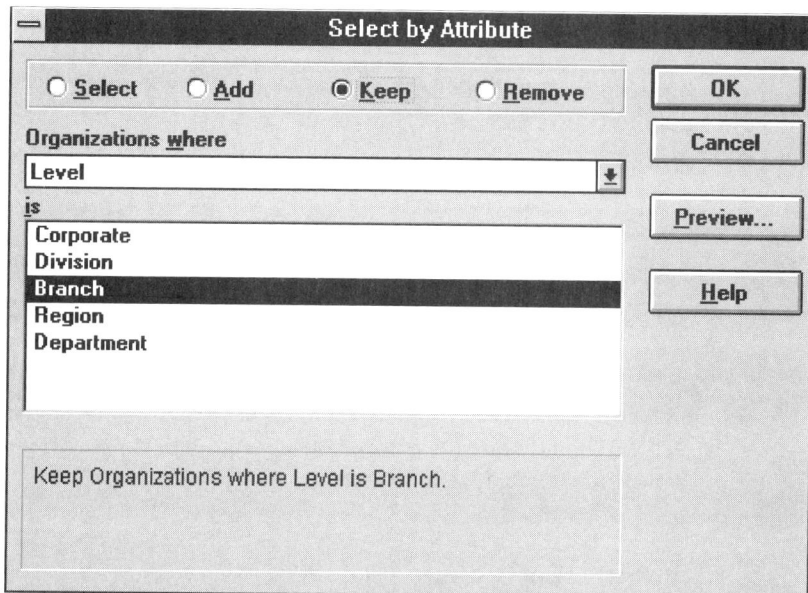

FIG 3.21   Select by Attribute – script generated in 'English'

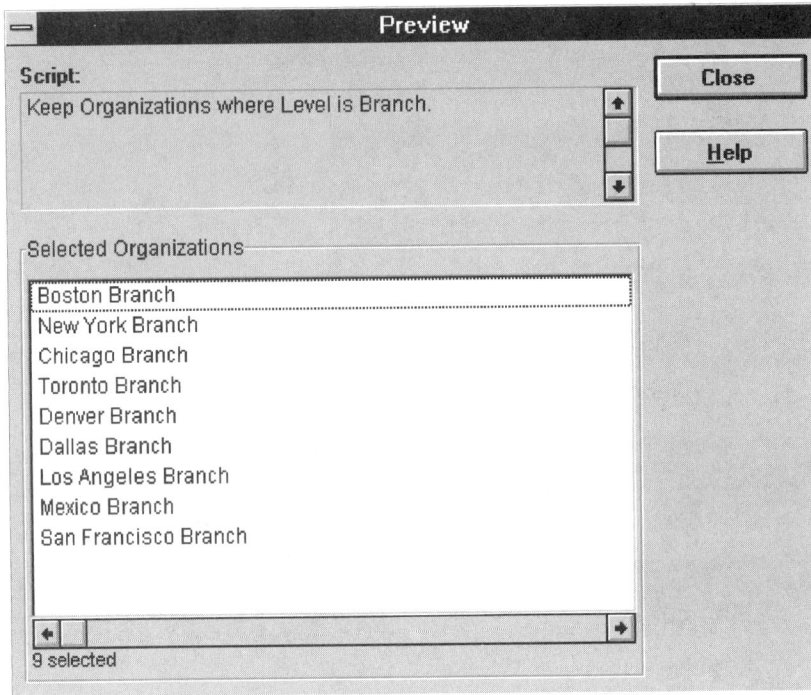

FIG 3.22   **Preview results before proceeding**

Other examples are:

- extracting account lines based on a classification, e.g. indirect, variable, personnel expenses;
- identifying products by brand, pack size, or store-keeping unit (SKU).

Select using Family

Oracle Financial Analyzer exploits the intelligence embedded in the user-defined OFA Hierarchies. Users can select specific elements of a Hierarchy. For example, to create a Worksheet for all 'input' organizations, i.e. at the lowest level in a hierarchy, the user would use the 'last descendants' option to extract all the leaf nodes in a reporting hierarchy. In the example shown in Figure 3.23(a) and (b), this would extract all the branches, for which a bottom-up budget could then be defined.

The elements of a hierarchy are:

- parents – values above the one selected;
- children – values one level below the one selected;
- siblings – values on the same level, but with the same parent;

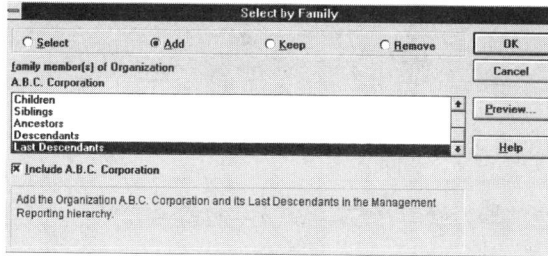

(a)

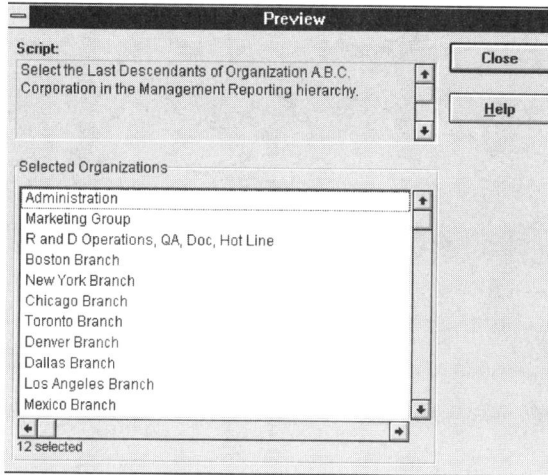

(b)

FIG 3.23   **Select by using the intelligence of hierarchies**

- ancestors – all values above parent;
- descendants – all values below the one selected;
- last descendants – just the leaf values of the one selected.

Select using Match

The Match facility allows users to define, combine or refine selections based on matching user input text strings against system-held descriptions (Figure 3.24).

As Oracle Financial Analyzer is designed to support the reporting and analysis of thousands of products, customers or organizations, this facility is an effective way of identifying ad-hoc data that may cut across the more predefined attributes or hierarchies. An example could be 'find all the accounts with "salary" in the description'.

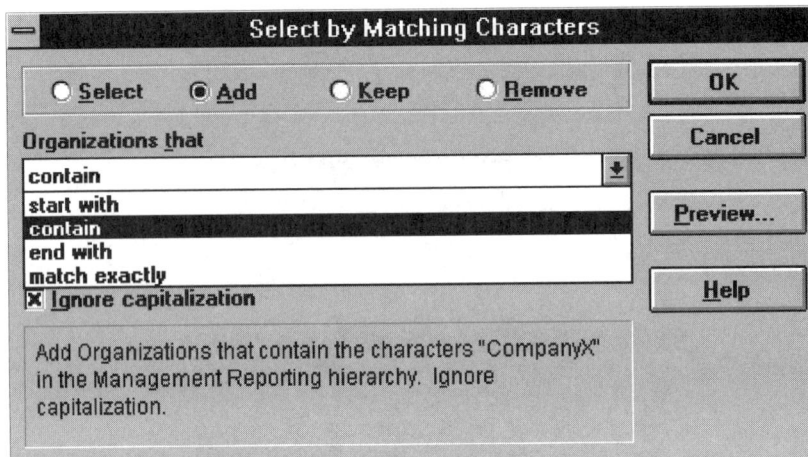

Select by matching text

Select by Exception

Criteria can be specified to select the appropriate values based on *exception* as in Figure 3.25. For example, they can be used to find:

- all organizations within the Northern Division with sales greater than £1 million for the current month and where adverse variance from budget is less than 10 per cent.

The Exception tool can be used to narrow down the view progressively until the desired data set is shown. In this way, relatively complex queries can be broken down into a number of steps, each of which uses simple exception criteria, thus:

1. Identify the organizations meeting the exception criteria shown in Figure 3.26, with the Exception tool, using the Select option.

2. Then narrow the selection further by use of the Exception option to Keep a subset of the data selected (Figure 3.27).

Select top/bottom performers

The Selector has a Top/Bottom tool which permits the user to conduct selections such as:

- find the top and/or bottom *n* products on year-to-date revenue;

- give me the organizations that contribute *n* per cent of the total business;

- give me the top five organizations with variances on overtime for the current month (Figure 3.28).

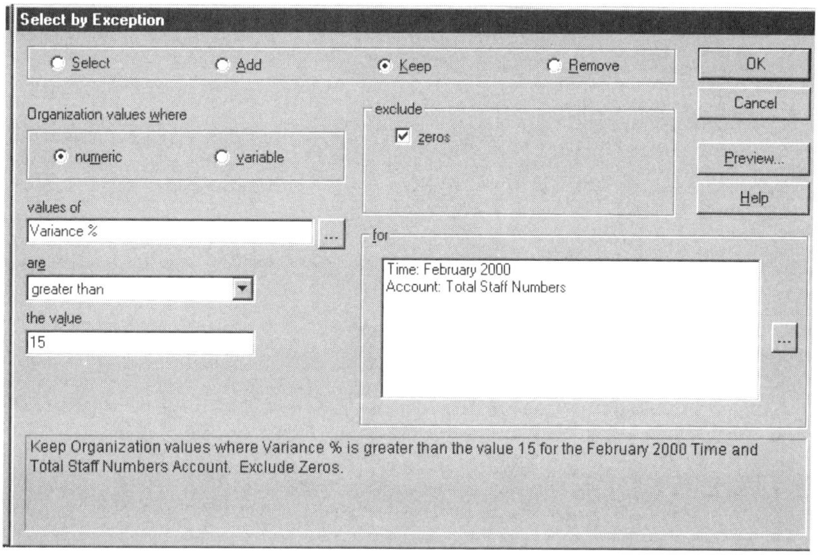

FIG 3.25   Select by exception

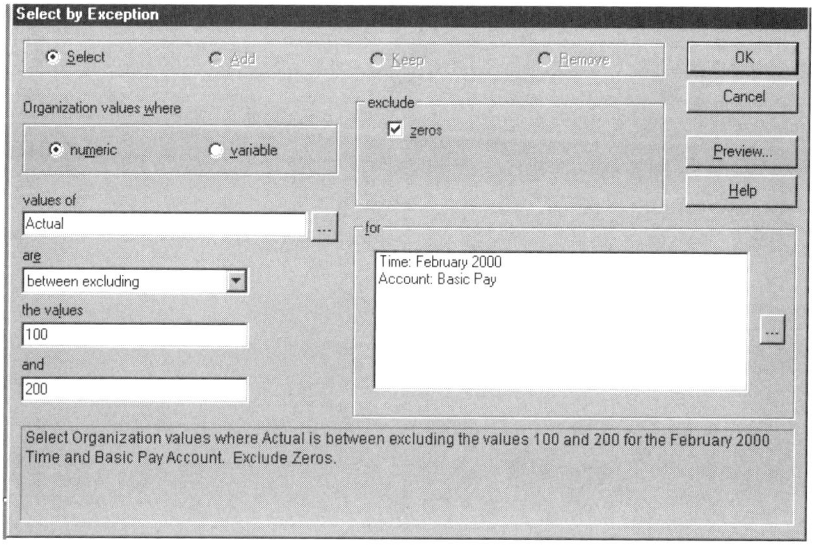

FIG 3.26   Make an initial selection

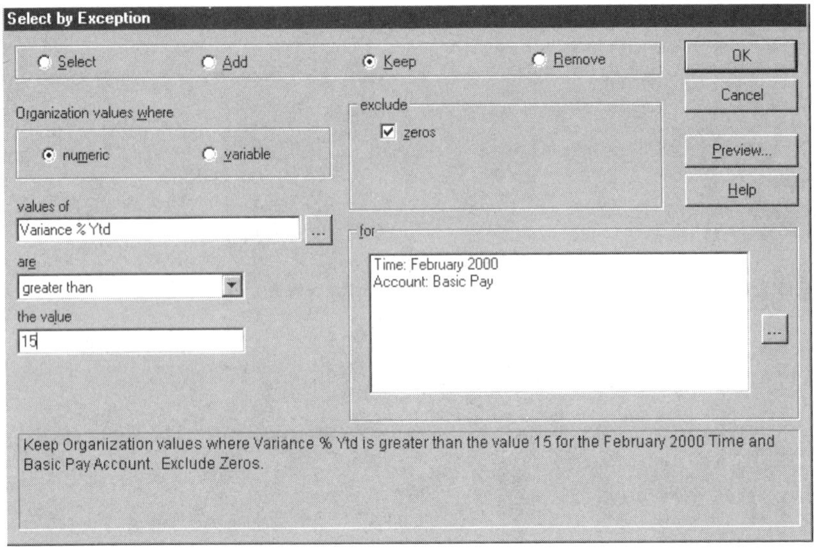

FIG 3.27   Narrow the selection

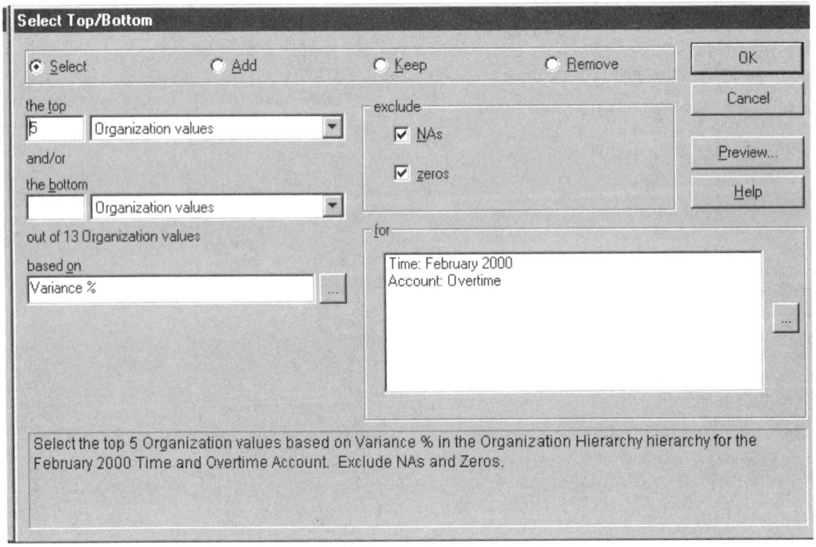

FIG 3.28   Select the top or bottom performers

The Exception and Top/Bottom tools have been superseded to a certain extent by the introduction of ranking and exception reporting in OFA 6.3, which is covered later. This provides greater reporting potential because it is sensitive to the paging dimensions chosen. The Exception and Top/Bottom tools are essentially static with regard to different pages within the report.

Sorting output

Once the dimension values have been selected the values can be sorted (Figure 3.29):

- alphabetically, ascending or descending;
- in database order, forward or reverse;
- based on a data value, i.e. by performance;
- manually, drag and drop values to place them in any order chosen;
- by selected hierarchy.

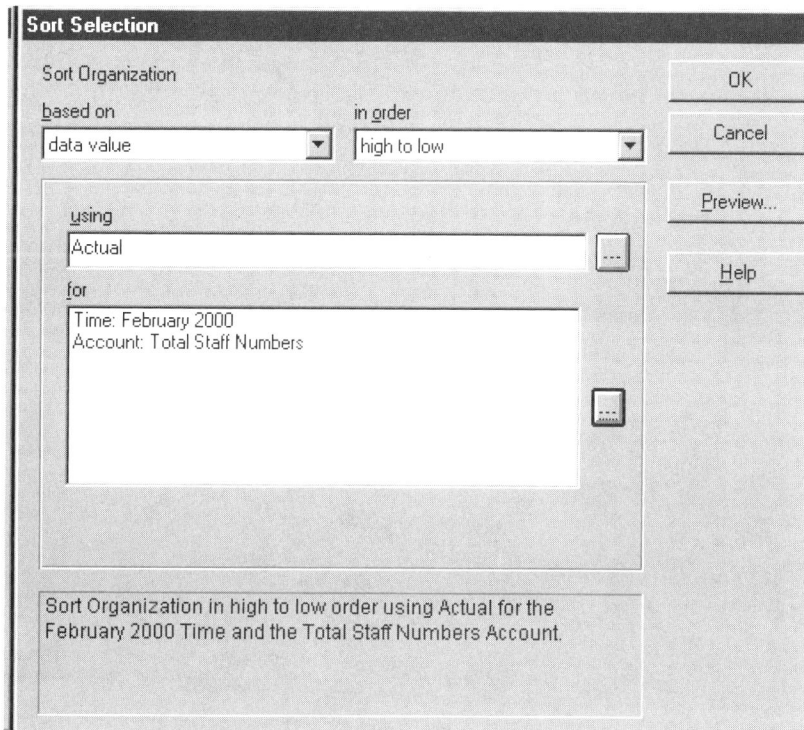

FIG 3.29   Sorting the selected items

Ranking/Exception, and Ranking/Exception combination reports

When creating reports, it is possible to combine the Exception tool with Ranking to create combination reports (Figure 3.30).

The report types available are:

- Ranking – displays data sorted according to ranking criteria specified, on one dimension per report.

- Exception – displays unsorted data associated with dimension values that meet specified criteria.

- Ranking then Exception – creates a ranking-then-exception report which ranks the dimension in the down-the-page position, then applies specified criteria to the ranked dimension to find any exceptions.

- Exception then Ranking – creates an exception-then-ranking report that enables selection of the values for the dimension in the down-the-page position, then applies sort criteria to that data to get ranking results.

Inserting calculations in a report

The Shared Database contains the results of calculations and aggregations performed on the production data loaded and gathered from OFA users into OFA. The Selector is a tool to retrieve data from the Shared Database to form a Report, Graph

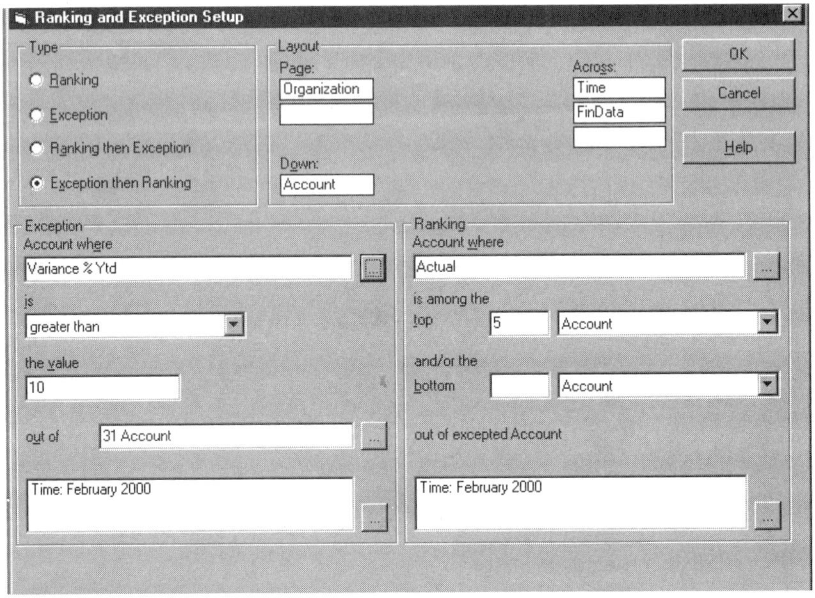

FIG 3.30   Ranking and exception reports

or Worksheet and does not offer functions to perform further calculations and aggregations. However, there may be a need to perform further calculations and aggregations on the Shared Data in a Report for a specific purpose. This is supported by functionality which allows for a range of calculations to be performed on the data, after new rows are inserted in a Report from the Edit menu.

In Figure 3.31, the user has inserted a row called Total Staff Numbers, and is about to select the three rows using the Values tab, before applying the SUM function from the Functions tab.

The functions supported include totalling, averaging and MIN/MAX, which can add considerably to the options available in the report, without burdening the Administrator with requests for further calculations and aggregations, which may not have wider applicability. They take time to develop and hence if there is a general need for such calculations, they should be done in the Shared Database.

More than one dimension can be shown down the page

In the example report shown in Figure 3.32, both organizations and line items are now displayed as rows. Up to three 'dimensions' can be nested in this way. However, it should be kept in mind that when dimensions are nested in the rows it is not possible to drill on any of the dimensions.

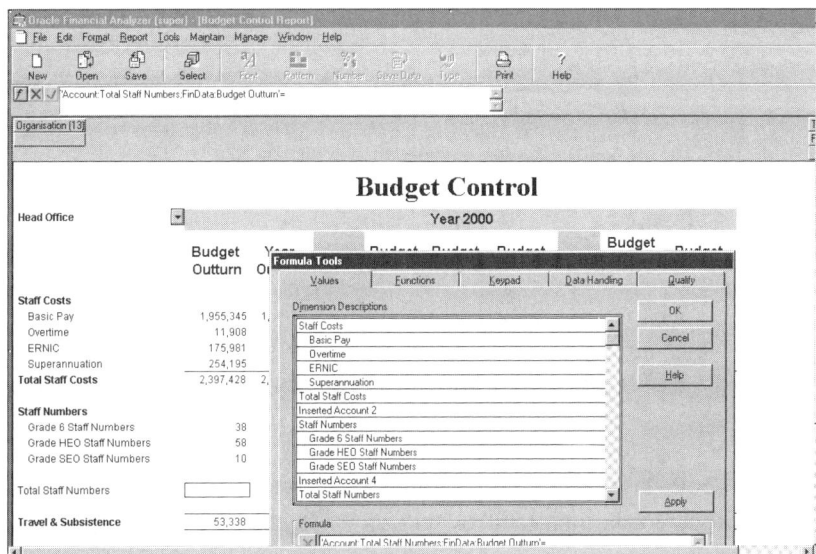

FIG 3.31   Inserting calculations in a report

Cost Analysis

September 2000

	Actual	Budget Final Version	Variance %		Actuals Ytd	Budget Ytd	Variance % Ytd
Basic Pay							
Head Office	147,838	172,086	14		880,710	991,291	11
Division 1	74,116	83,891	12		442,129	489,541	10
Division 2	73,722	88,195	16		438,581	501,750	13
Overtime							
Head Office	2,420	890	(172)		14,984	6,415	(134)
Division 1	1,213	446	(172)		7,428	3,210	(131)
Division 2	1,207	444	(172)		7,557	3,205	(136)
ERNIC							
Head Office	10,346	15,488	33		63,136	89,216	29
Division 1	5,186	7,550	31		31,614	44,059	28
Division 2	5,160	7,938	35		31,523	45,157	30
Superannuation							
Head Office	18,985	22,371	15		115,412	128,868	10
Division 1	9,788	10,906	10		57,786	63,640	9
Division 2	9,198	11,465	20		57,626	65,227	12
Head Office							
Division 1							
Division 2							
Travel & Subsistence							
Head Office	6,242	4,058	(54)		37,286	29,039	(28)
Division 1	3,102	2,060	(51)		18,684	14,525	(29)
Division 2	3,140	1,997	(57)		18,602	14,514	(28)

FIG 3.32   More than one dimension down the page

Saving selections for minimal maintenance

To minimize reporting maintenance work and to improve administrative/end-user productivity, the selection of dimension values can be stored as saved selections. These selections can be stored as scripts, which are evaluated every time a report or worksheet is opened, or as fixed lists of values.

Lists, such as the account lines that make up a summary P&L or detailed expense schedules, are defined once and can be shared across multiple reports and graphs.

■ *Lists* contain fixed selected values.

Scripts are combinations of selection criteria defined using the Selector tools, which are re-applied every time a report is run (Figure 3.33). They are dynamic with the underlying data or structures. For example, a profitability report that extracts all branches in a region can immediately reflect any changes made to that region's organizational hierarchy. If responsibility for a branch is moved from one region to another, the effect can be immediately reflected in the reports using that script. This approach ensures consistency, reusability and efficiency in defining reports.

■ *Scripts* select values based on functions, such as:
  - line items in a class, e.g. personnel expenses or office expenses;
  - organizations in a level, e.g. branch or region;
  - children of a parent, e.g. all organizations reporting to a Division.

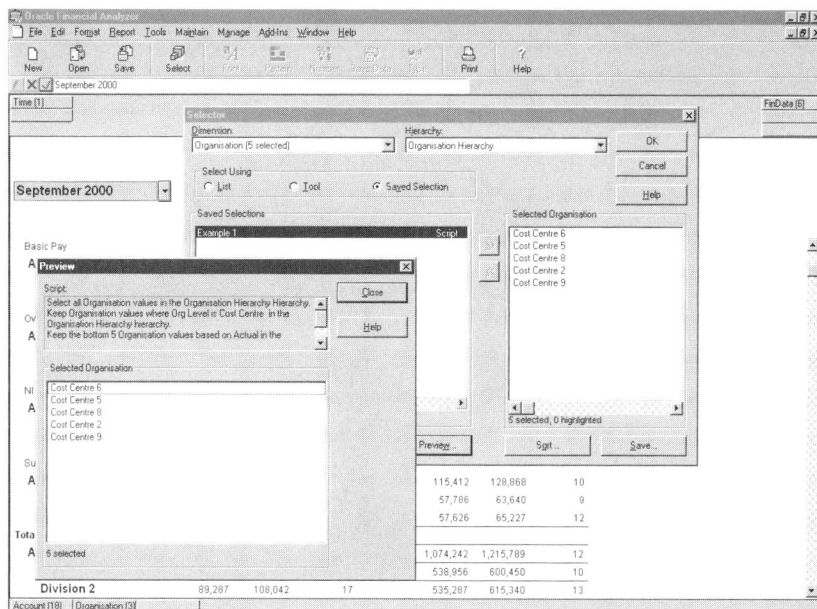

FIG 3.33 English script easy to understand

By capturing a sequence of selections in a script (using Select, Add, Keep and Remove options), sophisticated combinations of selection criteria can be strung together and then regularly applied. The advantage of scripts is that they dynamically substitute the current values that meet the specified criteria at the time the report is generated. They essentially act as macros on selections created using any of the Selector tools.

It is also possible to create custom saved selections, for instance to use the current month, whatever the month is when the data is loaded.

Drill-down capability

Analysis is often a manual process of reviewing a large number of reports, with further investigation often requiring reference to further reports for more detail. Oracle Financial Analyzer automates this process by providing drill-down analysis on any dimension (Figure 3.34).

Hence the same report can be used as the starting point for dynamic drill-down analysis. Click on a row with a + sign and the supporting detail will be revealed. In the example shown in Figure 3.35, clicking on total Division 1 and Division 2 will automatically break out costs by cost centre and dynamically refresh the screen. If time was the down dimension, drilling down on time will break the year into quarters, and quarters into months, and so on down to the lowest time unit that the business requires. Drilling on the account dimension will provide detailed account

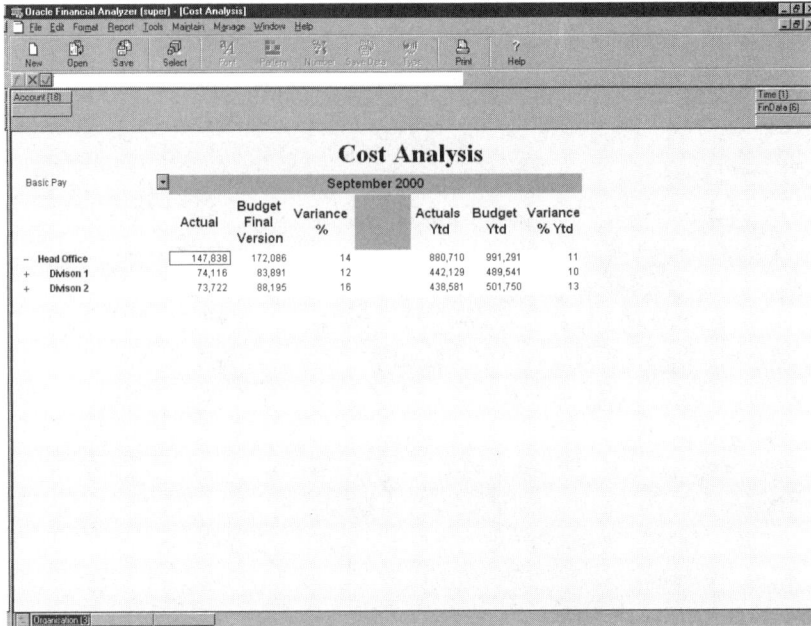

FIG 3.34   Drill down on any dimension

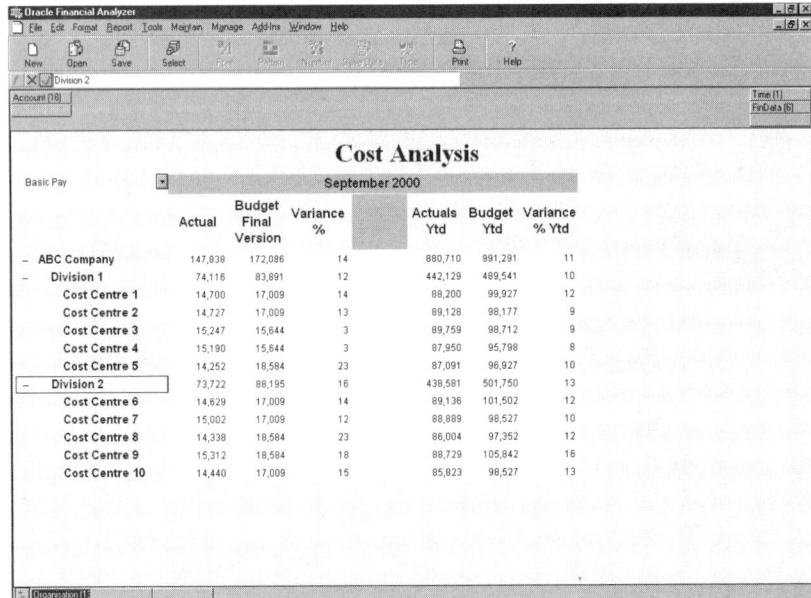

FIG 3.35   Drilling down on the selected hierarchy

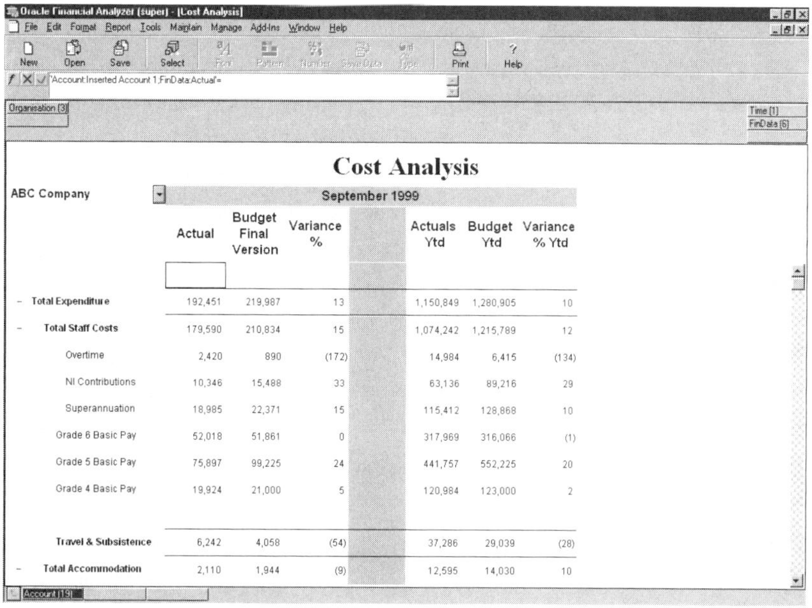
Oracle Financial Analyzer (super) - [Cost Analysis]
File Edit Format Report Tools Maintain Manage Add-Ins Window Help
New Open Save Select Print Help
'Account:Inserted Account 1;FinData:Actual'=
Organisation (3)
Time (1)
FinData (6)
Cost Analysis
ABC Company
September 1999
Actual
Budget Final Version
Variance %
Actuals Ytd
Budget Ytd
Variance % Ytd
Total Expenditure 192,451 219,987 13 1,150,849 1,280,905 10
Total Staff Costs 179,590 210,834 15 1,074,242 1,215,789 12
Overtime 2,420 890 (172) 14,984 6,415 (134)
NI Contributions 10,346 15,488 33 63,136 89,216 29
Superannuation 18,985 22,371 15 115,412 128,868 10
Grade 6 Basic Pay 52,018 51,861 0 317,969 316,066 (1)
Grade 5 Basic Pay 75,897 99,225 24 441,757 552,225 20
Grade 4 Basic Pay 19,924 21,000 5 120,984 123,000 2
Travel & Subsistence 6,242 4,058 (54) 37,286 29,039 (28)
Total Accommodation 2,110 1,944 (9) 12,595 14,030 10
Account (19)

FIG 3.36 Drilling down on the Account hierarchy

analysis. Swapping the organization with the account dimension allows drilldown on the accounts hierarchy, as in Figure 3.36.

The screen shots above are from the client/server interface; with the Web interface, it is possible to drill across rows, as well as drill down, as we shall see later.

It is important to note from the foregoing that no programming needs to take place, nor predefinition of screens or actions; an end user may accomplish the required reporting and analysis without any database administrator or user programming. Combining the power of drilldown with exception scripts permits analyses which can be run on a regular basis with, effectively, automated maintenance. This should free up the analyst's time and provide the framework for devolving more responsibility to operational management. This follows the principle of doing it better – not just mechanizing existing practice.

Creating graphs

Charting the data in Oracle Financial Analyzer follows a similar approach to defining a report (Figure 3.37). Exactly the same Selector facilities are used to identify the data to be graphed. A comprehensive range of graph styles is available.

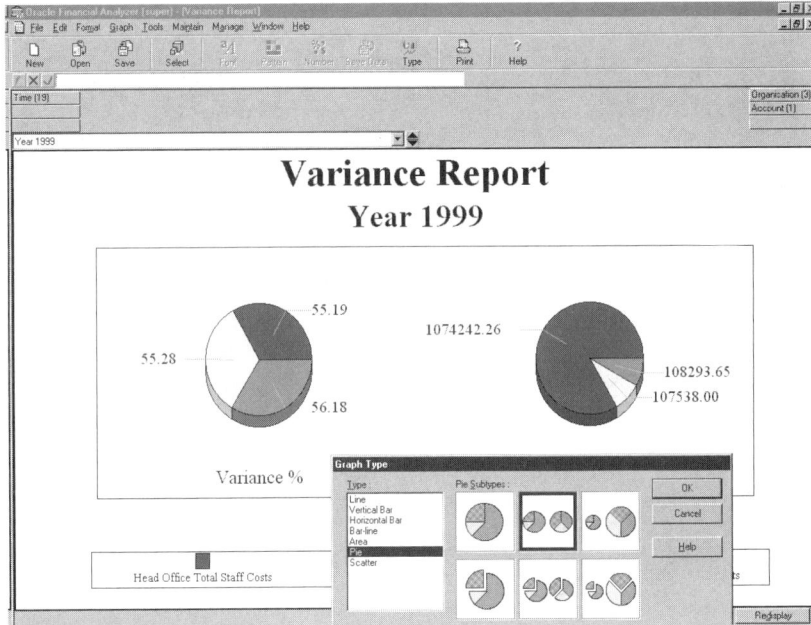

FIG 3.37   Defining a graph type

Reporting and analysis facilities in summary

- Direct, on-screen control of report and graph layout is provided through drag and drop techniques.
- Drill down through the data in reports.
- Open multiple reports and graphs at the same time – together with a Worksheet for data input and 'what-if?'.
- Reports and graphs support up to 10 dimensions.
- Control number formatting, including the number of decimals displayed, positive and negative formats, display/hide leading zeros, thousands separators, decimal separators, currency symbols and percent symbols.
- Display documents support all fonts available within the Windows environment.
- Use description, column or row dimension labels in reports and graphs.
- Control alignment of labels and data values, row height and column widths.
- Add descriptive rows and/or columns to a report as per a spreadsheet.
- Control background colours and borders of components in reports and graphs, including dimension labels, data cells, titles, subtitles, and footnotes in reports and graphs.

- User-definable colour palette.
- Save an existing report under a new name and use the saved report as a starting point for a new report.
- Report maintenance is assisted by recording date, time, user, search keywords and the definition of document folders.
- Both reports and graphs can be held in folders, which can be printed as a reporting pack.
- User-defined default report and graph formats.
- Use all printing devices supported by Windows.
- Include headers and footers on printed documents. Headers and footers can include text, bitmap images, date stamps, time stamps and document names.
- Insert calculations in reports.
- Combine Ranking with Exceptions when formatting reports.
- Copy and paste whole Reports/Worksheets or selected cells/columns/rows, including labels.

3.1.19 Applying OFA features and functions to business processes

We can now turn to see how Oracle Financial Analyzer features and functions can be used to deliver key business processes, before considering some more detailed functionality, and particularly the distributed architecture.

Planning, budgeting and forecasting

Enterprise business processes are typically devolved and iterative in the sense that there is a process of creation, review and amendment across a community of users, for example iterative budget preparation. Through the use of the Manage menu functions OFA can control submission of input across departments, divisions and companies, with automated consolidation (Figure 3.38).

Crucial to controlling such iterative processes is the Task Processor.

The Task Processor

It is a design feature of Express databases that only one process at a time can have write access to a database. In order to manage an OFA community of users who may all want to update the Shared Database, OFA uses a single process which has write access to the database and through which all updates flow. This process is called the Task Processor. It acts as a queuing device, sequentially processing the user updates submitted.

For those familiar with GL transaction processing systems, such as the Concurrent Processor in Oracle GL, the screen shot shown in Figure 3.39 gives an immediate sense of what the Task Processor does. An OFA user, in this case a Data

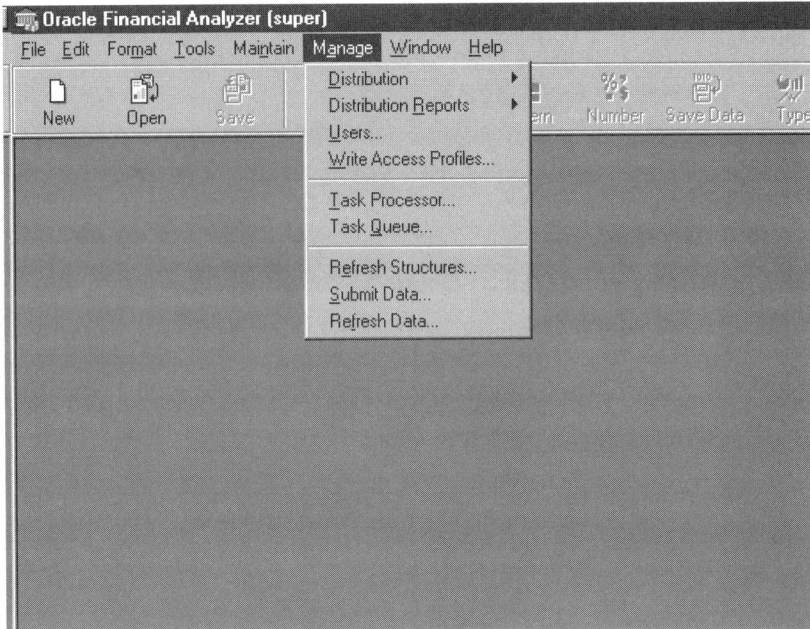

FIG 3.38   The Manage menu and the Task Processor

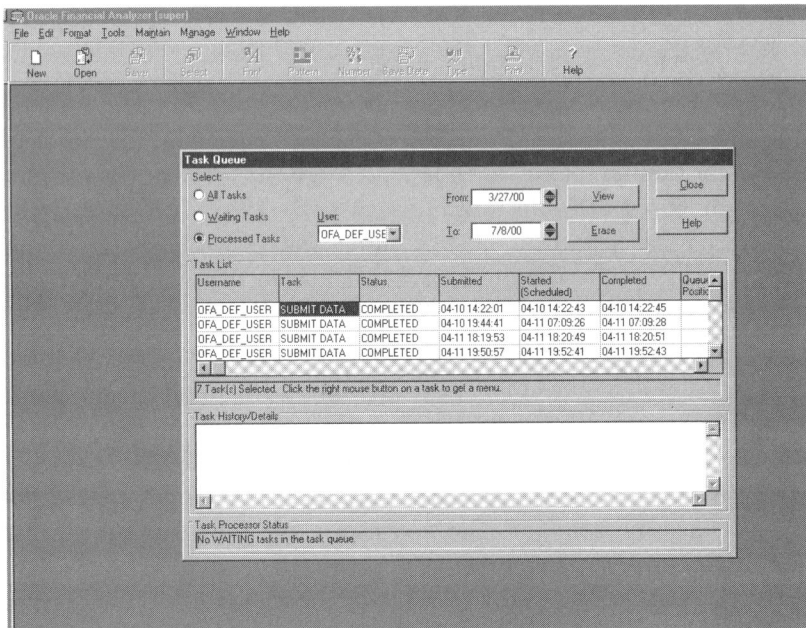

FIG 3.39   The user's data is processed by the Task Processor

Entry Form user (to be discussed later), has been submitting data for entry into the Shared Database. The submissions have all been completed at the times indicated. The Administrator has then started the process of taking the data into the Shared Database at the times concerned and can see that each process was completed at the times indicated.

It is, however, not possible for the Administrator to preview the effect on the Shared Database. The Administrator is essentially controlling a queue of tasks, and can only ask for a resubmission if the results are not acceptable. The level of detail available to the Administrator about the task submitted is at two levels.

History

The Administrator will know the OFA User Name, OFA_DEF_USER in the screen shot shown in Figure 3.40, and that this user submitted text, 'Budget Commentary', in the screen shot. The second level of detail available to the Administrator about the task submitted is about the dimensions and dimension values of the submission.

Details

The text submitted will be referenced to one or more of the 22 values in the Account dimension, which are listed in detail: Basic Pay, Overtime, etc. (Figure 3.41).

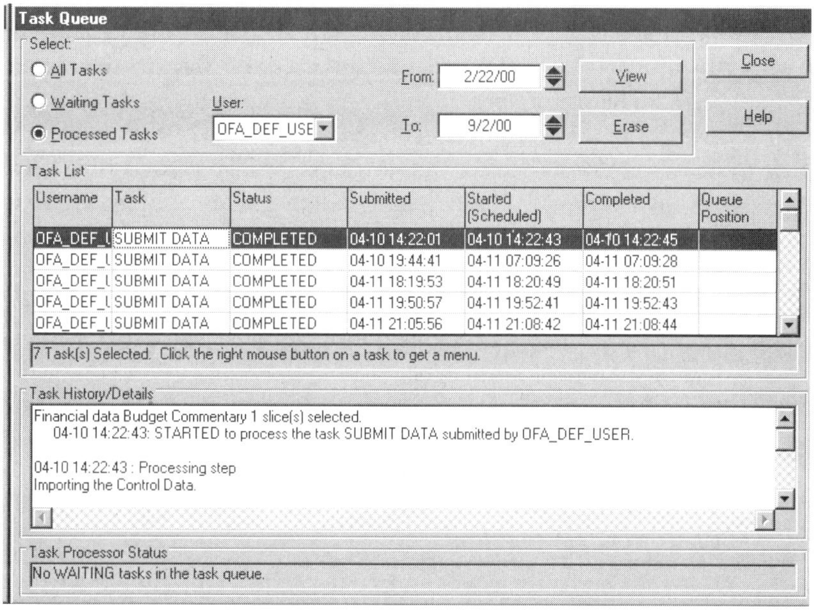

FIG 3.40   The Task Queue log history

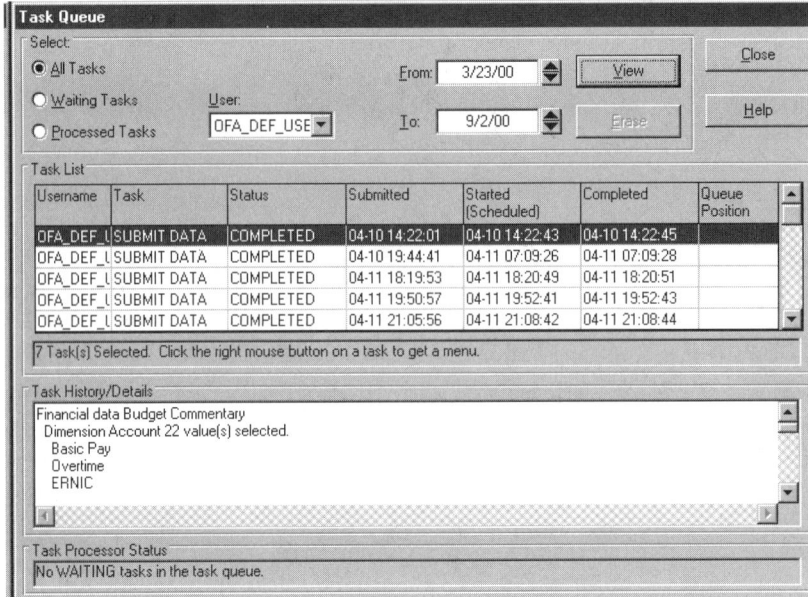

Task Queue

Select:
- ● All Tasks
- ○ Waiting Tasks   User:
- ○ Processed Tasks   OFA_DEF_USE ▼

From: 3/23/00
To: 9/2/00

[View] [Erase] [Close] [Help]

Task List

Username	Task	Status	Submitted	Started (Scheduled)	Completed	Queue Position
OFA_DEF_L	SUBMIT DATA	COMPLETED	04-10 14:22:01	04-10 14:22:43	04-10 14:22:45	
OFA_DEF_L	SUBMIT DATA	COMPLETED	04-10 19:44:41	04-11 07:09:26	04-11 07:09:28	
OFA_DEF_L	SUBMIT DATA	COMPLETED	04-11 18:19:53	04-11 18:20:49	04-11 18:20:51	
OFA_DEF_L	SUBMIT DATA	COMPLETED	04-11 19:50:57	04-11 19:52:41	04-11 19:52:43	
OFA_DEF_L	SUBMIT DATA	COMPLETED	04-11 21:05:56	04-11 21:08:42	04-11 21:08:44	

7 Task(s) Selected. Click the right mouse button on a task to get a menu.

Task History/Details

```
Financial data Budget Commentary
  Dimension Account 22 value(s) selected.
  Basic Pay
  Overtime
  ERNIC
```

Task Processor Status
No WAITING tasks in the task queue.

FIG 3.41   The Task Queue log detail

Iterative processes and 'versions of the truth'

Some multidimensional databases have a single cube approach. Express provides OFA with the ability to create as many cubes as are required to meet the business process requirement. During iterative processes such as planning, budgeting and forecasting, the multiple cube facilities of Express enable OFA to create many 'versions of the truth' to be maintained as the iterations proceed, providing a path towards the final version. In the screen shot shown in Figure 3.42, six Budget cubes – Financial Data Items – are created to control iterations through various versions of the Budget.

In this way, by combining cubes, users can compare alternative plans, budgets or forecasts. Scenarios typically merge data for actuals with different plans/budgets/ forecasts, and use a formula cube to calculate comparative values, e.g. variances = actual – budget, variance percent = (actual – budget)/budget, monthly change = actuals – previous period actuals. The Budget Difference cube in the screen shot is a formula cube. Since it is only evaluated when the user opens the Report, no data is stored, which controls database size. Later we will consider the implications of formula cubes in terms of the inevitable conflict between response time for the user as the formula is calculated, and database size issues.

Generating new versions

Different budget versions can be developed to evaluate alternative scenarios, e.g. best case with assumptions for growth, worst case assuming the recession continues, etc. To minimize time spent preparing data, the Financial Analyzer provides a Copy

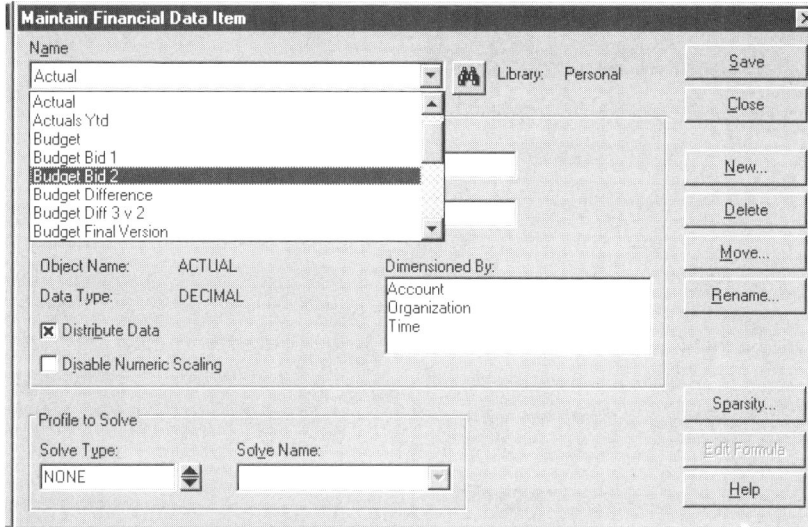

FIG 3.42   Multiple cubes

Data facility – the user identifies the data to be copied from one scenario to another, using the Selector tool. For example, the development of a new (worst case) scenario could start with the base budget, but applying differing absolute or percentage cuts to sales and expense lines during the copy (Figure 3.43).

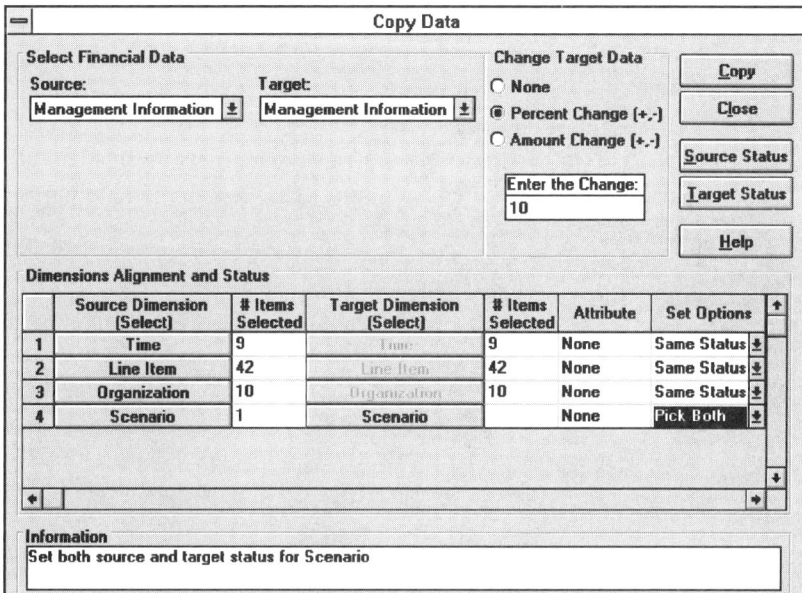

FIG 3.43   Creating an alternative scenario by copying existing data

3.1.20 Potential control problems

It will be clear by now that it is possible to:

▪ create new cubes easily;

▪ populate the new cubes with data which can be transformed during the process.

The Shared Database must be protected from unintentional changes. The Task Processor offers a queuing device to control changes submitted to the Shared Database. However, as we have seen earlier, it does not allow preview of the changes, and changes should only be made when they are important shared information. The Shared Database must be completely protected from some users and by restricting what other users can do. The careful use of access rights is crucial to avoid uncontrolled changes to structures and data in the Shared Database and in particular to avoid data integrity problems.

Access rights to see and change data (structures can only be created or changed by an Administrator)

Control over data integrity is achieved as follows:

▪ OFA users are restricted to the appropriate OFA user type: Super Administrator, Administrator, Budget, Analyst, Workstation or External user type. Since OFA user types can only be mapped to legitimate users at the operating system level, this first level of security is essentially defined at the operating system level. For instance, we map an OFA Super Administrator user type to a user at the operating system level, who can then create new users at the operating system level with inferior rights.

▪ Only the structures and data which are appropriate to them are distributed to OFA users. Therefore, the second level of security is under the control of the Task Processor in Distribution mode. Design precedes implementation of a Distribution; each user group must first be described on paper in some detail as to their entitlement to access:
  - structures
      Dimensions
      Dimension Values
      FDIs
      Hierarchies
      Attributes
      Models
      etc.
  - data
      Actuals
      Budget
      Forecasts
      etc.

Then the appropriate Distributions are made. Until the structures and data are distributed, regardless of the user's access to a Workstation or as an External user type, there will be nothing to see.

■ Write access rights in terms of data are scoped separately for each OFA user. We noted that each user group must first be described on paper in some detail as to their entitlement to access both structures and data. The Administrator then creates the OFA Users and distributes a set of structures and data to users so that they can view data in the Shared Database. An External user type can only have read-only access to the Shared Database under normal circumstances. The other OFA Workstations may have their access rights scoped in terms of their ability to change data. An Administrator can submit data upwards to the Shared Database at a higher level, a Budget Workstation can submit data to the Shared Database and an Analyst or Data Entry Form user can use the Submit Data or Submit button to provide data for inclusion in the Shared Database. However, data access controls can be set up to decide what will happen at the Shared Database level, achieved by creating a Write Access Profile.

A Write Access Profile is created to control user access to data in the Shared Database. A Write Access Profile links Financial Data Items and Dimension Values to users who have access to that data in view mode and prevents those users from writing data to the Shared Database for specific Dimension Values in the slice (Figure 3.44).

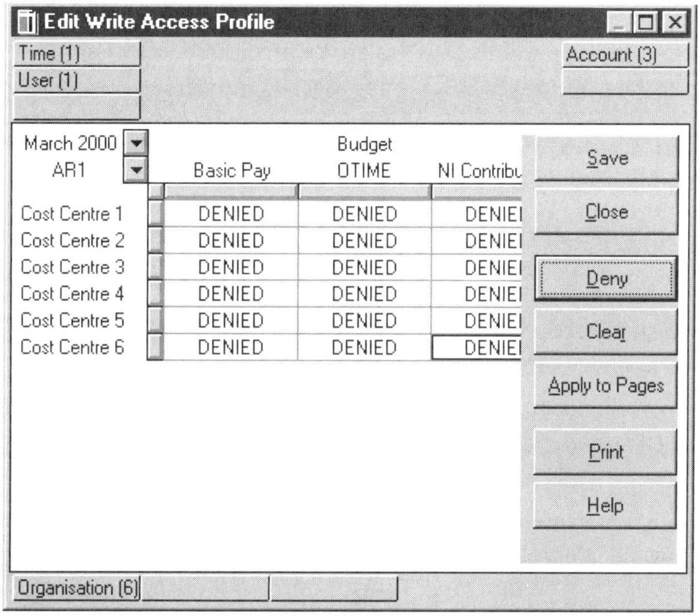

FIG 3.44   Creating a Write Access Profile

(Note: After creating the Write Access Profiles, it will be useful to use the facilities to print this important information for inclusion in the Administrator's Manual.)

Managing the user's expectations of the system

We have seen from the foregoing that we can achieve control at three levels:

1. by restricting OFA users to the appropriate OFA user type;
2. by distributing only the appropriate structures and data to users;
3. by restricting users' rights to have their data incorporated into the Shared Database by Write Access Profiles.

To the user, step 3 becomes visible when he or she tries to save data for which access is denied; with the Data Entry Form, the protected cells are greyed out. However, to the user, the role of the Task Processor as a queuing device is invisible. This has consequences, as considered in the following scenario:

> Two users have access to the same structures and data. If they both submit changes to the data and have rights to change that data, then the last to send a task into the Task Processor queue will be successful; the first will have his or her data overwritten. Both might think that they have succeeded in changing the Shared Database to their view; only one will have in fact achieved this.

> The Administrator is only able to see the impact on the attempted changes after incorporating them in the Shared Database, and hence can only ask for a resubmission of the last Task to be processed if he or she notices that the last Task has produced an unsatisfactory result.

The comments made above are a recognition that the Task Processor is just a queuing device and will simply control the submission of tasks, under the control of the Administrator. As with all systems, the processes outside the system boundary need to be as carefully handled as those delivered within it. There are three steps which are necessary to ensure that the expectations of users are met:

1. Documenting user profiles should be a planned project activity, scheduled to be completed before roll-out.
2. The Super Administrator and Administrators must keep detailed documentation of the users' profiles as to structures, data and data access. Some of this is possible within OFA, for instance by saving distributions.
3. The rights of users to have their data consolidated into the Shared Database must be communicated to them by the appropriate training or other communication method. One objective is to instruct the user that the Administrator can allow the Submit or Save to be overwritten by other users.

(Note: It is possible to create a security dimension. Users 'own' dimension values in the security dimension, and are distributed only the defined values for each user. Stored FDls are distributed to users, restricted to values defined in the security dimension. This makes it impossible for users to choose dimension values which will overwrite one another.)

3.1.21 The top-down and bottom-up process

The budgeting process often commences as the planning department identify high-level goals and resource constraints. Goals can be defined top-down, allowing corporate expectations to be set, and major assumptions and key operating parameters to be specified. Using the facilities described earlier, Oracle Financial Analyzer provides the facilities to create plans, high-level forecasts etc. As we saw with the OFA Worksheet, plans created at an aggregate level can be spread down to supporting units. Thus OFA can be used to build an annual plan at Head Office level, phase the plan over time and cascade/allocate sales/costs to reporting/operational organizations, perhaps by customers and products, based on a number of methods, for example using the current distribution profile of last year's actuals by business units.

Bottom-up plans are readily created by collecting and consolidating budget input submitted by distributed users. Typically, bottom-up budgeting requires departments to submit their budgeted figures for consolidation to the next level of the organizational hierarchy where they are reviewed and potentially changed. Where Head Office controls certain items, such as salary grades and overhead allocations, these can be determined at a corporate level and passed down to operating divisions.

This controlled separation of budgets and goals supports the ready exchange, comparison and negotiation of budgets throughout the organization. Local empowerment is achieved, with local conditions driving the detailed numbers, while consistency with assumptions generated top-down is achieved. Oracle's own use of OFA is a good example, as shown in Figure 3.45.

Oracle's own implementation of OFA allows information not only to be shared in finance across departments, divisions and the company as a whole, but also between finance and other functions, such as sales and marketing.

3.1.22 Solving data for the enterprise

We have seen how Worksheets provide a window on a sub-section of the data, and how the user can manipulate that sub-section of data. Data can be modelled, recalculated and aggregated via a Worksheet by choosing the appropriate Models and Hierarchies and then viewing the results on screen. These functions are very powerful in providing for local modelling with manual interaction. However, the Shared Database, the central 'one view of the truth', is unaffected by the user's iterations on that sub-section of the data. When performing calculations and aggregations for

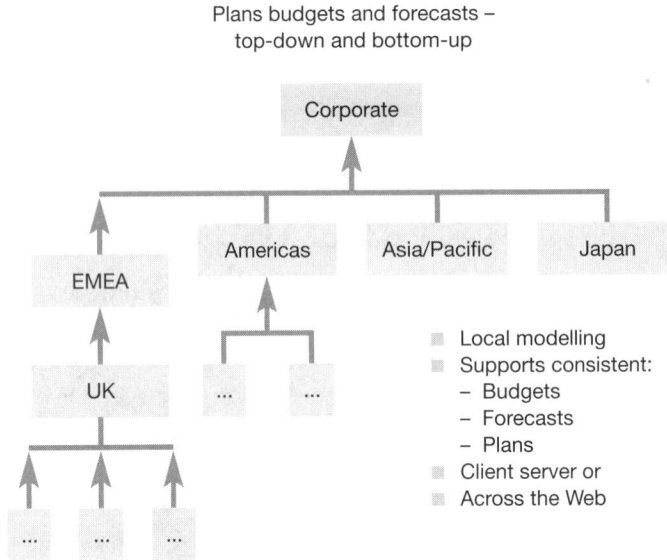

Plans budgets and forecasts –
top-down and bottom-up

Corporate

EMEA

Americas   Asia/Pacific   Japan

UK

...   ...

▪ Local modelling
▪ Supports consistent:
  – Budgets
  – Forecasts
  – Plans
▪ Client server or
▪ Across the Web

...   .

FIG 3.45   **Oracle's own implementation of OFA**

sharing with others at the business unit or at the global level, we must use Solve Definitions. A Solve Definition scopes what is to be calculated and how, ensuring that shared data is calculated and added up using the definitive standard Models and Hierarchies. To automate global calculations, a series of Solve Definitions can be set up and linked together.

In the example shown in Figure 3.46, the Budget will be recalculated by applying an OFA Model on the Account dimension to 13 organizations in the Organization hierarchy, the results of which are then aggregated up that hierarchy, for the 34 time periods, e.g. 12 months, 4 quarters, and the 2 years concerned, using the standard OFA Application Time hierarchy.

Linking these definitions together in Solve scripts automates regular processing and consolidation. They enable a series of different Models to be applied in sequence either to the same data, to different subsets of the same data or to a series of different scenarios.

Having now reviewed most of the features and functions of OFA, we consider their application in more detail, commencing with the critical issue of how OFA provides process flow over data and the structures that manipulate the data.

3.2   CONTROLLING THE FLOW OF STRUCTURES AND DATA

We now consider in more detail how OFA controls the flow of structures and data. Formal analysis techniques applied to the design of relational database systems

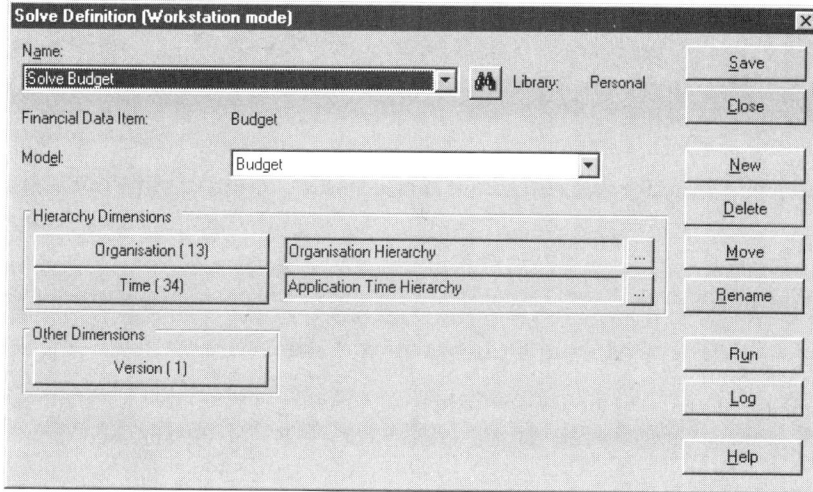

FIG 3.46   Solve Definition

separate **structures** from **data**, for example by modelling entities and their relationships separately from the data which will populate and flow through the
structures. With OFA, it is necessary to apply the same analytical process to
production data and data gathered from OFA users, distinguishing structures separately from the data itself. Controlling the flow of structures and data requires two
issues to be addressed:

1. An enterprise will need to define carefully the roles of those involved **at each
   level** in the enterprise, distinguishing their role in respect of **structures**
   separately from their role in regard to **data**.

   For example, in Head Office, the corporate financial controller may have
   designed a model which will calculate the Profit and Loss account line items,
   which is a **structure** applicable to all the business units for reporting purposes.
   Within one of the business units of the enterprise, a cost centre manager may be
   involved solely in submitting **data** regarding headcount. He cannot **change**
   structures. The finance manager at the business unit level may wish to add a
   sub-account level to the Profit and Loss Model for local purposes, which creates
   a local **structure**. The finance manager must be permitted to do this, but the
   data collected at the business unit level must be aggregated into the corporate
   Profit and Loss account headings when he submits the data upwards to the
   corporate financial controller.

2. Those controlling the process (either as the ultimate controller or as a sub-
   controller in a tiered architecture) must be able to control all changes to
   structures and to the **data** populating the structures, by **controlling proposed**

changes to structures and data separately. The alternative is some form of file transfer and aggregation process, in which the files transferred merge structures and data, making it difficult to provide scoping of user rights, as set out in (1) above. Furthermore, a file transfer and aggregation process, for example one based on using spreadsheets for the transfer process, is undesirable because it produces an onerous administration burden, typified by e-mail attachments, complex target directory structures and manual processes which are prone to error.

3.2.1 Personal Databases and the Workstations

Key to the process by which OFA manages the flow of structures and data throughout the enterprise is the concept of the Personal Database. Certain types of OFA user have to make an initial connection to a Personal Database on the server. Depending on which type of Personal Database is attached, different functionality is available. The different types of OFA Personal Databases are:

- Super Administrator (SuperDBAs)
- Administrator (SubDBAs)
- Analyst
- Budget

Users however, are not aware of the concept of the Personal Database, only the features which are available to them, collectively known in the User documentation as the Workstation, thus:

- Administrator Workstation
- Budget Workstation
- Analyst Workstation

A Personal Database can be attached for update by only one user at any one time. (This can present a design problem if many users need to access the Super Administrator's Personal Database, for instance, during development of the system, and there is only one Super Administrator Workstation.)

Figure 3.47 sets out an example of how Personal Databases interact with the Shared Databases, and it is important to understand what precisely the arrows mean.

The sideways and downwards grey arrows mean an OFA Distribution, set up by an Administrator (and executed through the Task Processor), as in the screen shot shown in Figure 3.48. A Distribution may be of **structures** or of **data**.

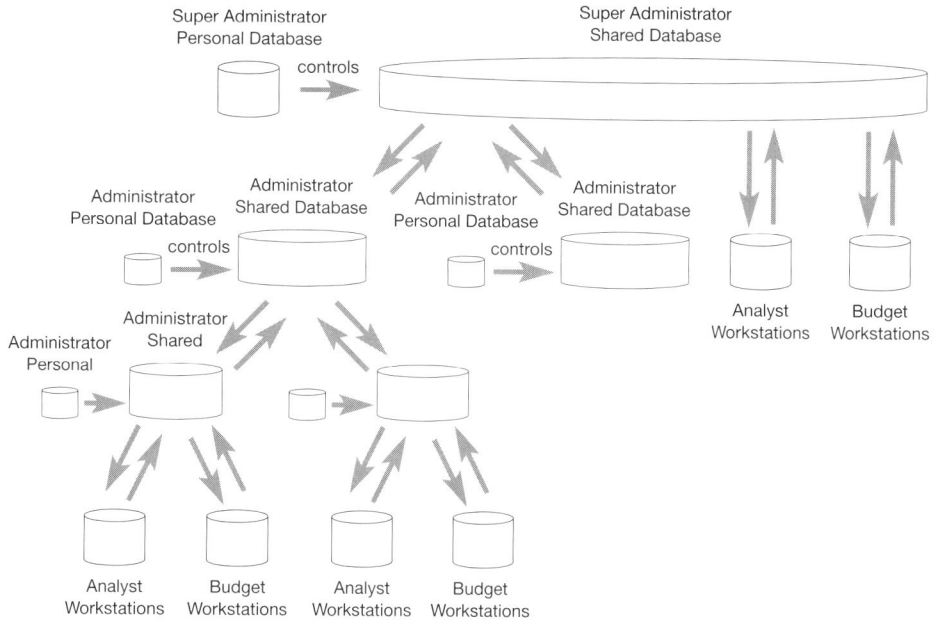

FIG 3.47   How Personal Databases interact with the Shared Databases

Structures

Structures flow **across** or **down** in the diagram. The Administrator is either:

- distributing structures **across** from his or her Personal Database to the Shared Database, so that they are available as part of the 'one view of the truth', or

- distributing structures **down** from the Shared Database to a Sub Administrator for sideways distribution to the lower-level Shared Database, or

- distributing structures **down** to a Workstation.

Figure 3.48 shows an example of distributing structures.

Data

Unlike structures, which can (with one exception to be discussed later) never flow upwards, the flow of data can be down, up or across. Thus the upwards arrows from Workstations mean that data is being submitted to a Shared Database. The upwards arrows from the Sub Shared database to the Super Shared database reflect the Administrator's role in submitting data upwards for consolidation into the Super Shared Database. Figure 3.49 shows an Administrator submitting data across from his Personal Database to the Shared Database. This in fact will rarely occur, since, in a normal production environment, the Administrator will wish to keep data in the Shared Database, rather than duplicate it in his Personal Database.

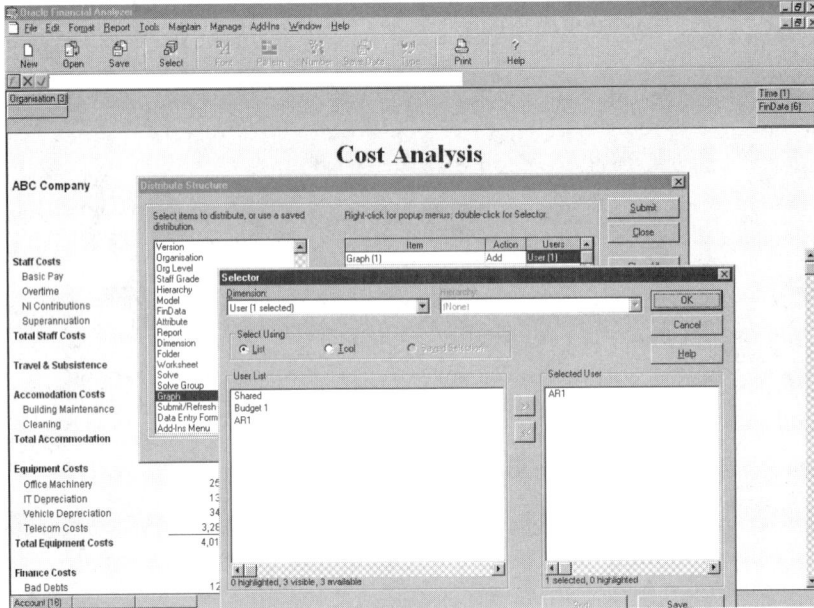

FIG 3.48   A graph is distributed to the selected user

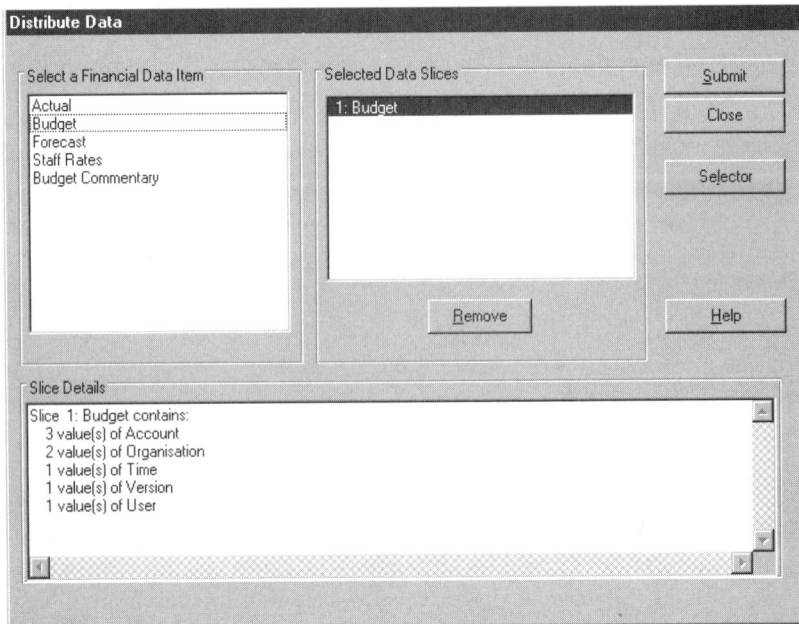

FIG 3.49   Distributing a slice of data

In designing an OFA system:

1. Any number of Administrators can be set up to model the **tiered** architecture of large enterprises. Each tier has its own Shared Database/s. Super Administrators and Administrators perform operations on their Shared Databases via their Task Processors and hence are subject to the control imposed by this queuing device. Analyst and Budget Workstations can then be set up to access these Shared Databases.

2. Super Administrators and Sub Administrators can create and maintain OFA **structures** (Dimensions, Financial Data Items, Hierarchies, Attributes, Models, Solve Definitions etc.) in their Personal Databases and can then distribute them to their Shared Databases and to their users. They do not work directly on their Shared Database. (Furthermore, any reports they open will look at their Personal Database, which would normally be empty of data.)

3. OFA **structures** can be distributed **down** from a Super Administrator to a Sub Administrator, but cannot be distributed back **up**. **Data** can be transferred down **and** up – subject to security and to control via the Task Processor.

4. Analyst Workstations **cannot** create OFA **structures**, nor can they initiate Solves without custom development. They report directly against the one Shared Database which they have been set up to access. They can open Worksheets for data entry – the changes are saved to the Shared Database via the Task Processor. They can create their own Reports and Worksheets, which are saved in the Analyst Personal Database.

5. Budget Workstations can **create** OFA **structures** (including Solve Definitions) for their personal use, to support the structures distributed to them by their Administrator. These personal structures cannot be distributed **up** to their Administrator without custom development. Budget Workstations report directly against their Personal Database, so data needs to be refreshed from the Shared Database using the Refresh Data function, if Budget Workstations are to be kept up to date with the latest data distributed by their Administrator.

   Budget Workstations can open existing Worksheets or create their own Worksheets for data entry – these are saved into the Personal Database, and then the Budget Workstation uses the Submit Data function to transfer data upwards to their Shared Database.

   A Budget Workstation needs to be proactive in using Submit and Refresh Data to transfer data in step with required business processes. Since there is a danger that an inexperienced user will not perform this operation correctly, designers may restrict the use of these Workstations unless a specific business need exists, e.g. where local detailed structures are required to model local business processes.

3.3   MORE WORKSTATIONS AND THEIR FUNCTIONALITY

3.3.1 The Express Spreadsheet Add-In

For many users, Excel is a natural interface. The Express Spreadsheet Add-In user is an 'External' user type, offering access to Express functionality. The Express Spreadsheet Add-In user has no Personal Database and will normally attach to a Shared Database in read-only mode. Once attached to the Shared Database, use is made of the Express Wizard in Excel to query Financial Analyzer data and perform hypothetical, 'what-if' analysis, but not make permanent changes to the database, since the analysis is being done on the Shared Database, the 'one view of the truth'.

The Express Spreadsheet Add-In can also be used for the collection of new or modified data. For this purpose, the Add-In user must be set up to attach to a **personal** database – an Administrator or Budget personal database. Essentially the Commit command (as in Figure 3.50) allows the data to be committed permanently to a Personal Database, which can then be submitted on to a Shared Database, under the control of the Task Processor.

The foregoing facilities available with the Express Spreadsheet Add-In enable those who prefer Excel as a natural interface to work in Excel, but in a structured environment and on a reliable view of the truth. They can add *structures to the*

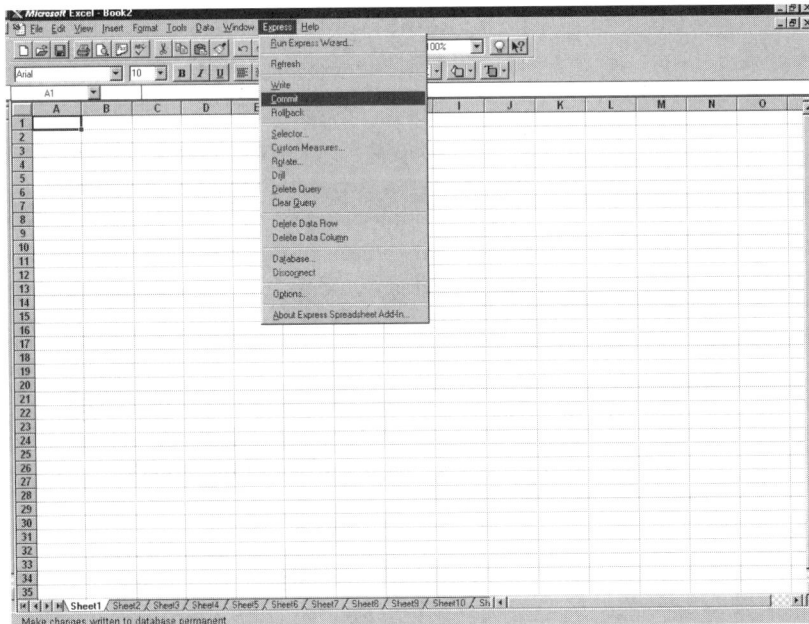

FIG 3.50   The Spreadsheet Add-In and the Commit option

spreadsheet to underpin calculations, but only commit data that fits within the common structures which the Administrator has distributed to the Shared Database. Like all systems, OFA imposes uniformity, and that can be resented. The Express Spreadsheet Add-In user must negotiate with the Administrator to provide new structures if he or she feels they are required. Even with early agreement, there will be a delay while the Administrator creates and distributes the new structures. It would be logically incorrect to blame OFA for not being 'user-friendly' because of any perceived 'unacceptable' delay; the software is, after all, designed to provide control. However, without careful handling, the imposition of control can often be resented. Transference of blame to the software by both the controller and the controlled may be a widespread misplaced emotion during OFA implementations and require careful change management. This topic is considered further in Sections 5.3 and 5.8.

3.3.2 The Data Collection Toolkit

Write back directly, under the control of the Task Processor, into the Shared Database is enabled by the Data Collection Toolkit (DCT). The User Guide refers to this as:

> the Financial Analyzer data collection toolkit for use with Microsoft Excel.
> This toolkit enables you to create a lightweight data entry mechanism for
> infrequent users of Financial Analyzer.

A more precise definition of 'lightweight' is required to support the decision on when to use this data entry mechanism. Scoping for this client type is considered later in Chapter 5. The Data Collection Toolkit as provided with Financial Analyzer is actually a Visual Basic script which requires some knowledge of Express to configure it appropriately. It uses a spreadsheet as a template with a fixed view (but many pages) for data input. The limitations are that it is a fixed view, with the user entering data page by page, and kicking off one Solve ('Recalculate') to review the results before submission ('Submit') (Figure 3.51).

How might the DCT be used?

The Administrator will use e-mail with attachments to send out a request for data. With only a spreadsheet file, a small connection file and an OFA user name to distribute, there should be few hardware/network bandwidth implications in requesting data and data submission, provided the data volumes are 'lightweight'. The recipient will simply fire up Excel, load the file, enter the OFA user name and password and be connected to the Shared Database. After entering data, and pressing Recalculate to review the results of any Solve, all that is required to submit is pressing the Submit button.

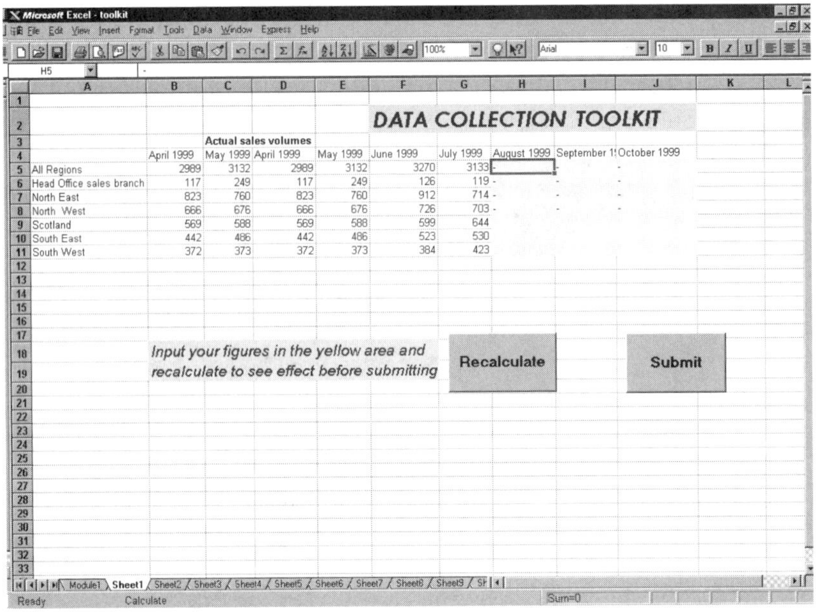

FIG 3.51   A Data Collection Toolkit example

3.3.3 Web-based data collection by OFA Data Entry Forms

Version 6.3 introduced this new function whereby a Workstation user or an External user who has a Web browser can use OFA Data Entry Forms to accomplish the following tasks:

- enter new data into the Shared Database under Task Processor control;

- make changes to existing data in the Shared Database under Task Processor control;

- run a Solve on the data to review the impact of the new or changed data.

As with all Web deployment, the aim is to expand the existing user community by a simple-to-use tool which is efficient in terms of implementation time and hardware requirements. The Administrator authors a template, a new structure in the File New drop-down window (Figure 3.52) called a Data Entry Form which can be set up in exactly the same way as a Report, Graph or Worksheet by selecting the appropriate dimensions and dimension values from the default selection.

Associated with the DEF is a Solve for recalculation purposes, in much the same way that a Worksheet has a recalculation option. The DEF is then distributed to the Shared Database and users in the normal way. The DEF is a fixed format data entry screen just like the Data Collection Toolkit. There is no Rotate, Selector or full formatting function available. In fact there were only three main buttons – 'Submit', 'Recalculate' and 'Column Width' in the 6.3 version. The 11i version of the Data

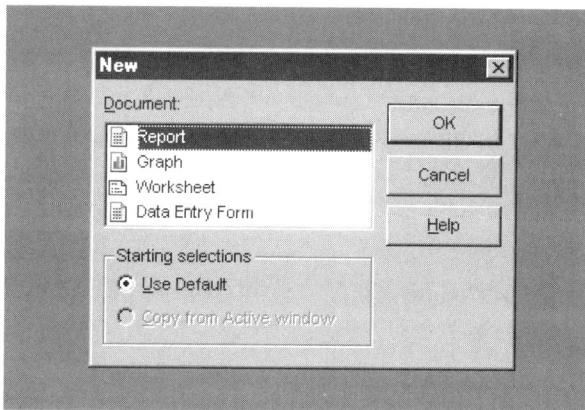

FIG 3.52   The New menu option and the Data Entry Form

FIG 3.53   The arrowheads indicate drilldown or drill across

Entry Form added the ability to drill on the down and across dimensions and to export to a spreadsheet format, as shown in Figure 3.53.

The stated aim in the User Guide is to **gather data** in a controlled way; the DEF supports Web-based data collection (not modelling – our words). Although users can enter data and run predefined calculations (one Solve), they cannot use the DEF to prepare budgets, forecasts, or conduct 'what-if' analyses other than in the sense of entering new data and running one Solve.

For the purpose stated, the advantages of Web writeback are set out below:

- As with the DCT, the DEF is **simple to use**, primarily because there are only two main buttons, 'Submit' and 'Recalculate'. Hence, if an individual can use a Web browser, it is reasonable to assume they can use the DEF, and hence little, if any, training is required. Note that this argument also applies to OFA Web reporting.

- No software deployment is necessary. The users only require a **browser**, Internet Explorer or Netscape.

- Referential data can be included and **protected** on the DEF, e.g. the Actuals can be provided to assist the user in entering budgets, but can be protected if required.

- The calculation logic, the Solve, is set up and maintained once in OFA and then accessed by the DEF – hence maintenance occurs **once**, in one place.

- Validation and control occurs at **point of collection**, since the user can run Recalculate and sense-check the numbers online.

- The numbers and **text for annotation purposes** can be gathered on the same screen (Figure 3.54). The screens are customizable; for example, the administrator could set up Hyperlinks to other Web sites. The DEF supports multiple FDIs on the same form whereas Worksheets only supported one FDI. This would enable, for example, budget numbers and text to be input on the same form.

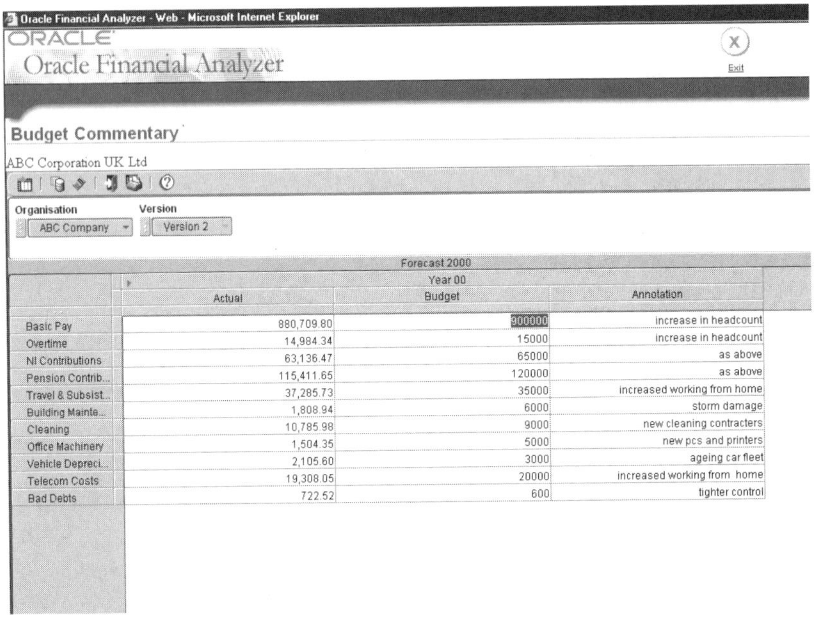

FIG 3.54   Text, as well as numbers, captured using the Data Entry Form

■ The DCT exists as an option for 'lightweight data entry'. However, one advantage of Web data collection is that there is **no programming required** to set up the DEF, whereas a modest amount is required to set up the DCT. One could reasonably expect a Finance DBA to author a DEF for data collection without any significant experience of programming.

■ It is **easier to deploy** than the DCT, since users require only a Web browser and the request for information can be sent out under control of the Task Processor, rather than as an e-mail attachment, with no auditable log of to whom it was sent.

When should the DEF be used? Early statements from the development people indicated that the DEF is aimed at those who are required to submit a volume of data once only and infrequently. The version 6.3 Release Notes set the cell limit to 4,000 cells, but this should not normally be a limit, since it implies a fairly substantial number of rows and columns.

(**Note: The Data Entry Form and copy and paste:** OFA 11i replaced the HTML-based DEF with a Java table-based DEF. At time of writing, OFA 11i 6.3.2 is scheduled to allow copy and paste from a spreadsheet to the DEF table. With 6.3 and 11i, copy and paste into the HTML-based and a Java table-based DEF can only be performed one cell at a time.)

3.3.4 Reporting and analysis

We have now looked at the **data gathering** options. For **reporting and analysis**, the client types are:

1. *OFA Web Reporting*

   An OFA Web-only user is provided (an External user type, in addition to the Budget, Analyst and Administrator user types), for which the Administrator creates a Web site to which a Web user can gain access in read-only mode to reports created and distributed by the Administrator.

   In this way, an expanded (read-only) user community can access reports, rotate, drill down and do simple selection in a secure environment, equipped only with a Web browser, which has been OFA-enabled.

2. *Excel interface*

   As discussed earlier, for many users, Excel is a natural interface and an Excel interface is provided through the Express Spreadsheet Add-In, another External user type. The Express Spreadsheet Add-In user will normally attach a Shared Database in read-only mode. Once attached to the Shared Database, use can be made of the Express Wizard in Excel to query Financial Analyzer data and perform hypothetical, 'what-if' analysis, but not make permanent changes to the database, since the analysis is being done on the Shared Database, the 'one view of the truth'.

3. *Direct use of the OFA-maintained Express database by Express Objects and Express Analyzer clients*

Direct access to the OFA-maintained Express Shared database is available to Oracle Express Objects (OEO) and Oracle Express Analyzer (OEA) clients (Figure 3.55). They provide an Object Linking and Embedding (OLE)-enabled interface to the Shared data, allowing a mixture of text, graphics, sound, video etc. to be used with OFA data, either within a heavily customized OEO interface or the more packaged interface provided by OEA. This can increase the user community to those for whom a number-centric reporting style is inappropriate, so enlarging the potential user community.

4. *Direct use of the OFA-maintained Express database by Web Publisher or Web Agent*

Direct access to the OFA-maintained shared Express database is made possible through **Web Publisher** or **Web Agent**. This provides an interface to the Shared data through the Internet/intranet, allowing a wider range of options as in (3). above to be used with OFA data, either within a heavily customised Web Agent interface or the more packaged interface provided by Web Publisher. Again, this can increase the user community to those for whom a number-centric reporting style is inappropriate, so enlarging the potential user community.

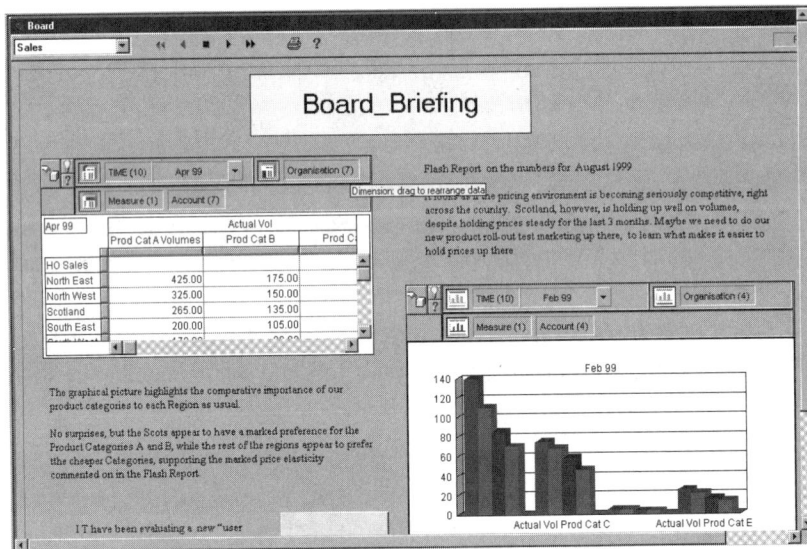

FIG 3.55   **A Board Briefing prepared using Express Analyzer**

3.3.5 The Shareable Report, Graph or Worksheet: an exception to the rule

The rule stated earlier is that **structures** flow down only, whilst **data** flows down and up. An exception to the rule was created by version 6.3. A process for enabling and using shareable documents was introduced whereby the Administrator can authorize users to create shareable documents. When the user so authorized submits a new document, the document goes to the Shared Database and is made available on Refresh Structures to the Administrator. The Administrator can distribute the document using one of the following distribution action options:

- Add – makes the document available to the users to whom it is distributed. The owner of the document can make modifications and submit them. Other users can use the document, but *cannot submit changes to it.*

- Add with Write Access – makes the document available to the users to whom it is distributed. All users can use the document *and submit changes to it.*

This exception only provides an option to share **Reports**, **Graphs** and **Worksheets**, not any other OFA objects. Where, for example, a report created 'in the field' is deemed to be more widely useful across the organization, it provides a controlled way to manage the distribution process. For example, the report will appear on the Distribution Report, enabling the Administrator to review to whom the report has been distributed. (Practical note: it is easier to develop reports in an Analyst Workstation where the reports will display data rather than in the Administrator's personal database which normally will not contain data.)

3.3.6 Version 11i and some reporting issues

OFA 11i deals with many Web delivery issues, in line with the philosophy of larger user populations which browser-only access makes possible. Five important features included for Web **Analyst** clients were:

1. Analyst users are given the capability to define and save personal Reports and Graphs via their Web client. In earlier versions, they could only open existing Reports, as distributed by the Administrator. Formatting facilities are provided, such as number formatting, alignment, font type, font size, foreground colour, background colour etc. for a specific report, and saved.

2. Improved facilities to manage documents within folders by drag and drop.

3. An API is provided to start OFA and directly open a specific document. The obvious application of this feature is to allow OFA documents to be launched from within other Web applications, such as a Web portal.

4. Run-time selection of the OFA Web client language, which hitherto had to be specified at install time. Enterprise roll-outs across global multilingual communities make this feature crucial.

5. The Web Analyst client also includes traffic lighting reporting/colour coding, a feature of the other Express clients which had not been made available to OFA client server workstations.

Finally, as far as Oracle Applications were concerned, which have all been Web-enabled in Release 11i (and re-badged as the Oracle E-business Suite), single sign-on was enabled for OFA.

3.3.7 The current Web-enablement status of OFA

Since many projects may be contemplating a Web-only implementation, the current Web-enablement status of OFA is important.

Analyst Workstations; is their functionality replaced by the Web Analyst?

Release 11i makes it possible for much of the Analyst Workstation functionality, such as reports and graphs, to be created over the Web, as an OFA Web External user. However, the 11i Web interface does not replace all the Analyst Workstation functionality, as it will not support:

- report calculations;
- row and column inserts.

If such functionality is required of a read-only client type, the client/server Analyst Workstation presents the only option, and hence precludes Web delivery. However, it is unlikely that these constraints will outweigh the advantages of Web delivery, especially since Web delivery allows drilling in both rows and columns whereas OFA clients can drill only in the row dimension.

Administrator and Budget Workstations

Administrator and Budget Workstations which exist as OFA users can use the Web interface to access the Shared Database, and will get the same data access profiles as they enjoy when accessing through client/server mode. However, they cannot access their Personal Databases through the Web. Hence they cannot perform the functions which are restricted to these types of workstation, such as creating new structures. For all practical purposes, they remain client/server, and will do until Analytic Solutions 12.

In summary, pure Web access will only come with Analytic Solutions 12, the pure Java Beans version when all client/server interfaces will be replaced.

4 Enterprise Oracle Financial Analyzer, ERP and the Data Warehouse

ROAD MAP

The laudable goal of most enterprises is to consolidate all information systems, including GL, into one so-called Enterprise Resource Planning system (ERP hereafter) for which all information flows to the user. This goal is better viewed as a process rather than an outcome, since it is likely to be hard to achieve for a number of reasons. Mergers and acquisitions, for example, interfere with attainment of the goal. Chapter 4 considers how Oracle Financial Analyzer can make a significant contribution to attainment of the goal.

In Section 4.1, we cover the GL Link between Oracle GL and OFA. Where Oracle GL is in use or planned, the GL Link can facilitate the transfer of information to and from OFA, for example to populate OFA with Actuals and to pass Budget data collected and modelled in OFA back to the GL. Higher level issues are covered in this section while more detailed hints and tips are covered in Appendix C, allowing the reader to choose the appropriate level of detail. We then consider other ERP systems and Oracle Financial Analyzer, Section 4.2 being concerned with getting the structures and data out of non-Oracle ERP into the files to be loaded into OFA.

So far, we have been discussing the options on how OFA can be loaded with structures and data from an ERP, Oracle, SAP, Peoplesoft etc. There may however be a separate data warehouse in existence or contemplated at the time that the OFA project is being considered. The corporate data warehouse clearly can be a source of structures and data, albeit only of production data. In Section 4.3, we consider how the orthodoxy about data warehouse architectures can be enriched by using OFA to add data gathered from people.

For many enterprises, moving to 'one view of the truth' by rolling out a data warehouse is a very large step. In Section 4.4, we consider the option to use OFA to provide the basis for a 'start small, think big' approach. Using this approach, an OFA project can start with one business process, an OFA Data Mart. As data volumes grow, the source systems can be redirected to an RDBMS-based data warehouse, from which appropriate volumes of data can be staged into Express.

4.1   THE ORACLE GENERAL LEDGER AND ORACLE FINANCIAL ANALYZER

This section covers how the GL Link enables the flow of structures and data between Oracle GL and OFA. We note the constraints which exist within the GL Link, those which accrue from the way the Oracle GL may have been set up or managed, making suggestions for workarounds where appropriate.

(Note: In Appendix C, we cover some hints and tips at a detailed level on load procedures, load performance issues, transitioning from a test environment, and troubleshooting. These will be useful to the reader who has some knowledge of Oracle GL, the GL Link, OFA and Express.)

4.1.1 Oracle Financials General Ledger and the GL Link

In most General Ledger packages, there is the concept of a Chart of Accounts, a pre-defined account code structure. In Oracle Financials General Ledger, the structure of the Chart of Accounts is described as being made up from a number of segments. Segments are essentially sub-sections within the Chart of Accounts.

The GL Link provides an interface between the Oracle Financials General Ledger (GL) and OFA that enables population of OFA with structures and data directly from GL, and the writing of data prepared in OFA back to GL. It also allows user reporting in OFA to drill down to the detailed transactions in GL. The functionality offered by the drilldown is at present limited. It only works for FDIs created in GL. The user must also identify and navigate to leaf nodes in each dimension before the drill will operate. Users cannot always easily determine if they are using FDIs created in GL and what Dimension Values are GL leaf nodes.

The GL Link creates Dimensions, Dimension Values, Hierarchies and FDIs in OFA based on metadata in GL.

The flow of structures from the GL does not conform to the usual OFA architecture (Figure 4.1). Structures from the GL are loaded directly into the Shared Database, bypassing the SuperDBA. The SuperDBA must then refresh his or her own Personal Database in order to make the structures available to distribute onwards to the OFA users.

If analysts have already been distributed the structures, which is usually the case, then the new values are immediately available to them. This can lead to confusion

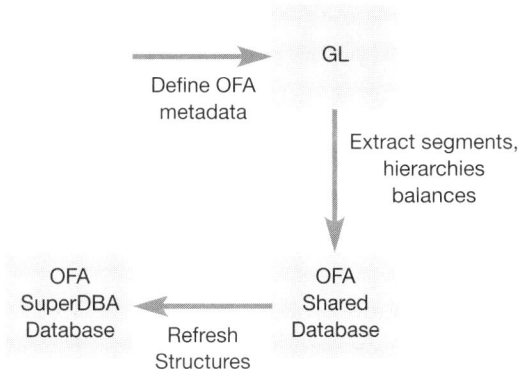

FIG 4.1   **GL Link data flow**

as the SuperDBA has an older view of the static data until he or she performs a refresh of his or her Personal Database. While looking at this older, out-of-date view, the SuperDBA should take care not to perform a distribution prior to refreshing, otherwise he or she will overwrite the changes that have just come in from the GL.

4.1.2 Oracle Financials General Ledger

In many cases the GL will already have been designed and implemented before the OFA project commences. However, there are some features of the GL Link that will materially affect the design and use of GL with OFA. The link does not support all of the GL functionality available. If the GL is already live when the OFA project is undertaken, the limitations of the GL Link may preclude its use without changing the GL design, which may not be a practical option.

4.1.3 Design of the Chart of Accounts

The link supports only one named Chart of Accounts. This has a potentially significant effect on the design of the GL, because all balances that are to be transferred to OFA must use this single Chart of Accounts. This means that there cannot be a different Chart of Accounts for different organizations in the GL. They must all share the same one.

The GL design often includes a consolidated set of books to consolidate a multi-organization GL. This set of books usually has a summarized Chart of Accounts. The link does not support both the summarized and detailed Chart of Accounts, so the summarized accounts must be included within the detailed Chart of Accounts if OFA requires both levels of detail.

4.1.4 Disabled segments

The GL allows the disablement of a redundant segment value; for example, a cost centre that is no longer used. This stops any future posting to the segment. However, the segment extract does not reference this flag, and will extract disabled segment values as well as live ones. This is not a problem in itself. It just leads to unnecessary segment values cluttering up the OFA application. This could be more significant if the GL is an old, established implementation, with a large number of disabled segment values.

If the clutter is significant and hence there is a need to exclude these disabled values from the OFA users, they should be excluded from the distribution down to users, and any SubDBA systems. It is possible to build an attribute on the relevant dimension to identify the disabled values to aid the control of their distribution. This attribute would have to be maintained manually by the DBA, unless a custom routine is written to load the disabled flag from the GL. Suppression of disabled segment values is always subject to the need to distribute values if any historical data needs to be available in OFA.

4.1.5 Cross-validation rules

Cross-validation rules are used by GL to define valid combinations of segment values. The table used by GL to define the rules consists of multiple ranges of segment values. In a budgeting and forecasting OFA system it is often very useful to have this information in OFA to validate data entry. However, the table is not included in the GL Link interface, nor is it easy to use a custom routine to extract the table and load it into OFA by other means. The way the rules are defined in GL is not easily reflected in Express structures. An alternative is to create Attributes and/or text financial data items in OFA to duplicate the validation rules. These can then be used to validate OFA data, possibly before it is submitted back to GL. This, of course, means maintaining the rules in two places, which is not ideal. We know of no OFA site that has successfully loaded the cross-validation rules table from GL into OFA.

4.1.6 Dependent segments

A dependent segment in GL is one whose meaning is dependent on another segment value. An example would be that of a sub-account segment whose meaning differs depending on the primary account segment value with which it is associated, e.g. sub-account 001 means 'Photocopy Paper' when used with the primary account '100 – Stationery', but means 'Contractors' when used with the primary account '200 – Consultancy Costs'. The dependent segment value only has meaning when associated with another segment value. It is really a special kind of cross-validation rule.

The GL Link will bring only the base values of the dependent segment across to OFA, not its varying meaning. In our example, sub-account 001 would be brought across, but the interaction with primary accounts 100 and 200 would be lost. If the meaning of the sub-account is required in OFA, customization of the interface is necessary to bring the combination of the two related segments into OFA.

4.1.7 Currencies

Currency is one of the defining factors of a set of books in GL. A set of books must have a primary or functional currency, and can have two or three other optional currencies. These are called Local, Foreign Entered and Foreign Translated. To load balances across multiple currencies into OFA it is necessary to define a Financial Data Item for each currency type. It is not necessary to define the Financial Data Items with a currency dimension. The data items can then be joined in OFA using a formula which is dimensioned by currency.

4.1.8 Attributes

Descriptive **flexfields** from GL cannot be loaded as part of the extract. These structures function in GL much like Attributes do in OFA, but there is no facility available to load them using the link. They must be maintained manually in OFA, or read using a custom routine.

4.1.9 Hierarchies

Multiple GL segments may be mapped to a single, combined, dimension in OFA. For example, certain Account Segments and Cost Centre Segments could be combined to create one dimension. This dimension can incorporate the Hierarchies of both base segments to provide drill capabilities for OFA users.

If the multiple segments all have Hierarchies defined in the GL, and these Hierarchies are required in OFA, there is a potential explosion of parent values in the single OFA dimension. This comes about because of the exponential growth in the number of parents required from multiple hierarchical segments being combined into one dimension. To illustrate this, assume that there are three segments each with three base values. Each segment has one hierarchy with a single parent node. If all combinations are valid, there will be 27 (3^3) base values of the new dimension. But there will be 81 (3^4) values of the dimension in total needed to build all the parents needed for the three Hierarchies now required on the new dimension. This problem becomes significant if there are a large number of base values in the segments. The hierarchy parents will be densely populated, so the database will potentially be large and slow to aggregate.

To avoid this problem, it is necessary to exclude some or all of the Hierarchies on the combined segments, and build them directly in OFA in a summarized form. If the Hierarchies from GL are a definite requirement it is necessary to monitor the number of Dimension Values, or the number of composite values (if composites are applied to the Financial Data Item) in the OFA Shared Database. The final number of composite values will only be evident in the Shared Database after the balances have been aggregated, using the extracted Hierarchies.

4.1.10 The extraction process

Here is a summary of the extraction routines available from GL:

- Extract Segment Values. Dimension Values are created in OFA when the associated segment value has a balance in GL. There is an option to load all segment values.
- Extract Hierarchy. Parent/child relationships are only updated if the Dimension Values have already been extracted from GL to OFA.
- Extract Balances. Data is only loaded for Dimension Values that already exist on OFA.
- Extract Calendar. This only needs to be run on initialization, and when new years are enabled in GL.
- Extract Currency. This only needs to be run on initialization, and when new currencies are enabled in GL.
- Extract Period Rates. Rates data is only loaded for currencies that exist in OFA.

From the above dependencies it is clear that the 'Extract Segment Values' option should be run in conjunction with 'Extract Hierarchy' and 'Extract Balances' to ensure that OFA is synchronized with GL.

4.1.11 The load process

A example of the OFA procedures required to load GL structures and balances into OFA will be something like this:

1. Run the GL extracts.
2. Load the extracts into the Shared Database.
3. Refresh the SuperDBA to update structures into the SuperDBA's Personal Database.
4. Update any associated Attributes and Hierarchies.
5. Distribute the updated structures to users and SubDBA systems.
6. Run Solve Definitions to aggregate and Model the loaded data.

This process is very procedurized, requiring the DBA to run the tasks in a strictly defined order. If a step is missed, or the order changes, the result is unlikely to be successful. As a result, it is advisable to have the procedures well documented. The process can be automated to a certain extent. The task to load the extract into the Shared Database can be made to wait until the extract file from GL is produced. The task will wait for the files' arrival until a task-defined date and time, before aborting.

This OFA task must be submitted and it is necessary to ensure that the Task Processor is running before the extraction process in GL is started. To enable the auto load from GL, the Administrator must run the extractions in the normal way, then run the 'Analyzer-Load Extracts' program in GL. When this program completes, it alerts the waiting OFA task that the extract has completed.

When the extract has been loaded, the Task Processor will process any other tasks in the queue. Any relevant Solves can therefore be submitted after the extract task to aggregate and Model the data. This will not include any manual DBA maintenance that might be required, so there may still be the need for manual intervention by the DBA, but this offers significant scope for overnight batch loading and aggregation of GL data.

4.1.12 The load destination in OFA

Data can only be loaded via the GL Link into a SuperDBA. There may be situations where SubDBAs want control of data loading from their local GL, to allow for, perhaps, a review process before submission to the SuperDBA. This might allow for corrections and adjustments to be made at the transaction level prior to a second data load. This conflicts with the OFA Model which demands that consolidated GL data is loaded into the SuperDBA directly and then passed down to relevant SubDBAs.

There is no easy solution to this problem to load data directly into the Shared Database of a SubDBA, because a SubDBA does not contain the metadata required by the GL link to facilitate the load. Possible solutions are:

- Create multiple SuperDBAs to allow local data loading, then via custom code, consolidate these to a 'Super' SuperDBA.
- Temporarily convert the SubDBAs to appear to be a SuperDBA to the GL Link. This requires a significant amount of customization.
- A commonly used workaround is to create custom data loaders to read in extract files of GL data, thus avoiding all the restrictions of the GL Link and allowing treatment of non-Oracle GL data.

4.1.13 Budget write back

Before write back can proceed, a Budget organization named 'ALL' must exist in GL. GL will recognize the ALL organization as a special case. It is not necessary to set up Accounting Flexfield ranges, as would be necessary with the creation of a normal organization.

When submitting data back to the GL it is possible that new segment combinations will have been created in OFA that did not exist in the original extract from GL. These combinations must pass any cross-validation rules, as we discussed earlier. Even if the new combinations do pass these rules the combination may not exist in the GL.

If dynamic insertion is switched on in the GL configuration, the combination will be created when the data is written back. If dynamic insertion is off, then the combination must be opened before the write back will succeed. The combination is opened in GL in the 'Code Combinations' screen. Even if the combination is open, it still needs to allow Budget posting. The option to allow Actual and Budget posting is in the same 'Code Combinations' screen. The GL administrator should be consulted for more details on opening combinations in GL.

4.1.14 OFA formulae

The financial data items loaded from the GL extract are often not in an ideal state for end-user reporting. The GL Link will load period movements for Revenue and Expense account types, and year-to-date balances for Balance Sheet account types. An OFA formula will be required to produce the following types of data:

- data dimensioned by Currency;
- year-to-date P&L;
- variance analysis;
- period trial balance.

See the section on Reporting requirements in Section 5.5.13 for more information on these techniques.

One point to remember when creating financial data item formulae is that the GL Time dimension has a different order from the standard OFA Time dimension. This means different formula syntax from the standard Time dimension for such scenarios as period-to-period variances.

If average daily balances are enabled in GL then Period average to date and Year average to date balances can be loaded into OFA.

4.2   OTHER ERP SYSTEMS AND ORACLE FINANCIAL ANALYZER

For non-Oracle sites, depending on the detailed requirements, the process for loading of actuals from any GL into OFA, including the ERP GLs, normally involves exporting structures and data to files and then creating data loaders (which load both structure and data). Data loading into OFA is discussed in Appendix B; this section is concerned with getting the structures and data out of the ERP into the files to be loaded.

The first step should always be to establish whether there is already a routine to download files in existence. Often this has been done to support existing processes, perhaps to feed a spreadsheet-based approach to reporting, budgeting, analysis or other process which requires downloads from operational systems. The existing process may well have encountered issues such as data quality problems and addressed them already. If there are no existing downloaded files, options to create them must be considered.

In considering those options, keep in mind that the operational systems which hold the data are tuned for performance to meet their operational requirements. The IT function must protect operational systems from invasive demands outside their service level agreement with the operational users. Imagine a routine being set up to query the tables for data for off-line OFA purposes, which issues the 'query from hell' and damages performance of the operational system.

The four main options are described below.

a) Using the ERP report generator to dump a flat file, to be used in a loader program

The ERP data is highly structured, and ERP in-built maintenance facilities allow changes in structures to be made easily, hiding the complexity of the underlying relational tables where the data is held. Clearly it is better to utilize these structures – the metadata – in the process of extracting the data. It harnesses the end user's view – the business view – of the data, in using the ERP report generator to set up the routines to dump the file/files. OFA and Express maintain essentially a business view of the data, and so the download process should also be defined in business terms. Specifying the data extract in business terms, rather than technical terms, means that there is no translation of the requirement from a business view to an SQL program, with the attendant possibility of misunderstanding between specifier and programmer. However, this solution lacks elegance from some points of view:

- It may be difficult to schedule the process, necessitating manual intervention.

- The files written may combine structures and data, so that the data loader program must separately validate and load the structures to check for changes and then load data.

However, it should not be invasive, because the report generator functionality is an optimized and controlled part of the operational system and hence IT should not be concerned about impact on operational performance.

Note that report generators vary in sophistication; experience suggests that the report generator user creating the files should have a good understanding of the underlying GL table structures, so that the files written are 'intelligent'. By this, we mean that there is immediate recognition if the files do not carry meaningful information and that the structures created anticipate the OFA requirements, by ordering the files in a sensible way.

b) Extracting data using purpose-built data extractor software

This option is attractive because purpose-built data extractor software should provide not just data files but files which are 'intelligent' in the sense set out above, by providing:

1. the metadata, for example product, organization and account hierarchies, which map directly to OFA structures;

2. the data itself, in well-structured relational tables.

There are usually facilities to schedule the process, restricting manual intervention to the minimum. However, the ability of such purpose-built data extractors to be 'intelligent' is dependent on the underlying ERP implementation being a 'vanilla' implementation, i.e with no customization. If customization has changed what the extractor expects to see, the files produced may be opaque.

Particular problems relate to providing a product for extracting SAP data. For historic reasons relating to constraints during development of the Oracle RDBMS to its current version, the clustered or pooled Oracle tables within SAP contain many structures, not just simple entities as in the classical relational model. Only the so-called transparent tables are normalized tables conforming to the classical relational model. In 1997, Oracle produced the SAP Toolkit and introduced a replacement, the SAP Integrator, in 2000. There are many other vendors. All of these tools may suffer a lack of 'intelligence' about how to create logical data entities from physical data storage in the 17,000 transparent, clustered or pooled tables which make up a SAP database. They concentrate on the mechanics of extracting data rather than on its business meaning. It is therefore best to recognize that, as observed in option (a) above, if there is in-house knowledge of the SAP tables, it makes sense to use these skills when using any tool to create files from SAP.

c) Querying data in the ERP's relational data warehouse such as SAP's Business Warehouse

Where the ERP vendor provides a staged data warehouse, such as SAP's Business Warehouse, which provides a staging operational data store and some data marts which are fed from the data store, SQL can be written to extract structures and data direct from the Business Warehouse operational data store database, or from the data marts which are sourced from it. There is obviously a maintenance overhead between the ERP source and the files, since the SQL extract routines will need to be changed if there are changes in the source tables. The link between the SAP Business Warehouse clearly must be managed outside the OFA system boundary, with the extract programs scheduled to:

▪ provide timely updates, and

▪ flag changes in structures in SAP

with appropriate routines set up to act on changes in the SAP structures.

An architecture which adds to the relational tables underlying the ERP, and the ERP off-line data store, file readers staging data into OFA's Express database may not appeal to the purist technical architect. He or she might say 'we now have three databases to maintain'. One might usefully comment that, if we are replacing spreadsheets, we are moving from possibly hundreds of personal databases to only three enterprise databases.

The different development paths of OFA and OSA are relevant in this area. In a project involving SAP's Business Warehouse, SQL was written to extract structures and data from the source into an Oracle relational database configured as a star schema. Thereafter, Oracle Sales Analyzer was used to access the data in the Oracle relational database using RAA/RAM, which gives a multidimensional view 'on the fly'. The RAA/RAM link between OSA and Oracle relational database does not require the onerous maintenance of file readers; the Relational Access Manager facilities allow graphical re-mapping of the metadata, leaving just the link between SAP Business Warehouse and OSA to be managed outside the system boundary as above. However, the development paths of OFA and OSA diverged, with RAA/RAM being provided within OSA, but not OFA. OFA cannot therefore harness the RAA/RAM option to provide a more appealing technical architecture involving less than the three database option discussed above.

d) Direct querying of production data in the underlying ERP relational database tables

It is also possible to extract data by direct querying of production data in the underlying ERP relational database tables using, for example, ABAP programs to retrieve data from the SAP source tables. In this case, rather than harnessing the metadata in the ERP end-user facilities, there is a requirement for translation of the data requirements from a business view to ABAP, with the attendant possibility of misunderstanding between programmer and business person specifying the data required, as noted above. This option does not appear attractive.

4.3   OPERATIONAL DATA STORES, THE DATA WAREHOUSE AND OFA

We have been discussing the options on how OFA can be loaded with structures and data from an ERP, Oracle, SAP, Peoplesoft etc. The structures are metadata about the data which is in such systems, which are operational data stores, in the sense that they contain data to support operations. There may, however, be a separate data warehouse in existence or contemplated at the time that the OFA project is being considered. The corporate data warehouse clearly can be a source of structures and data, albeit of production data, since it typically stores data already in many operational data stores, to provide 'one view of the truth'. A number of issues arise.

4.3.1 Staged and real-time data access

OFA typically operates on data which is staged into Express at intervals driven by the nature of the business. This could be quarterly, for example in the upstream part of the oil business, monthly in the public sector, weekly in the retail sector and daily in the banking sector, where there is a need for 'average daily balances'. But not real-time, since to borrow an expression from Ralph Kimball (1996), when analyzing data, we should not be looking directly at a 'twinkling' database, an operational database which 'twinkles' as a transaction is processed. In any case, the operational systems will have query tools already optimized for retrieval of data from the operational data stores. Since the detailed transactions are in the operational data store, an issue arises when it is necessary to go from OFA to the detailed transactions, 'drill to detail' in common usage.

4.3.2 Drilling to detail

'Drilling to detail' within OFA

The data staged into Express will often be aggregated up product, account and organization hierarchies within OFA. When the user looks at a report, the report is likely to be at the top of these hierarchies and hence the user can 'drill to detail' by bringing the required dimension down the page and drilling to the leaf level.

'Drilling to detail' from OFA to the operational data store or data warehouse

The detail, we shall assume, is in a relational database. To go back to the source system data, there are three options:

1. If the data is in Oracle GL, and the supporting sub-ledgers, AR, AP, PO, OE etc., then the user can drill to the required cell in OFA, invoke the Applications Desktop Integrator and drill back through summary balances, to journal entries, to the source sub-ledger, ultimately to, say, the purchase order itself in PO, as discussed in Section 4.1. If the data is not in Oracle GL, but instead a relational source, then

2. Custom coding can be used to attach SQL queries to a cell, enabling the source data set to be retrieved for the SQL query attached to that cell. This option, being a highly bespoke and hardwired process, may not provide an easily maintainable solution. However, we can

3. Use the appropriate tool for drilling to detail in the source system after the OFA user has identified the information required in Express dimensionality terms. For instance, the OFA user would first navigate, using the Selector, to the required set of cells, e.g.

Dimension	Dimension value
Account	Sales Revenue
Organisation	Business Unit 3
Product	Product 50026
Time	January 2001

The user can then invoke the appropriate tool which executes 'canned' SQL queries against the relational source, for example Oracle's Discover product. The metadata of Express, as in the above Selector query, should match the metadata of the ad-hoc query tool, assuming that careful analysis and documentation of common metadata took place before implementation of both OFA and the 'canned SQL' ad-hoc query tool. In Web delivery mode, the 'portal' which allows OFA to be accessed can contain an embedded URL to kick off the ad-hoc query tool so that the process of 'drilling to detail' is relatively seamless.

4.3.3 Drill to detail: ROLAP, MOLAP and HOLAP

The ad-hoc query tools which 'can' SQL for easy end-user multidimensional query-ing of relational databases, of which Oracle Discover is one, are collectively known as relational online analysis processing (ROLAP) tools. However, OFA relies upon data physically staged out of the source system and held in Express in a physical multidimensional format specifically for multidimensional online analysis process-ing (MOLAP). Oracle Sales Analyzer offers hybrid online analysis processing (HOLAP), as it enables, through RAA/RAM, a multidimensional view to be taken 'on the fly' of data held in relational tables, which can be physically cached if required. Note that HOLAP will work only where the source tables are structured as a star schema, or can be visualized as such. OFA does not support HOLAP, as discussed above in the discussion on data extracts, and hence drill to detail, albeit to data held in a star schema, is not possible with OFA.

4.3.4 The generic OFA process model and the data warehouse

Most of the business processes discussed in Chapter 2 contemplate merging produc-tion data with data gathered from people in OFA. There is a commonly held view that all required data can be extracted from production systems, cleaned and trans-formed (calculate and aggregate) and loaded into the data warehouse and then out to the users – including OFA users. The flaw in this view is that gathering data from people is not simply a data entry and validation process, as discussed in Chapter 2. Instead the data is reviewed by business people and can be potentially changed as it is submitted to the Super Shared Database or passed upwards through a tiered struc-ture of Sub Shared Databases. Likewise, further calculations and aggregations may need to be performed on this richer data set. Hence there is conflict between the generic OFA process model and current data warehousing orthodoxy.

4.3.5 The current data warehouse orthodoxy challenged

A key objective of the data warehouse is to enable access for all decision support to one consistent view of the enterprise's data. One obvious benefit should be the replacement of the widespread spreadsheet phase between production systems and final submitted reports. However, the spreadsheet problem still exists. Why?

We start with the textbooks, which influence practitioners. The classic textbook view of the data warehouse contemplates implementation steps of data extraction, transformation and loading, architecting the appropriate data warehouse schema and then – and critically for this discussion – choosing the appropriate query and reporting tool. The data warehouse orthodoxy is offering the model shown in Figure 4.2.

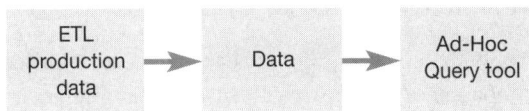

FIG 4.2   **The data warehouse process model**

The transfer to the data warehouse of production data is well supported, through tools supporting what has become known as the ETL (Extract, Transform, Load) process. There is rich support for the design of warehouse schemas and a mini-industry providing tools capable of filling the ad-hoc query box, from canned SQL to data mining. IT departments conduct feature/function vendor appraisals to 'select the appropriate query tool'.

Kimball (1996) states that the owner of the dimensional data warehouse needs to qualify and select a number of query tools for different purposes in the organization. What is meant by 'query tool'?

Kimball states that a query tool can be:

1. a standalone software package more or less limited to building SQL statements, or

2. a standard spreadsheet with embedded SQL statements, or

3. a report writer with facilities for displaying and formatting reports in both textual and graphical modes, or

4. a monolithic decision support application with a custom user interface perhaps programmed in Visual Basic or Powerbuilder.

Option 2 above could be very damaging to the 'one view of the truth' if the 'standard spreadsheet with embedded SQL statements' introduces data gathered from people in an utterly uncontrolled manner to stand alongside production data which has been subjected to controlled data entry.

But users actually need to supplement the production data in the data warehouse with data gathered from people in business processes such as planning, budgeting and forecasting, etc. A sales forecast carries as much importance as an analysis of historic sales, if not more. Hence it is important to ensure that only the agreed version of data gathered from people, such as a sales forecast, is used. Kimball actually quotes from experience that 'nothing drives senior management crazier then to have two people present the same business result but with different numbers', but it appears that the numbers contemplated are only the historic data set or production data, rather than the complete data set of production data and data gathered from people which together drive business decisions.

The spreadsheet phase in reporting and analysis enables two processes:

1. merging of data gathered from people with production data;

2. a calculation, aggregation and analysis process, sometimes including 'what-if' analysis of that data.

Preventing users doing these things, by restricting a data warehouse architecture to production data and a read-only query and reporting tool, is to invite certain users to export the data back to the spreadsheet to complete the job – and our senior executives might legitimately feel that we are back to square one.

Data gathered from users is not restricted to numeric information. Text data can be even more valuable, for example input of variance explanations can be invaluable to high-level management. And looking down the responsibility tree, divisional managers could input queries to department heads.

The actual requirement, certainly as far as the processes that OFA supports are concerned, is the diagram used throughout this book (Figure 4.3).

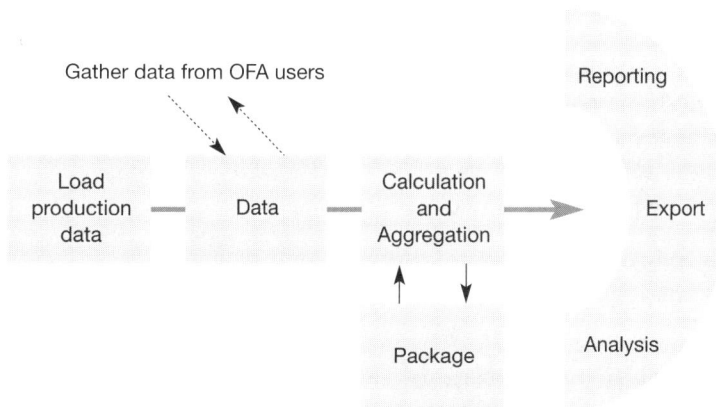

FIG 4.3   **The generic OFA process model**

The textbook orthodoxy simply does not currently support the process implied by the words 'Gather data from people' and assumes that all data transformation processes occur during the ETL phase.

A richer data warehouse model is required to meet the requirements of the user more closely than the simplistic production data-driven model. It might look like the diagram shown in Figure 4.4.

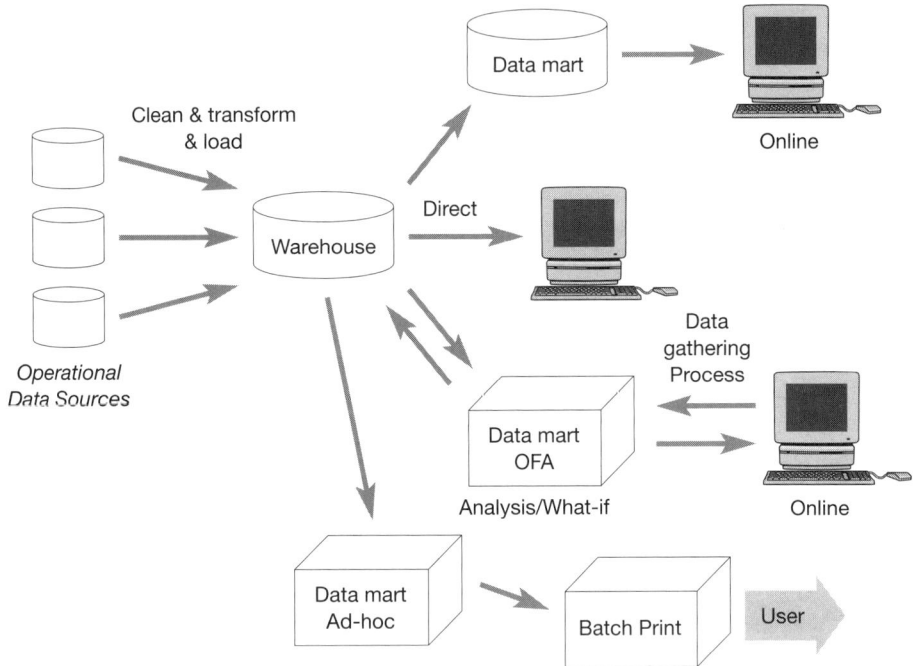

FIG 4.4   **A richer data warehouse process model**

The warehouse provides cleaned and transformed production data, a reliable source for a number of data marts and against which direct ad-hoc queries may be made if required. The clients on the right represent some generic user types of a business process-led, rather than a data-driven, warehouse.

All types of user can be supported:

1. online ad-hoc query against a read-only data mart;

2. online ad-hoc query against the read-only data warehouse;

3. writing to an OFA data mart, enabling modelling and analysis on both production and data gathered from people;

4. batch print from a data mart.

It includes OFA as a data mart, because the logical requirement includes data gathered from people in a controlled way, and must permit calculations and aggregations which go beyond what happens during the ETL process. This architecture can support many key business processes while still delivering the benefits of a read-only data warehouse model.

4.3.6 Are there signs of change in data warehouse orthodoxy?

In May 1999, the National Computing Centre published, as one of their Guidelines for IT management, a paper entitled 'Closing the Loop – Using Data Warehousing to Deliver Business Benefits'. Of particular interest is the following comment:

> data warehousing increasingly needs to be integrated into business processes rather than driven by business data. The failure to integrate data warehouses into business processes … results in warehouses which are too ambitious, too complex, too expensive and too focused on technology.

We have considered the role of the spreadsheet in some processes which are reasonably central to running a major enterprise, for example in reporting, sales and financial planning, budgeting and forecasting etc. The need for a data mart/warehouse architecture is clear in these processes, but one accommodating enterprise methods of handling all sources of data and allowing controlled further modelling to take place.

The NCC paper takes the point about data further in discussing 'failed' data warehouse projects, quoting Gaskin (1998). Note the first of three factors described as being ubiquitous:

> 'Data that is required is not collected or not accessible.'

> 'Not enough time was spent prototyping or understanding the real business needs in depth.'

> 'Besides the initial project approval, senior management did not provide much direction in terms of priorities, resulting in a disconnect between the data needed and the data gathered.'

The absence from textbook orthodoxy on data warehousing of any serious reference to the problem of managing data gathered from people permits one to suspect that the 'missing' data referred to above might include this type of data. If during the data warehouse scoping stage, analysts do not recognize the validity of data gathered from people and the importance of managing it in a robust enterprise way, it is hardly surprising that the business needs are not met. That which is not designed most certainly cannot be built.

4.4   OFA, TACTICAL SOLUTIONS AND THE DATA WAREHOUSE

For many enterprises, moving to 'one view of the truth' by rolling out a data warehouse is a very large step. One option is to use OFA to provide the basis for a 'start small, think big' approach. Using this approach, an OFA project can start with one business process, an OFA Data Mart, perhaps implemented locally in the business unit or even enterprise-wide, to demonstrate value. Then the process is moved out to the enterprise level and/or another business process is supported with another OFA Data Mart. Initially all the data to support the OFA Data Marts can be stored in Express. The actual interfaces with the user may be through a custom Web Agent front end, rather than OFA, but the management of data and structures will be enabled by OFA to provide the control required. As source data volumes grow, the source systems can be redirected to an RDBMS-based data warehouse, from which appropriate volumes of data can be staged into Express.

4.4.1 A scenario

Consider a scenario in which OFA is used to deliver a number of tactical solutions, such as (Figure 4.5):

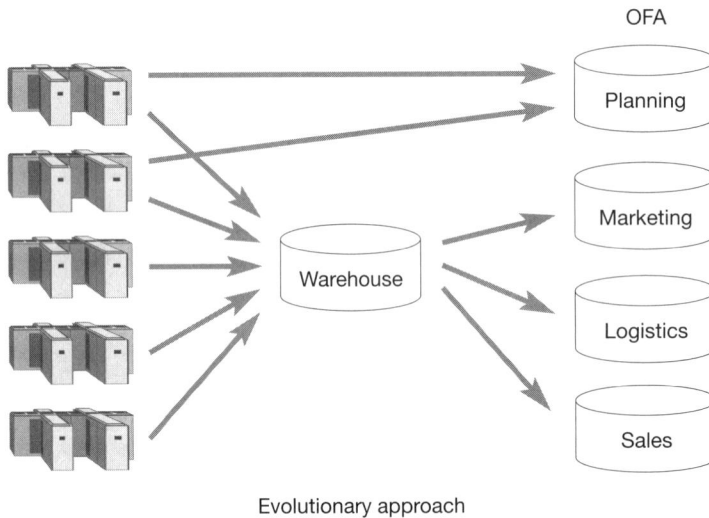

Evolutionary approach

FIG 4.5   An evolutionary approach to the warehouse using OFA

■ initially a Planning Data Mart with highly aggregate sales and cost data requirements, then

■ a Marketing Data Mart populated with some syndicated market research data against which an aggregate view of sales is compared, then

- a Logistics application which needs a more granular view of sales, plus a data set on production numbers, then

- a Sales Data Mart offering an even more granular view of sales, say for segmentation analysis (age band, marital status, etc.).

The scenario offers an evolutionary approach. Initially files would have been exported to enable loading of some aggregate sales and cost data to the Planning Data Marts. Subsequently the files created for sales data import will have forced out a progressively more detailed view of that data; the sales data in the Planning Data Mart is at a highly aggregated view, but becomes progressively more granular as successive OFA Data Marts are rolled out. Now consider that there may be an ultimate objective to perform customer-level profitability analysis on sales data, requiring the most granular view of the data to be taken.

The 'think big, start small' approach means designing the evolving warehouse to accommodate future business processes. In the scenario, this is enabled by the following:

- Value to the user is proven and tuning of the user interface and user functionality is stabilized during the incremental roll-outs.

- The OFA structures – which clearly must be meeting users' requirements – provide design input for structuring the data warehouse,

- The OFA data feeds – which clearly must be meeting users' requirements – are re-mapped, by the most appropriate method from the ETL options, into the evolving data warehouse to populate the structures.

- The progressively more detailed view of sales data required for the OFA Data Marts validates the structures by which sales data is held. This delivers a template for designing the warehouse schema to accommodate a detailed customer-level view of the sales, a longer-term objective of the warehouse.

In this way, the enterprise data warehouse can be implemented in an evolutionary way, while allowing 'quick wins'. Furthermore, the approach allows evolution towards the superior technical architecture for which the argument was made in Section 4.3, as shown in Figure 4.6.

The architecture shown in Figure 4.6 supports data loading and data gathering from people. However, the data may need to be aggregated in different ways. Aggregations can be performed in either the relational or multidimensional engines, allowing the appropriate environment to be selected, depending on the task to be performed. Provision is made to take copies of the central information into smaller data marts, for modelling or performance reasons. In summary, an architecture which provides:

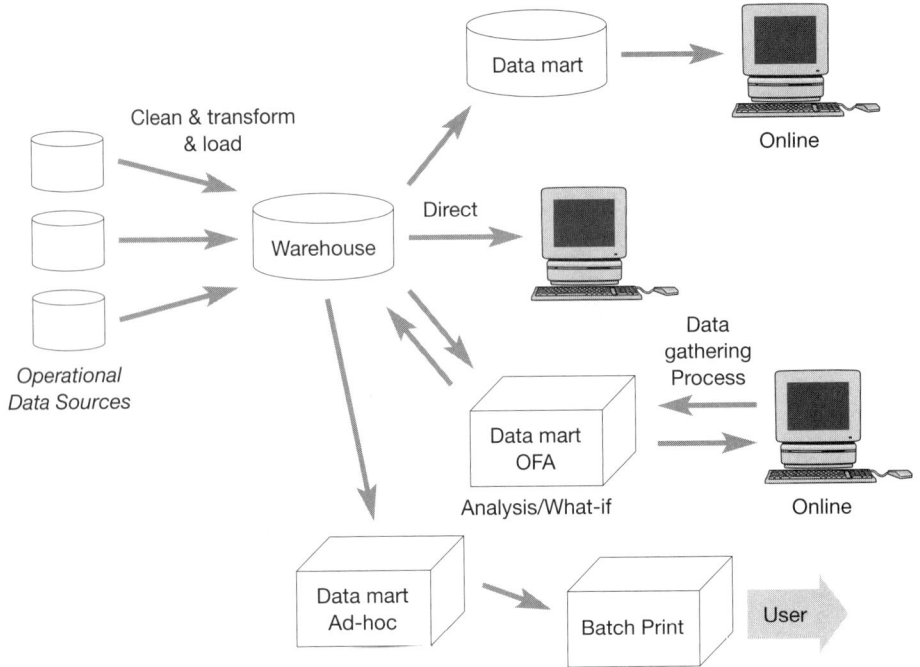

FIG 4.6 **A richer data warehouse process model**

- relational data warehouse for totally scalable data volumes;
- end-user RDBMS ad-hoc query tools;
- multidimensional database for calculation and analysis;
- multidimensional query tools;
- control over capture of low volume enterprise-wide data gathered from people.

4.4.2 The benefits

Consistent metadata

Because:

- all relevant production data for managing the business is gathered into one place; and
- control is exercised over the gathering of data from people to support further analysis; and
- control is exercised over the calculations and aggregations applied to all the data; and
- all users are able to access the same data and its transformations (subject to their seeing only the data which is relevant to their role).

Ability to derive new structures

Users will be able to create new structures which may lead to an improved understanding of the business drivers by modelling in the controlled OFA environment. If required across the enterprise, the structures and data can be transferred to the warehouse from the OFA-maintained database.

Resource saving

Because the architecture provides for control over data gathering, calculation, aggregation and of standardized reporting from a single source of data for all users, duplication of data capture and processing will be removed, allowing more people to make use of information instead of simply providing it.

Simplification of systems

The reduction in the number of systems owned, to be maintained and train staff to use will have obvious benefits in making the IT infrastructure more efficient.

5 Project principles

ROAD MAP

We now have OFA mapped to an appropriate business process which exploits some or all of OFA's key features, and have considered the issues relating to ERP, principally the GL and the Data Warehouse. We now consider how a particular project can be approached, using project principles abstracted from common experience across a number of projects. This chapter considers those principles in the classical order of the software life cycle, from sponsorship of an OFA project, through design/implement/roll-out to backup and recovery. There are nine sections:

5.1 Sponsorship

5.2 Business process modelling

5.3 Change management planning

5.4 Design of the application architecture

5.5 Database design

5.6 Infrastructure specification

5.7 Documentation

5.8 Roll-out and continuing change management

5.9 Backup and recovery

As each section is covered, the tight linkage between the following issues is brought out:

Business process defined precisely in terms of 'who', 'what' and 'when'
⟶ Application architecture defined to meet processes
⟶ Database designed to provide structures required
⟶ Infrastructure defined to host logical application architecture

The strict sequence is crucial in delivering **performance**, defined in terms of:

▓ functionality provided to the user, both initially and after roll-out;

▓ adequate response times provided to the user;

▓ and for the Administrators:

– *speed* of data load/calculation/aggregation;

– *manageability* of the Task Processor queue;

– *maintainability*, in terms of change in source data and metadata, change of calculation and aggregation rules, and change in the structure of the user population;

– *maintainability*, such as creating natural windows of opportunity for system maintenance, backup and disaster recovery.

Performance is 'designed in' by this approach. An OFA project would be like any other, but for the separation of structure from data and the top-down maintenance of such structures; bad design at any stage in the project cycle will be heavily penalized in terms of:

▓ failure to deliver functionality at each level of a tiered architecture;

▓ failure to deliver performance at each level in terms of:

– unsatisfactory response times;

– unmanageable task queues;

– inflexibility in face of change.

However, change management is also viewed as a necessary 'before and after' issue, and the issues peculiar to OFA considered. As the system should be functional and performant, an OFA system *should* not encounter user resistance from a management perspective, but the nature of the processes which OFA supports often leads to resistance at roll-out. The processes to which OFA is applied are inherently complex both in software terms and also in the way in which they require people to interact. There is development, roll-out and operational risk. We believe that containment of risk starts with the application of principles which this chapter seeks to communicate.

5.1   SPONSORSHIP

Sponsorship in OFA projects is critical since implementation normally requires change, which may be resisted without sponsorship from the appropriate level of decision-making in the organization. The mechanisms for user engagement in the change process such as feedback loops, road shows etc., which seek close involvement of all users in project implementation, are discussed later in Section 5.3. Here we discuss getting sponsorship from key decision makers.

When considering sponsorship, we need to keep in mind that OFA projects can be standalone or part of a large programme extending over a number of years. In either case, getting sponsorship from key decision makers is important. Furthermore, we need to consider situations where, although there may be sponsorship at the executive level, there is a need to gain sponsorship from all business units.

A common model requires that four steps are taken:

1. *The programme is sponsored*
   Executive Sponsors and Business Owners are agreed for each of the projects identified as part of the overall programme. The Executive Sponsor is the board member responsible for ensuring that their project delivers the desired benefits to the business. The Business Owner is nominated by the Executive Sponsor to be their representative and functional expert who works with the Project Manager on a day-to-day basis to ensure that the project content is accurately defined.

2. *Programme Director appointed and Programme Office set up*
   All projects are controlled by the Programme Director (with administration under the control of the Programme Office Manager), who will identify project managers to plan, manage and deliver the individual project. The project's implementation plan must be approved by the Executive Sponsor and Programme Director.

3. *Individual project implementation planning*
   Plans are defined at project start-up and agreed by the business prior to any work starting. These plans define the 'what', 'when', 'who' and 'how' for each project – and ensure that, for those involved in shaping the content of the projects, they deliver the benefits expected.

4. *Implementation review mechanism set up*
   A mechanism is set up to measure the benefits of the programme during execution, so that timely and appropriate action can be taken if the expected benefits are not delivered.

Are there issues with the foregoing for OFA implementations?

5.1.1 The Board vs. the business unit: contentious issues with OFA implementations

The Board may have made a commitment to the programme through individual Board members nominating projects, but lack of attention to business unit (BU) management requirements/agendas may leave business units resistant since there is 'nothing in it for them'. For instance, our planning and budgeting system may provide a top-level view of BU detail. However, if an existing opaque spreadsheet-based management information system prevents drilling down into detail from the top-level view, why should BU management assist in removing it? In such a situation, project implementation activities such as conference room pilots to demonstrate progress for validation are dangerous; it is easier for those resistant to change to say they do not like the software or how it is being implemented, rather than that they object to the project's objectives. In Section 5.2, we cover the use of business process modelling to provide the business case for project sponsorship, design documentation for the implementation and the criteria for review as the project is implemented. This approach can provide an objective approach to winning sponsorship across the business.

5.1.2 Role of IT and OFA implementations

IT have a custodial role in protecting the corporate technical architecture from inconsistent, piecemeal projects while seeking to deliver projects which give business benefit on reasonable timescales. Spreadsheets and packages potentially threaten the corporate technical architecture by introducing risk of data loss or data isolation in a package which cannot be integrated.

However, the business sponsor may see procurement of a package as a means of gaining business benefit on reasonable timescales. The arguments made for the use of OFA within enterprise systems in Chapter 2 and in Sections 4.3 and 4.4, should enable IT to sponsor OFA as being a better solution than a number of packages, all of which will require maintenance at the interface level if 'islands of data' are to be avoided.

5.1.3 Role of the major consultancies and OFA implementations

The major consultancies may have two roles in their relationship with an enterprise which have an impact on the sponsorship of OFA implementations:

1. If engaged in business process re-engineering which contemplates the use of OFA, their work may precede the actual OFA project by a number of months. For example, if reviewing efficiency in the reporting and analysis process, a great deal of work is required to define the 'to-be' reporting and analysis model before the OFA implementation project can proceed. A three-month OFA implementation may follow a nine-month modelling exercise. During the definition phase, it is important that the nature of OFA is made clear to the business sponsor, so that the strengths of OFA over packaged solutions are understood. Otherwise the implementation plan may appear onerous, with no demonstrable benefits.

2. On the other hand, the major consultancies may simply conduct 'package evaluation' exercises for clients, to support the implementation of their plans. If

OFA's functionality as an application development framework is confused with a package, it is unlikely that a meaningful exercise will be conducted; the exercise will compare apples with pears.

5.1.4 Sponsorship beyond Finance

During the sponsorship process, the name Oracle Financial Analyzer can be misleading for the sponsors. It is common for OFA to be used when the ownership of all the data may not be the Finance function.

Planning is a good case in point. The 'look ahead for five-years' forecast of market size, market share and the associated volumetrics associated with these is typically undertaken by the Marketing or Sales function. The five-year plan should roll forward, providing Year 1 as the basis of the Budget. Until that point, the user group and owners of the data will not be Finance. Seeking sponsorship from all the owners of the data is therefore crucial. It is clear that sponsorship should be sought from all functions, supply chain as well as demand chain, and extending to well beyond what is often called the back office, namely Finance.

5.2   BUSINESS PROCESS MODELLING

OFA provides an application development framework for certain business processes, which utilize some or all of the features of the generic OFA process model, as captured in the diagram we have used throughout the book (Figure 5.1).

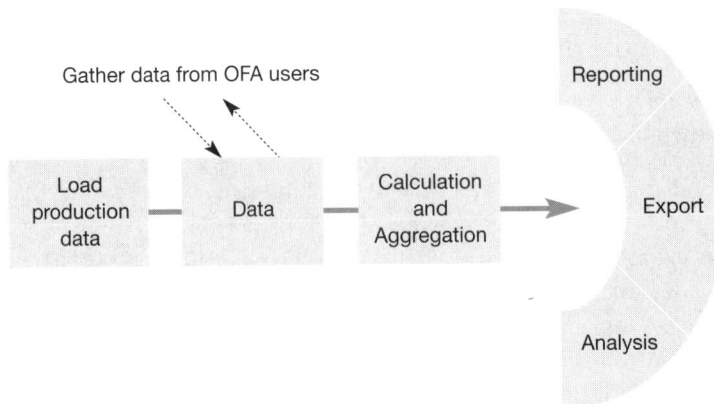

FIG 5.1   The generic OFA process model

We now look at the need for the analyst to prepare explicit business process models during the analysis/project justification phase. These can be used to map to, and specify, the OFA generic processes, especially for the following:

a) gather data from OFA users;

b) perform calculations and aggregation;

c) provide the results to users for reporting and analysis purposes.

Why do we need to prepare business process models prior to implementation?

There are two reasons:

- for use in designing the system;

- to provide a business case for project sponsorship and criteria for review during and after the implementation.

5.2.1 Designing a functional and performant system

The business processes supported by (a), (b) and (c) above involve people performing a number of tasks, sometimes in a defined order and at a particular time, and sometimes not. There are obvious implications for performance of the built system, even if the OFA generic process models map well to the requirements. For example, OFA may be a good match to the business requirements, but if a large number of users are all doing the same task at the same time with large amounts of data, the design must consider a tiered architecture to avoid contention for the Task Processor, as discussed below.

Consider the OFA process to **gather data from OFA users**.

In looking at a particular process, the analyst first needs to consider whether the business process contemplated maps to the OFA process model for gathering data from users. For instance, a data entry application involving validation on a field-by-field basis, a transactional level of granularity and which does not involve any request or review process is not naturally supported by OFA. Correct mapping of the proposed application to OFA in this case is dependent on the analyst performing **detailed** analysis on any requirement to gather data from people. If we assume that the mapping exists, the next set of issues are:

- Are there a number of tasks?

- Are they in a defined order?

- At a particular time, or ad-hoc?

- How many people will be performing the tasks?
- What are the volumes of data contemplated?

As the complexity and number of users increase, the need to gather information efficiently about the process also increases. The designer has to consider how best to use the options available with the OFA tiered architecture and client types to allow meaningful review as the data is submitted. For example, the number of Shared Database tiers will have implications for the numbers of Tasks submitted to the Task Processor. There are limits to the ability of an Administrator to manage the Task Queue in a meaningful way if there are too many Tasks being submitted.

Now consider the process to **perform calculations and aggregation**.

The project proposed might be to reimplement in OFA some existing calculations and aggregations, perhaps where a spreadsheet or package-based solution has reached capacity limits. In this case, the analyst needs to separate business rules from data since they are merged in the existing spreadsheets or may be concealed within the package. The project proposed may be to reimplement a business process that has become inefficient, involves calculation and aggregation, and is expensive in resources. In this case the analyst has to work with the business to design the new system logic, and ensure that the new logic can be mapped easily into OFA functionality, as supplemented by Express SPL programs. First, there must be a business process model extracted from the business to provide the overall functional specification. Thereafter the program specifications for any Express SPL custom programs required to supplement the OFA front-end functionality can be captured in cube maps and supporting pseudo-code (see Section 5.7).

Finally, consider the process to **provide the results to users for reporting and analysis purposes**.

End users may be conducting simple read-only reporting at one end of the spectrum, with use of the Selector providing all the functionality required. However, at the other end of the spectrum, other users may be performing advanced modelling; manipulating the existing data or performing more complex analysis by modelling new structures, inputting new data and reviewing the results. The progressive replacement of the OFA front end with Web clients means that these users scale up to potentially very large populations. There is an obvious need to separate the users into user groups on the basis of the tasks they undertake, so the same questions as above can be asked:

- Are there a number of tasks?
- Are they in a defined order?
- At a particular time, or ad-hoc?
- What are the volumes of data contemplated?

It follows that there is a need for careful modelling of the required business processes. Furthermore, this needs to be done at the analysis stage of a project. Large complex calculations and aggregations obviously require more documentation, smaller implementations less.

5.2.2 Use of analysis and design methodologies for OFA projects

The development of the relational database model, pioneered by Oracle amongst others, has led to structured methodologies for system specification, such as SSADM. These methodologies are typically data-centric, concentrating on processing within the system boundary, rather than people, and process-centric, recognizing the role of people outside the system boundary. This may explain why it has not been normal practice to document the required processes that OFA can deliver with methods applied to relational database design.

Do methods for the analysis and design of data warehouses provide an option for specifying OFA projects? As discussed in Chapter 4, the data warehouse development might have been expected to embrace the need to manage data gathered from people with the same rigour as production data, but did not so do.

The 'quality management' developments of the early 1990s were influential in driving the development of business process modelling software as an aid to systems design and redesign of the people processes outside the system boundary. We consider this option next.

5.2.3 Business process modelling software to support analysis for OFA projects

Most business processes to which OFA is applied require tasks to be performed outside the OFA system boundary, which are integral to the overall process. For instance, the business planning group may need to gain agreement from the Sales function as to sales forecast assumptions, before issuing a Data Entry Form to capture revised half-year plans.

Business process modelling software can be used to capture a logical definition of the business processes to be implemented, the 'to be' as well as the 'as is' system. In the screen shot shown in Figure 5.2, from Kaisha Active Modeller, there is an example of swim stream process modelling, in which the process flow is left to right, each process is resourced (the ellipses) and there is full documentation support for each process. Packages such as these define what is done, the sequence in which each task is performed, and permit resourcing and costing of the processes. Figure 5.2 shows both people processes, occurring outside the system, and the processes within the system which are executed by software. They can be very explicit about processes which involve the interaction of people, such as budgeting and planning, which are typical of OFA. For instance, a group may be engaged in the process of gathering the sales forecast data. A role/process analysis sheet might be as below:

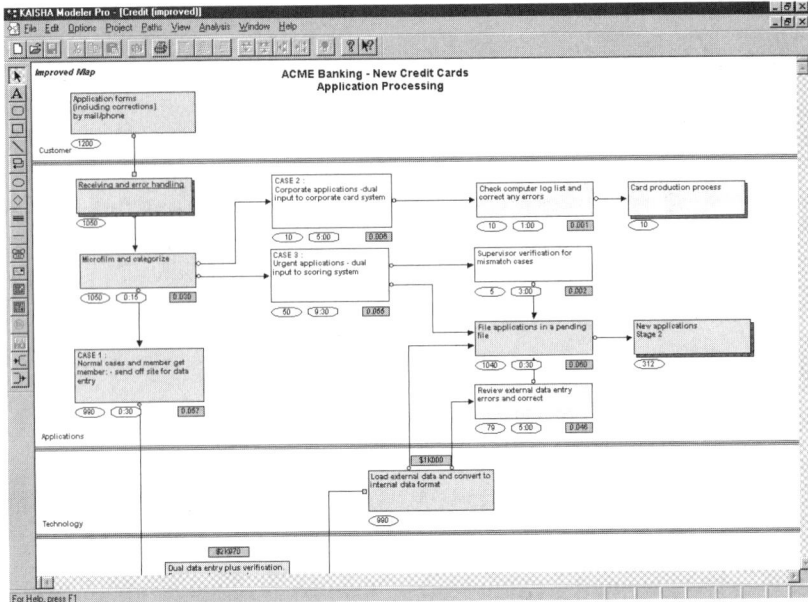

FIG 5.2   Screen shot from Kaisha Modeller Pro showing a process model

TASK GROUP:	**FORECASTING**	OUTPUT:	**MONTHLY FORECAST**
DATA TYPE:	**Spreadsheets**	DATA VOL:	**500 MB**
WHEN:	last Friday of month	WHO:	PM, 3 analysts

The ability to attach such documents to each process – or sub-process – enables the analyst to describe the required process down to a low level of detail, for instance to the psuedo-code level to define required calculations. The software captures all processes, whether they can be automated or must be performed by people.

With a clear specification of the processes, they can be mapped to OFA functionality with confidence:

Process	*Mapping to OFA*
1. Ask for forecasts	DEF sent out
2. Forecast prepared	DEF user enters/recalculates to check sense
3. Send to planning dept	User submits DEF
4. Check all forecasts received	Administrator reviews Task Processor queue
5. Consolidate forecasts	Administrator kicks off Solve
6. Review results	Administrator uses Analyst Workstation
7. Consolidated plan issued	Users alerted to access the Shared Database
8. Management review	Selector in Reports, perhaps OEA
9. Planning respond to review	Copy Data, Add Version, send out DEF

5.2.4 Use of business process modelling in creating the OFA project business case

While use of business process modelling packages can contribute to good require-ment analysis and design, they can also be used in creating the business case. For example, 'as is' and 'to be' scenarios can be resourced and costed to identify the benefits of using OFA to implement process changes, providing some precision in making the business case.

Project justifications for OFA are commonly about **intangibles**, such as to increase the time spent on analysis and reduce unproductive time spent on data handling. However, in some cases, the justification can be made on **reducing costs** through more effective utilization of human resources, as in these examples:

> 'all of their marketing analysis was done on Excel spreadsheets, which left a lot of room for error. Manual entry of retail information alone took nearly 60 hours a week. Loading the data directly eliminated most of this time.'

> 'implementing helped it reduce its inventory on hand from 120 to 80 days, which will save millions of dollars a year.'

> 'used to distribute information on spreadsheets across Europe, and the process took two weeks … it now takes two hours with OFA. Updating plans on multiple spreadsheets took days and days … it now takes half an hour.'

> 'the need to identify areas within the budget for cost reduction analysis was confounded by the cumbersome process by which budgets were created. It took three months to prepare the budget, during which time there was little opportunity to actually conduct the analysis required. The OFA solution made it possible to radically reduce the cost of operations, by creating trans-parency regarding the source – the business drivers – of costs. The benefits of the OFA solution were a strategic plan which could be produced with integrity and robustness in four days and, through enabling clarity in cost analysis, yielded a £1M saving in operating costs.'

A business process modelling package may be used to provide an ROI (return on investment) justification for the project, since:

1. The recurrent resources and hence costs of the 'as is' processes can be estimated.
2. The recurrent resources and hence costs of the 'to be' processes can be projected.
3. (1) minus (2) gives the project benefits in cash flow savings.
4. The project cost estimate provides the cost of implementation.
5. The net cash flows can be discounted at the appropriate discount rate to provide the Internal Rate of Return of the project.

Note: All of the projects referred to above indicate time saved and by extension cost saved, but do not reveal total project cost. The external cost of consulting, licences and external support are precise, being an invoiced amount, whereas the internal staff costs of the project may be more of an estimate. How much internal time was consumed? This time must be costed – but at what rate? The costs and benefits of the 'as is', 'to be' and 'as built' systems requires this complete view of an implemented project.

5.2.5 Current practice in use of business process modelling for OFA projects

It has not been normal practice to use business process modelling software to capture a logical definition of the business processes to be implemented in OFA, split between those inside the system boundary and those outside it. Instead, the business process requirements are typically gathered in a number of other ways – from more formal functional specifications, or less formal system requirements documents, assisted by conference room pilot processes, workshops, etc. We will discuss how this informality is managed through documentation in Section 5.7, but now also need to look forward to what may be expected of the current interest in workflow enablement of the Oracle Analytic Solutions.

5.2.6 Workflow enablement

The current options to model the required business processes are:

- a fully functional business process modelling package,
- a diagramming tool which simply provides convenient functionality to represent the process flows, or indeed
- on paper.

These do not provide a seamless link to implementing OFA. If the implementation process of OFA was workflow enabled, the project would start with inputting the business process model, allowing each business process to be modelled within OFA in diagrammatic form. At run time, the OFA application would take its cues from the business process model in knowing when to prompt for activity outside the system boundary. An example:

Activity:	Amend a budget
Condition:	Needs re-authorization
Event:	Re-authorization received
Activity:	Submission to corporate level
Condition:	If it is accepted then
Event:	Notification (Alert)

The development plans for OFA take this route, making the case for preparing explicit business process models prior to implementation even stronger.

CHANGE MANAGEMENT PLANNING

Project sponsorship has been attained and, through the use of business process modelling, there is precision about the processes to be delivered in OFA and also the role of those outside the system boundary. With some critical questions answered, we now have to address the next logical set, those that deal with change management planning. The theme of this short section can be summarized by asking the questions:

1. Why should those asked to actually operate the new processes be committed to the pain of transition and to maintaining them thereafter?

2. The investment decision is typically taken by a few decision makers. Substantial effort goes into the preparation of the investment proposal for the attention of this minority. There is a very much larger group involved in operating the system. Why should the effort in persuading this much larger group not be the appropriate order of magnitude greater than that involved in the investment proposal?

5.3.1 Spreadsheets and change management during OFA roll-outs

Typically, there are large numbers of spreadsheet users involved in sites where OFA is to be rolled out. We have discussed in Chapter 2 why this is the case. As we noted in that chapter, some of the major consequences are experienced as a business pain only at the organizational level, without being measurable at the individual level. The organization bears the heavy and unmeasurable cost of rekeying and data integrity issues, but few metrics exist to assess the efficiency of the spreadsheet user. The users may argue that the spreadsheet is 'easier to use' and make a case for the new system to replicate exactly the functionality of a spreadsheet, for example the ability to create new logic, or structures which are not shared across the enterprise. Some of the budgeting packages have provided, as OFA does, a spreadsheet inter-face. However, the Manage menu functionality represents control; the Spreadsheet Add-In cannot create new structures when submitting data, and the Administrator must be asked to create them and distribute them from the Shared Database.

The issue of 'ease of use' is difficult to handle in a meaningful way, since it involves the user's views after a comparison process between:

1. the product the user currently uses and therefore knows about,

2. an application development product the user does not know about and will need to learn,

3. and sometimes a single-process package which is already configured, in the sense that OFA is not, and hence appears very easy to use.

Users often only participate in a simple one or two feature/function review sessions prior to new software acquisitions, and any one individual may not actually know the overall requirements. Since OFA is an application development framework, it can perform both simple and complex functions, but they are not necessarily 'out of the box' in the sense of a package, and the user cannot casually see what the ultimate solution would look like.

Involving users in the process of defining the requirement at the earliest stage will engage them in suggesting how the solution can be made easy to use, and in recognizing that this is the task of the implementation team. Key users should then be involved in the requirement analysis process, participating in the requirements definition. The analyst should work directly with these users to identify whether OFA can or cannot do the job. Generally, management has the attitude that if a tool can do the job, and is cost effective, then time to learn to use the tool is a good investment. If the users believe the first, there is some chance that they will concur with the second. Some OFA projects have taken the spreadsheet issue up-front, put OFA on the managing director's desk, made clear at that level what it would and would not do, and asked the MD to resist any complaints about the change from spreadsheet to OFA. In particular, to resist requests for marginally important functionality which can contribute to scope creep.

5.3.2 Planning the change process

Roadshows in which all the members of the user community participate have been used in many OFA projects. The roadshow approach will present:

- benefits to the company of the OFA implementation;
- benefits to the user group of the implementation with different messages for:
    - those involved in the data gathering process;
    - those involved in the reporting and analysis process.

An OFA prototype may be useful in explaining the project scope, but for the reasons discussed earlier, it should emphasize the benefits to users and de-emphasize the control aspects of how OFA works.

5.4   DESIGN OF THE APPLICATION ARCHITECTURE ROAD MAP

In this section, we discuss the design of our application architecture:

- We consider in more detail the concept of the tiered architecture.
- We discuss the advantages and disadvantages of four types of architecture.
- We introduce the different client applications that can be used, and discuss the advantages and disadvantages of each for reporting and data entry.
- Finally, we review the roll-out issues for each client.

5.4.1 Introduction

In many implementations of OLAP systems, there is a need to balance the requirement to define and control the application centrally with the need to allow flexibility to individual areas. This is appropriate, for example, in budgeting and forecasting applications, where different business areas may want to have different ways of creating a budget or forecast, but the central group still need to be able to collect, consolidate and analyze the budget or forecast effectively. It is also appropriate in management reporting applications, where individual businesses may want to store additional detail specific to that business, or may want to summarize their detail in a different way.

OFA is unique in its ability to meet this requirement, in that there are a number of possible architectures that can be implemented. The purpose of this section is to describe the architectures available, and highlight their advantages and disadvantages.

One of the ways in which the requirement can be met is through the use of 'tiered' architectures, and an example of this is described below.

5.4.2 Example tiered architecture

A tiered architecture (Figure 5.3) can enable the following functionality:

1. Ability for a group of users to set up 'local' structures, i.e. Dimensions and Dimension Values, Financial Data Items, Hierarchies, Attributes, Models. For example, a business unit may want to set up additional budget versions for their own use or create additional Financial Data Item(s) to store and report on additional management information.

2. Ability for a group of users to work on their own copy of the data. For example, a business unit may want to work privately on their own copy of the data when preparing and reviewing a budget, and then to submit the final version for public review, or perform 'what-if' analysis on a local version.

3. Ability to treat business units as logically distinct areas. If an organization has a philosophy of autonomous business units then it cannot implement centrally run systems to support the critical business decision-making of its units.

4. Ability for the different business areas to be managed and administered effectively without contention for the SuperDBA Database. As only one user can attach the SuperDBA Personal Database at a time, it is important that the architecture does not generate contention for this database. For example, in a budgeting implementation, there are usually high periods of activity close to deadlines, and it is important that the architecture being used does not restrict the business processes.

SuperDBA
Personal Database

controls

Super Shared Database

SubDBA   Sub   SubDBA   Sub
Personal Database   Shared Database   Personal Database   Shared Database

controls   BU1   controls   BU2

Clients

Clients   Clients

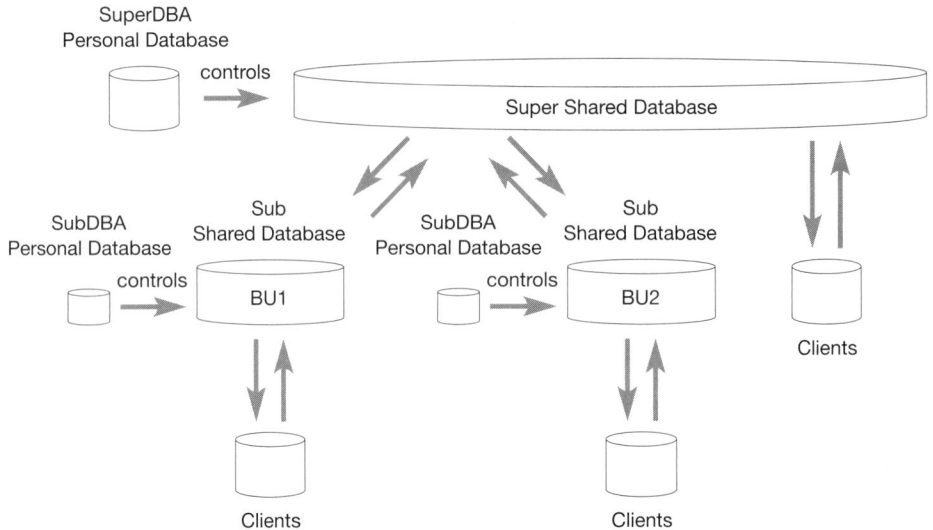

Note on terminology

In the OFA documentation, the SuperDBA is referred to as the Super Administrator and the SubDBA is referred to as the
Administrator. The terms SuperDBA and SubDBA will be used for brevity.

FIG 5.3   **Example tiered architecture**

However, the use of a tiered architecture means that there are additional tasks to be
performed in the administration of the system. The system architecture as above is
not unduly complex, but is sufficiently complex to be useful as an example. Let us
assume that all the clients are Analyst Workstations. In the example above, the following tasks arise:

▫ *Set-up of Analyst users for the Sub Shared Databases*
There will need to be Analyst users set up for the Sub Shared Databases
(assuming that Analyst users for the Super Shared Database have already
been set up). This is because an Analyst Workstation reports from only one
Shared Database.

▫ *Distribution of structures from SuperDBA to SubDBA*
Distributions are required, for example when a new OFA user is created, or when
a standard report is to be distributed. As the number of structures in the system
increases, more distributions will need to take place. Essentially, whenever the
SuperDBA is maintaining a structure via the OFA Maintain Menu, he or she
should ask whether that structure needs to be distributed. This will be the case
the majority of the time. The distribution process can be made efficient through
use of the functionality, available in version 6.2 and later, to ' save' distributions.

It is very important that only the relevant structures are distributed to the relevant SubDBA. If all structures are distributed to a SubDBA, there is a danger that the SubDBA will submit the forecast or budget for these structures back to the Super Shared Database, and overwrite the data that is already in the Super Shared Database. Note that the exact content of the distributions will depend on what the SuperDBA wants the SubDBAs to see, but it will make the system easier to use if they are not distributed structures they clearly do not require.

It is often useful to create a custom automatic distribution which will redistribute updates to structures which have already been manually distributed. This can be used by the SuperDBA or the SubDBA without worrying that any security is jeopardized, but ensures that all users have up-to-date dimension descriptions, hierarchies, attributes and report definitions.

Distribution of structures from SubDBA to users
Distributions from the SuperDBA are sent to the SubDBAs, and are refreshed at login time, or by performing Manage – Refresh Structures. At login time, the SubDBAs can choose whether to view a Refresh Preview via Tools – Application Options. In practice the Refresh Preview option is of little value as if the SubDBA cancels the refresh he or she effectively blocks any further refreshes, which is not usually practical. SubDBAs need to be aware that receipt of these new or amended structures into their Personal Databases has no effect on their Sub Shared Database or their users until they themselves perform a distribution. In Figure 5.3 the word 'controls' covers this issue. Again, saved distributions which send all relevant structures to the appropriate users would make administration more efficient.

Initiation of Solves in the Sub Shared Databases
SubDBAs are also responsible for initiating Solve Definitions. This enables models to be applied to Financial Data Items, and hierarchies to be rolled up. SubDBAs may choose to use the Solves that are distributed to them, or create their own. Consideration should be given, before creating new Solves, to ensure that there is no equivalent Solve already in existence. There is a risk that if the Solve Definitions are not well maintained, duplicate processing takes place.

Refresh of data from the Super Shared to the Sub Shared
(This assumes that the SubDBA is running in 'Administrator Mode' as set in Tools – Application Options.)

If, for example, forecast data has been generated in the Super Shared Database, then this needs to be refreshed into the Sub Shared Database using the Manage – Refresh Data function. The use of Refresh Data can be made more efficient through the use of the Refresh script.

■ *Submission of data from the Sub Shared to the Super Shared*

(This assumes that the SubDBA is running in 'Administrator Mode' as set in Tools – Application Options.)

Data can be submitted from the Sub Shared Database to the Super Shared Database via use of the Manage – Submit Data function. The use of Submit Data can be made more efficient through the use of Submit scripts.

Let us now consider four different options for architectures. For the time being, we will ignore the different client types that are available to access these databases – these will be considered later.

5.4.3 Option 1: One SuperDBA and no SubDBAs (the 'flat architecture')

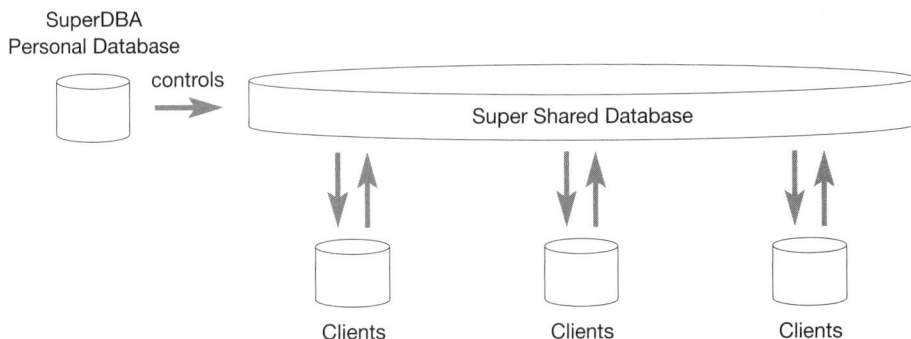

SuperDBA Personal Database — controls → Super Shared Database — Clients   Clients   Clients

FIG 5.4   **Option 1: A SuperDBA and no Sub DBAs (the 'flat architecture')**

This is the simplest scenario (Figure 5.4), without any SubDBA workstations. The functionality is as follows:

1. Where a group of users require a 'personal' structure, this must be added by the SuperDBA.

2. Where an individual user requires a 'personal' structure, this would have to be added by the SuperDBA, or a Budget Workstation would need to be set up for that user.

3. For a group of users to be able to work on a personal data set, extra cubes or extra values in a version dimension would need to be set up in the SuperDBA. This would need to be coupled with security within the Super Shared Database, so that only the appropriate user/user group could access their personal data. This could be achieved by using a nominated security dimension, as discussed in Section 3.1.20.

4. Where an individual user requires to work on his or her own copy of the data, a Budget Workstation would need to be set up.

5. There is no provision for business units to be logically separate.

6. The SubDBAs for the different application areas have to share the single SuperDBA Workstation.

Option 1 advantages

1. *Simplicity*
    This is the most straightforward solution, as there is only one SuperDBA and Shared Database. This is an appropriate architecture for a highly centralized organization, where individual businesses are afforded little or no autonomy. This could potentially lead to a reduction in the training effort required, balanced against the need to train an alternate administrator for the system.

2. *One Shared Database*
    Within a 'tiered' architecture, individual business units have their own Shared Database to work with, and must clearly understand that their database is not the corporate view. The 'flat' architecture, however, means that there is only one Shared Database, and the potential for users reporting from the wrong Shared Database is removed.

3. *Low administration*
    Some of the administration tasks associated with the 'tiered' architectures do not apply. For example, transfers of structures from a SuperDBA to a SubDBA are not required.

4. *Reduced disk space*
    In a tiered environment, the Sub Shared Databases store a copy of their 'slice' of the database, which takes up extra disk space. Depending on the sizes of the slices and the additional local structures held in the Sub Shared Databases, the size of all the Sub Shared Databases together could exceed the SuperDBA Shared Database.

Option 1 disadvantages

1. *High contention for SuperDBA access*
    Individual businesses require access so that they can maintain the components of the application that are unique to their business. There is therefore likely to be huge demand for access to the SuperDBA workstation at certain times, resulting in a loss of productivity when access is not available. Practically, this could mean that processes such as budgeting, planning and forecasting cycles take a longer elapsed time. It could also mean that administrators would be

restricted in their ability to respond in a timely way to requests or changes from their business. This is potentially disastrous in a Business Intelligence application, where users need to feel that the system can be responsive to change.

2. *Preparing data 'off-line' to the Super Shared Database*
Groups of users cannot prepare their data 'off-line', since access to the Super Shared Database is required to maintain consistency through the Task Processor. The 'tiered' architecture specifically provides the functionality of groups working together, unconnected to the Super Shared Database until they are ready to submit data.

3. *No single point of responsibility for SuperDBA Personal Databases*
As the SuperDBA contains all the 'local' structures, the contents of this database would grow significantly over time. There would be no one person with sufficient knowledge of all the structures to know which could be deleted and which were current. The only way to address this would be to make one person responsible for all administration activities within the SuperDBA database, but it is likely that this would be a difficult job, and would present bottlenecks to the use of the system.

4. *Usability of the system is reduced*
Related to point 3, there is a high risk that the choices and picklists available to users accessing the system become confusing. With a large number of people adding objects to the SuperDBA Database, there would be no common naming convention across the application. For example, each business unit accessing the SuperDBA Database could set up reports which are specific to their business. These could then be distributed to users, giving them a bewildering choice of reports. Also, as individual businesses create additional FDIs for their own management information, these again could be viewed by users, making it complicated for them to create a new report.

5.4.4 Option 2: One SuperDBA and multiple SubDBAs, but one tier only

This has been the most frequently used scenario in implementations of OFA in large organizations (Figure 5.5), with a SuperDBA controlling those parts of the application common to all, and SubDBA Workstations controlling aspects of the application specific to a group of users. The majority of users would be Analyst Workstations viewing their Sub Shared Database. Budget Workstations could be used where appropriate. The exception to this would be users who require to see data across all business units, who would have an Analyst Workstation viewing the SuperDBA Shared Database. A single user can be both an analyst of a Sub Shared Database and an analyst of the Super Shared Database by having workstations defined at each tier. SubDBAs would also be given an Analyst Workstation viewing the SuperDBA Shared Database, so that they can verify that the data they have submitted has been successfully received.

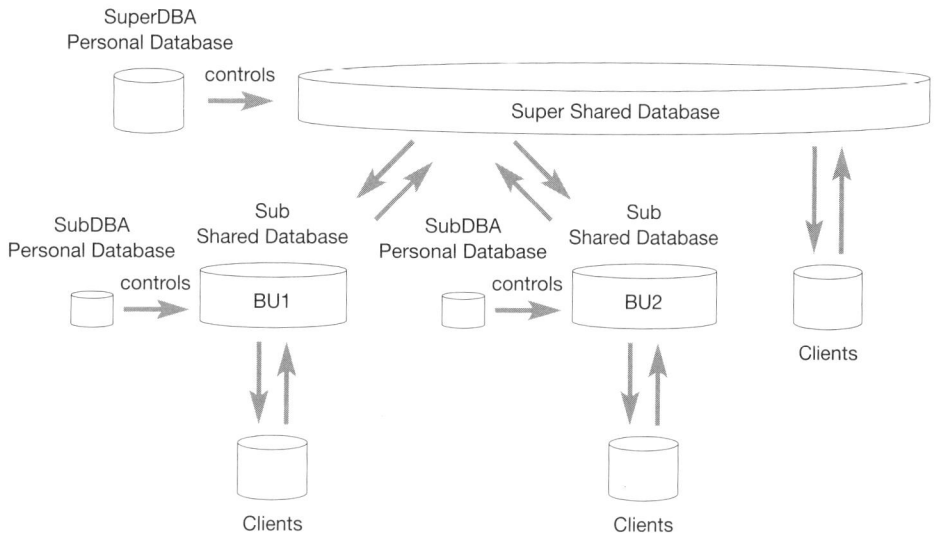

FIG 5.5　　　　Option 2: A SuperDBA and multiple SubDBAs, but one tier only

The features provide functionality as follows:

1. Where a group of users require a 'local' structure, this would be added by the appropriate SubDBA.

2. Where an individual user requires a 'personal' structure, this would have to be added by the SubDBA, or a Budget Workstation would be set up for that user.

3. For a group of users to be able to work on a local data set, this would be available by default in the SubDBA Shared Database.

4. Where an individual user requires to work on his or her own copy of the data, a Budget Workstation would be set up.

5. The need to recognize separate logical entities would be handled by having multiple SubDBAs. The SubDBAs would be identified as a result of an organizational design exercise, not as a software issue; typically they would map to business units.

6. At a lower level in the business organization, particular business processes may require a high degree of administration. Such areas would be set up as a separate SubDBA. For example, a costing process could lend itself to be set up as a SubDBA with a separate Shared Database. Costing requires a reasonably high

level of administration, as allocation rules are set up and volume drivers are established, so a separate SubDBA may be appropriate for this. A Shared Database storing costing data would enable costing users to review their unit costs prior to submission to the Super Shared Database, and if necessary to modify allocation rules appropriately.

Option 2 advantages

1. *Highly functional*
   This architecture often provides the highest fit with business requirements of medium to large enterprises.

2. *No contention for SuperDBA*
   The high degree of contention described in the disadvantages of option 1 would not be a problem with option 2. Each SubDBA would have 100 per cent access to his or her **Personal** Database. Furthermore, using the example in (6) above, the costing SubDBA would have 100 per cent access to administer his or her business process.

3. *Reduces risk of system being seen as 'not our system'*
   For most users, the primary Shared Database will be that of their SubDBA, since for a particular business unit user, the majority of his or her work will be performed looking at the business unit Shared Database. This means that the list of options, e.g. reports he or she has to look at, is restricted to those of interest to his or her business unit.

Option 2 disadvantages

1. *Multiple Shared Databases – user awareness required*
   Whilst being a benefit in many ways, it should be pointed out that multiple Shared Databases can cause confusion to users who are not aware of the application architecture. There is a risk that if users are given access to both the Super Shared and SubDBA Shared Databases, they might not choose the correct database to report upon. This can be addressed through education and training in the application architecture as part of the change management process, which should have, as its aim, a thorough awareness of the business processes being supported.

2. *More administrative tasks for the SubDBAs*
   In the 'tiered' architecture, there are some additional tasks that a SubDBA would have to perform. Some of these are existing tasks as discussed in option 1, which have been delegated to the SubDBAs, such as:
   - creation and maintenance of users and their security profiles;
   - maintenance of hierarchies and reports specific to a business unit;
   - initiation of Solve Definitions to process data, e.g. calculate a costing model, aggregate data using a local Hierarchy.

Others are new tasks, such as:

- distribution of structures that have been distributed by the SuperDBA to the SubDBA, e.g. the latest version of a product hierarchy;

- submission and receipt of data, e.g. submission of budget data.

These tasks can be modelled in detail in a process modelling package as part of the sponsorship process, and the time required costed. This cost can then be weighed against the business benefits: extra flexibility and functionality delivered.

3. *Additional disk space*

Additional disk space will be required. Although the cost of disk space is negligible in comparison with total project costs, it is an issue if the system is undersized and additional space needs to be added in an unplanned way.

4. *Data mismatches*

As some of the same data will reside in the Super Shared and the Sub Shared Database inevitably the data will become out of step. Budget or forecast data in the Sub Shared Databases will be updated and reviewed before it is changed in the Super Shared Database by submission. Similarly, new high-level targets may be defined in the Super Shared Database before being passed down to the Sub Shared Databases. There is therefore scope for disconnects between analysts at the Super Shared level and analysts at the Sub Shared level when they discuss the 'same' data item. It is important that each user community knows the current date of their data. This can be achieved by publishing a standard report which gives details of the current dates for FDIs, e.g. 'Budget amendments to 08/21/2000' or 'September actuals were reloaded 09/02/2000'. If this is insufficient then key analysts at each level need to have Analyst Workstations defined at the other level in order that they can see the same data at the other tier. A user with workstations defined at multiple tiers can open those workstations simultaneously in different windows and view 'the same' report from each shared database to compare the data.

5. *Data confusion*

An advantage of this configuration is that SubDBAs can create their own structures and FDIs. This can also be a source of confusion between users at the different levels. For example, a SubDBA may create an account hierarchy that reflects country-specific statutory reporting requirements, which include a roll-up point 'Total Revenue'. The Sub Shared FDIs will then be rolled up using this hierarchy and an analyst at this level will review this account in reports. If there is also a Super Shared account hierarchy with a roll-up point called 'Total Revenue' or similar, but defined differently in terms of its children accounts, then 'the same' account will have different values in each hierarchy.

To avoid this situation the organization should adopt a naming convention which clearly identifies the ownership of hierarchies and their roll-up points. A common method is to designate the first letter of the dimension code to define which Shared Database owns the dimension value.

6. *Data overwrite*
    Distributions from a SuperDBA will overwrite definitions created at a SubDBA. For example, a SubDBA might define an account hierarchy roll-up point called 'Distribution Costs' in response to a request from his user community. If subsequently the SuperDBA defines an account using the same code, then the distribution of the account from the SuperDBA will destroy the existing account in the Sub Shared Database.

    This problem is also avoided by strict use of naming conventions.

5.4.5 Option 3: One SuperDBA and multiple SubDBAs, i.e. >1 tier

Option 3 advantages

The benefits of option 2 also apply here:

1. Highly functional.

2. No contention for SuperDBA.

3. Reduces risk of system being seen as 'not our system'.

The additional benefit comes from the creation of the extra level, so that, in this example (Figure 5.6), two groups of business units can be treated as separate SubDBAs, below a SuperDBA. Where the business conducted within the two groups of business units is substantially different, autonomy is permitted in designing the appropriate structures, while preserving one view of the truth when consolidating upwards.

Option 3 disadvantages

1. *Multiple Shared Databases – user awareness required*
    As in option 2, there are multiple Shared Databases, but the effect here is more significant. There is a much higher risk of users becoming confused about the location of their data, regardless of the extent of their initial training. Also, the issue of data mismatch is greater as the time delay between updates flowing between the Super Shared and the Sub Sub Shared Databases tends to be greater.

2. *More administrative tasks for the SubDBAs*
    As in option 2, there are additional tasks inherent in a tiered architecture. However, these will become more onerous as the number of tiers increases, and it is possible that these will outweigh the benefit of an additional tier.

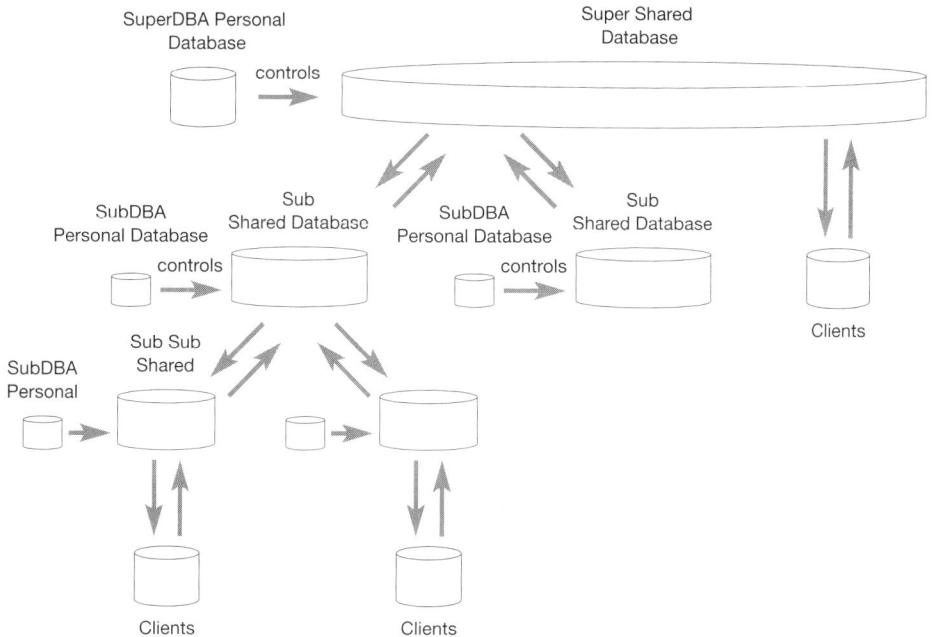

FIG 5.6   **Option 3: A SuperDBA and multiple SubDBAs, >1 tier**

3. *Additional disk space*
   In certain circumstances, each extra tier could take up additional disk space
   equivalent to that of the Super Shared Database.

4. *Data mismatch and overwrite*
   Strict naming conventions become even more important, as the number of local
   structures increases as the number of tiers increases.

5. *Data confusion*
   This is likely to be more of an issue as the amount of time that the various
   databases are out of step in respect of common structures and data will increase.

6. *Time delay during data submission*
   With tight budgeting timetables, the time delay as users submit data from one
   tier to another can be a problem.

5.4.6 Option 4: Multiple SuperDBAs

In this option (Figure 5.7), SuperDBAs are used instead of SubDBAs and essentially
model an organization which would like business units to use OFA autonomously.

All the databases would be distinct, and there would be no opportunity to view data from separate databases summarized. If such facilities were required, there would need to be Express custom procedures developed to facilitate distribution of structures and data between separate databases, as there exists no standard functionality to enable this.

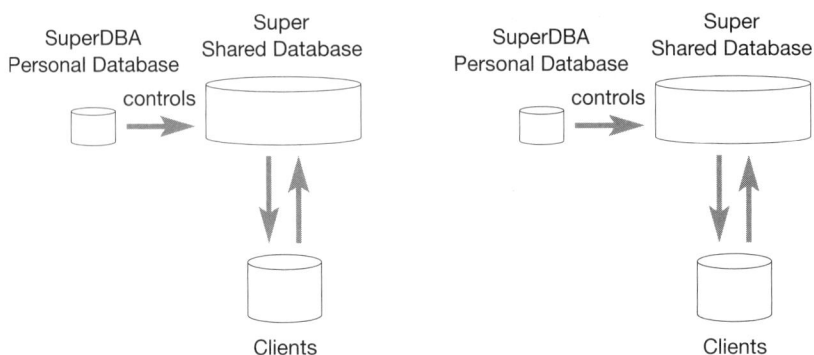

FIG 5.7   Option 4: Multiple SuperDBAs

Option 4 advantages

1. *Delivers devolved flexibility*
   This meets the requirement for individual businesses to be able to maintain their own structures and data. There is no possibility of the users seeing data for business units that they are not responsible for.

2. *No contention for SuperDBA*
   As in option 2, the existence of multiple SubDBAs removes the possibility of contention for a single database.

3. *Reduces risk of system being seen as 'not our system'*
   Again as in option 2, the risk of the system being seen as 'imposed' is reduced.

4. *System independence*
   The different SuperDBAs could be on separate OFA versions on different versions of Express on different platforms. In a tiered architecture, the different businesses can be on separate platforms and operating systems, but the versions of OFA and Express must be common.

5. *GL interface*
   As discussed in Section 4.1, The GL–OFA interface works only at the SuperDBA/Super Shared level. Multiple SuperDBAs enable the GL–OFA interface to be used without customization by many businesses.

6. *Data mismatch, confusion and overwrite*
   As no data is exchanged or duplicated in the Shared Databases there is no danger of mismatch, confusion or overwrite.

Option 4 disadvantages

1. *Common structures may need to be maintained*
   As standard, there is no facility within OFA to transfer structures between separate SuperDBAs. There may be a need for common structures to be shared between these applications.

   Whilst pointing this out as a disadvantage, the effect of this can be mitigated. Through use of a standard Express routine across all businesses, these common structures could be imported from an underlying relational database (such as a data warehouse) or set of flat files. Express procedures for exporting and importing data between systems are relatively quick to develop, providing that there are matching structures between these systems.

2. *More administration*
   In comparison to option 1, and similar to option 2, there will be more administration with separate databases.

5.4.7 Different client types

In an OFA implementation, the user has the ability to access the OFA data using a number of different Express client front ends, of which the OFA client is one. This does not mean that all these client types need to be used – again, if the requirements can be met through the roll-out of just one client type, then this should be done. It is important to fit the user to the optimal client type.

The clients can be grouped into four main types, with some variations within each type:

1. Oracle Financial Analyzer (OFA) client
2. Microsoft Excel client
3. Intranet/Internet client
4. Oracle Express Analyzer (OEA) client

These are now described in turn, together with their advantages and disadvantages. The ease with which each client type can be rolled out is also discussed at the end of this section.

OFA client

This is the 'standard' OFA client, and across all implementations is probably the most widely used. It is a proprietary client, developed solely by Oracle, designed purely for working with OFA databases. Technically speaking, the OFA client is a Visual Basic program that uses the Express API (SNAPI) to read from and write to the Express database.

The functionality within the OFA client depends on the type of Personal Database it is being used with, and so effectively is available in two variations. The two types of Personal Database are shown in Figure 5.8.

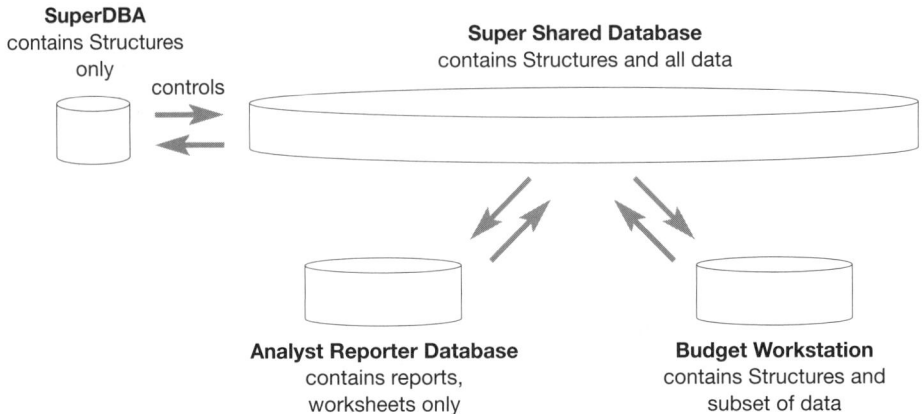

FIG 5.8   **Workstation types**

OFA client using an Analyst Reporter Personal Database

This has historically been the most commonly used client, enabling powerful reporting, together with relatively simple data entry and submission. It is suitable for a wide variety of users, and typically would be the preferred client for management, accountants and other finance staff and management who work with OFA data regularly.

In its simplest form, a user can open a report and print it, or can open a Worksheet, enter data, calculate and save it directly to the queue. In its most complex form, a user can create a presentation-quality analysis, and share that report with others.

The OFA client has a standard Windows graphical user interface, and in some ways has the look and feel of a spreadsheet, so it can be considered for roll-out to a wide user audience of infrequent users. However, as described later, there are other client types which infrequent users may feel are easier to use on an occasional basis. Also, the effort involved in rolling out and maintaining the OFA client needs to be considered. This is discussed in detail at the end of this section.

Advantages and disadvantages of OFA client with Analyst Reporter Personal Database for reporting

Advantages

■ Reports are directly from the Shared Database, with standard functionality to select, rotate and drill within the report.

■ Row and column calculations can be added in the report.

- Individual row and column formatting of fonts, borders, patterns, width, height is supported.

- Row and column labels can be overtyped within individual reports.

- Nested reports are supported, as are 'asymmetric' reports, where not all the combinations of the nested across or down dimensions are shown.

- Standard reports can be distributed using the Distribute Structure functionality, and personal reports can be saved. Reports can be transferred back to the administrator for sharing with other users, subject to security.

- Multiple reports can be open at a time.

- Reports can be exported to Excel as static Excel files, including the OFA formatting. One or multiple pages of a report can be printed from the Print dialog box.

- Print Preview and Fit to Page are supported.

- Reports can be grouped into folders, and multiple reports can be printed directly from the menus.

- Custom options exist to run a Visual Basic (VB) executable from the Tools menu, with the VB program having knowledge of the current cell. This can be used to provide 'drill down to transactions', showing the underlying transactional detail from GL or some other source. This has been seen to be a very popular facility for users throughout the organization.

- Simple 2D graphs are supported.

- Cut and paste to Excel or any other OLE applications.

Disadvantages

- Only one report or graph can be printed on one page.

- Individual cell formatting as available in Excel is not supported.

- Colour coding of individual cells based on the data value is not yet supported.

Advantages and disadvantages of OFA client with Analyst Reporter for data entry

Advantages

- Copy and paste multiple cells within the Worksheet, or from another Windows application such as a spreadsheet, is supported.

- Tools are available in the Worksheet to grow, increase and spread data.

- Menu options exist to associate a Hierarchy or Model with the Worksheet, to enable recalculation of the data.

- Ability to select, rotate and drill is supported as per reports.

- Row and column formatting is supported as per reports.

- When data is saved, it goes directly to the Task Processor queue of the relevant Shared Database without the user having to use Manage – Submit data. When data is read into the Shared Database, a 'partial' Solve can be processed, recalculating only those parts of the FDI impacted by the change. The dimension selections made in the Worksheet when the user pressed 'Save' are stored as details in the task queue.

- When data is saved to the Shared Database, the data write access controls set up by the administrator are checked to see if the data is permitted to be saved.

- Custom options exist to run an Express Stored Procedure as data is saved. An example of this would be to remove unnecessary zeros from the data submission.

Disadvantages

- Nested rows and asymmetric use of dimensions are not supported.

- Only one Worksheet can be open at a time.

- Only one stored Financial Data Item can be viewed in a worksheet . This is often seen as a major drawback when users want to see protected Actuals alongside their Budget or Forecast, or users want to input text assumptions alongside their data. The workaround is to copy the Actuals data into the Budget FDI. If the user inadvertently changes the Actuals data this can be overwritten by a refresh of Actuals during the budget calculation Solve.

- Automatic recalculation is not supported.

- No detail audit trail of data before/after a change is stored.

- Row and column calculations are not supported.

- Security is evaluated when the user saves the data and not when he or she enters the data into the individual cell. There is no individual cell protection in the Worksheet without customization. If the user attempts to save data that he or she is not permitted to save, he or she sees a message box indicating that this is the case, but this doesn't show which cells were protected.

OFA client using a Budget Workstation Personal Database

Budget Workstations are not frequently used, as effectively they require users to take a copy of the data that they wish to work with, and there is the risk that this gets out of synchronization with the Shared Database. This client has the greatest functionality of all, enabling users to create their own models and hierarchies and to recalculate their own data, and so is generally reserved for 'power users' who use OFA very regularly and want to make the most of its power. There is standard functionality to transfer data to/from the Shared Database, and the selections made in these transfers can be saved and reused.

Advantages and disadvantages of OFA client with budget workstation for reporting

▨ Reporting is as per an OFA client using an Analyst Reporter Personal Database, except that the Database being reported upon is the Budget Workstation Personal Database. This has advantages and disadvantages, in that the Budget Workstation user has the flexibility to perform his or her own calculations and aggregations, but also has the responsibility of refreshing core data from the Shared Database.

Advantages and disadvantages of OFA client with Budget Workstation for data entry

▨ Data entry is as for an OFA client using an Analyst Reporter Personal Database, except that the data is saved directly to the Budget Workstation Personal Database. The user can then initiate Solve Definitions to apply calculation models and hierarchies to the data. This gives almost unlimited flexibility to the modelling and manipulation that can be performed.

▨ There is no automatic functionality to perform a 'partial' Solve, as described for an OFA client using an Analyst Reporter Personal Database.

▨ Budget workstations are useful for modelling sensitive data (e.g. staff remuneration) away from the shared database.

Excel client

All structures and data in an OFA application are stored in an underlying Express database, so any client application that can interact directly with Express can also interact with OFA. One of these applications is Excel, through the use of the Express Spreadsheet Add-In. An Excel Add-In has been developed by the core Express development team and this enables data to be read from and written to any Express database, subject to security. This can be used in its raw form against an OFA database or in conjunction with the OFA Data Collection Toolkit, as described in the following sub-sections.

Express Spreadsheet Add-In

The Express Spreadsheet Add-In always appears initially to users as an attractive option for reporting, as it gives the power of selection, rotation and drilldown, combined with the power and flexibility of Excel with which they are familiar. It is therefore appropriate to infrequent and frequent users of the application, as even though a user may be unfamiliar with OFA, it is likely that he or she will be familiar with Excel. It can therefore be considered as an appropriate client when the OFA application is being rolled out as a reporting tool to users outside the Finance function, e.g. cost centre managers, product managers, project managers and other managers who may be infrequent users. However, the detail advantages and disadvantages need to be examined before a decision is made as to whether this client should be used for reporting.

The Express Spreadsheet Add-In on its own is very rarely used for data entry, as it effectively requires a Budget Workstation to be set up and maintained for each user. This is explained in detail below.

Advantages and disadvantages of Express Spreadsheet Add-In for reporting

Advantages

- A user can combine Excel functionality with OFA functionality such as select, drilldown and rotate.
- Formatting of individual cells or ranges of cells is supported through standard Excel functionality.
- Row and column calculations can be added in the report using standard Excel functionality.
- Nested reports are supported, and asymmetric reports are also supported, in that unwanted rows or columns can be manually deleted.
- Multiple tables and graphs can be printed together on one page – this is a common requirement in implementations where the reproduction of an existing management reporting pack is required.
- Multiple reports can be open simultaneously.
- Reports can be transferred to other users via e-mail or via a Shared directory on a server.
- Colour coding of individual cells based on the data value is supported using Excel functionality.
- Sophisticated Excel 2D/3D graphics are supported.

Disadvantages

- Printing multiple pages, e.g. a page for each cost centre, is only supported by storing each cost centre report on a separate sheet, which can lead to large spreadsheets.
- Printing multiple reports (i.e. reports in separate workbooks) is only supported via Excel macros.
- Data is not automatically refreshed when a report is opened – the user has to choose the Refresh Data option from the menu to do this.
- Changes in the dimensionality of the report will overwrite calculation cells entered manually into the spreadsheet.

Advantages and disadvantages of Express Spreadsheet Add-In for data entry

As described above, the standard Express Spreadsheet Add-In functionality enables the user to read from and write to an Express database.

However, the design of the add-in assumes that the user is the only person who is updating the database at that time. This is because Express allows only one user to update a database at a time. In this context, updating a database could mean saving data from a data entry session, lasting only seconds, or could trigger Solve Definitions to recalculate models and/or hierarchies which could last minutes or hours.

Unless every user is given their own Personal Data database, i.e. an OFA Budget Workstation, there is a risk of users not being able to save their changes because the database is being written to by another user.

If users attempt to share a database, either a Shared Database or a Budget Workstation Database, then there is a risk of the users not being able to save their changes. This therefore would not normally be recommended, except in certain cases where the users work closely together in the same geographical location, and where all Solves are performed overnight according to a predefined timetable. This situation occurs rarely in real life and is the reason that this option for data entry is rarely implemented.

We will see later that the Data Collection Toolkit uses the OFA task queue mechanism to save data, and therefore enables multi-user data entry from Excel.

Assuming that we can live with the limitations described above, the advantages and disadvantages are as follows:

Advantages

- Multiple stored and formula financial data items can be used in the sheet.
- Multiple workbooks can be opened simultaneously.
- Calculations can be added into the Excel Workbook which can then be automatically recalculated as per standard Excel functionality.
- Formatting, printing and Workbook sharing is as per reporting.
- Ease of use of Excel data entry, including cut and paste/linked cells etc.

Disadvantages

- OFA models and hierarchies cannot be used for recalculation. This means that, in practice, OFA calculations need to be duplicated in Excel. At a minimum, this creates a maintenance overhead – in the worst case, calculations between OFA and Excel become out of sync, leading to data reconciliation problems.
- No security checks are performed when writing back to the database. If a user is writing to a Budget Workstation, security would apply when the data is submitted to the Shared Database.

Express Spreadsheet Add-In together with Data Collection Toolkit

This combination offers the benefits of the Express Spreadsheet Add-In for reporting, together with a Data Collection Toolkit that removes some of the data entry limitations associated with using the spreadsheet add-in on its own.

It can be considered as an appropriate client for infrequent users of the application, as described above.

It requires knowledge of the Excel macro language VBA to implement, together with knowledge of the Express Stored Procedure language.

It is recommended only for small data entry applications where a small number of data cells are captured.

Advantages and disadvantages of Express Spreadsheet Add-In together with Data Collection Toolkit for reporting

- As in the previous sub-section.

Advantages and disadvantages of Express Spreadsheet Add-In together with Data Collection Toolkit for data entry

Advantages

- Data can be recalculated using OFA Models and Hierarchies.
- Data can be submitted to a Shared Database via the task queue.
- Multiple stored and formula financial data items can be used in the sheet.
- Formatting, printing and Workbook sharing is as per reporting.
- A user can input text alongside numbers.
- A user can enjoy the ease of use of Excel data entry, including cut and paste/linked cells etc.

Disadvantages

- The Data Collection Toolkit is applicable only for small data entry applications.
- Only one Data Collection Toolkit workbook can be open at a time.
- Only one Solve Definition can be associated with a Data Collection Toolkit workbook.
- Knowledge of Excel VBA and Express SPL is required for implementation and maintenance.

OFA Web client

In the same way that the OFA client has been the most commonly used client historically, the OFA Web client is likely to be the most commonly used client in the future. One of the reasons for this is the ease of roll-out of a Web client to large user populations, together with the fact that many users are now familiar with Web browser interfaces. Other reasons are that the Web clients are feature rich, well integrated with the OFA application, and easy to implement. OFA reports can be distributed to a Web client user for reporting, and OFA Data Entry Forms can be distributed for data collection.

Advantages and disadvantages of OFA Web client for reporting

Advantages

- The Web clients are easy to roll out.
- The Web clients are easy to use for users of browser applications.
- Reports are directly from the Shared Database, with standard functionality to select, rotate and drill within the report.
- Formatting of fonts, borders, patterns, width, height is available for row, column and page headers (but not individual rows/columns).
- Nested reports are supported.
- Standard reports can be distributed using the Distribute Structure functionality, and personal reports can be saved.
- Reports can be exported to Excel as static Excel files.
- One or multiple pages of a report can be printed from the Print dialog box.
- Print Preview and Fit to Page are supported.
- Colour coding of cells based on data value is supported.
- 2D/3D graphs are supported, including the ability to drill down within a graph by clicking on the graph.
- Drill columns as well as rows, which is not supported in the OFA client.

Disadvantages

- Only one report or graph can be viewed/printed on one page.
- Individual cell formatting as available in Excel is not supported.
- Individual row/column formatting is not supported.
- Row/column calculations are not supported.

Advantages and disadvantages of OFA Data Entry Forms for data entry

Advantages

- Data can be recalculated using OFA Models and Hierarchies.
- Data can be submitted to a Shared Database via the task queue.
- Pending tasks in the task queue can be viewed.

■ Multiple stored and formula financial data items can be used in the same form.

■ A user can input text alongside numbers.

■ An administrator can easily create a new Data Entry Form using the OFA Administrator GUI.

■ Protected cells are visually highlighted to the user and input is prohibited at the entry stage.

Disadvantages at the time of publication

■ There is a limit of 4,000 cells per Data Entry Form.

■ A user cannot copy and paste multiple cells in the current version.

Other Web clients

As well as the OFA Web Reporting clients and OFA Web Data Entry Forms, there are other Express Web clients which should be considered. In the same way as the Express Spreadsheet Add-In has been developed as a generic tool for accessing Express data from Excel, there are generic tools for accessing Express data (and therefore OFA data) from a Web browser.

Express Web Publisher

This is the simplest of the Express Web clients, enabling reporting via a Java or HTML table/graph with very similar functionality to the OFA Web Reporting client. There is less integration with the OFA distribution function, in that the list of reports is common to all users and not specific to the user that logs in.

Advantages

■ There is similar functionality to the OFA Web client for drill, select, rotate.

■ OFA security is inherited during login.

■ The user interface is easily set up and maintained via the Express Web Publisher GUI.

Disadvantages

■ There is no integration with the OFA Distribute Structure function.

■ There is no data entry facility – only reporting.

■ A user can view only one table/graph per page.

Express Web Agent Developers Toolkit

This toolkit allows the Express developer to build custom Web sites that enable a user to report from and interact with OFA data. Reports and graphs can be created with a single Express Stored Procedure call, and these have the same look and feel as the Java/HTML tables described above.

Advantages

- Similar functionality to OFA Web client for drill, select, rotate.

- OFA security is inherited during login.

- Multiple tables/graphs on a page are supported.

- Custom HTML forms are supported. These enable the user to select a dimension value, e.g. enter an exception threshold for an exception query.

- Linked tables can be created.

- Formatted text and data can be integrated into the same page.

- Hypertext links can be inserted between pages.

- Frames on pages can be dynamic.

- Pages can be assigned a corporate look and feel and made available via a corporate portal.

- Access can be granted to users outside the corporate firewall.

- Oracle provides a useful series of working samples which amply illustrate the functionality available.

Disadvantages

- This requires knowledge of Express Stored Procedure Language to set up and maintain.

- There is no data entry facility – only reporting.

Express Analyzer/Express Objects

As well as the Excel and Web clients, there are two more proprietary clients that can access Express databases and therefore OFA-maintained databases. These clients were originally developed to deliver executive information systems, and are optimized for ease of use and rapid assimilation of information by an executive. To this end, they include functionality such as colour coding to quickly identify areas for attention, and they allow for the combination of different information in tables and graphs on the same page. They also allow for inclusion of buttons to aid navigation, and other Windows objects such as Word documents and Excel spreadsheets to enable information to be collected together in one screen.

Express Analyzer is controlled through a GUI interface and requires no programming to implement. Consequently the functionality that can be delivered is more limited in comparison to Express Objects, which has its own object-oriented development environment to deliver sophisticated functionality. Express Objects briefings can include features such as colour-coded maps, speedometers, dashboards, traffic lights and other mechanisms for rapid assimilation of information.

Owing to the ease of use inherent in these types of systems, these clients are therefore applicable not only to senior executives, but also to infrequent users of the OFA application. These clients can support data entry as well as reporting, subject to the constraints outlined below. The ability to control the look and feel of the user interface also makes it applicable to those users who find that the other clients contain too much functionality, and who require a simpler, easily navigable application.

Advantages and disadvantages of Express Analyzer/Express Objects for reporting

Advantages

- Access to standard tools for select, rotate, drill.
- Can customize look and feel and content of the application.
- Can include buttons for ease of navigation.
- Can include multiple tables and graphs on a page.
- Can include other EIS tools for ease of assimilation (maps, dashboards etc., Express Objects only).
- Inherit OFA security during login.
- Can format row header, column header and body.
- Custom options exist for 'drilldown to transactions' (Express Objects only).

Disadvantages

- Asymmetric reports are not supported.
- Row and column insertions and calculations are not supported.
- Individual cell formatting as available in Excel is unavailable.
- Individual row/column formatting is unavailable.

Advantages and disadvantages of Express Analyzer/Objects for data entry

Advantages

- Control over look and feel and content as in reporting.
- Multiple stored and formula financial data items can be used in the same form.
- Can input text alongside numbers.
- Ease of set-up via OFA Administrator GUI.

Disadvantages

- As in the Express Spreadsheet Add-In, requires access to a Personal Database, i.e. Budget Workstation, to avoid risk of database not being available to read/write.
- OFA models and hierarchies cannot be used for recalculation. Calculations would need to be performed in the Budget Workstation.

No security checks are performed when writing back to the database. If a user is writing to a Budget Workstation, security would apply when the data is submitted to the Shared Database.

5.4.8 Installation considerations

Having discussed the functional advantages and disadvantages of each client, we now discuss the relative ease with which these clients can be rolled out and maintained within a large user community.

OFA client

Installation

The OFA client is installed using the Oracle Universal installer and must be installed on each client PC or on a local area network (LAN) server. Administrator rights are required to perform the installation and a reboot is required at the end. Scripting tools have been used to automate the installation, and in some sites SMS has been used to create an OFA package for remote installation. Citrix Metaframe has been used in some sites to provide a three-tier architecture and to reduce the roll-out effort.

There is significant effort and planning involved in upgrading OFA versions when using OFA clients. This is due to the fact that OFA has both a client and server code. When the server code is upgraded all the clients must be moved in step. This can be logistically difficult if they are geographically or time zone dispersed. There is often an upgrade process run automatically when a user first logs in after a server upgrade. This can be confusing for the user community, but if done centrally will take considerable elapsed time.

Excel client

The Spreadsheet Add-In client is installed using the Oracle Universal installer and can be installed on each client PC or on a LAN server. Administrator rights are required to perform the installation and a reboot is required at the end. The user then needs to attach the add-in within Excel manually. Connection utility and connection files need to be installed and kept up to date on each PC.

Problems can arise if the path variable is not correctly configured on the user's PC and problems removing and installing a new version in Excel are common.

Web client

No client installation is required as the Java applet is downloaded from the server as required. However, this doesn't necessarily mean that any client PC with a browser can access OFA, as the Java applet requires a reasonable amount of memory together with recent versions of browsers/Java Development Kit.

Users must be advised of the URL and login process.

Express Analyzer client

The Express Analyzer client is installed using the Oracle Installer and can be installed on each client PC or on a LAN server. Administrator rights are required to perform the installation and a reboot is required at the end.

Connection utility and connection files need to be installed and kept up to date on each PC.

As with the OFA client, there is significant effort and planning involved in upgrading Analyzer versions if the application changes or the Express server is upgraded. Where the application changes to use new or changed structures in the Express database, all users must be distributed copies of the new application. When the Express server is upgraded, all the client Analyzers must be upgraded and the application may need amendment. This can be logistically difficult if the users are geographically or time zone dispersed.

5.5   DATABASE DESIGN

ROAD MAP

In this section, we look at the design of our database:

- We look at why design is important, and what are the effects of a bad design.
- We discuss how to identify our dimensions and how to assess what type of dimensions they are.
- We discuss how to design our cubes, including topics such as hypercubes vs. minicubes, stored cubes vs. formula cubes, sparsity, sizing and the use of reporting cubes.
- Finally, we look at detail design points.

5.5.1 Why is design important?

Most of us would agree that in a classic project life cycle the system design phase is inevitable. However, to validate that the design activity is worthwhile, and to focus on what we mean by database design, it's worth considering the implications of a bad design.

Poor batch performance

The most common symptom of bad design is poor performance, particularly in the processing of OFA 'Solve Definitions' where aggregations and calculations take place, and this affects everyone. For the users, it means frustrating delays waiting for calculations to finish, which can become even more frustrating when the calculations have to be reprocessed, perhaps because some of the input information has changed or because a structural change is required.

For the administrator, it also means that future flexibility is restricted. How can he or she deliver the additional calculations and analysis that users are asking for when the current processing is so excessive? For the IT department/manager, it means that valuable system resources are being over-used and stretched with possible knock-on effects if other applications are sharing the same hardware platform.

A further difficulty is that the system performance may not initially be an issue, and only when the system is used in anger and when the implementation team has been disbanded does the issue arise. A proven method for reducing the risk of this is to do significant volume and performance testing before the system goes live. However, this is one of the first tasks to be sacrificed or significantly reduced when timescales are tight.

Early warning of a batch performance problem is essential, but this processing is sometimes performed at night once the source information has been finalized, for example when the general ledger balances have been finalized and the accounting period has been closed. It is important, therefore, for an OFA administrator to monitor and be aware of the processing times taken by overnight batch jobs.

Poor online performance

The next most common symptom of bad design is poor online performance.

Poor online performance provides all the same problems as poor batch performance, but in many ways it can be worse as online performance is so much more visible. It is now not only the administrator and the IT function that are aware of poor performance, but also every user, possibly including some of the senior managers and business sponsors.

Users can quickly become frustrated with poor online performance and can end up making mistakes due to frustration/lack of concentration, and the system can rapidly end up with a bad reputation.

Reduced flexibility, excessive maintenance and administration

Bad design can also lead to situations where the system becomes inflexible, where the users either cannot be given the functionality they require, or where such functionality can only be provided with laborious and costly system maintenance and administration work.

5.5.2 Why do we need to worry about design now ?

Generally, online analytical processing (OLAP) systems are presented as being highly flexible and capable of accommodating change. OFA is no exception to this.

So it is valid to question whether we need to invest time in designing the system up front. Surely, if OLAP systems are as flexible as claimed, there will be no problem adapting the design in the future should we hit a performance bottleneck or have a need to add functionality?

The best way of answering this is by considering an example.

Assume that we have set up an Actuals cube with three dimensions, Cost Centre, Account and Time, and we need to add a fourth dimension, Project.

OFA has the functionality and flexibility to accommodate this change. Using the graphical user interface (GUI) in the OFA administrator, we can easily create a new cube with the four dimensions and copy the existing cube into a slice of our 4D cube. This can be accomplished without much effort. However, our users will need to modify their reports and worksheets to view the new cube, which can become a significant task. As the administrator, you will also need to set up new Solve Definitions to perform roll-ups and calculations on the new cube.

Finally, we will need to modify any data loading or data manipulation programs that we might have created, so that these will work correctly with the new cube.

In summary, there are enough tasks associated with a cube redesign to make it worthwhile to get the design right first time.

5.5.3 How do we make sure our design is right?

Prototyping

The most common technique for reviewing and validating the design is to build a prototype. This is a sensible approach as an OFA prototype can usually be created very quickly and users and other project team members can be involved in reviewing and commenting on the prototype. Users are particularly keen on prototypes as it helps them to visualize the solution being delivered. However, we need to issue health warnings with prototyping.

The most common danger is the 'runaway' prototype. A simple prototype is built and presented to the users. However, at this and subsequent presentations, the users feel 'they haven't quite seen enough' of the system via the prototype and ask for a 'bit more functionality' to be added. This can consume considerable time and money if not properly managed. One technique used for managing this is the 'time-boxed' approach to prototyping. If the users can describe the requirement and it can be built within the time window, then it can be included, otherwise it is excluded from the scope of the prototype.

Another danger with this approach is that if users' expectations are not managed correctly, they may see the prototype system as being appropriate enough for use in a production environment and start using it. Users rarely appreciate the effort involved in 'productionizing' a prototype, and so it helps to make this clear before the prototype is presented. An example of this 'productionization' may be the development of a data loading program or interface program to populate data in a cube automatically. A common mechanism for helping to describe the production-ization effort is the classic 80–20 rule, i.e. it takes 80 per cent of the effort to finalize the last 20 per cent of the system.

Obviously, if the users are happy or can be persuaded to forego the last 20 per cent, then there is an opportunity for quick delivery of a system that will meet the users' requirements, and this opportunity for a 'quick win' should not be missed. The extra 'bells and whistles' can always be added in a later phase.

5.5.4 Summary

In summary, a poor design affects the whole quality of the system, and so appropriate time should be invested initially in considering and reviewing the design of the OFA system. This investment in time should lead to a more successful implementation of OFA.

5.5.5 Identifying our dimensions and dimension values

A key aspect to getting our design right is identifying our dimensions.

How do we identify the dimensions and dimension values that are required?

The requirements for dimensions will come from a variety of sources. As in most approaches to systems analysis, we need to look at the existing systems in place that we are to replace and/or complement, and we also need to get input from our prospective users to identify requirements that are beyond the scope of existing systems.

(The existing systems are sometimes referred to as the 'as is' requirements, whereas the requirements beyond the scope of the existing systems are sometimes referred to as the 'to be' requirements.) If we first look at the existing systems, there are many different systems that we could be replacing/complementing. OFA is similar to other OLAP systems in that in the majority of cases, the existing system that we are to replace is likely to be a spreadsheet-based system, typically Excel. However, there are other cases where we might be replacing an existing OLAP tool, an existing PC data management tool (typically Access) or some other reporting or budgeting tool. Also, we could be enhancing the functionality of systems such as a general ledger – in this case, the OFA implementation could be running in parallel with the GL implementation or conversion, could be implemented shortly after the GL implementation as a subsequent phase, or could be being implemented some time after the GL implementation.

In each of these cases, we will first consider how to identify our dimensions from our existing system, and then we will go on to identify our 'new' requirements.

Replacing existing OLAP systems

The simplest existing system to replace is the existing OLAP system, where the dimensions and dimension values will have already been identified. Although this might be seen as a rare case, OLAP systems have been in existence for a number of years now. As the OLAP marketplace consolidates around a smaller number of larger suppliers, this situation is likely to occur more frequently. Of particular concern here, of course, is to ask why the system is being replaced, and to ask what the perceived limitations and boundaries of the existing system were.

Complementing general ledger systems

We are not going to be replacing a general ledger with OFA, but instead we are likely to be complementing the GL functionality with enhanced reporting and/or budgeting.

In most general ledger packages, there would be the concept of a chart of accounts or account key, and this would have a predefined code structure. In Oracle General Ledger, the structure of the chart of accounts is described as being made up from a number of segments, and so this term will be used to refer generically to the sub-sections within the chart of accounts key.

When we initially review the chart of accounts structure, we might instinctively think of a 1:1 relationship between the segments within the chart of accounts and our dimensions. This is valid in many cases, but we also need to raise two questions:

Are the segments in any way dependent on each other?
Is there 'subanalysis' within the segment code?

To answer these, we may need to look beyond the chart of accounts structure and get input from our users on how the GL is used. We may need to look at reports that are being produced directly from GL, and we may also need to look at reports that are being 'hand crafted' in spreadsheets to produce the required results. 'Getting input from our users' could take a number of forms, including the review of requirements documents, interviews, workshops, and classical systems analysis techniques.

Dependent segments

The best way of considering the question of dependent segments is via an example. For instance, if the chart of accounts segments were:

Company
Business
Cost Centre
Account
Product

then we would want to ask the following questions:

■ When we post journals to a cost centre, do we always use and have we always used the same business for a particular cost centre?

■ If we do this now, are we guaranteed to continue doing this in the future?

If the answer to both these questions is Yes, then we are more likely to create a 'Business' hierarchy rather than have separate dimensions in our stored cube. In other words, Business is simply a roll-up of cost centres.

Alternatively, if we identify a report that shows cost centres going down the page, and businesses going across the page (see example below), then this would identify that at a minimum we need to be able to report on these dimensions separately.

Sample report showing costs by cost centre and business

Jun 2000 £'000	Credit cards	Personal loans	Mortgages	Savings and Investment
Operations	1,012	567	389	876
Finance	88	45	23	92
IT	305	144	104	256

Analysis within the segment

Again, let us consider an example.

Assume that we have a three-digit code for the cost centre. However, on closer examination of the cost centre values and on discussion with the GL administrator who is responsible for maintaining segment values, it emerges that the first digit always represents the type of cost centre, and the second and third digits represent the location.

Sample list of cost centre values

101	Call Centre Edinburgh
102	Call Centre Dublin
103	Call Centre Bristol
202	Bad Debt Dublin
203	Bad Debt Bristol
301	IT Edinburgh
302	IT Dublin
303	IT Bristol

On investigation of the ad-hoc reports being produced manually within spreadsheets, we find that there is a report showing costs by cost centre type and location:

Sample report showing costs by cost centre type and location

June 2000 £'000	Edinburgh	Dublin	Bristol
Call Centre	3,212	883	595
Bad Debt	1,634	422	358
IT	804	228	156

This points to us having cost centre type and cost centre location as dimensions, as well as cost centre itself. Later we will discuss how to design our cubes to handle this requirement.

As before, we also need to ask ourselves whether this coding convention will be used for ever or whether there will come a time when it won't be possible to continue with this convention as we 'run out' of codes. In the example above, we will have a problem if we ever have more than 36 cost centre types (26 alpha + 10 numeric) – obviously this problem would be even worse if the segment had been defined as numeric only.

Other examples of this kind of reporting occur with the product dimension where there may be a number of product attributes embedded within the product code, e.g. product type, product flavour, product pack type, etc.

Usage of GL segments

The last question we need to ask ourselves when we are implementing OFA to complement GL functionality is:

> Are the segments and segment values actually used for management
> reporting and information?

Sometimes the segments in the GL do not actually reflect the way in which the business wants to see their information.

There are a number of possible reasons for this:

- The GL implementation was performed some time ago, and the focus of the business management has moved on from when the GL was implemented.
- The GL chart of accounts structure may have been imposed on a business as it is part of a larger multinational group, and so it may not reflect the local needs.
- The GL chart of accounts structure may have been influenced heavily by the financial controller to provide statutory and regulatory reporting.
- The GL implementation may have been influenced by the data structures in key operational systems. If a key source system stores data in a certain way, then it may have been beyond the scope and budget of the GL implementation to change that source system, and it is possible that the cost of modifying the data structures via the interface and appropriate mappings was too high.

Again, in this case we need to go beyond the chart of accounts structure, and get input directly from our users, as described previously.

Replacing spreadsheet-based systems

Identifying the dimensions when replacing a spreadsheet-based system is a harder task, as there is typically far less structure and methodology with spreadsheets. This is not a criticism of spreadsheets – in fact, it is one of the reasons they are so popular, and their use should be encouraged for the right type of application.

However, spreadsheets have limited flexibility to handle true multidimensional structures. Whilst they have rows, columns and pages, there is no easy way of rotating the report or input area, and so they have been described as $2\frac{1}{2}$ dimensional. This is why many spreadsheet-based systems end up being replaced by OLAP systems – the $2\frac{1}{2}$ dimensional nature means that sophisticated spreadsheet links and macros need to be constructed to provide the reporting required, often requiring the latest and fastest PC processor to perform in a reasonable time. Alternatively, pivot tables can be used to perform OLAP-style rotation, but this requires the data to have been stored in a database-style format.

The absence of structure and methodology will manifest itself in many ways, but we will focus on two common symptoms:

1. It is very likely that there is no design document showing the key data structures available, meaning that we have only the spreadsheets to look at to understand the design.

2. The nature of the spreadsheet system means that it is likely that there will be many spreadsheets linked with formulae and macros, making it a time-consuming task to understand the system.

Essentially, to identify the dimensions and dimension values in a spreadsheet-based system we have to work through the rows and columns within the reports being produced. In a budgeting and forecasting system, we also have to work through the spreadsheets to identify cells that are input, and for those that are calculated, the essential syntax of the calculation.

The simple technique of looking at the rows and columns will be recommended also when we are replacing other types of reporting systems, but it needs to be qualified in two ways:

1. We need to make sure that the report we are looking at is still used and is still required, and if so, whether it is important to maintain the format, layout and presentation of the report.

2. More importantly, we need to look at the header, footer and title(s) of the report, together with getting input from our users, to see if any additional criteria have been applied to the data in the report.

For example, we might see a report showing types of expenditure going down the page, with cost centre groups going across the page. We can see from the header that the report is for a particular month, and so we would assume that we would have three dimensions – cost centre, account and time.

Sample report showing costs by cost centre and account

June 2000 £'000 Business as usual	Call Centre	Bad Debt	Finance
Salaries & Benefits	2,543	1,345	340
Premises	678	388	28
IT	1,228	670	120
Other	244	120	30

However, upon closer examination, we might find that the numbers in the report are for 'Business as Usual' only, and exclude any project-related costs incurred within the cost centre. Or we might find that the costs are only those that have been incurred within a certain legal entity or country. This analysis of our 'paging' dimensions is essential at this stage so that we can understand *all* the dimensions within our system before we design our cubes.

Replacing other reporting systems

Examples of other reporting systems are PC-based data management tools such as Microsoft Access or custom reporting solutions using relational databases. The techniques for identifying the dimensions in these systems are essentially a combination of the techniques described above:

- Identifying the data structures in the existing system, which are likely to be represented by key fields within the relational database.
- Identifying if any of the fields within the database are dependent on each other or whether there is 'subanalysis' within the field.
- Reviewing the reports provided by the system, and looking at the row, column and 'paging' dimensions.

Identifying dimensions from new requirements

As described earlier, our analysis of the dimensions required will come partly from our existing systems, and also from getting input from our users on what they would like to see. When interviewing our users, we will find that there are some keywords that we can look out for in our users' responses.

For example, our senior manager says:

'I want to see profitability by product and by channel for the UK business.'

The 'by' keyword gives us a clear indication of a dimension, but we should also pay attention to the 'for' keyword. In the example above, is the UK the only business that we need to produce the profitability report for, or are there other countries that will require the same report, in which case we might add a business or region dimension to our product and channel dimensions?

We will also need to break down and understand each key phrase within the sentence. The manager wants to see 'profitability', so this becomes the 'cube' we want to report upon – but what do we mean by 'profitability'? Does he just want to see one number for the profit for a product for a channel, or does he actually want to see a detail Profit and Loss? Does he want to see it every month or every quarter? Does he want to see Actual and Budget profitability?

Another example might be:

'I want to see the split between Business as Usual and Investment costs.'

Again, the 'split' keyword gives a clear indication that a dimension is required.

Typical dimensions

To assist in recognizing dimensions, some typical dimensions are shown below:

- *'Organizational'-style dimensions*: Company, Business, Legal Entity, Cost Centre, Location, Department, Branch
- *'Account'-style dimensions*: Account, Line Item, Expense Type
- *'Product'-style dimensions*: Product, Product Group, SKU
- *'Product attribute'-style dimensions*: Product Type, Product Class, Product Size, Product Variety etc.
- *'Customer'-style dimensions*: Client, Customer Group, Market, Channel, Delivery Point
- *'Project'-style dimensions*: Project, Programme
- *'Activity'-style dimensions*: Process, Activity
- *'Version'-style dimensions*: Version, Scenario, DataType, Data set, Currency
- *Time-style dimensions*

Non-typical dimensions – essentially transactional

Conversely, it seems appropriate to mention dimensions that would not normally be seen in an OFA system:

- *'Transactional'-type dimensions*: Purchase Order, Purchase requisition, Invoice
- *'Large' dimensions*: Large dimensions with over 100,000 values tend to be avoided. Owing to the large number of values being transferred to the client, these would tend to cause long delays on start-up and when accessing the selector. Also, certain administrative functions, such as the distribution of dimension values, become very slow with large dimension lists, as well as the potential maintenance headaches associated with such a large value set.

Other dimension types

As well as the standard type of dimensions we have identified so far, it is worth mentioning some of the rarer varieties of dimensions, but which can still add significantly to the functionality of the system. Understanding the role of these types can help during our analysis when identifying dimensions.

Shadow dimensions

Shadow dimensions are usually copies of an existing dimension, with the same or a similar set of values used to provide a specific report. The best example is 'target cost centre' in a cost allocation Model where costs are transferred between cost centres, e.g. IT, HR and Facilities all allocate their costs to other departments. The creation of a 'target cost centre' dimension will enable users to see where allocated costs have come from, and where allocations are going to. A health warning needs to be applied here. When we consider designing a shadow dimension, we must give careful consideration to how it will be maintained, allowing not only for additions but also for deletions. There are many implementations where a shadow dimension becomes cluttered with 'old' dimension values.

Shadow dimensions are also used when we need to be able to report on internal OFA structures, but using the standard OFA front-end reporting. For example, OFA stores internal dimension(s) containing the names of each Hierarchy for a dimension. If we wanted to report on (say) the number of orphans in a Hierarchy as a control check, we can create a shadow dimension which is automatically maintained from the internal dimension.

Integer dimensions

As the name suggests, integer dimensions contain numeric values. They can be used in a number of ways, including being used to store different items, events, iterations, etc. For example, cost centre managers may want to budget for their IT hardware expenditure by breaking it down into a series of items, where the items budgeted for differ from one cost centre to another. In a cost allocation example, we might want to keep track of the iterations that we perform whilst resolving a 'circular' allocation where cost centres are allocating costs to each other. Other examples of integer dimensions are simple 'row' and 'column' dimensions, which might be used to control 4GL Express programs that use data read from or written to a spreadsheet.

Reporting dimensions

Reporting dimensions are used to control the appearance of data in a report, so that the user can control the appearance via an extra 'tile' in the report. One example of this might be to control whether data is displayed as monthly or YTD data, or whether it is shown in local or one or more main currencies. An extra 'Scale' tile is an example of a common reporting dimension. Although number scaling has been introduced in OFA, a scale dimension can still be used as it enables a user to see easily the scale of the numbers when the report is viewed on screen or printed out. It also provides a controlled approach to scaling, ensuring that all numbers are scaled and not just selected columns. Other examples of reporting dimensions are where several Financial Data Items are grouped together into one 'hypercube' using a reporting dimension to indicate the different stored and comparative data. The use of reporting dimensions is covered further in the section on reporting cubes.

5.5.6 Base and attribute dimensions

Now that we have gathered our list of potential dimensions, we need to decide which of these will be 'base' dimensions on our stored cube or cubes, and how we are going to handle our 'attribute'-style dimensions.

Let us consider an example of two dimensions – product and product group, and let us assume for the moment that a product belongs to only one product group. We would describe product as one of our 'base' dimensions, as the lowest level of detail in our system is stored by product. We would consider 'product group' as one of our 'attribute'-style dimensions as it is essentially a characteristic of product. We may want to use the product group 'attribute' in a number of ways:

1. We may want to look at our sales information summarized by product group.

2. We may then want to be able to drill down to individual products within the group.

3. We may want to select the products within a product group.

4. We may want to input information, e.g. marketing spend at a product group level, and allocate or 'spread' that down to individual products.

We now need to consider which type of OFA structure is most appropriate, i.e. whether we want to use an Attribute, a Hierarchy or both. Let us look at each of the requirements in turn, and decide which of our OFA structures we should use:

1. The most common way of summarizing data is via a Hierarchy, and so for the moment we should assume that if we need to see this summarized data, we should use a Hierarchy. Later, we will discuss whether we will store the summary data (or 'parents') in the Hierarchy or whether they are calculated at run time or 'on the fly'. We will also discuss advanced ways of using attributes to calculate summary information on the fly.

2. The only way of providing drilldown is via a Hierarchy, so if we need to provide this functionality, we should use a Hierarchy.

3. In the Selector we can use the Hierarchy or Attribute tool to make selections (Figure 5.9). The use of the Hierarchy tool assumes that the product group that

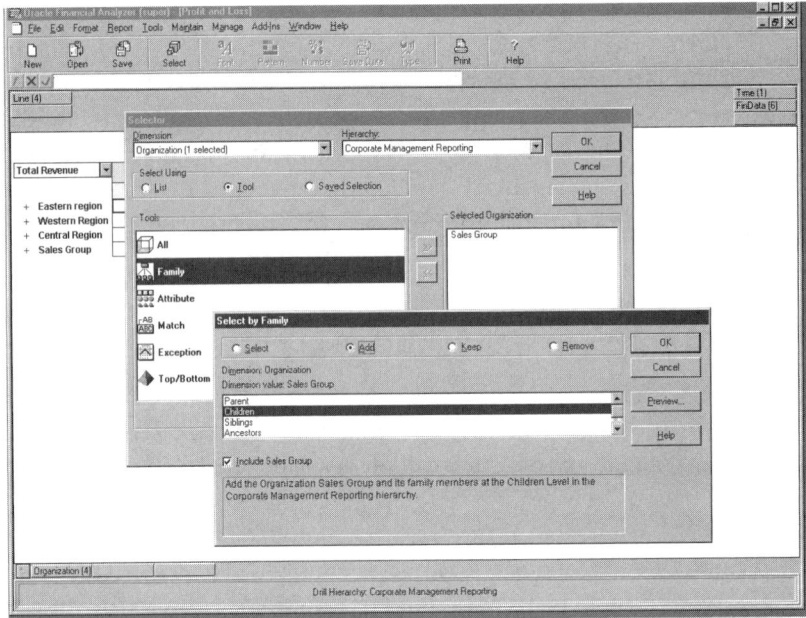

FIG 5.9   The Family tool in the Selector

we want to select from is selected, i.e. on the right-hand side in the selector list window, and is the currently selected row on the right-hand side if more than one row exists there. Furthermore, if we wanted to select products within a number of product groups, we would need to use the Family tool once for each group. In contrast, the Attribute tool doesn't have these limitations and presents very little system overhead, so an Attribute would be the recommended way of meeting this requirement.

4. This requirement can be met using either a Hierarchy or an Attribute. If we are using a Hierarchy, then we can use the standard spreading functions in the worksheet to allocate the numbers down the Hierarchy. If we are using an Attribute, we will use the product group dimension as a 'base' dimension in a separate cube called 'Marketing spend' and then use a Model to allocate that to individual products.

Many-to-many relationships

In the last example, we assumed that a product belonged to only one product group, but the relationship between two dimensions may not always be a many-to-one relationship. So we need to examine the relationships between our dimensions. In the discussion of dependent segments when implementing OFA alongside a GL system, we discussed the example of two dimensions – cost centre and business. We questioned whether data for a particular cost centre would always be stored against one business or whether it would be stored against many businesses. When we examine this relationship, we can end up with three possible scenarios.

1. Data for a particular cost centre has always been and will always be stored against the same business. In this case, we can use a Hierarchy or Attribute to store this relationship. Another example of this is where the account segment is broken down into two dependent segments – one controlled by Head Office, the other 'sub account' segment being available for local use by the business.

2. Data for a particular cost centre can be posted to any business. This is most likely where the cost centre dimension represents 'functional' groupings that are common across the businesses, and do not represent individual cost centre managers. In this case, we would need our stored cube to have both cost centre and business dimensions.

3. Data for a particular cost centre has been posted to a specific business for selected periods, but after a reorganization on a specific date it is now posted to a different business. In this case, we are likely to use one dimension containing cost centres and businesses, with multiple hierarchies representing the structures at different points in time. We would need to assess how many hierarchies would be required and whether we want to keep them all – if the number of hierarchies becomes excessive, then we might revert to case 2 and the solution provided there.

Examining the relationships between our dimensions is critical to getting our design right, so appropriate investment in time should be made here.

Many-to-many Attributes

We can set up an Attribute as many-to-one, or as many-to-many. It is worth clarifying at this point that a many-to-many Attribute is not the solution in case 2 above. Many-to-many Attributes are useful for selecting dimension values, but do not affect how the underlying data is stored.

For example, in our payroll modelling example, assume that we have a number of allowances for our staff such as first aid allowance, large town allowance, clothing allowance, commuting allowance. If different grades are entitled to different allowances, then we could set up a many-to-many Attribute so that we can select the grades entitled to a specific allowance. The Maintain Attribute screen for this many-to-many Attribute would look similar to this:

	First aid allowance	Large town allowance	Clothing allowance	Commuting allowance
Grade 1	Yes	Yes	No	No
Grade 2	Yes	Yes	Yes	No
Grade 3	Yes	Yes	No	No
Management	No	No	No	Yes

Detail design

Before we focus on the detail design and set-up of our dimensions, e.g. width, type etc., let us consider our Financial Data Items, and later we will revisit the detail design of dimensions.

5.5.7 Cube design: hypercube vs. minicube

So far, we have focused on the dimensions within our system, but we need to think about how we are going to use and combine our base dimensions into Financial Data Items. As noted earlier, Financial Data Items are also referred to as FDIs, or as 'cubes'.

Let us consider first the cubes that we will use to store data, i.e. our 'stored cubes'. Essentially we have two approaches for our stored cubes:

- the hypercube approach where we define a cube containing all of our base dimensions;
- the minicube approach where we define a number of smaller cubes containing only the data and/or dimensions that are relevant to that cube.

To illustrate the difference, let us consider an example:

> We are building our expenses budget by cost centre, account and time. We want to be able to calculate our staff costs (salaries, benefits, NI, cars) based on a series of input drivers (heads, average salary, bonus %), and this model will need to have an additional grade dimension, as the average salary and bonus % within a cost centre will vary by grade.

The hypercube approach would design the cube as follows:

> We would have one Budget cube dimensioned by Cost Centre, Account, Grade and Time. The Grade dimension would have a 'default' value so that for all our costs that are not analyzed by grade, we can store them against a grade dimension value. If we are linked to Oracle GL, then the most likely value for this 'default' value is 000 (assuming that the segment is 3 digits wide). The Account dimension would include all our expense accounts, together with all the input drivers required for our staff cost model.

The minicube approach would design the cubes as follows:

> We would have two cubes – one Main Budget Cube dimensioned by Cost Centre, Account and Time and one Sub Cube dimensioned by Cost Centre, Payroll Line, Grade and Time. The Main Cube would hold the result of the staff cost model for the total of all grades – a Model would be set up to achieve this. The Sub Cube would hold the detail by grade, with the Payroll Line dimension containing the input drivers and resultant calculations. These resultant calculations would include either a subset of the chart of accounts, or a mapping to a subset of the chart of accounts. (This is described in more detail in Section 5.5.10, 'Linking multiple cubes'.)

Let us now consider the pros and cons of the two approaches.

Hypercube approach

The overriding benefit of the hypercube approach is its simplicity. Set-up time is reduced as there are fewer cubes, dimensions and Models to build. A simpler design will also require less ongoing maintenance and support. There are many OFA implementations where a hypercube approach has been used to deliver business benefit quickly and effectively. In many other OLAP products, the hypercube is the only available approach.

However, there are some disadvantages to this approach, and these can be summarized as follows:

- Users will always see the additional dimensions, e.g. grade, as an extra 'tile' – they will have to select the correct value for additional dimensions whenever they use the selector, i.e. in Reports, Graphs, Worksheets, Copy Data, Solves, Submits/Refreshes of data. Of particular concern is when they are doing data entry via a worksheet – users commonly check that they have the correct row and column selections, but frequently fail to check the 'page' selections. When doing data entry this can be frustrating for users if they have to re-enter data that they have entered into the wrong place, e.g. if they had input into the 'Total Grade' value rather than the 'Default' value.

- There is currently a limit of 10 dimensions in any one Financial Data Item, and this limit may come into effect in a hypercube approach.

- Solve times may well be longer in a hypercube situation. The reason for this will be explained in detail later when roll-up of data is discussed, but in general the larger the number of dimensions, the longer the roll-up times will be.

- In a hypercube it is easy to lose the data by not selecting the appropriate dimensions for a report. To overcome this, each dimension should have a hierarchy in order that the dimension can be effectively discarded by selecting its top value in a report.

Minicube approach

The pros and cons of the minicube approach are essentially the opposite of the hypercube approach.

The benefits are:

- Generally the Solve times will be faster as the number of dimensions are fewer.
- When preparing reports or performing data entry via a worksheet, only the relevant dimensions are displayed. This ease of use for data entry can become an important issue when the OFA data entry worksheet or an OFA Web Data Entry Form is being rolled out to a large population of users for data collection.
- The 10 dimensional limit on one FDI is far less likely to be reached.
- The minicubes can be combined into a hypercube for reporting.

The disadvantages are:

- The design is more complex, requiring more set-up time.
- There may be a reporting requirement which requires us to bring all the data into one 'reporting cube'.
- FDI naming conventions will be needed in order for the users to identify easily which FDIs contain the data they require for their report.

The decision between these two approaches is made based upon a number of factors – the design of an OFA system is less of a science and more of an art, and different situations will require different solutions. There is generally no right or wrong answer. There may also be a compromise where a combination of the two approaches is required.

Some of the best implementations of OFA are where a straightforward solution has been quickly designed and implemented, but the requirements may not always allow this and a more sophisticated design may be required. The role of this book is to educate the reader about these design options, and to discuss the flexibility of OFA and its underlying Express database in handling these. The next sections will go on to discuss some of these options and their benefits.

5.5.8 Cube design: stored vs. calculated cubes

The next key design question that we need to explore is what cubes we store and what we will calculate at report time or 'on the fly'. The flexibility of OFA and the Express database gives us many options here and we will discuss these in turn.

The extremes

To illustrate the design implications of storing data vs. calculating data at run time, let us consider two extremes.

We could store every cell. This would give the fastest possible online response as every cell would just be retrieved straight from the disk. It would give us the slowest batch time as every cell would be calculated and stored, and this would give us a huge database. It would be inflexible to changes in calculations as we would need to re-run the batch, and would be very intensive on disk space usage. At the other extreme, we could store purely the base data required for the calculations. This would give us the slowest online response due to calculation time; zero batch calculation time would give us high flexibility for changes to calculations, low disk space usage, and flexibility to add lots of calculations with very little system overhead.

We can see that neither extreme is usually acceptable, but as we choose a point of compromise somewhere between these two extremes, it gives us an idea of the implications of our decisions.

Stored cubes vs. formula cubes

Our first decision on whether we store or calculate would be made on a cube-by-cube basis. For example, if we have a stored Actuals and Budget cube, then we would normally calculate Actuals–Budget at report time, i.e. within the OFA Maintain Financial Data Item dialog box, we would define Actuals–Budget as a 'formula', as opposed to a stored cube.

Other typical examples for cubes set up as a formula would be:

- Other comparatives, such as
  - Variance – Actuals – Budget %
  - Variance – Actuals – Actuals Last Period
  - Variance – Actuals – Actuals Last Period %
  - Variance – Actuals – Actuals Same Period Last Year
  - Variance – Actuals – Actuals Same Period Last Year %
  - etc.
- Year to Date/Monthly calculations
- Movingtotal formulae
- MovingAverage formulae
- Simple additive calculations, e.g. Net Actuals = Input Actuals + Adjustment
- Simple currency conversion

Essentially, we will define the whole cube as a formula when we know that the calculation will be processed quickly and when we know that the calculation can be easily defined, i.e. the logic of the calculation is relatively simple and does not introduce unacceptable complexity.

Ratios in formulae

The main watch point when using formulae is the need to calculate ratios within the formula. For example, we may have decided to store our Actuals as a Monthly movement, and then to calculate the Year to Date figure using a formula. If we then needed to calculate a ratio such as Staff Cost / Total Cost % based on the Year to Date data, we need to consider how we will achieve this. This is because the YTD figure in the formula will be incorrect as per the example below:

	Jan Month	Jan YTD	Feb Month	Feb YTD
Staff Costs	100	100	121	221
Total Costs	1000	1000	1100	2100
Staff Costs/Total Cost %	10 %	10 %	11 %	10.52 %

As we can see, the ratio for February YTD needs recalculating as it is clearly not equal to 10%+11%.

The standard OFA mechanism for calculating ratios is to use a Model, and then apply the Model using a Solve Definition. Unfortunately, this only applies to stored data, and so we need an alternative solution for formulae. We have a number of options from which to choose:

- Calculate the ratio within the report using the on-screen formulae, by inserting a row calculation. This means that the calculation needs to be defined more than once.

- Embed the calculation for the ratio in the formula in a nested if..then..else statement. This means again maintaining the syntax of the calculation in more than one place, plus if there are many calculated ratios there will need to be many levels of nesting in the if..then..else statement

```
if view eq 'YTD'
    then actuals
    else if view eq 'MONTHLY'
        then if not ratio.flag
            then actuals_mon
            else if acc eq 'STAFFTOTEXPRATIO'
                then actuals_month(acc 'STAFF')*100/actuals_mon(acc 'TOTEXP')
            else if acc eq 'PROPERTYTOTEXPRATIO'
                then actuals_month(acc 'PROPERTY')*100/actuals_mon(acc 'TOTEXP')
            else if acc eq 'TRAVELTOTEXPRATIO'
                then actuals_month(acc 'TRAVEL')*100/actuals_month(acc 'TOTEXP')
                else na
```

assuming that a formula FDI called actuals_month has been defined to return the monthly movement. This FDI would probably be defined as:

```
if account_type eq 'FLOW'
    then actuals – lag(actuals 1 ctime)
    else actuals
```

(The lagdif function has been deliberately not used as it ignores the setting of the Express naskip2 option.)

▨ Use a Model to store the calculation of the formulae, with a function to calculate it on the fly.

▨ Reconsider whether to store the whole formula cube.

▨ Consider whether to store that part of the formula cube that is required for the calculation, and use standard Model/Solve Definition functionality to calculate the result.

▨ Calculate the ratios using a Model and store them in one of the stored cubes as statistical items.

Storage of Month vs. Year to Date

Having raised the question of ratios when reporting Year to Date data, it is worth highlighting the design decision on whether to store the monthly movement or the year to date balance or both. (This issue is primarily addressed at 'flow' items, e.g profit and loss accounts, cash flow accounts, although occasionally users will request to report upon the movement in a balance sheet account.) Typically, only one of these two would be stored, but there have been cases when storing both has been seriously considered to improve online reporting performance. The way data is stored is also driven by the users' requirements for data entry via a worksheet or data entry form, which looks directly at the stored data. Commonly, users entering budget data would want to enter P&L movement data as this is a traditional method of data entry. This also enables the worksheet tools such as spread, grow and increase to be used, as these would not be appropriate with YTD data. This would suggest that we should always store our data as movement, but we should consider the converse, in that the calculation for Year to Date requires more cells to be brought into memory and calculated. In the worst case, a YTD calculation based on Monthly Movement data being stored will require 12 cells to be retrieved. More cells would need to be retrieved if additional time periods are used for opening balances, adjustment periods etc. The Movement calculation based on YTD data being stored will require only two cells to be retrieved, as the movement is calculated as this month's YTD value minus last month's YTD value.

In a large report, this factor of 6× slower can make a difference. Again, there is no right or wrong answer, and the design will depend on the circumstances and requirements, e.g. is worksheet data entry required?

5.5.9 Cube dimensionality: the 'version' dimension

As we finalize the list of stored cubes within our system, we need to consider a question that comes up frequently in OFA implementations.

Assume that we are considering an example where we have two main stored cubes, Actuals and Budget. There is only one version of Actuals, but there could be more than one version of Budgets. Should we store each data type/version separately in a separate cube, e.g. Actuals, Budget1, Budget2, Budget3? Should we store the Budgets in one cube with a version dimension? If we do this, should we store Actuals as an extra dimension value within this version dimension?

The last question is probably the easiest to answer first. As our Actuals data is likely to have far more combinations than our Budget data, the roll-up time for Actuals will be slower than that for Budget. Putting the two data sets together into one FDI is likely to make the Budget roll-ups significantly slower as Express will have the overhead of manipulating a much larger object. There will be other characteristics that are specific to the Actuals cube, e.g. how we want to store and recalculate history for Actuals, how we want to apply security to Actuals, etc., that make it a logically separate cube. Overall, the Actuals cube is stored separately in the majority of implementations.

Let us now consider the pros and cons of separate FDIs against using a version dimension for storing our budgets and forecasts:

Advantages and disadvantages of separate FDIs

- Batch performance is likely to be quicker as the object is smaller and therefore will fit more easily into memory.

- We can easily define formula FDI showing difference between versions, and show these as columns with our FinData tile going across the page.

- The set-up and administration will take more time – we need to define the FDI itself, we need to define any new comparatives to other FDIs, we need to define associated Solves, we need to define Access Controls if appropriate, we need to define reports/worksheets to access the new cube, etc. Consequently, adding a new budget version can take a non-trivial amount of time.

- The FDI list can easily become cluttered when we define all the possible formulae and comparatives, e.g. Budget1, Budget2, Budget1 YTD, Budget2 YTD, Budget1–Budget2, Budget1 YTD – Budget2 YTD, Actuals – Budget1, Actuals – Budget 2 etc.

Advantages and disadvantages of a Version dimension

- We can easily define an extra dimension value, and this will be reflected across our system automatically in reports, worksheets, Solves etc.

- We need to set up fewer comparative FDIs as we can set up Actual – Budget and let the user choose via the Budget version tile which version is being compared against.

- Any custom Solves that reference the object name require no further development.

- The roll-ups will be slower as the object is larger, although if version is the slowest varying dimension then this may not have a significant effect.

- Defining comparatives between budgets and showing them in the report as columns alongside Budget1, Budget2 can be achieved but is not as straightforward as for multiple FDIs.

In general, where there is a variable number of versions of a reasonable size, a Version dimension would be used. Conversely, in cases where a fixed number of large budgets exist, then separate FDIs would be used.

We have considered storing Budgets here, but similar arguments apply when storing Forecasts and Long Term Plans – we need to decide whether to store Budgets, Forecasts and Long Term Plans in one cube or in multiple cubes.

5.5.10 Linking multiple cubes

To date, we have considered relatively simple designs with straightforward cubes such as Actuals and Budget. As discussed earlier, if the requirements can be met quickly and easily with a simple design, then this obviously should be used. However, the option to use minicubes differentiates OFA from other OLAP tools and in many ways gives OFA its power and flexibility, so we ought to discuss how minicubes work in practice.

The design of the minicubes will vary from one application to another, but in general the design should be illustrated via a cube map. An example of this for the payroll Model we described earlier is shown in Figure 5.10.

In every case of a minicube implementation, there will need to be a mechanism to feed or link data between cubes, so we should discuss how this can be achieved.

Firstly, we have to identify the relationship between our cubes. There are three main cases:

1. Relationship is 1:1. In some cases, the relationship between the cubes will be 1:1, with both source and target variables having matching dimensions and values.

2. Relationship is 1:1 after manipulation in the source cube. In other cases, there may be some manipulation or calculation within the source cube before the data is transferred to the target cube. For example, in our example payroll Model, the resultant accounts in the chart of accounts could be calculated within the payroll Model using a Hierarchy or using an OFA Model. It is then possible to transfer the data between the cubes, as although the source and target dimensions are different, there is a 1:1 match on a range of dimension values.

For example, the payroll Model would contain the following dimension values and calculations:

Payroll Sub cube
dimensioned by Payroll Line,
Grade, Cost Centre, Time

Grade

Cost
Centre

Time

Payroll
Line

Main cube
dimensioned by Cost Centre,
Account, Time

Cost
Centre

Time

Account

Depreciation Sub cube
dimensioned by Asset Line,
Asset Group

Asset
Group

Cost
Centre

Time

Asset
Line

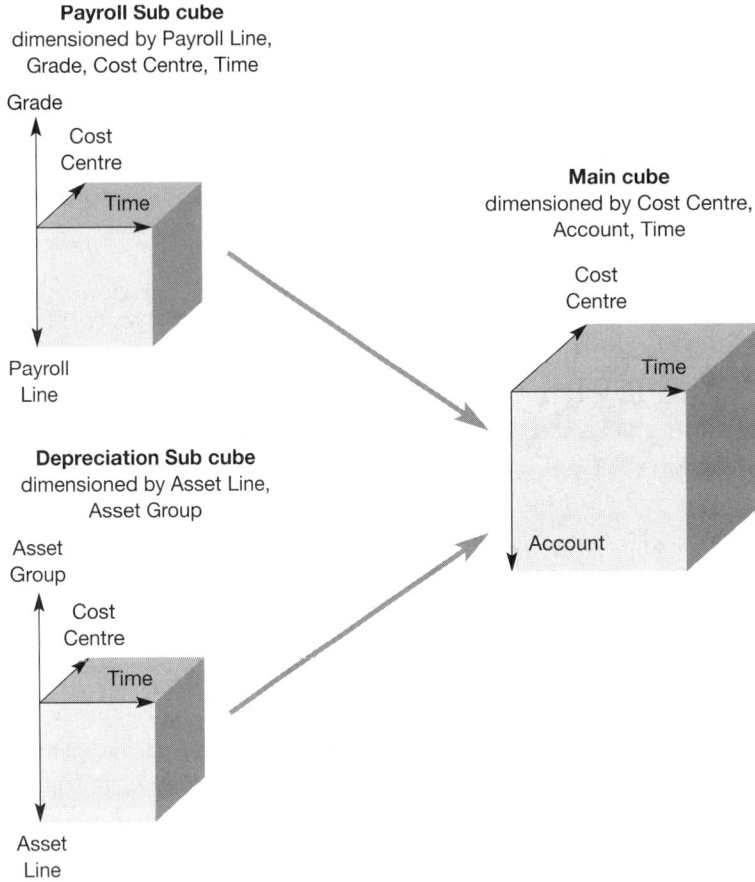

FIG 5.10   Cube map for payroll Model and other models

Payroll Line dimension	*Calculation*
P100 Headcount End of Period	
P110 Average Headcount	(P110 + lag(P110 1))/2
P120 Average Annual Salary	
P130 Salary	P110 * P120/12
P140 National Insurance	P130 * 0.09
P160 Discretionary Bonus	
P170 Contractual Bonus	P130 * 0.03
P180 Housing Allowances	(P130 + P160) * 0.05
P190 Clothing Allowance	(P130 + P160) * 0.01
A500 Salaries account	P130
A510 National Insurance account	P140
A520 Bonus account	P160 + P170
A530 Allowances account	P180 + P190

The Pxxx values in the Payroll Line dimension represent the workings of the calculations, with the Axxx values in the Payroll Line dimension representing the resultant calculations that will be transferred into our Account dimension which has the same values.

Account dimension values and description

A500 Salaries account
A510 National Insurance account
A520 Bonus account
A530 Allowances account

3. Relationship is many-to-one and is handled in the transfer. In this case, there are likely to be OFA Attributes which provide many-to-one or one-to-one mappings between source and target dimension values.

For example, if we reuse our payroll line example from before, the Payroll Line dimension would contain the following values:

P100 Headcount End of Period	
P110 Average Headcount	(P110 + lag(P110 1))/2
P120 Average Annual Salary	
P130 Salary	P110 * P120/12
P140 National Insurance	P130 * 0.09
P160 Discretionary Bonus	
P170 Contractual Bonus	P130 * 0.03
P180 Housing Allowances	(P130 + P160) * 0.05
P190 Clothing Allowance	(P130 + P160) * 0.01

The Account dimension would contain the following values:

A500 Salaries account
A510 National Insurance account
A520 Bonus account
A530 Allowances account

and there would be a many-to-one Attribute between Payroll Line and Account:

Payroll Line	*Account*
P130	A500
P140	A510
P160	A520
P170	A520
P180	A530
P190	A530

There are a number of options for then transferring the data between the cubes.

The first option is not to physically move the data or summary data between the cubes at all. Reporting cubes are discussed later in this chapter and are a common way of 'joining' minicubes together. The benefit of this approach is that data is not replicated, so there is no batch processing overhead. There is also no additional disk space requirement. However, the downside will be that online reporting performance may well be slower.

The second option is to use the Copy Data function. We can save a particular Copy Data process as a script, and then reuse this later or call it from within a Group Solve definition. This has led to a growing use of 'staging' cubes – temporary cubes used during a process where data is manipulated, which give great visibility and audit trail as to how a process has worked.

For example, assume that the GL interface is being used to populate an Actuals cube with monthly movements, but that the designer wants to store Actuals data as YTD for reporting performance.

We might then create three FDIs:

ACT_GL	Actuals staging cube (populated from GL)
ACT_TRANSFORM	Actuals formula to convert to YTD values
	e.g. movingtotal(ACT_GL, 1-month.num, 0, 1, time)
ACT_STORED	Stored Actuals YTD cube

Copy Data would then be used to copy from the ACT_TRANSFORM cube to the ACT_STORED cube.

The Copy Data function allows for the transfer between cubes of differing dimensions, providing an Attribute exists between the dimensions. However, this functionality makes use of the Express TOTAL and this has been seen to make significant use of system resources while aggregating the data. Also, in releases prior to 6.2 of OFA, the Copy Data function was highly inefficient when copying sparse data, and so ruled out this option in many cases.

The third option is to use a standard OFA Model called by an OFA Solve Definition, where the source is specified for each target dimension value. In the example of our payroll line flowing into the chart of accounts, we would use our existing payroll line Model to populate the resultant calculated lines, followed by a new Model to transfer the data between cubes.

Again, considering our payroll line example, and assuming that:

▥ the payroll cube is called PAYCUBE;

▥ the payroll cube has an additional grade dimension, which has TOTGRADE as the total in the PLINE dimension Hierarchy;

we could then define a Model on the Account dimension, with the following syntax:

```
A500 = paycube(pline 'A500')
A510 = paycube(pline 'A510')
A520 = paycube(pline 'A520')
A530 = paycube(pline 'A530')
```

Alternatively, we could handle the mapping between the dimensions in the Model itself:

A500 = paycube(pline 'P130')
A510 = paycube(pline 'P140')
A520 = paycube(pline 'P160') + paycube(pline 'P170')
A530 = paycube(pline 'P180') + paycube(pline 'P190')

The benefit of this approach is that no Express SPL development is required. Also, data is being physically copied so there is no online reporting performance issue. The disadvantage is that if a chart of accounts value is added, the Model needs to be maintained and distributed.

The final option is to use a 'custom Model' which makes a call to an underlying Express routine, and this gives us the option of using the power of Express to manipulate and transform the data.

The benefit of this approach is that frequently the Express SPL will describe the flow of data in a high-level language and so will be easily readable and maintainable. Again, data is being physically copied so there is no online reporting performance issue. The downside is that the development of Express SPL routines may be seen as onerous for those unfamiliar with Express development. This may also be more efficient in terms of resources as clauses such as 'across' can be specified to reduce the looping over the dimensions.

5.5.11 Cube design for sparsity

What is sparsity and why do we need to worry about it ?

Sparsity arises when some of the cells in our stored cube(s) are unpopulated. As the number of dimensions increases, the likelihood of sparsity increases. As the number of dimensions increases, the number of possible combinations of dimension values increases, and the chances of every combination of these dimension values containing data reduce.

If sparsity is not managed correctly, the data storage can become inefficient, resulting in slower than optimal batch and online performance. In extreme cases, the data storage will be many orders of magnitude less efficient, with the resulting effect on batch and online performance.

Different types of sparsity

There are essentially two types of sparsity – controlled and random. Controlled sparsity occurs when the designer of the system knows that certain dimension 'ranges' within the cubes will be empty, i.e. not populated. For example, we might have an Actuals cube dimensioned by Cost Centre, Account and Time where the time dimension spans not only the historic months, say January 1999 to June 2000, but also the future months from July 2000 to December 2001. The designer will know that the Actuals cube will be empty from the current month onwards for all cost centres and accounts, and so can design the cube appropriately. Random sparsity occurs when the designer does not know which combinations of cells will be populated. In our example above, the designer is likely to have very little knowledge of which combinations of cost centres and accounts have been used. Even if the designer can predict this, he or she cannot guarantee that this situation will continue in the future.

How to manage sparsity

The obvious answer to sparsity problems is not to store the cells that are not used, but this is generally easier said than done. To understand this, we need to consider how Express stores data. Let us consider our three-dimensional Actuals cube, and assume for the moment that it is defined as a standard variable without any special sparsity management (which is normally referred to as an 'open' variable). Let us also assume that the cube is dimensioned in the order Cost Centre, Account, Time. Then the cells in the cube would be physically stored in the following order:

Cost Centre	Account	Time
CC1	Acc1	Time1
CC2	Acc1	Time1
...		
CC99	Acc1	Time1
CC1	Acc2	Time1
CC2	Acc2	Time1
...		
CC99	Acc2	Time1
...		
CC1	Acc99	Time1
CC2	Acc99	Time1
...		
CC99	Acc99	Time1
CC1	Acc1	Time2
CC2	Acc1	Time2
...		

CC99	Acc1	Time2
CC1	Acc2	Time2
CC2	Acc2	Time2
...		
CC99	Acc2	Time2
...		
CC1	Acc99	Time2
CC2	Acc99	Time2
...		
CC99	Acc99	Time2
...		
CC1	Acc1	Time99
CC2	Acc1	Time99
...		
CC99	Acc1	Time99
CC1	Acc2	Time99
CC2	Acc2	Time99
...		
CC99	Acc2	Time99
...		
CC1	Acc99	Time99
CC2	Acc99	Time99
...		
CC99	Acc99	Time99

In this example, cost centre would be described as the fastest-varying dimension and time would be described as the slowest-varying dimension.

Express then stores data in pages, with the size of the page depending on the platform: 4 Kbytes on 32-bit platforms and 8 Kbytes on 64-bit platforms. If any cell in that page is populated, the whole page is stored. If all the cells are empty, the page becomes an 'NA page', taking up no space and very little system overhead. Consequently, we need to calculate how many cells need to be consecutively empty before the page is not stored.

The number of bytes that each cell takes up depends on the data type as follows:

Short Integer	2 bytes
Integer	4 bytes
Short Decimal	4 bytes
Decimal	8 bytes

Assuming that we are using decimal data, a page will consist of 4096/8=512 cells, meaning that if 512 contiguous cells are empty then the page won't be stored.

With this knowledge, the designer of the cube has some options when dealing with controlled sparsity, where 'ranges' of data are empty. By choosing an appropriate dimension order, redundant pages need not be stored and therefore do not need to have an impact on performance. In the example above, where Actuals data is not stored for future months, all the cells associated with the future time periods would be stored contiguously and would therefore be treated as 'NA pages'.

This illustration helps to show how difficult it is to manage random sparsity using standard 'open' variables. In our example above, let's now assume that we define our cube with the Time dimension first. If we had, say three years in our Time dimension, comprising 12 months, 4 quarters and 1 year, then each combination of Cost Centre and Account would take up 51 cells. If the number of cells per page was still 512, then we would need 10 sequential combinations of Cost Centre and Account to be empty before the page was treated as an NA page. Whilst this might happen in some cases, we need a better approach to optimize our data storage.

This improved approach is the use of 'composite' dimensions, where effectively only the combinations used are stored. In versions of Express prior to version 6, there existed a similar concept called 'conjoints' but these would typically have to be maintained programmatically. Version 6 introduced the concept of 'invisible conjoints' to reduce the effort of achieving this more efficient data storage and these were then called 'composites'. A composite is very similar in structure to a conjoint dimension and in fact the objects can be easily switched using the CHGDFN command.

One might think therefore that all variables would be defined with one 'composite' dimension containing all the 'base' dimensions. However, this is not practical for two reasons:

▓ Roll-ups or aggregations of a variable defined with all dimensions in the composite typically take longer than those based on a variable with at least one dense dimension.

▓ The size of a composite itself can be considerable, so that it needs to be established that a composite is more efficient in data storage than an 'open' variable. In most cases with more than three dimensions the size of the composite will be small compared to the size of the 'open' variable, but the size of the composite should be calculated to confirm this. The size of a composite can be calculated using the following algorithm:

Size of Composite = Number of Composite Values * (14 bytes + 10 bytes per dimension)

For a composite with 1,000,000 values and five dimensions:

Size = 1,000,000 * (14 + 5*10) = 64 Mbytes

We can therefore establish if the benefit of a composite is outweighed by its size and its disk I/O requirement.

Some other general rules that apply to the use of composites that are of particular note when implementing OFA:

■ Wherever possible, composites should be shared. This requires the object to be redefined and the Financial Data Item Catalog (FD.CATALOG) to be updated, after the FDI has been defined initially in the GUI.

■ The dimensions in the composite should be ordered by their size to improve aggregation performance.

■ The number of segments should be managed to ensure optimal processing, particularly if time is the fastest-varying dimension, and only one month is processed at a time.

■ The composite should not necessarily contain all the dimensions except time. The number of composite values and disk space required should be assessed for a number of different scenarios.

These topics are discussed in more detail in *Oracle Express: Performance and Database Design Guide*.

Sparsity in a tiered architecture

In a tiered architecture, the sparsity at different levels may be different, so the OFA designer needs to allow for this. The designer has two main options:

1. Choose a compromise design to allow for different sparsity at different levels, with the associated impact upon storage and batch performance.

2. Choose to create local cubes to optimize sparsity at specific levels, with additional processes to transfer data to/from the centrally defined structures for submission and refresh of data.

The decision about which option to take will depend mainly on how different the sparsity is across levels, and therefore the feasibility of option 1.

5.5.12 Cube design for aggregation

Once we have decided to have a stored cube, e.g. Actuals, and we have decided how to manage its sparsity, we need to decide how best to optimize the aggregation and calculation stage to fit within our batch window.

First, it is worth understanding what is happening during the aggregation phase, and this can help us to improve its speed.

Let us consider the following example:

■ A two-dimensional cube Actuals by Cost Centre and Account.

■ All combinations of cost centres and accounts are populated.

■ There are 60 base-level accounts with 40 parents.

■ There are 60 base-level cost centres with 40 parents.

Base-level Accounts Parent Cost Centres	Parent Cost Centres and Accounts
Base-level Cost Centres and Accounts	Base-level Cost Centres Parent Accounts

We can calculate the size of the 'base' data as 60 * 60 * 8 = 28,800.

However, we can see that the total size, including parents, is 100 * 100 * 8 = 80,000.

So, although the base dimension values occupied 60 per cent of the dimension, the base data occupied only 36 per cent (60% * 60%) of the total. This worsens as the number of dimensions increases, and as the number of hierarchies and parents increases to the point where the ratio of base data to total data is very small. There have been cases where the base data fitted on a floppy disk, but the summarized data needed more than 1 Gb of disk space.

The situation also worsens when the base data is sparse or a dimension has more than one hierarchy.

Consider the following dimensions and hierarchy levels, assuming that the hierarchies have a fixed number of levels. Although this is rarely the case in an OFA implementation, it is sufficient to illustrate the point.

Organization hierarchy levels

Branch
Region
Total Organization

Account hierarchy levels

Sub Account
Account
Account Group
Total Account

Project hierarchy levels

Project
Project Type
Total Project

If we start with one base-level combination of Org, Sub Account and Project, then after rolling up all the hierarchies, the following combinations would be produced:

Parent combinations

Region	Sub Account	Project
Total Org	Sub Account	Project
Branch	Account	Project
Region	Account	Project
Total Org	Account	Project
Branch	Account Group	Project
Region	Account Group	Project
Total Org	Account Group	Project
Branch	Total Account	Project
Region	Total Account	Project
Total Org	Total Account	Project
Branch	Sub Account	Project Group
Region	Sub Account	Project Group
Total Org	Sub Account	Project Group
Branch	Account	Project Group
Region	Account	Project Group
Total Org	Account	Project Group
Branch	Account Group	Project Group
Region	Account Group	Project Group
Total Org	Accoun Group	Project Group
Branch	Total Account	Project Group
Region	Total Account	Project Group
Total Org	Total Account	Project Group
Branch	Sub Account	Total Project
Region	Sub Account	Total Project
Total Org	Sub Account	Total Project
Branch	Account	Total Project
Region	Account	Total Project
Total Org	Account	Total Project
Branch	Account Group	Total Project
Region	Account Group	Total Project
Total Org	Account Group	Total Project
Branch	Total Account	Total Project
Region	Total Account	Total Project
Total Org	Total Account	Total Project

So starting with one base combination, we end up with 35 parent combinations. This becomes worse if the number of dimensions increases, the number of hierarchies increases, or the number of levels within the hierarchies increases.

Against this, as the number of base combinations increases, some of the parent combinations will be reused, particularly in the levels near the top of the hierarchies.

However, even taking this factor into account, we can see that a huge amount of summary data is created, with many of these cells unlikely to be accessed by a user, and this gives us an opportunity to speed up our aggregation process using the Aggregate command and Aggregate functions. This is covered in more detail in the document *Oracle Express: Performance and Database Design Guide*.

Whilst these features were new in 6.3, the concepts have been around since Express was first released, and there are many implementations prior to 6.3 where these techniques have been used. A common technique prior to 6.2 was to store the base-level data in a small compact conjointed form which could easily and quickly be aggregated on the fly.

Aggregate functionality gives us the ability to calculate parts of our cube on the fly and this should be used in cases of large cubes. At the same time, and as discussed in Section 5.5.1, we have to be careful not to trade bad batch performance for bad online performance. We should be very careful in setting users' expectations for response times if certain cells are being calculated on the fly.

There are other ways of improving aggregation and calculation performance, which should be used alongside the aggregate command/function. Essentially these concentrate on reducing the amount of 'work' that the system has to do, either by 'storing less' and therefore reducing the amount of disk I/O required for processing, or by 'processing less' of the data that is stored. The details of these techniques will vary from one implementation to another, but the general ideas are shown below:

General approach to 'storing less':

Reducing the number of dimensions in the cube
Reducing the number of hierarchies used
Reducing the number of levels in the hierarchy
Archiving unwanted data to another database, such as a Budget Workstation
etc.

Whilst it might appear difficult to reduce the number of levels in a well-established hierarchy, there may be cases where budget and forecast data is not being gathered at the lowest levels of all the hierarchies. In this case, 'cut off' hierarchies or 'dummy nodes' at higher levels in the hierarchy can be used to effectively reduce the number of levels stored. In this scenario, care must be taken to roll up the cut-off hierarchies only from the input-level rather than the base-level values.

General approach to 'processing less':

Processing less frequently
Processing fewer hierarchies on certain occasions
Processing fewer time periods, e.g. current year only

In a budgeting and forecasting example, a typical use is to perform 'partial' roll-ups when a user submits his or her data, rather than wait for all the data to arrive before solving. This is well catered for using the 'Solve Profile' facility within OFA, whereby a Solve Definition or Solve Group can be 'assigned' to a Financial Data Item. When a user saves data for, say, one cost centre in an Analyst Worksheet, OFA sets the status of the Solve so that only parents impacted by the change are recalculated.

This feature is relatively under-used considering the benefits it can give. It can be used to process standard Definitions and Group Solve Definitions, and can also be used for custom Solves, as the status of the dimensions is set appropriately before the Solve is executed.

5.5.13 Reporting cubes

There has been a lot of discussion about storing, linking and aggregating cubes, but ultimately the users of the OFA system will be happiest if they are able to do the reporting and analysis they want. OLAP systems are by their very nature strong on reporting, but the combination of OFA and Express makes OFA exceptionally flexible for reporting and analysis.

Shown below are some examples of the kinds of reporting formulae that can be set up in OFA. This list is not exhaustive, but should give an idea of what can be achieved.

Reporting hypercubes

Frequently the Financial Data Item list in OFA contains many values, and so it becomes harder for a user to select the values he or she wants. One way of reducing the risk of this is to create a reporting hypercube, which uses an additional dimension to join together cubes that are reported together. Let us assume that this extra dimension is called Scenario, although in practice it has been given other names such as data type, view, and format.

In its simplest form, the administrator creates the dimension values for the Scenario dimension and then creates a new formula Financial Data Item with the following formula:

```
if Scenario eq 'ACTUALS'
then ACTUALS
else if Scenario eq 'BUDGET'
then BUDGET
else if Scenario eq 'FORECAST'
then FORECAST
else if Scenario eq 'VARIANCE'
then VARIANCE
else na
```

where Scenario has the values ACTUALS, BUDGET, FORECAST, VARIANCE and there are existing FDIs called ACTUALS, BUDGET, FORECAST, VARIANCE.

This effectively joins all the cubes together, so we can educate our users always to select the reporting hypercube, which we would usually put at the top of our Financial Data Item list. A variation on this form is where we don't need to define all our comparatives as FDIs, but instead can embed the calculation within the reporting hypercube formula, e.g.:

```
if Scenario eq 'ACTUALS'
then ACTUALS
else if Scenario eq 'BUDGET'
then BUDGET
else if Scenario eq 'FORECAST'
then FORECAST
else if Scenario eq 'VARIANCE'
then ACTUALS–BUDGET
else if Scenario eq 'VARIANCEPERCENT'
then (ACTUALS–BUDGET)*100/BUDGET
else na
```

We can become more sophisticated than this and embed the calculations in a text variable or in a Model, and then use a function to evaluate the calculation. In this case, the function would be built using the Express technique of dynamic program building, where a program or function is built from variables already stored within Express. If we used a text variable, it might look like this:

Scenario	Calculation
ACTUALS	ACTUALS
BUDGET	BUDGET
VARIANCE	ACTUALS – BUDGET
VARIANCEPERCENT	(ACTUALS–BUDGET)*100/BUDGET

This makes the creation of new comparatives very easy, and the calculations can be easily viewed and printed. This approach is discussed in more detail in the case studies.

From a reporting perspective, the hypercube also gives us more flexibility for ratio reporting. Given that all the different data types (Actuals, Budget, Forecast) are now in one cube, we can offer the user the ability to look at a ratio for any account for any data type by adding a new FDI such as:

Object name	RATIOTOTREV
Description	Reporting Cube / Total Sales %
Calculation	HYPERCUBE * 100 /HYPERCUBE(ACC 'TOTREV')

Crosstab reporting

Assume that we have a product dimension with two attributes – Flavour and Pack Type – and that we have a Sales cube dimensioned by Product and Time. Crosstab reporting enables us to see Sales by Flavour and Pack Type by adding a new FDI such as:

Object Name	SALESFLAVPACK
Description	Sales by Flavour and Pack Type
Calculation	TOTAL(SALES, FLAVOUR, PACKTYPE)

This would normally be evaluated within an Express function to ensure that the status of the base dimension (in this case Product) is appropriately set. As with any Express implementation, the developer should not assume that the status of the base dimension will be set to all.

Breaking out dimensions

Assume that we have a Costs cube dimensioned by Cost Centre and Time, and the Cost Centre dimension has the following values:

101	Call Centre Edinburgh
102	Call Centre Dublin
103	Call Centre Bristol
202	Bad Debt Dublin
203	Bad Debt Bristol
301	IT Edinburgh
302	IT Dublin
303	IT Bristol

The cost centre code is made up of cost centre type and location. We can create two new dimensions, Cost Centre Type and Location, with the values:

Cost Centre Type

1	Call centre
2	Bad Debt
3	IT

Location

01	Edinburgh
02	Dublin
03	Bristol

We can now report on our costs by Cost Centre Type and Location by adding a new FDI such as:

Object name	COSTS_TYPE_LOCN
Description	Costs by CC Type and Location
Calculation	COSTS(CCTYPE extchars(CC 1 3) LOCATION extchars(CC 4 2))

We should also use the isvalue function within an if..then..else function to validate that the cost centre exists for this cost centre type and location.

Paging by Attribute dimensions

Assume that we have a Sales cube dimensioned by branch and time, and that we have an Attribute from branch to region. We already have a Hierarchy between branch and region, and this enables us to report at region level and drill down to branch, or to select all regions and their branches using the Family tool. However, we have 100 regions and 3,000 branches and we want to print out the sales for our branches grouped by region, with a page break for each region. We don't want to create 100 separate reports, nor do we want to insert 100 page breaks manually into our report.

The solution is to create a reporting cube containing branch *and* region, with the data suppressed if the branch isn't within that region. We can then use the zerorow suppression to suppress the branches that aren't applicable for that region.

Object Name	SALES_BRANCH_REGN
Description	Sales by Branch and Region
Formula	if region eq region.branch
	then sales
	else na

where region.branch is the renamed attribute between branch and region.

5.5.14 Cube design: other cube types

We have discussed the design of the major cubes in our system, but in many cases, there are a significant number of additional FDIs defined, which should be included in our detail design. These are categorized below.

Small numeric FDIs

There are likely to be small numeric FDIs storing information required for calculation or in the reporting formula. Frequently these are dimensioned by our time dimension. Examples are shown below:

    number of days in the month
    number of days year to date
    the number of custom time periods in the year
    the number of custom time dimension values between a period and the same
    period last year

(these variables are populated automatically if the standard OFA time dimension is used).

Catalogs

Catalogs are small text FDIs used to store and/or report structural or system information. These are commonly used to provide parameters to processes that have been added to the Tools menu or to processes run from custom Solve Definitions – for example, in the case of loading data from a spreadsheet into a budget FDI with a version dimension, the catalog would store the budget version that data should be loaded into. The Tools menu allows for a dialog box to appear, prompting the user for one parameter, but there is no picklist or validation of this parameter without resorting to developing a form in Visual Basic. This is not a trivial task, as it requires the VB programmer to understand the structured N-dimensional API (SNAPI).

Catalogs enable these parameters to be stored and modified using a worksheet. Whilst there are still no picklists or validation (as standard) in a worksheet, at least the user has access to the menus to check his or her input.

Catalogs are also used to hold system information for interfaces, e.g.:

- the path and name of a file to be processed;
- the path and name of the detail log file to be produced.

Catalogs can also be used to report on summary information from an interface, e.g.:

- number of records processed;
- number of error records.

In this way, a user can access this information from the OFA GUI and doesn't have to access a log file located on the server. In UNIX implementations, the user would have to view this file from a telnet or ftp session, and whilst there are many easy-to-use GUI FTP tools available, many organizations discourage the use of ftp for security reasons.

The case studies give more examples of catalogs and their uses.

Text cubes

Text FDIs have been available for some time in OFA, but prior to 6.3 the limitations of one FDI per worksheet meant that data entry of text was not frequently implemented. In the two common cases of text usage, i.e. for budget assumptions input and for variance explanations input, the user would require to input the text alongside the associated numbers, which is not easily achievable. However, with the advent of 6.3 Web data entry forms, more use of text cubes is expected.

Nevertheless, there are potential problems with text cubes that need to be pointed out.

As there is no mechanism for 'rolling-up' text, the designer needs to identify a common hierarchy level at which text will be input and can therefore be accessed. Otherwise, different users will input their assumptions/explanations at different levels and these may well never be seen again. The alternative to this is to consider developing custom functionality to 'roll-up' text together using text manipulation functions, but the difficulties associated with doing this in a multidimensional cube should not be underestimated.

Text cubes can be slow to export, particularly if they are defined as 'open' variables and have a large number of dimensions.

5.5.15 Cube design: sizing of cubes

At some stage in the project, IT will need to know the amount of disk space that will be required on the production box.

In the case of a variable defined without composites, the size can be calculated by multiplying out the number of populated cells by the bytes/cell. The number of cells is derived by multiplying out the numbers of values in each dimension, allowing for the fact that if a range of cells is empty then the page will not be stored, as described in Section 5.5.11 when discussing sparsity.

The number of bytes per cell depends on the data type – this is covered in the detail design section.

For example, assume that our Actuals cube (decimal) is dimensioned by cost centre, account and time (in that order) and that we have 200 cost centres, 1,000 accounts and 5 years of data. Each year contains 12 months, 4 quarters and 1 year – only the first 3 years are populated, but these are stored contiguously.

The size would be 200 ccs * 1000 accts * 3 yrs * (12 months + 4 quarters + 1 year) * 8 bytes/cell = 81 Mbytes

In the case of a sparse variable, however, determining the number of composite values used is much harder.

One approach is to consider the number of base-level combinations, and then to take a worst-case scenario where a parent combination is generated for every level every Hierarchy for every dimension, and then to reduce this by a factor to allow for the fact that the parent combinations will be reused at the higher levels in the Hierarchy.

Using the same example as in Section 5.5.12, 'Cube design for aggregation', we would perform the following calculations:

Average number of levels in all Org hierarchies	3
Average number of levels in all Account hierarchies	4
Average number of levels in all Project hierarchies	3
Frequency of parent combinations reused	2
Ratio of parent to base combinations	3 * 4 * 3 / 2 = 18
Number of base combinations	20,000
Number of parent combinations	18 * 20,000 = 360,000
Dimension values outside composite (assume ctime only)	100
Number of cells	36,000,000

Assuming no controlled sparsity and decimal data

Cube size	256 Mbytes

Another approach is to consider the sparsity between pairs of dimensions (include parent levels) and then to multiply these out, allowing for any controlled sparsity on the slowest-varying dimensions outside the composite, to give an overall sparsity %.

Total number of Org values	200
Total number of Acc values	300
Total number of Project values	150
Total number of possible combinations	9,000,000
Sparsity between Org and Acc	30 %
Sparsity between Org and Proj	40 %
Sparsity between Proj and Acc	30 %
Expected number of combinations	$9,000,000 * 0.30 * 0.40 * 0.30$ $= 324,000$
Dimension values outside composite (assume ctime only)	100
Number of cells	32,400,000
Assuming no controlled sparsity and decimal data	
Cube size	259 Mbytes

Whichever theoretical approach is adopted, it is always best to try to confirm the theory through practice. A prototype can be put together relatively quickly to help confirm the likely size of sparse data when rolled up.

A large amount of space in an Express database can be taken up with page copies created by Express to maintain a consistent view of the data for each user. This occurs when an update process modifies the database while read-only users are attached. The larger the number of read-only users, the greater the number of copy pages will be used. Although this space is reused after the update is committed, the space can only be returned to the operating system by exporting and importing the whole database, which is a time-consuming and off-line process. In practice it is advisable to add 100 per cent to the computed size of the database to allow for this effect.

5.5.16 Sizing in a tiered architecture

Tiered architectures were discussed in Section 5.4 and have an obvious effect on the disk space requirements on the server(s). The logical architecture discussed in Section 5.4 will be mapped to a physical architecture – this will be discussed in more detail in Section 5.6, but we need to size every database in our tiered architecture. Database sizes will vary greatly by type (i.e. Analyst Reporter, Budget Workstation, DBA Personal, Super Shared, Sub Shared) and in most cases the only significant size databases would be the Super Shared, the Sub Shareds, and Budget Workstations.

In some cases, the lower 'tiers' in the architecture store the same data and level of detail, and it will be found that the sum of the databases in each tier adds up to the same size or greater than the Shared Database in the tier above. In this case, each tier effectively adds at least the size of the Super Shared Database to the disk space requirement.

However, in many cases the lower tiers will hold additional data, or data at a greater level of detail, and so these need to be thoroughly sized.

5.5.17 Express detail design

The majority of this section has considered the high-level design decisions, but there are a number of detail design decisions and OFA set-up issues which need to be considered.

Dimension definition

When setting up a new dimension in OFA, we are presented with some choices on the dimension object, i.e. name, width, type and prefix, along with choosing the dimension description. The dimension description can be easily changed at a later date, but none of the other decisions we make here can be easily changed. In fact, there is considerable work associated with redefining a dimension to change, say, its width. We would have to export the whole database to EIF files, create a new database, define the dimension with its new width and import the EIF files. Fortunately, the import command is tolerant of the redefinition of the dimension's width.

Let us consider all the dimension definition options in turn.

Type

A dimension can be of type text or time. The majority of our dimensions will be text dimensions, but if we are defining a custom time dimension, there are benefits if we define this as type time. If we do not, we will be losing the built-in time intelligence in OFA. This functionality enables appropriate calculation of quarterly and yearly data based on the type of account, and enables point and click use of the Express time-series analysis functions (lag, lead etc.) in the Model definition screen. It also enables the lag and lead functions to refer to a dimension value so that a Model does not need to refer to a Financial Data Item – this means that one Model can be used (if appropriate) across several FDIs and so reduce maintenance. For non-time-type dimensions, there would need to be a separate model for each FDI.

(Note: The GL time dimension currently defined by the GL–OFA interface is defined as text, not time.)

Width

For each dimension we have to specify a maximum width. Common sense suggests that we should not set our dimension width too wide as this will mean that more disk space and memory will be taken up managing the dimension, with an associated impact on performance. However, as described above, redefining a dimension's width effectively requires all structures to be reimplemented (or non-trivial Express commands to export/import the catalogs), so we need to set our dimension width to be wide enough to allow for future usage. We could consider redefining the dimension without a width if we are unsure about how the dimension values will change over time.

Dimension name/prefix name

OFA uses a six-character prefix to hold certain internal objects, e.g. ORG.DESC for the ORG dimension. This is because a number of objects are created using this prefix, e.g. FMSHREL.ORG, and as the maximum length of an Express object is 16 characters, there needs to be a limit on the prefix. Once chosen, this cannot be changed, so again it makes sense to choose a convenient name to start with. Common sense would suggest that if we keep our dimension names to six characters or less, then we can use the dimension name as the prefix name – this makes developing and maintaining Express routines easier as there is less to learn/remember about the system.

Maintain DBA sort order

This option enables the sort order in subsidiary Workstations to be kept in the same order as the DBA. It can be modified after the dimension has originally been defined, but it is worth setting straight away as it improves the speed of distribution. This cannot be changed if the dimension is sourced from GL and therefore owned by the Oracle GL.

Time dimensions

The standard time dimension allows for easy addition and deletion of all periods in a year, merely by specifying the year. A year is then made up of 12 months, 4 quarters and 1 year linked in a Hierarchy – the start of the financial year can be selected when the time dimension is first used. If the 12+4+1 time dimension values fit well with the requirements, then the standard time dimension should be used. However, in many reporting and budgeting implementations, there may be historic data or future data that is only stored at 'year' level, and it will be inefficient to keep the empty months and quarters associated with the standard year, as in many designs time will be the fastest-varying dimension. Also, one cannot create a personal Hierarchy from the standard time dimension. Whilst there is a small overhead in setting up a custom time dimension, additions and deletions occur rarely and so this does not present a significant administration overhead. Defining a custom time dimension gives extra flexibility without much overhead, e.g. many organizations now prefer their time dimension values to be MMMYYYY format (Mar2000) rather than the MMMYY format used in the standard time dimension.

The benefit of a standard time dimension is that there are a number of metadata objects (e.g. number of periods to same period last year) automatically created.

Financial Data Item definition

The decisions to be made when defining a new FDI are already likely to have been made or are easy to make, e.g. stored or formula, sparsity, object name. There is one decision, however, that may not have been thought through in detail – the data type of the FDI for a numeric cube. There are four options with differing size per byte, number of significant digits and size:

Short Integer	2 bytes/cell	–32767 to +32767
Integer	4 bytes/cell	–2 billion to +2 billion
Short Decimal	4 bytes/cell	7 significant digits
Decimal	8 bytes/cell	15 significant digits

The size of each cell is obviously going to have an impact on disk space required, memory required and therefore overall performance, so it's worth considering whether Integer or Short Decimal can be used for a cube. The instinctive reaction from accountants is to store the fullest detail, but the argument should be put that when budgeting and forecasting P&L and balance sheet items of millions and billions, it is spurious to examine any detail below thousands. The benefit of improved performance should also be explained. Against this, we should consider the implications of rounding if we are storing only seven significant digits.

Whilst it is not as difficult to redefine an FDI as it is to redefine a dimension, it would still require redefinition of Solves, reports and worksheets at a minimum, so it is worth making the correct decision now.

For FDIs sourced from the GL, the data type is fixed as Decimal.

5.6   INFRASTRUCTURE SPECIFICATION

Performance and flexibility are as much a function of a supporting infrastructure as good database design principles. This section is aimed at the technical and non-technical reader who has been assigned the role of system architect.

The task of engineering a supporting architecture is multidisciplinary. It can involve multiple functional areas and the commitment of individuals not immediately identified as part of the project. The system architects must be aware of their role, not only a technical authority but also as a facilitator, mediator and evangelist throughout the enterprise. They must also be aware that their activities may cut across internally politically sensitive areas, and understand how such relationships are to be managed.

The core aim of this section is to demonstrate that delivering a performant and flexible architecture can only be achieved if the system architect has the appropriate knowledge about the application, the business process and the existing enterprise infrastructure. To achieve this, a framework is given, by which system architects may conduct their analysis in an orderly fashion.

Infrastructure specification is commonly treated as a simple hardware sizing exercise. This is a gross over-simplification. The complexity of enterprise business processes makes such a view risky.

ROAD MAP

The section is structured as follows:

- An introduction to the range of Oracle Financial Analyzer architectures (**5.6.1**)
- A description of the analysis framework (**5.6.2**)
- An example framework, demonstrated by a simple scenario (**5.6.3**)
- Design of the physical architecture based on the understanding of the business process and the enterprise infrastructure (**5.6.4**)
- Summary (**5.6.5**)

5.6.1 OFA architecture overview

This section will discuss a range of Oracle Financial Analyzer architecture configurations, each with incremental complexity. The section aims to alert the reader to the range and flexibility of the Oracle Financial Analyzer architectures.

OFA application and architecture terminology

A brief review of official and commonly used terminology is provided here to aid understanding. (Some of these concepts have been addressed elsewhere in the book, but are reproduced here for completeness.)

- *Oracle Financial Analyzer* – the application.

- *Oracle Express Server* – Express server is the database management system that supports the Oracle Financial Analyzer application for data storage, retrieval and processing. Express server is a multidimensional database. The physical multidimensional structuring of the data generates significant performance improvements for complex and iterative analytical query patterns compared to other database technologies (for example, relational databases).

- *Super Administrator* – Oracle Financial Analyzer is typically structured to support hierarchical information flows. The OFA Super Administrator is the most senior Administrator in the hierarchy. The Super Administrator is responsible for declaring structure and processes. Each Oracle Financial Analyzer implementation must have at least one user assigned to the Super Administrator role.

■ *Sub Administrator* – For complex environments where a hierarchical structure is required to support the business requirement, a Sub Administrator role may be created by the Super Administrator to manage a subset of users. The hierarchical nature of Oracle Financial Analyzer deployments creates subsets of users based on the enterprise's own hierarchical and functional structure. For example, a Sub Administrator may be responsible for administering 10 users who create and report data for the manufacturing operations. An Oracle Financial Analyzer deployment may contain zero or many Sub Administrators.

■ *Database file*[1] – Oracle Express Server physically stores individual schemas as separate physical files in the file system. An Express database file may contain both data and executable logic using Stored Procedure Language (Express SPL). The objects held within the database can be classified as structures or data. Structures refer to the physical multidimensional structures used to index the data. Data can be either numeric or text.

A physical Oracle Express database file (version 6.X) has a maximum size limitation of 2 Gb. If the size of the physical data to be stored exceeds this threshold, then an extension file is created. For example, a database named 'super.db', would be extended into 'super.001', and then iteratively into 'super.N'. By default, Oracle Express is configured to place extend files in a default location. Importantly, the system architect must be aware of this issue. Failure to do so could result in a performance deficit or failure to perform a complete backup. Loss of any extension file will render the entire database unreadable.

■ *Personal Database* – Each OFA user is allocated a Personal Database. A Personal Database may contain structures (for example, dimensions and hierarchies) and data. Structures are added to the user's Personal Database file by an Administrator (SuperDBA or SubDBA) at creation time and can be modified by the Administrator as required. Either the user or the Administrator can add data to the Personal Database file.

■ *Super Database* – The Super Database is the Personal Database of the Super Administrator. Like any Personal Database it may contain both structures and data. The key difference is that it is extremely likely to contain all the structures and probably also sensitive data. The Super Database is therefore key to the entire operation of Oracle Financial Analyzer and the file must be carefully protected to ensure against accidental failure (backup and recovery, Section 5.9) and protected from unauthorized access (this section and Chapter 3).

---

1 In Oracle Financial Analyzer terminology, a user's database is analogous to a user's schema in the Oracle RDBMS world. Unfortunately the logical abstraction and physical implementation share identical descriptions, making discussions somewhat confusing!

■ *Shared Database* – Unlike Personal Databases or the Super Database, the Shared Database is multi-user, which may be read or written to by any Oracle Financial Analyzer user (subject to permissions). Again, the Shared Database may contain structures or data. It is likely that the Shared Database will contain the most accurate data, for example actual figures and accepted budgets and forecasts. It is probable, therefore, that the Shared Database is the largest file in the Oracle Financial Analyzer system both logically and physically (multiple extension files, see Database File above).

■ *Task Processor* – Oracle Express Server operates using a multi-read, single-write methodology. As a multi-read, multi-write application, Oracle Financial Analyzer requires the Task Processor. The Task Processor is effectively a virtual queue. The only file in the OFA system requiring multi-read, multi-write access is the Shared Database; all other database files are accessed exclusively by an individual or system user. Instead of each user issuing data writes to the Shared Database, the write operation is transparently written as a physical file to the server's file system.

The Task Processor is the only operation able to write to the physical Shared Database file. The Task Processor scans the task queue (a dedicated directory, for example '/ofadata/super/taskfile'), reads the oldest file and executes the operations, finally deleting the file before moving to the next.

The Task Processor can be configured to run in two modes: background or foreground. The background method allows the process to run continuously; the foreground method requires manual intervention of the Administrator to start and stop it. The business process will dictate which method is most applicable.

■ *Node* – Node is not official Oracle Financial Analyzer terminology. However, it is extremely useful for describing certain aspects of enterprise-scale deployments containing multiple layers of Sub Administrators and potentially thousands of users.

In this section, the word 'node' is used to describe a discrete grouping of an administrative user (Super or Sub), a Shared user and multiple Personal users (from a physical perspective: a Super Database, a Shared Database and multiple Personal Databases). Typically a node may represent a distinct business unit within the enterprise.

■ *Tier* – Tier is also not part of the Oracle Financial Analyzer terminology. The term tier is often used, however, to describe a layer within the organization hierarchy. A tier may contain one or more business units or nodes. Figure 5.11 is an illustration of an implementation containing three tiers.

■ *SNAPI* – Structured N-Dimensional Application Programming Interface. The protocol used by Oracle Express-based tools and applications to connect to Oracle Express Server. SNAPI (a C-based interface) is optimized for accessing multidimensional data sources.

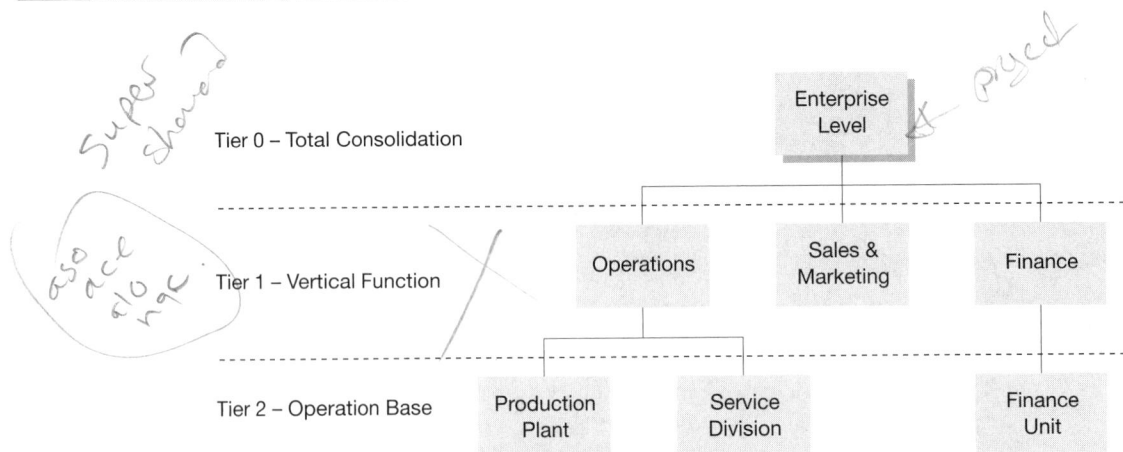

Tier 0 – Total Consolidation

Enterprise Level

Tier 1 – Vertical Function

Operations   Sales & Marketing   Finance

Tier 2 – Operation Base

Production Plant   Service Division   Finance Unit

FIG 5.11   **Illustration of a tiered OFA hierarchy**

SNAPI is an open and published API. For Microsoft Windows NT 4.0 environments, Microsoft's Remote Procedure Call (RPC) layer supports SNAPI. For UNIX environments, Oracle's implementation of RPC (Remote Operations) supports SNAPI. Both RPC implementations are TCP/IP based.

- Physical Server – The physical hardware hosting the Oracle Express Database software.

- Distribution – The process of the Administrator transferring structures to subordinate Administrators and users within their node.

- Submission – The process of users transferring data from the user to the Administrator.

- Thin client – Describes a configuration of the Oracle Financial Analyzer client. The client PC-based OFA application that connects to the remote OFA Server to access the user's Personal Database.

- Thick client – As per the thin client; however, the user's Personal Database is stored on the client PC, not the server. This configuration is designed for users who require the ability to work without being physically connected to the system, for example laptop users.

- Web client – A combination of HTML and Java applet client that allows access using only a Web browser. The functionality available is described in more detail in Section 5.4.

- Spreadsheet client – A plug-in to Microsoft Excel that allows users to read and write data from their Personal Database using a spreadsheet interface. The functionality available is described in more detail in Section 5.4.

Single node, single server

The single-node, single-server architecture is the simplest and therefore extremely common. In this scenario, all users are managed by a single Super Administrator and all processing is performed on a single physical server. The advantages of such architectures include:

- single point management and administration;
- reduced administration costs;
- standard implementation;
- standard migration path.

A single-node, single-server architecture is recommended for the following environments:

- tactical deployments where the scope of the business process is well determined;
- non-complex business process, with no requirement for individual business units, and the span of control – the ratio of users to administrators – is low.
- small number of concurrent users actively connected to the system (50 or fewer);
- all users are physically located in close proximity and are within the same time zone.

Unfortunately, the benefits of this architecture also produce negative features. The simple approach creates inflexibility to future growth in terms of:

- the physical limits of hardware, for example the number of CPUs, or memory capacity;
- an expansion of scope of the business process;
- an increase in the number of users.

Multiple nodes, single server

The multiple-node, single-server concept offers important benefits. By abstracting physical implementation (hardware and infrastructure) from the business process (application architecture), a flexible and modular architecture can be delivered. The modularity allows the architect to combine all the benefits of the single-node, single-server architecture without compromising future growth and flexibility. The required modularity can be achieved by spending minimal time at the analysis and design stages of the development process. The multiple-node, single-server architecture should be considered when:

- the business process requires multiple business units, or contains complex processing;
- the organizational or reporting structure is multi-tiered;

▓ keeping a manageable span of control between users and administrators is important;

▓ future growth may be dramatic, but is currently unquantifiable.

Oracle Financial Analyzer projects are often initially deployed to largely financial-oriented users. However, once the benefit of the improved business process is realized, the user community is often increased. Having engineered a modular architecture, the organization can rapidly increase the scope of the deployment with little rework required to existing processes, structures etc.

The multiple-node, single-server architecture has few negative features. Principally, the tiered nature of the deployment will require additional procedures and checks to ensure that data is being transferred. But the additional rigour is often viewed as contributing to the overall improvement of data quality.

Multiple nodes, multiple servers

The multiple-node, multiple-server architecture is logically identical to the multiple-node, single-server configuration except that certain logical nodes have been deployed on separate physical servers. The reasons for this type of architecture may be diverse:

▓ business – growth or acquisition of business units;

▓ environmental – geographical location;

▓ technology – hardware limitations (CPUs, memory etc.), infrastructure constraints (network links).

The multiple-node, multiple-server architecture can be advantageous where:

▓ Oracle Financial Analyzer is being deployed to implement a strategic requirement across the enterprise;

▓ the number of concurrent users is high (> 150);

▓ the user community is widely distributed;

▓ there is a need to support users across multiple time zones, denying a 'window of opportunity' for administrative tasks.

The disadvantages are that such distributed architectures are resource-intensive to administer, often requiring dedicated local resources, or enterprise management software to support remote management. However, from an application perspective, the process is no more complex than the multiple-nodes, single-server configuration. Figure 5.12 illustrates this architecture.

Architecture summary

This discussion has introduced Oracle Financial Analyzer terminology and outlined a number of architecture configurations available. However, each Oracle Financial

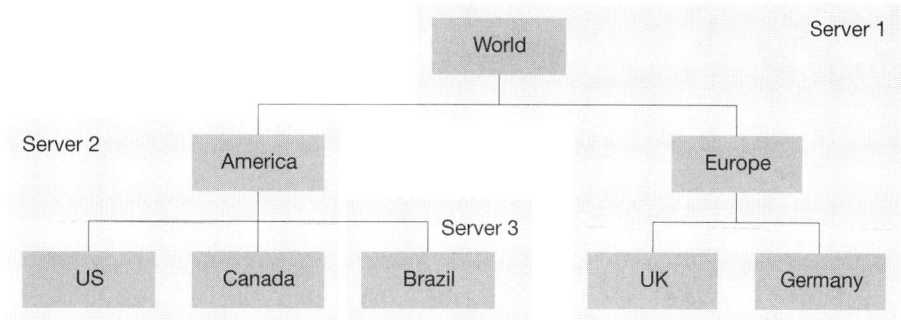

FIG 5.12   **Multiple-node, multiple-server logical and physical architecture**

Analyzer implementation will have individual requirements. The key to the design of performant and flexible architectures is the recognition that the process is one of understanding the requirements of the deployment rather than simply selecting an architectural option.

Understanding that the application can be considered as distinct logical and physical components allows the solution to focus closely on the business process and the physical infrastructure.

5.6.2 Understanding the enterprise infrastructure

It is a common failing within non-strategic projects that infrastructure issues are less well understood than functional requirements. Tactical projects are driven by business imperative and therefore have less IT/IS influence. The result is often non-alignment of infrastructure capability and functional requirements, creating deployment delays and operation problems.

This section highlights the relationship between the business process and the enterprise infrastructure using a framework methodology to identify inter-relationships. The aim of the framework is to structure understanding of all relevant issues (business and technical) that will influence the performance and flexibility of the architecture they deliver. The framework requires a wide range of skills and experience, particularly from IT functions. The system architect must recognise his or her role of coordinating framework activities. The framework elements have been grouped into two key categories:

■ logical elements – factors created by the project, for example user distribution by role, function and location;

■ physical elements – a metric that describes the enterprise infrastructure, for example the network bandwidth between two locations.

The techniques used in the framework may range from interviews to formal bench-marking exercises. Depending on the size of the implementation, the system architect may complete the exercise either singly or as a multidisciplinary team. Duration is also dependent on size as well as the depth/accuracy of any scoping study; however, the process must be rapid and delivered within several weeks for even the largest projects.

Understanding the logical elements

Logical factors drive how the application behaves when in use. If the system architect is to design architecture to support the behaviour of the application then logical factors must be understood; they are:

- distribution of the user community;
- the business process;
- users' involvement in the business process;
- the duration and frequency of the users' involvement.

User distribution

For smaller implementations, the majority of users will be contained within the same building. For enterprise-scale deployments, the user community is not only significantly larger but may also be separated by user role, divisional functions, country and, not unusually, time zone. By considering each of these factors the architect will gain a balanced view of users' dynamics.

System role

System role describes logical groups of users who perform like tasks. The number and detail of each group are related to the complexity of the business process and size of user community. Default categories may be:

- Administrators (business) – those users who have responsibility for maintaining the structure and operation of the system.
- Data generators – users who are required to submit information; typically, these are budget generators or people forecasting activity. Equally, a data generator user could be considered as the Administrator of a feeder system, for example an ERP providing actual data for retrospective periods.
- Information consumers – users who access the system to extract information, typically reporting of performance measures.
- Administrators (technical) – operators who have responsibility for performing system tasks such as backup, archiving, user security management etc.

Organizational function

For enterprise deployments, the business process will typically span multiple functional areas (e.g. manufacturing, sales, finance etc.) and also several organizational levels (e.g. sales person, plant manager, financial controller and board director). The system architect therefore needs to understand how the user community is distributed across the organizational structure. The information gleaned from this exercise may not be valid beyond the medium term because of continual change.

Geographic location

Most organizations have evolved through some degree of acquisition. Growth, whether internal or external, can result in widely distributed user communities.

Time zone

Understanding where users are located with respect to time zones has a significant effect on planning the management routines of any system. This information will again be used elsewhere in the framework. World commerce typically creates three core time zones: Europe and Africa, the Americas and Austral-Asia.

Understanding the business processes

An intrinsic relationship exists between business process, the supporting application and the load placed on the enterprise infrastructure. If the enterprise infrastructure is to be able to support an application and provide adequate performance, then it is essential that the system architect has a strong understanding of the business process. The primary aim of studying the business process is to be able to identify when the application will be generating peak load.

The load an application creates is often termed the 'application signature' and can be expressed using measures such as:

- average number of concurrent users;
- average volume of user-generated data;
- average volume of user-consumed data.

It is important to distinguish between peak and ambient application signatures. For example, planning and budgeting applications generate application signatures with massive variations between ambient and peak load. Variance may be caused by deadlines, when a high percentage of users perform the business process, often iteratively. Therefore, for applications such as Oracle Financial Analyzer, the above measures must be expressed for both ambient and peak times.

Quantifying the difference between the ambient and peak signatures is required to estimate user response times. If the enterprise commits to satisfying peak demand, the additional infrastructure will be under-utilized outside this period. In the opposite scenario, providing no additional infrastructure will create poor performance and potentially missed deadlines.

The goal is to gain sufficient understanding of the business process to provide appropriate resources for acceptable performance during peak usage.

Choosing a formal methodology or even a CASE tool to document the business process may be dictated by the complexity of the business process as well as being a project standard for larger projects.

User involvement in process

Understanding the business process is an excellent methodology for estimating the application's signature, but ultimately the application signature is driven by the quantity and type of users accessing the application. This section will decompose the deliverables of the previous task to group the user community into categories based on the type, duration and volume of user interaction. Later elements of the framework will physically quantify the load of each user category by:

- network traffic – the physical amount of data traffic that each user of this type will typically generate;
- connection times – to understand the frequency, duration and time each user type will connect to the system.

The number of user categories required to describe the user population is dependent on the business process complexity and the deployment size. Suggested categories are:

- Super Administrator – a special role of defining and distributing OFA structures and data.
- Sub Administrators – as Super Administrator, but on a reduced scope.
- Data generators – users primarily responsible for generating budgets and forecast.
- Data consumers – access granted primarily for reporting corporate information.

The representative quality of the categories will be greater if the business process has been analyzed. For larger deployments, particularly multi-tier architectures, it may be necessary to define sub-categories, particularly if the granularity of the data is reduced at higher tiers in the Oracle Financial Analyzer hierarchy.

Planning for future change

It is a key requirement that the application architecture must be sufficiently flexible to respond to future business/organization change without major reworking.

An example of such change may be the creation of a new business unit. If the architecture is flexible, another node can be logically and physically integrated into the existing application framework.

Investigating physical elements

Rarely will the enterprise infrastructure be a homogenous collection of technologies and standards. The goal of this section is to develop a clear understanding of the enterprise infrastructure with respect to the areas that will be influenced by the Oracle Financial Analyzer deployments. The technical skills necessary to create this part of the framework may not exist in the project team. The aim of the physical aspect of the framework is to:

- determine physical constraints – for example, network bandwidth, client PCs below recommended specification etc.;
- estimate the operation application signature;
- determine additional constraints – for example, security, access rights etc.

Network topology

The term network topology describes the architecture of the enterprise network. Few organizations will not be totally networked; however, a plethora of connection technologies exist (for example, ISDN, ATM, T1 etc.) meaning that simply knowing that office A can connect to system B is insufficient when attempting to attain performance targets.

Investigating network topology has two purposes: to identify network bandwidth between specific sites and to identify suitable hardware hosting locations.

The detail of the information required to describe topology is dependent on the complexity of the project and may have to be defined at several levels for projects involving multiple time zones and multiple countries.

Measuring the application signature

The section above, 'Understanding the business processes', introduced the concept of the application signature as the total load the application will exert on the enterprise infrastructure.

The application signature must be considered with respect to the logical information such as geographical user distribution and network topology. This combined view of application load and logical factors will be the key foundation in identifying where infrastructure is insufficient to support the application. The following sections will outline the methodology.

Network latency

Understanding that location A and location B are connected using a 64 Kbps ISDN connection is insufficient when ensuring performance. Connection speeds only describe the maximum bandwidth and it must be assumed that the link carries other traffic (for example, e-mail, files etc.).

Network latency is the term that describes available/usable bandwidth. Utilization of network links typically fluctuates across the working day. Enterprise organizations should track network latency as standard practice to determine infrastructure performance.

Benchmarking the user signature

For each of the user categories developed in the section above, 'User involvement in process', a list of standard tasks that user type will typically perform must be generated. This task list will represent the user profile. Examples include:

- Log on – client/server versions of OFA software exchange metadata information at the initialization of the session.
- Open sample document – this involves the transfer of the report data to the client; the number of FDIs and the dimension status will have implications.
- Change default selection – this task involves the transfer of incremental data.
- Rotate report – rotating a report can involve the transfer of incremental data and so can create network traffic.
- Drill down on Sales hierarchy – causes additional data for child level to be fetched.
- Submit forecast – submission of a small amount of data to the Shared Database.
- For Web clients only – the Oracle Financial Analyzer Web client downloads several Java applets. OFA applets are signed and therefore can be stored persistently on the client PC/browser, making the additional download a consideration only for the initial download. Apart from the initial download, the Web client will generate a similar network signature to the traditional client types.

The benchmarking must take place in a closed environment using a similar database design to the production system. The benchmarking exercise will quantify the traffic volume by task. Most IT departments have appropriate resources and equipment for such exercises. Figure 5.13 illustrates the configuration of the equipment required.

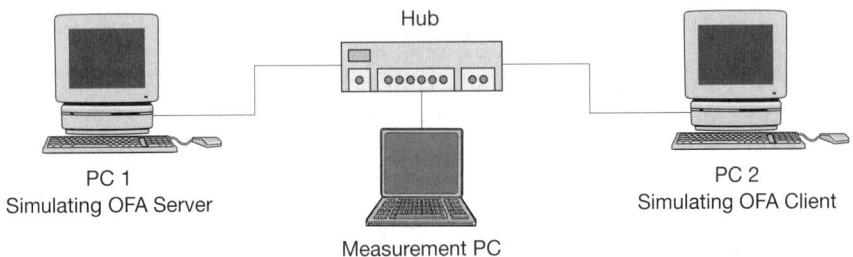

Hub

PC 1
Simulating OFA Server

PC 2
Simulating OFA Client

Measurement PC

FIG 5.13   Illustration of signature benchmarking equipment

The benchmarking exercise is best performed later in the development cycle, when database designs become more stable and prototype systems are available.

Propagation delays

Network propagation is a consideration for international deployments. It describes the time taken to establish a network circuit. The time delay caused by network propagation is only perceptible over extremely long connections (for example, transatlantic links) and may be in the order of 0.5–1 second per transmission. The delay is dependent on the distance and the technology. If applicable, propagation delay must be considered in estimating user response times.

Security

An Oracle Financial Analyzer system may contain sensitive information that can have a material effect on the enterprise if disclosed. The role of the system architect is to work with appropriate parties to establish both technical and operational risks and take appropriate measures. Common risk areas are:

- user authentication;
- user accounts;
- file system access.

The purpose of this section is to highlight common Oracle Financial Analyzer deployment issues, independent of operating system. The reader is recommended to consider specialist texts for more detail.

User authentication

User authentication is the process of identifying whether the user is who he or she claims to be. In the computing world we accept this as anyone who knows the identified person's password. Oracle Financial Analyzer as a product has an internal security model that controls a user's access to information. However, unlike other Oracle products such as Oracle8i, Oracle Financial Analyzer does not maintain a user database. Authentication is provided by the underlying operating system of the Oracle Express Server hosting the Oracle Financial Analyzer application. This is a low-risk methodology because by implication the organization trusts the operating system. Also, reuse of existing user accounts prevents duplication of account administration.

However, few organizations have integrated user authentication across multiple platforms. The majority of organizations use Microsoft or Novell systems to authenticate users; therefore OFA UNIX implementations require account duplication. The system architect must be aware of this requirement and specify a process to manage OFA account administration.

User accounts

For security best practice, each Oracle Financial Analyzer user should be allocated an individual user account to preserve integrity. In addition to human users, Oracle Express Server also requires three system accounts transparent to OFA application users. These accounts are inherently part of Oracle Express Server, and perform tasks on behalf of Oracle Express Server including file access, memory management etc. The account roles are:

▨ Database Administrator Account – this 'dba' role refers to physical system processes rather than a human administrator. By default this role is allocated to an account called 'oesdba'. This account performs all operations with the operating system on behalf of, and transparently to, the user. This account is therefore granted higher operating system permissions than standard users (see OES platform-specific manual for details).

▨ Initialization Account – this account would be better named background process account, because of its role. By default the role is allocated to an account named 'oesinit'. In the Oracle Financial Analyzer environment, the background Task Processor (the queuing mechanism to update the Shared Database) is performed under this identity.

▨ Default Access Account – this role is by default allocated to an account named 'oesguest'. In the generic Oracle Express Server environment this account allows access to unauthenticated users. In the Oracle Financial Analyzer environment this type of unauthenticated access is a security weakness and must be disabled.

Oracle Express Server is configurable, so the actual account allocated to each role may be modified. From a security perspective, the 'oesdba', and 'oesinit' accounts are a potential weakness. Because they are system accounts, Express Server constantly requires access to them and therefore stores their passwords, albeit in an encrypted format. As system accounts, there is no reason why a human user would require the password, and ideally the passwords should not expire after a set time. Failure to 'freeze' the passwords or change them in an integrated manner commonly results in the entire Oracle Financial Analyzer system suddenly failing because a password has expired. Often, dispensation from internal security functions is required to create static password accounts. A compromise is to expire the password on a less frequent basis, for example every 90 days. Appropriate administrative processes must be implemented to support this requirement.

File system access
Oracle Express Server and therefore Oracle Financial Analyzer applications store data directly in operating system file systems. Thus each new user results in a new physical file being created on the server's file system. See the section, 'Application and architecture terminology'.

This method is different from other database management systems such as Oracle RDBMS that separate logical and physical storage. The Oracle Financial Analyzer security model for restricting data access therefore uses file system privileges to control physical access. For example, user A cannot open user B's database file because the operating system physically prevents the action. In addition, if a user were able to circumvent this mechanism, an internal system of checking user credentials serves as an additional security layer. OFA ensures that the user ID has been given access to the user database by the Administrator.

Figure 5.14 illustrates how a file system structure may appear. Note that the file system represents a hierarchical deployment with one super-node ('super') and three sub-nodes ('sub_db', 'sub_fr' and 'sub_uk'). The system policy in this example dictates that each user has a personal directory under the 'users' directory to store their Personal Database. This policy is simpler to maintain from a file permissions perspective, because it is directory rather than individual file based. Each user will require read and write privileges within their personal directory but only read privileges in the 'shared' directory (the location of the Shared Database, 'ofas.db'). Standard users should not require any file permissions beyond those mentioned unless specific customizations dictate otherwise.

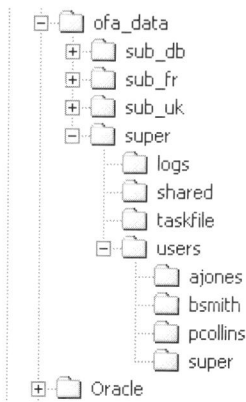

```
⊟ ☐ ofa_data
    ⊞ ☐ sub_db
    ⊞ ☐ sub_fr
    ⊞ ☐ sub_uk
    ⊟ ☐ super
            ☐ logs
            ☐ shared
            ☐ taskfile
        ⊟ ☐ users
                ☐ ajones
                ☐ bsmith
                ☐ pcollins
                ☐ super
    ⊞ ☐ Oracle
```

FIG 5.14   **Typical file structure for a multi-tiered OFA system**

Exceptions to this rule are the Super Administrator user who should have access to each user's personal directory and database for administrative and support purposes. Also, note that physical file read/write operations are performed by an Oracle Express Server system account. By default this role is performed by the 'oesdba' account; see the section on 'User accounts' above. The 'oesdba' account therefore requires full privileges on the entire super directory structure.

User access

The Shared Database may contain all data and structures. Whilst users are able to open the Shared Database, they are limited to being able to read only the subset for which they have corresponding structure. A user's Personal Database may contain data of its own. The Super Administrator is responsible for making structures available to the user community and allocating user IDs to OFA users.

This model is successful in practice, but like so many other application security models, it relies heavily on the integration of two key processes:

- System administration – consistency and correctness depend on the frequency with which the server administrator checks the users' file permissions. Commonly the business process and technical processes are disjointed, so that users who leave the organization or change responsibility do not have their file access privileges altered, leaving scope for unauthorized access.

- Business process administration – the responsibility of identifying logical data access privileges must be defined at a granular level within the specification. The task of allocating data access to individual users in the operational world falls to the Super (or Sub) Administrator. In smaller deployments, the Administrator is likely to have a very clear understanding of the users' data access requirements. This is not always true for larger deployments, and thus the process of distributing access must be controlled and accountable.

General security weaknesses

The previous security discussions outlined passive security implications caused by the poor operation and administration of internal procedures and systems. We now discuss weaknesses caused by active attempts to violate security. Active security violations fall into two key categories: denial of service and system infiltration.

The purpose of 'denial of service' attacks is to prevent the normal operation of the system. Denial of service attacks are usually initiated from outside the enterprise and are often targeted at external-facing applications. The purpose of such attacks is to cause maximum inconvenience.

The majority of enterprises take adequate precautions to insulate internal systems from the external world (e.g. Internet) using technologies such as firewalls. As a consequence, internal systems such as Oracle Financial Analyzer are at lower risk of external attack. Denial of service attacks initiated from within the enterprise are easily traceable so will cause short-term inconvenience only. Internally originating denial of service attacks are rare and are usually targeted at operating systems or application servers.

System infiltration attacks are more insidious. Unlike the denial of service attack, the aim is to extract information without detection. The risk of this attack is directly proportional to the sensitivity of the information. This type of attack may be initiated from within the enterprise as an act of espionage. There is little protection from this type of attack other than integrated administrative processes such as:

- reviewing user access permissions;

- instantaneous termination of an employee's user account on termination of employment;

- instructing employees not to share passwords;

- forcing users to change passwords regularly;

- limiting user scope by physically partitioning the application (e.g. multiple-node architectures with a low ratio of users to administrators).

More opportunistic attacks can occur at infrastructure weak points. Such attacks are rare. The sensitivity of the information stored will determine the appropriate protection. Examples of infrastructure weaknesses include:

- External connections – any connection using a public network such as the Internet or modem dial-up is susceptible to a range of attacks, such as eavesdropping.

- Office hardware such as PC monitors emit radiation. Equipment is available to intercept and reproduce the images being displayed on the original monitor.

These risks are generic security problems and are not specific to Oracle Financial Analyzer.

Client hardware audit

As part of the physical deployment it may be necessary to upgrade the PC hardware of some users. Typically only a very small number of users require hardware upgrades. The deliverables from this process are, for each user's PC:

- operating system, version number – for example, Windows NT, 4.0 Workstation;

- CPU speed – for example, 600 MHz;

- memory – for example, 128 Mbytes;

- available disk space – for example, 2 Gbytes;

- for users who will connect via dial-up connections, modem speed – for example, 56 Kbps;

- For international deployments only, the local language settings – for example, English (United Kingdom).

Some enterprises may already hold such information. Should a PC require replacement or upgrade, the appropriate budget holder must be identified.

Infrastructure summary

The purpose of the framework is to allow the system architect to consider all the relevant information he or she will require when designing the physical architecture.

5.6.3 Example Enterprise

In this section we introduce a fictitious organization called 'Example Enterprise' to demonstrate how the framework discussed above may be applied in practice.

Business vision

Example Enterprise has grown rapidly over the past seven years. Their principal markets have traditionally been in the UK and Western Europe. In the past three years they have expanded into Scandinavia and opened an office in the US.

Example Enterprise manufactures network equipment for the telecommunications industry. They have two manufacturing plants in the UK and Mexico. Figure 5.15 illustrates the Example Enterprise organization chart.

Historically, Example Enterprise relied on forecasting, budgeting and reporting using a manual process of interconnected spreadsheets. The process became increasingly inaccurate and difficult to manage. Example Enterprise requires a system to deliver faster, more detailed information to sales and manufacturing divisions. Oracle Financial Analyzer was selected to support this application.

Logical elements

This section examines the user base and the business process.

System role

Table 5.1 is a breakdown of the initial user community by system role.

Organizational function

Table 5.2 is a breakdown of the initial user community by organizational function. Note: the table includes the support personnel who do not directly affect the Oracle Financial Analyzer business process.

Geographic location

Table 5.3 shows the user community by geography.

Time zone distribution

Table 5.4 shows the user community by time zone.

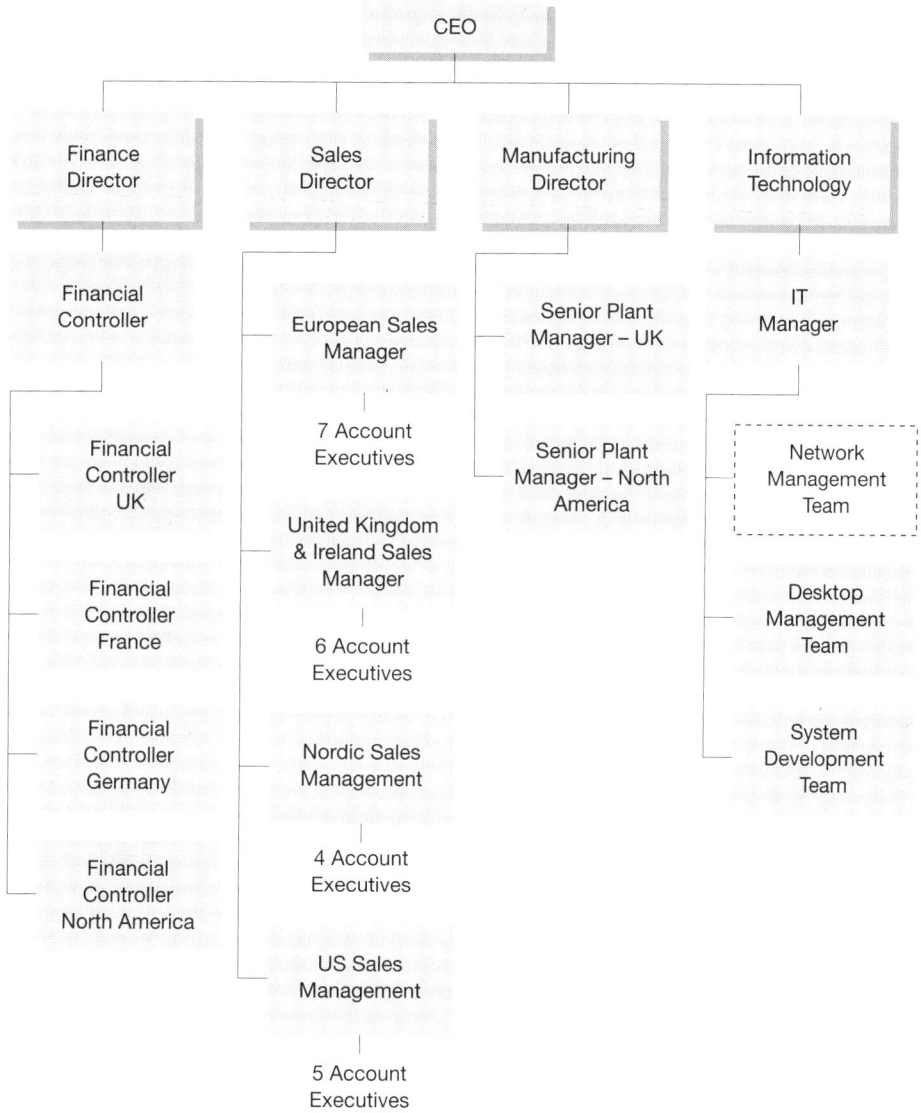

FIG 5.15   Example Enterprise organization chart

TABLE 5.1   **Breakdown of Example Enterprise user community by system role**

Role	Group/User
Administrators – 4	Super Administrator – UK Sub Administrator – UK (UK & US) Sub Administrator – France (Europe) Sub Administrator – Germany (Nordic)
Data Generators – 28	All Sales Managers (4) All Account Executives (22) All Senior Plant Managers (2)
Information Consumers – 48	CEO All Board Directors (4) All Financial Controllers (5) All Territory Sales Managers (4) All Account Executives (22) All Senior Plant Managers (2) All Assistant Plant Managers (10)
Technical Administrators – 3	Desktop Management Team (3)
Total Users:	83

TABLE 5.2   **Breakdown of Example Enterprise user community by function**

Organizational function	Group/User
Senior Management – 5	CEO Finance Director Sales Director Manufacturing Director IT Director
Finance – 5	Financial Controller Financial Controller – UK & Ireland Financial Controller – Europe Financial Controller – Nordic Financial Controller – US
Sales & Marketing – 4	Sales Manager – UK & Ireland Sales Manager – Europe Sales Manager – Nordic Sales Manager – US
Manufacturing – 12	Senior Plant Manager – UK Senior Plant Manager – Mexico Assistant Plant Manager – UK Assistant Plant Manager – UK Assistant Plant Manager – UK

Organizational function	Group/User
Manufacturing – 12 continued	Assistant Plant Manager – UK
	Assistant Plant Manager – Mexico
	Assistant Plant Manager – Mexico
	Assistant Plant Manager – Mexico
	Assistant Plant Manager – Mexico
	Assistant Plant Manager – Mexico
	Assistant Plant Manager – Mexico
Support – 4	Desktop Management Team – UK
	Desktop Management Team – UK
	Desktop Management Team – UK
	Desktop Management Team – UK

TABLE 5.3   Breakdown of Example Enterprise user community by country

Country	Location	Users
United Kingdom – 23	London – 15	CEO
		Finance Director
		Sales Director
		Manufacturing Director
		IT Director
		Financial Controller
		Financial Controller – UK & Ireland
		Sales Manager – UK & Ireland
		Account Executive – UK (4)
		Desktop Management Team – UK (3)
	Manchester – 8	Senior Plant Manager – UK
		Assistant Plant Manager – UK (4)
		Account Executive – UK (2)
		Desktop Management Team – UK (1)
France – 7	Paris – 7	Financial Controller – Europe
		Sales Manager – Europe
		Account Executive – Europe (5)
Germany – 8	Bonn – 8	Financial Controller – Nordic
		Sales Manager – Nordic
		Account Executive – Nordic (6)
United States – 7	New York – 7	Financial Controller – US
		Sales Manager – US
		Account Executive – US (5)
Mexico – 7	Mexico City – 7	Senior Plant Manager – Mexico
		Assistant Plant Manager – Mexico (6)

TABLE 5.4   Breakdown of user community by time zone

Time zone	User
Greenwich Mean Time – 23 GMT 00:00	CEO Finance Director Sales Director Manufacturing Director IT Director Financial Controller Financial Controller – UK & Ireland Sales Manager – UK & Ireland Account Executive – UK (6) Senior Plant Manager – UK Assistant Plant Manager – UK (4) Desktop Management Team – UK (4)
Central European Time – 15 GMT + 01:00	Financial Controller – Europe Financial Controller – Nordic Sales Manager – Europe Sales Manager – Nordic Account Executive – Europe (7) Account Executive – Nordic (4)
Eastern Standard Time – 7 GMT – 05:00	Financial Controller – US Sales Manager – US Account Executive – US (5)
Central America – 7 GMT – 06:00	Senior Plant Manager – Mexico Assistant Plant Manager – Mexico (6)

Figure 5.16 illustrates how global working patterns overlap. Such exercises are required for multi-country or multi-time-zone deployments where a window of opportunity for essential administrative tasks is required. In our example, a working day from 08:00 to 19:59 local time (11 hours) is assumed. It is important that the working day includes peak usage times; for example, working hours may be extended immediately prior to a budget deadline.

The architect should perform this task with respect to each office within the enterprise, not each country, because a country may contain multiple time zones. For example, if Example Enterprise were planning to open an office in San Francisco (Pacific Standard Time, GMT – 08:00 hours), the window of opportunity would reduce from seven hours (01:00–07:59 GMT) to five hours (04:00–07:59 GMT).

For multi-country/multi-time-zone deployments, the output of this exercise has direct influence on the configuration of the architecture selected for deployment, as defined in Section 5.6.1, 'Architecture overview'.

Office/Time (GMT)   00 01 02 03 04 05 06 07 08 09 10 11 12 13 14 15 16 17 18 19 20 21 22 23

UK, London

UK, Manchester

France, Paris

Germany, Bonn

Sweden, Stockholm

Mexico, Mexico City

US, New York

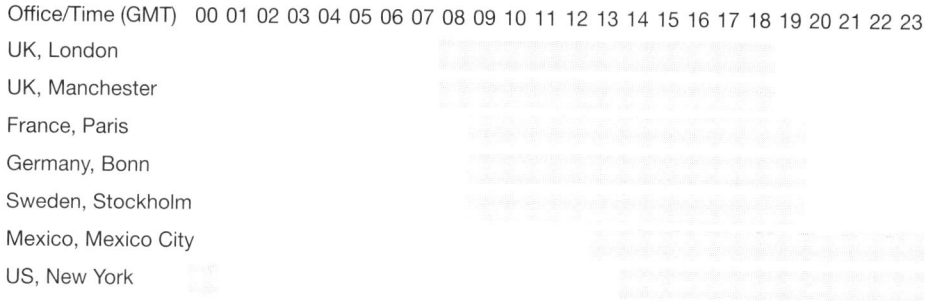

FIG 5.16   **Window of opportunity**

Understanding the business process

The purpose of implementing Oracle Financial Analyzer for Example Enterprise is to create an integrated system to produce a 'single truth' of the organization. As a distributed and multi-currency, multilingual organization, Example Enterprise has discovered that an unmanaged collection of spreadsheets fails to provide a consistent enterprise view. For this scenario, Example Enterprise requires the following functionality:

▧ monthly forecast of production for all manufacturing plants by product line;

▧ monthly sales report for each market region by sales person.

Given the organization structure and the business process, the Oracle Financial Analyzer application architecture is illustrated in Figure 5.17.

User involvement in process

Table 5.5 illustrates the common tasks by the four user groups of this deployment. Note: some tasks require multiple iterations (for example, tasks 3.3 and 3.4) that must be accounted for when calculating the application signature.

Defining the application signature

Table 5.6 contains the benchmarked data for common tasks of the business process. Table 5.6 quantifies each individual task but does not account for actual users or the frequency at which the tasks will occur; it is therefore not the application signature. Table 5.7 illustrates how the individual benchmark data can be extrapolated to derive the application signature. It is important that the application signature is defined with respect to a time period (for example, quarter or year). The time period (or cycle) should be the longest period; in this limited example it is quarterly. This methodology means that the stated application signature represents each task/process being executed at least once, and is therefore truly indicative of the business process.

```
                          Super
                       Administrator

Finance Director                    Financial
Sales Director                      Controller
Manufacturing Director
IT Director


UK – Senior Plant Manager
Mexico – Senior Plant
Manager
UK – Assistant Plant
Manager
UK – Assistant Plant
Manager
UK – Assistant Plant
Manager
UK – Assistant Plant     Financial      Financial      Financial      Financial
Manager                  Controller     Controller     Controller     Controller
Mexico – Assistant Plant  – UK           – Europe        – Nordic        – US
Manager
Mexico – Assistant Plant
Manager                  Uk & Ireland Sales  European Sales   European Sales   European Sales
Mexico – Assistant Plant Manager             Manager          Manager          Manager
Manager                  Account Executive   Account Executive Account Executive Account Executive
Mexico – Assistant Plant Account Executive   Account Executive Account Executive Account Executive
Manager                  Account Executive   Account Executive Account Executive Account Executive
Mexico – Assistant Plant Account Executive   Account Executive Account Executive Account Executive
Manager                  Account Executive   Account Executive                  Account Executive
Mexico – Assistant Plant Account Executive   Account Executive                  Account Executive
Manager                                      Account Executive
                                             Account Executive
```

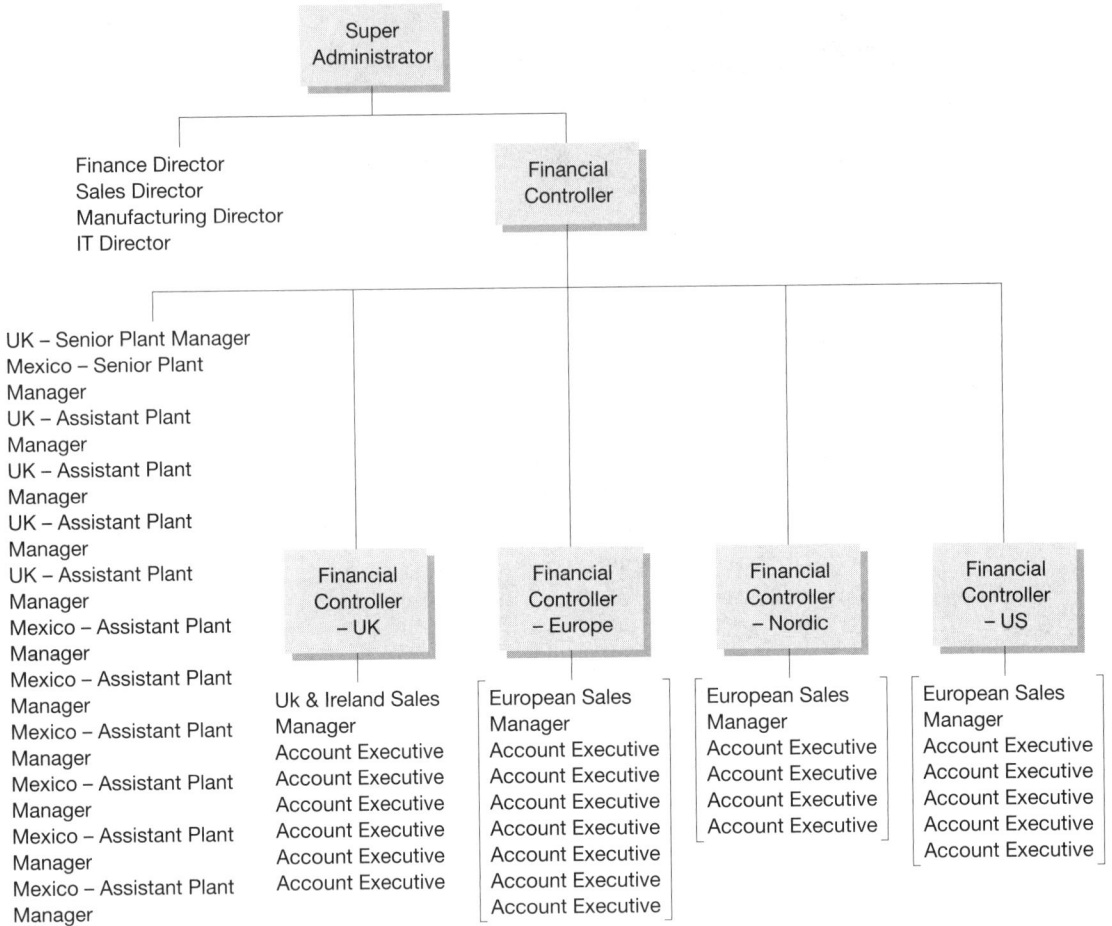

FIG 5.17   OFA structural hierarchy

TABLE 5.5   Common OFA tasks by user group

Role	ID	Common task
1. Super Administrator	1.1	Distribution of data to Sub Administrators
	1.2	Reconciliation of budgets
	1.3	Reporting of global manufacturing activity
	1.4	Reporting of global sales activity
2. Sub Administrator	2.1	Distribution of data to Sub Administrators
	2.2	Reconciliation of budgets
	2.3	Reporting of regional manufacturing activity (where applicable)
	2.4	Reporting of regional sales activity

Role	ID	Common task
3. Budgeteer	3.1	Production of monthly sales forecast
	3.2	Production of quarterly budget
	3.3	Review/re-submission of administrator forecast changes
	3.4	Review/re-submission of administrator budget change
	3.5	Reporting of monthly regional activity against forecast
4. Reporter	4.1	Reporting of monthly regional activity against forecast

TABLE 5.6 **Network traffic volume analysis**

Task		Network traffic vol (bytes)		Total
		Client to Server	Server to Client	(Kbytes)
1	**Super Administrator**	**210,960**	**1,227,150**	**1,438**
1.1	Logon	32,230	320,500	353
1.2	Distribution of data to Sub Administrators	93,500	510,300	604
1.3	Reconciliation of budgets	57,330	210,000	267
1.4	Reporting of global manufacturing activity	15,500	102,450	118
1.5	Reporting of global sales activity	12,400	83,900	96
2	**Sub Administrator**	**172,730**	**958,650**	**1,131**
2.1	Logon	32,230	299,450	332
2.2	Distribution of data to designated users	72,100	350,000	422
2.3	Reconciliation of budgets	48,500	150,000	199
2.4	Reporting of regional manufacturing activity	7,500	75,300	83
2.5	Reporting of regional sales activity	12,400	83,900	96
3	**Budgeteer**	**56,630**	**337,920**	**395**
3.1	Logon	32,230	240,970	273
3.2	Production of monthly sales forecast	4,000	3,200	7
3.3	Production of quarterly budget	3,700	4,500	8
3.4	Review/re-submission of administrator forecast changes	2,000	1,650	4
3.5	Review/re-submission of administrator budget change	2,300	3,700	6
3.6	Reporting of monthly regional activity against forecast	12,400	83,900	96
4	**Reporter**	**44,630**	**254,200**	**299**
4.1	Logon	32,230	170,300	203
4.2	Reporting of monthly regional activity against forecast	12,400	83,900	96
	Total	**484,950**	**2,777,920**	**3,263**

TABLE 5.7   Defining the application signature

Task	Data volume (Kbytes)	Frequency per cycle	Number of users	Volume per user	Volume per role (Kbytes)
1	1,438		1	24,375	24,375
1.1	353	17		5,996	5,996
1.2	604	12		7,246	7,246
1.3	267	16		4,277	4,277
1.4	118	32		3,774	3,774
1.5	96	32		3,082	3,082
2	1,131		3	16,297	48,890
2.1	332	12		3,980	11,940
2.2	422	12		5,065	15,196
2.3	199	16		3,176	9,528
2.4	83	12		994	2,981
2.5	96	32		3,082	9,245
3	395		28	5,872	164,417
3.1	273	15		4,098	114,744
3.2	7	12		86	2,419
3.3	8	12		98	2,755
3.4	4	15		55	1,533
3.5	6	15		90	2,520
3.6	96	15		1,445	40,446
4	299		48	2,391	114,751
4.1	203	8		1,620	77,772
4.2	96	8		770	36,979
Application Signature					**352,433**

The application signature for Example Enterprise is therefore 352 Mbytes per quarter. For simplicity, it is assumed that there are no end-of-year procedures, and that all quarters are equal.

Physical elements

This section examines the physical constraints of Example Enterprises' existing infrastructure.

Network topology

Figure 5.18 represents the network topology of Example Enterprise. For illustration purposes, Example Enterprise is less complex than a real deployment. The scale of the organization often makes it difficult to illustrate individual PCs on a single diagram. This representation was produced using Visio.

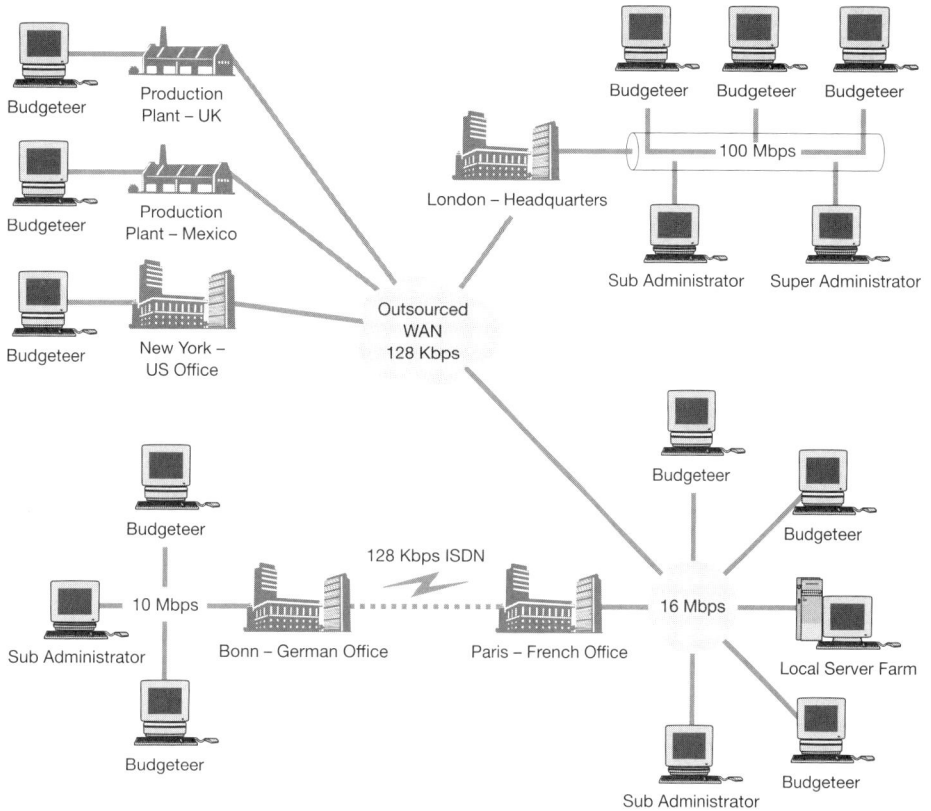

FIG 5.18   **Example Enterprise network topology**

Example Enterprise has six offices (London, Manchester, Mexico City, New York, Bonn and Paris). All locations are connected by an outsourced WAN of 128 Kbps, except for Bonn where the connection is routed through Paris first. TCP/IP is the principal networking protocol. The Paris office still retains a token ring network that was in place when the operation was acquired. Scandinavian operations are based in the Bonn office.

Estimating response time

Estimating user response times is complex because the architecture has not yet been selected. This task is key in the influence of the final architecture because the system architect develops a strong understanding of how and when information will flow across the network.

Table 5.8 illustrates the latent bandwidth of the outsourced WAN network. The average latent bandwidth represents only core business hours.

TABLE 5.8   **Example Enterprise WAN latent bandwidth**

Link	Type	Max. bandwidth (Kbps)	Average latent bandwidth (Kbps)
WAN – London	ISDN	128	20
WAN – Manchester	ISDN	128	60
WAN – Mexico City	ISDN	128	35
WAN – New York	ISDN	128	80
WAN – Paris	ISDN	128	35
Paris – Bonn	ISDN	128	40

Table 5.9 illustrates the process to estimate user response times in seconds. The information is listed by location, latent bandwidth of location and task ID. For simplicity, only four tasks are shown. For this illustration it is assumed that a multiple-node, single-server architecture has been implemented in the London office. Note:

- London latent bandwidth is therefore that of the LAN, not the WAN.
- Bonn traffic routes via Paris; the latent bandwidth is therefore that of the slowest part of the link (WAN – Paris).
- Processing delay has been ignored.
- Grey cells indicate tasks that take more than 6 seconds to complete.

Security

Example Enterprise has a global authentication method based on Windows NT 4.0 domains. All users' accounts are based in the same domain.

TABLE 5.9   **Estimated response time (by location and task, in seconds)**

Location / Task	Bandwidth	1.1	1.4	2.1	2.4
London	50000	0.01	0.00	0.01	0.00
Manchester	60	5.88	1.97	5.53	1.38
Mexico City	35	10.09	3.37	9.49	2.37
New York	80	4.41	1.48	4.15	1.04
Paris	35	10.09	3.37	9.49	2.37
Bonn	35	10.09	3.37	9.49	2.37

5.6.4 Designing the physical architecture

The entire rationale of Section 5.6 has been to highlight the factors that drive the performance characteristics of Oracle Financial Analyzer implementations. To summarize, the process up to this point has been to qualify and where appropriate quantify those drivers. A common failing in any system implementation, including Oracle Financial Analyzer, is to ignore the behavioural drivers and enter directly into hardware specification. The risk of the direct approach is:

- performance – the cost of under- or over-estimating the hardware platform;
- inflexibility – failure to address infrastructure issues, thus constraining future change and expansion.

However, this section will illustrate that having completed the framework process, the task of specifying the Oracle Financial Analyzer physical architecture is not only intuitive but also accountable. The key tasks within the specification process are:

- locating physical hardware – choosing the optimal location(s) to physically site server platforms;
- hardware specification – physical requirements, including fault tolerance;
- infrastructure upgrade – upgrading infrastructure to support additional loading of new application;
- operational processes – operational processes can be defined for supporting the application.

Locating physical hardware

All of the decisions made in this section are based on findings of the framework, so an initially daunting task may have already been decided by other factors. The three key inputs to this decision are logical architecture, distribution of the user community and network topology.

Logical architecture refers to the application architecture adopted to support the business process. Sections 5.4 and 5.6.1 outlined the key OFA logical architectures (single and multiple node). The choice of appropriate logical architecture can be driven only by business process requirements, not technical considerations. Therefore the system architect must rely on the application architect role to define the application architecture early in the process.

If the application architect has specified a single-node architecture, the decision of physically locating the supporting server is to identify the central point of the infrastructure, thus creating equal response times for all users. Unfortunately, the other influences of user distribution and network topology complicate this decision because the geographic centre of the infrastructure may not necessarily be the same point as the response centre. The response centre is the point where the time taken for a packet of information to reach the boundary is the same for all locations. Similarly, it is probable that the user community is biased towards a specific location. For Oracle Financial Analyzer deployments, this is naturally the Finance department. Figure 5.19 illustrates this problem graphically, which is present in the Example Enterprise scenario of Section 5.6.3.

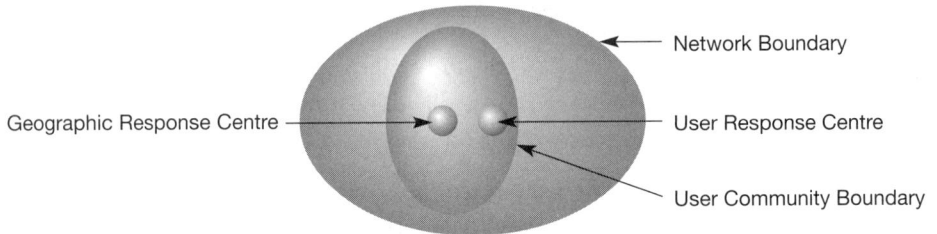

FIG 5.19   **Differentiating the central point of the network**

It is possible to calculate accurately the precise user response centre by taking the network latency information (see Section 5.6.2) and then weighting it by the user application signature and user distribution. However, there is unlikely to be a suitable facility to host the server at this theoretically exact fulcrum, and therefore heuristic experience can be relied on to identify an optimal compromise.

Note: outsourced enterprise networks tend to have virtual response centres (i.e. at the point of outsourcing), making almost all locations non-optimal, especially for highly distributed user communities like those in Example Enterprise (Figure 5.20). In such situations the system architect must seek a professional opinion. It may be desirable to outsource the hosting of the OFA server also. This complex problem may be an indication that the logical application architecture is unsuited to the business process for the reasons originally referred to in Section 5.6.1: single-node architectures are suited to tactical deployments supporting non-complex business processes of concentrated user communities.

For multiple-node architectures, the process of identifying the user response centre should be repeated for each logical node in the architecture. For the multiple-node scenario, the process of defining the user response centre is less complex because the scope constraints of user distribution and network topology can be considered at a lower level of detail and therefore have fewer implications, considerations or interdependencies. However, the system architect should avoid specifying a unique location for each logical node because of the incremental cost of purchasing and support. A node should only be located separately because of an insurmountable problem/requirement, for example security or network bandwidth. If the constraint is insufficient latent bandwidth (i.e. user response times), the cost

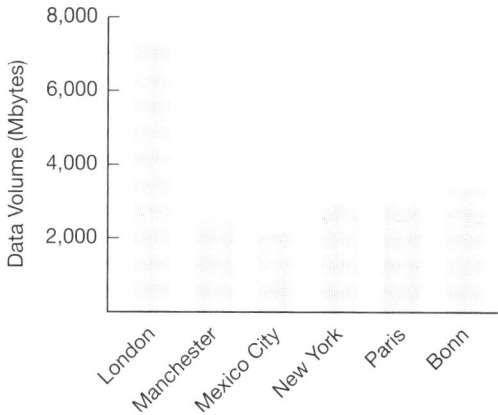

FIG 5.20   **Example Enterprise network traffic volume by location**

of increasing the bandwidth versus the cost of purchasing and supporting dedicated hardware over the system write-off period, typically five years, must be evaluated. An advantage of choosing to upgrade bandwidth is that the cost can be apportioned against the entire business unit.

Note: if the multiple-node architecture is aligned to support individual business units (BU), then in the vast majority of examples the user community will be concentrated and the above statements will be generally true. Conversely, if this is false and the BU has a highly distributed user community, the problem of selecting a location will be similar to that of the single-node deployment outlined earlier. Again, this may be an indication that the logical architecture is unsuited to the business process and should be addressed.

Hardware specification

This section will develop physical hardware specifications. Having selected the optimal location for the logical application nodes and knowing the application profile generated by that aggregation of the user community, hardware specification is a far less risky task than the alternative methodology of guessing and adding a percentage for contingency. (Note: if the user community is small, the best approach to hardware specification may be simply to conduct benchmarking on the batch load and roll-up, as the build nears completion, on the Oracle recommended base case specification machine.)

For applications built using Oracle Financial Analyzer the critical components of hardware sizing are CPUs, memory and disks. CPU and memory have a direct correlation and are therefore sized in parallel. The configuration of the disk array is as critical as the size.

CPUs

Specifying the number of processors is highly dependent on the current specification and underlying chip architecture; however, the process is relatively simple.

To size CPU and memory, the architect must be aware of which performance criteria the solution must satisfy, for example ambient or peak. The recommendation is to satisfy peak periods plus expected growth within the first two years of operation. Some vendors will recommend upgradable hardware platforms (for example, start at two CPUs, upgradable to four), especially if the project is to be deployed in phases. However, in reality, obsolescence in the sub-£20,000 hardware market makes this option less practical and often more expensive in the longer term.

Oracle's recommendations for Windows NT deployments of Oracle Financial Analyzer are that the server contains one processor per 25–50 concurrent users, within a minimum of two CPUs. The user banding is designed to accommodate the fact that some user profiles generate more intensive activity than others. As Intel chip speeds are commercially achieving speeds of 1 GHz, it is our opinion that an OFA implementation of standard planning and budgeting, running on a dedicated server with moderate tuning, will routinely support 50–75 concurrent users per CPU.

Memory

Memory requirements can be split into two distinct components: working memory and a page buffer. Express Server reserves a portion of physical memory for use as a database page buffering system. The remainder of memory available is then used to process data for each concurrent session.

Working memory sizing is a relatively simple calculation; for each concurrent processing-intensive user (i.e. Database Administrators, Budget Workstations, using roles developed in Section 5.6.3), a minimum of 8 Mb of memory is required. For each concurrent non-processing-intensive user (i.e. data consumers), a minimum 6 Mb of memory is required. These figures are close to those recommended in Oracle Financial Analyzer release notes.

The architect must remember to add the paging buffer memory required by Express Server to these figures. It is strongly recommended that the sizing of this requirement should be reviewed in partnership with the implementation team to ensure that assumptions made are correct. An exacting methodology can be employed to define memory paging requirements precisely, but the calculations are highly dependent on knowing the number of dimensions, dimension members, data attributes, specifics of models etc.

Disk

At date of writing, the recommendation for Oracle Financial Analyzer disk space is to multiply the total file requirement (summation of system and user databases, see Section 5.6.1 for descriptions of Oracle Express Server file systems) by 2.5 to allow for maintenance and growth during user access. As the scale of Oracle Financial Analyzer deployments increases, this metric is onerous because it implies infrequent use of a large proportion of the disk space. Experience with version 6.3 of Express may reduce this figure.

The underlying disk architecture must also be considered. Oracle suggest that RAID10 (RAID0 + RAID1, e.g. mirrored stripes) provides the optimal balance between speed and resilience. Ideally the disk array should include a self-recovering hot disk utility; this allows the hardware to handle recovery of media in the event of a disk failure without requiring the application to be halted. For performance, all server disks must be SCSI; however, fibre channel SAN (Storage Area Network) technology provides much greater transfer rates and is becoming increasingly more cost-effective.

Similar to many DBMS packages, RAID5 can cause performance bottlenecks for disk-intensive applications and should therefore be avoided.

Other issues

Enterprise-scale deployments may demand hundreds of concurrent user connections. It is therefore advisable to consider what type of network adaptor is appropriate. In certain circumstances fibre connections may be required, or additional adaptors in case of failure.

In high availability environments, it may be necessary to specify backup power systems. This precaution is only required if the hosting data centre does not make provision for this risk.

Hardware vendors will be able to advise on specific options.

Performance tuning

Oracle Express Server is a highly tunable data server. Tangible performance improvements can be recognized with only simple tuning (i.e. less than five parameters).

Oracle provides documentation with the installation CD, in addition to several practice-based white papers. It is important to remember that a large number of installations are not optimally tuned and it must never be assumed that the default installation-tuning configuration is appropriate to the application.

Unfortunately, tuning is a heuristic task:

- Define the tuning profile – select whether the tuning configuration should be biased to general performance, improving complex models, loading external data sources etc.

- Define a baseline – select a task and benchmark the time to complete. Take steps to ensure that the result is not influenced by background processes or users.

- Alter the tuning profile and repeat.

After several iterations, the most influential parameters will become apparent. Tuning should ideally be performed prior to deployment and periodically checked. Always define the tuning objective (e.g. 10 per cent reduction) prior to commencing the exercise; it is very easy to become trapped in a tuning cycle. Note: the behaviour of parameters may not be consistent across all supported operating system platforms.

Simulating application signatures

An extremely useful and little-known utility of Oracle Express Server is the test engine facility. Test engine is designed to simulate user activity. Test engine uses standard Express SPL scripts to define the workload; for example, attach a Personal and Shared Database, open a report, change the status, perform a what-if calculation etc. If the server is started and the test engine parameter is specified with an integer, the server will run the script simulating that number of users. When defining test scripts, remember to add some degree of dynamic randomness, otherwise the exercise will demonstrate only the effectiveness of database caching when 600 users serially read the same data.

Test engine can be used prior to deployment to ensure that:

- the hardware is correctly sized;
- the configuration tuning strategy is optimum;
- the database design performs well.

Defining administration procedures

- User account administration
- System account password management
- Database file system permissions

5.6.5 Summary

The purpose of this section was to make the reader aware of the complex and interdependent relationships involved in implementing Oracle Financial Analyzer systems.

The continuous theme has been to deliver application architectures that are both performant and flexible, where performance is defined within defined user response levels and must be flexible enough to accommodate future change in terms of user growth or infrastructure change.

The purpose of the framework methodology is to structure analysis and quantification of the logical business process and physical enterprise infrastructure. The reader is reminded once more that the approach is not prescriptive. The deliverables of the framework should be:

- a clear understanding of the logical business process;

- quantification of the application load that the logical process will generate;

- an appropriately detailed understanding of existing infrastructure capability;

- final physical architecture design;

- identification of existing infrastructure to be upgraded.

An important element of the framework is the involvement of specialist skills throughout the process.

Finally, the result should be a clear technical specification of necessary hardware. It is important that this is recognized as a deliverable, but that the knowledge influencing the design is the key factor to success.

<table>
<tr><td>5.7</td><td></td></tr>
</table>

DOCUMENTATION

Chapter 5 is about the common project principles which characterize well-executed OFA projects. This section considers documentation. All project implementation methodologies require some formality in documentation. We will describe OFA-specific documentation requirements. These complement any particular project methodology, rather than replace any part of them.

The normal justifications for documentation apply to OFA projects, for example:

- to provide 'as built' documentation;

- to enable maintenance by individuals other than just the original implementer;

- to be able to conduct impact analysis on proposed changes;

- to ease the preparation of administrator and end-user documentation, testing, and escrow documents.

Any method is designed to support good practice, rather than enforce it. For example, if there is no real commitment to performing quality management, the primary reason for quality management can become lip-service compliance, 'going through the motions', with little effect on delivered quality, despite lots of documentation.

5.7.1 What is different about OFA documentation?

Two questions occur:

1. Why is documentation important in an OFA implementation?

2. What is so different about OFA documentation that it will not automatically be captured in whichever project implementation methodology is being used for the project?

Firstly, documentation forces key decisions to be taken. It is axiomatic that what is not designed tends not to be built, or at least not built in a robust and maintainable way. In the road map to this chapter, we have argued that performance is designed in by the sequence of activities suggested by Sections 5.1 to 5.6. We must avoid leaving to the system builder any important key design decisions to be taken 'on the fly'; for example, decisions about structures or processing which might have large performance implications. Documenting such decisions ensures that they *can* be implemented; through documentation, the project plan should take care of ensuring that they *are* implemented.

Secondly, documentation of the required OFA structures and the process flows which perform calculation and aggregation is often done incrementally, particularly when prototyping and conference room pilots are being used to gain user commitment during implementation. In contrast, many project implementation methods require extensive up-front documentation. The high-level processes can still be documented in advance of the creation of detailed structures, ideally, for example, by using business process modelling software as discussed earlier.

5.7.2 Business requirement definitions supported by a more detailed functional specification document?

Whether or not there has been extensive use of prototyping, there should exist some form of high-level business requirements definition. The document need not necessarily be supported by a more detailed functional specification document; detailing the business requirements definition as work proceeds to provide 'as built' documentation has worked successfully in relatively complex projects. It is important to note, however, that the calculation and aggregation process had been defined with precision and good business process modelling had been conducted prior to commencement of the software implementation phase in such projects.

Some form of documentation for all of the steps reflected in the generic OFA process model, as in Figure 5.21, is crucial. We need to document the complete system at some level of detail, rather than just the OFA calculation and aggregation processes, which often receive a disproportionate amount of time. Consider each of the processes shown in Figure 5.21.

5.7.3 Documenting the loading process for production data

The production data will often include GL data, which is subject to standards imposed by the chart of accounts (for example, all cost centres start with 9) and to very detailed reconciliations, performed to ensure that the accounts balance and that the subsidiary ledgers agree with the general ledger. The data will have been subject to external audit and hence be an important 'one view of the truth'.

Gather data from OFA users

Reporting

Load
production — Data — Calculation
and
Aggregation

Export

data

Analysis

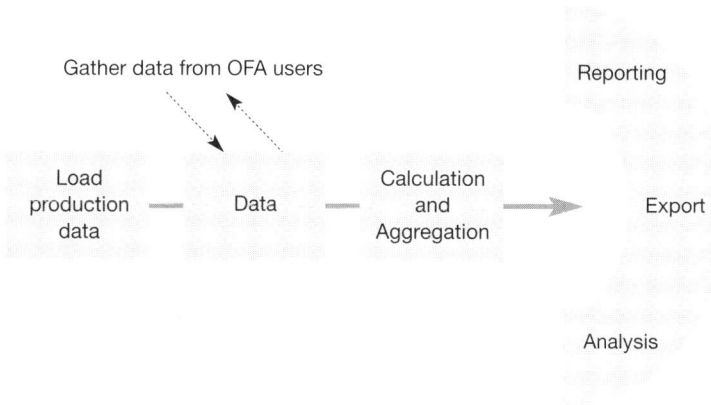

FIG 5.21 **The generic OFA process model**

The load process requires:

a) 'history' load, where the structures which order historic data must be loaded first, followed by the Actuals for the period which has closed;

b) 'operational' loads, which may be the monthly, weekly, daily or annual refresh of structures and data.

The working assumption will be that, since the data is audited, it is 'correct'. OFA often permits access to views which otherwise might be hard to achieve in a GL report writer. It is therefore not uncommon for the user to become aware of problems with the source data, and hence the project can deliver a 'quick win' by simply providing a flexible report writer on the source data to reveal such problems. However, this ease of access to different views of the data can also lead to challenges that the OFA data is not 'correct', and that the load process is suspect. Without a test data set, a disorderly situation can occur of accusation and counter-accusation regarding the effectiveness of the data load. Clearly the ability to prove that the 'historical' load and subsequent 'operational' loads have been achieved successfully is important. Hence the normal project activity of documenting a test data set for use in comparing the data loaded from the source system and obtaining sign-off for this project activity is even more important in OFA projects.

5.7.4 Documenting the processes involved in the gathering of data from people

The processes of gathering data from people have been discussed in Chapters 2 and 3, and in Section 5.2. The gathering of data is clearly a highly OFA-specific process involving possible review of data, amendment and approval. This must be distinguished from the data load and validation process of mainstream IT systems. The data gathered, particularly across a tiered architecture, involves a complex series of processes, before being merged with the data loaded from production systems.

The business processes often require activities to be performed in a particular sequence of steps as data is gathered. For example, all of the data submitters must have completed their Save Data or Submits before the Administrator kicks off Solves to perform calculations and aggregations. After review, the Administrator may need to perform a Submit to the Super Administrator, who then needs to ensure that the Task Processor is run, a Solve kicked off, and the users alerted when the Solve is finished.

Documenting the processes, perhaps by using a business process modelling package or at least by a Visio-type diagram with supporting notes, will enable clarity in designing the application architecture, as discussed in Section 5.4. Furthermore, documentation of 'who does what and when' is obviously critical to preparation of the User and Administrator Manuals, roll-out and training, as discussed later in Section 5.8.

5.7.5 Documenting the calculation and aggregation processes

Cube diagrams are used to document the calculation and aggregation processes for OFA. The cube diagram focuses on data transformation by inter-cube arithmetic, in which all of the Financial Data Items from initial data load to final reporting cube are shown along with the processes that transform them. The cube diagrams, together with text describing the structures – FDIs, dimensions, hierarchies, attributes etc. – and the processes – the inter-cube arithmetic – provide the core documentation of the required OFA Super Shared Database. Figure 5.22 shows a typical cube diagram.

Despite the relative maturity of the multidimensional database in the IT industry, no standards have been promulgated on how cube maps should be constructed. The conventions we have used to annotate the cube diagrams later in this book are as follows:

- **Data loads**: these are indicated by an arrow from a disk icon.
- **Data gathered** by Worksheet/DEF: these are denoted by a rectangle containing the relevant words.
- **Cubes:** the dimensions are named and the FDI name is included in the cube. If the FDI is a formula it is indicated by dashed lines forming the cube, as in Figure 5.23.
- **Hierarchies:** these are represented by a triangle diagram and are numbered if more than one hierarchy exists on the dimension.
- **Solves:** these are indicated by a hard line between relevant cubes and are numbered as P1 to Pn.
- **Attributes:** Attributes are simply documented in our cube maps with a numbered dashed line indicating which dimensions are related, supported by text description.

The cube maps need to be supported by narrative, discussed next.

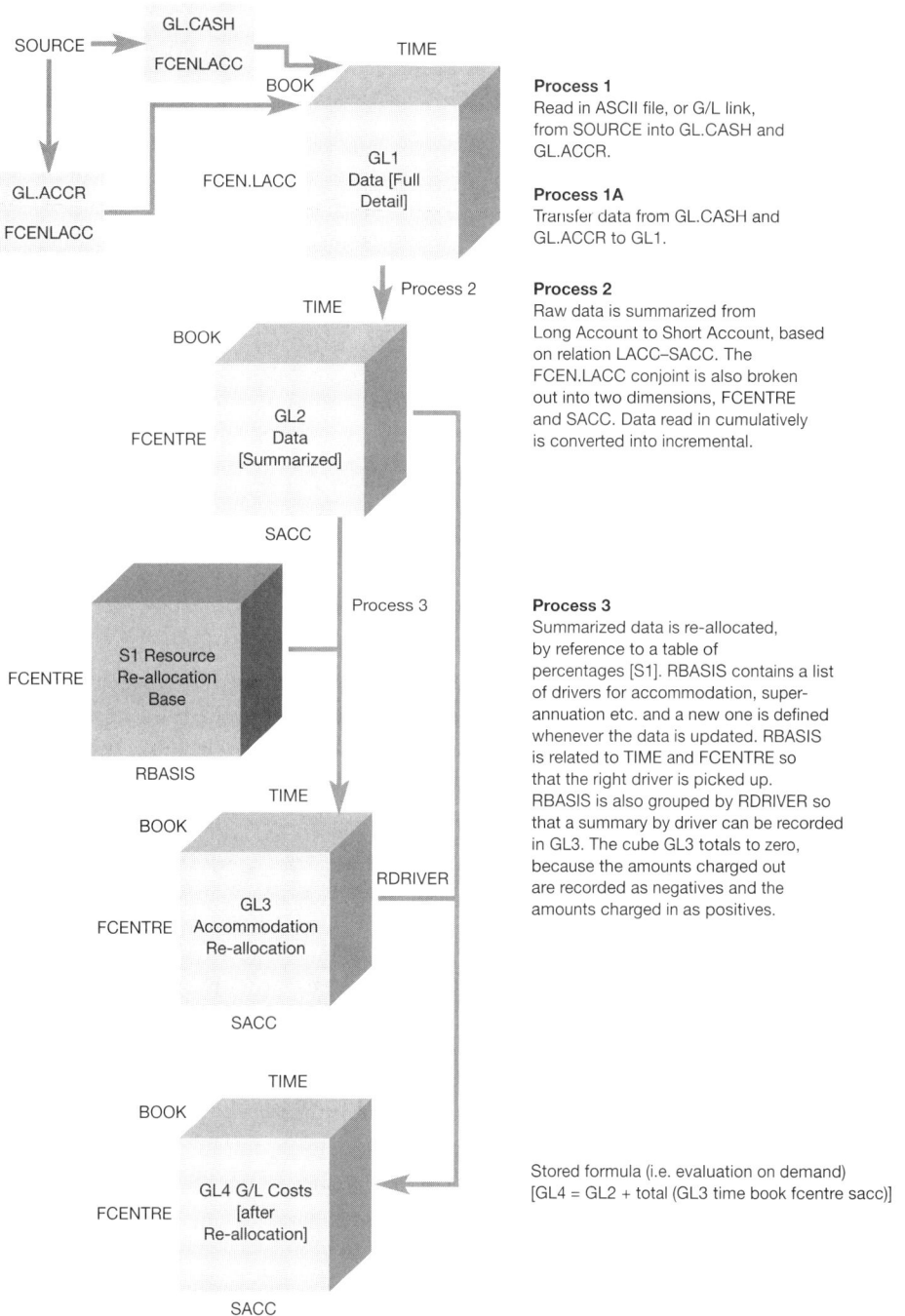

Process 1
Read in ASCII file, or G/L link, from SOURCE into GL.CASH and GL.ACCR.

Process 1A
Transfer data from GL.CASH and GL.ACCR to GL1.

Process 2
Raw data is summarized from Long Account to Short Account, based on relation LACC–SACC. The FCEN.LACC conjoint is also broken out into two dimensions, FCENTRE and SACC. Data read in cumulatively is converted into incremental.

Process 3
Summarized data is re-allocated, by reference to a table of percentages [S1]. RBASIS contains a list of drivers for accommodation, super-annuation etc. and a new one is defined whenever the data is updated. RBASIS is related to TIME and FCENTRE so that the right driver is picked up. RBASIS is also grouped by RDRIVER so that a summary by driver can be recorded in GL3. The cube GL3 totals to zero, because the amounts charged out are recorded as negatives and the amounts charged in as positives.

Stored formula (i.e. evaluation on demand)
[GL4 = GL2 + total (GL3 time book fcentre sacc)]

FIG 5.22   A typical cube diagram

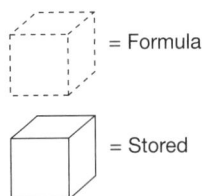

= Formula

= Stored

FIG 5.23   **Formula FDI indicated by dashed lines**

5.7.6 Narrative documentation of the OFA structures, where maintenance is done, and related matters

Table 5.10 shows the dimensions of a typical multi-tiered OFA and provides documentation under four headings:

- Maintenance: how and by whom maintenance is done;
- Scoping: by whom the scoping is undertaken and what is scoped;
- Hierarchies: which hierarchies exist, on what dimension, and how maintained;
- Attributes: which attributes exist, what is the base dimension, and how maintained.

Each of the FDIs should be supported by a narrative description, covering issues that will influence database size, such as whether the FDI is a formula or stored and whether the format will be Decimal, Short Decimal, Integer or Short Integer. It is likely that these design decisions were needed anyway for database sizing calculations, long before the system builder requires such information when using the Maintain screen as in Figure 5.24.

Dimension values and hierarchies will often be supported by a physical file, and hence the documentation can simply refer to the actual file. For example, the Account dimension will be populated from the chart of accounts from the GL, dumped as a flat file, CCACC.doc. The Accounting hierarchy can also often be saved from the GL report writer, dumped as HIER.doc.

5.7.7 Documentation of the Solves, which may include Express SPL programs

We observed in Chapter 3 that OFA can harness the underlying Express database effectively as a fourth-generation language, which can be used to build custom programs, utilizing a library containing arithmetic, mathematical, logical and statistical functions. Such functions are supportive of modelling, forecasting and simulation and are particularly important where allocation processes are involved. The system builder will create Express SPL programs when the OFA front end cannot provide the required functionality, and embed the calls to these programs in a custom Solve.

TABLE 5.10   A typical multi-tiered OFA, documenting structures and roles

Dimension code	Dimension description	Max. width	Maintainance			Scoping			Hierarchies							Attributes – base dimension									
			How?	By: Dept	By: Local	Dept	Local	End-users	FCENTRE	DCENTRE	OCENTRE	LACC	SACC	REGIME	TIME	RG.AT.SA	OC.RG.AT.SA	RGATSA.LA.PR	OC.RGATSA.LA.PR	OT.RG.AT.SA	OT.RGATSA.LA.PR	TIMESCEN	LACC	FCENTRE	RBASIS
FCEN.LACC	Centre-Account Combinations	Conjoint	1	●		●	●		○			○													
OCENTRE	Centre [Operational]	10	2		●	○	●	●			○					○		○							
OC.OT.RG.AT.SA	Output-Centre-Activity Combinations (Std)	40	3		●	○	●	●			○		○												
OC.OT.LA.PR	Output-Centre-Activity Combinations (Local)	40	4		●	○	●	●			○		○												
AT.SA	Activity-Subs	15	5	●		●	●	●																	
FCENLACC	Centre-Account Pseudo-Conjoint	30	CENTRE	●		●																			
FCENTRE	Centre [CENTRE]	10	CENTRE	●		●	●	●	■																
LACC	Account [Long]	10	CENTRE	●		●	●	●				■													
OC.RG.AT.SA	Centre-Activity Combinations	30	Conjoint		●	○	●	●			○		○												
OC.RGATSA.LA.PR	Centre-Activity Combinations [Local/Transient]	30	Conjoint		●	○	●	●			○		○												
OT.RG.AT.SA	Output-Activity Combinations (Std)	40	Conjoint	●		○	●	●																	
OT.RGATSA.LA.PR	Output-Activity Combinations (Local)	40	Conjoint		●	○	●	●																	
RG.AT.SA	Activity Combinations [Dept.-wide]	21	Conjoint	●		●	●	●					○			○	○		○						●
RGATSA.LA.PR	Activity Combinations [Local/Transient]	30	Conjoint		●	○	●	●					○						○		○				
TIMESCEN	Scenario/Time	13	Conjoint	●		●	●	●							○										
ACTTYP	Core/Non-Core	5	Fixed			●	●	●								●									
APPORTMETHOD	Trace [DCS or Consistent]	10	Fixed			●	●	●																	●
BOOK	Cash/Accruals	8	Fixed			●	●	●													●				
ACTIVITY	Activity [Main]	7	OFA	●		●	●	●								○									
UNIT	Unit	10	OFA	●		●	●																		●
DCENTRE	Centre [Departmental]	10	OFA	●		●	●				○					●									
LOACT	Local Activity	7	OFA		●	○	●	●									○		○						
LOOUT	Output [Local]	7	OFA		●	○	●	●									○		○						
OUTPUT	Output [Dept.-wide]	7	OFA	●		●	●	●												○	○				
PROJECT	Project	7	OFA		●	○	●	●									○		○						
RBASIS	Accrual Re-allocation Basis	10	OFA	●		●																			
RDRIVER	Accrual Re-allocation Driver	10	OFA	●		●	●	●																	●
REALLDRIVER	Re-allocation Driver	10	OFA	●		●	●	●								●									
REGIME	Regime	7	OFA	●		●	●	●						●		○									
SACC	Account [Short]	10	OFA	●		●	●	●					○											○	
SCENARIO	Scenario	5	OFA	●		●	●	●																○	
SUBACT	Sub-Activity	7	OFA	●		●	●	●								○									
TIME	Time	8	OFA	●		●	●	●							○									○	

Values & Definition ●   ● Maintained in OFA
Definition only ○   ○ Automatically Maintained
                ■ Maintained by Centre

1 By program CA.CENTRE
2 When FCENTRE is refreshed
3 When FCENTRE, OUTPUT or RG.AT.SA are refreshed
4 When FCENTRE is refreshed or where RGATSA.LA.PR or OT.RGATSA.LA.PR are maintained
5 After RG.AT.SA is amended

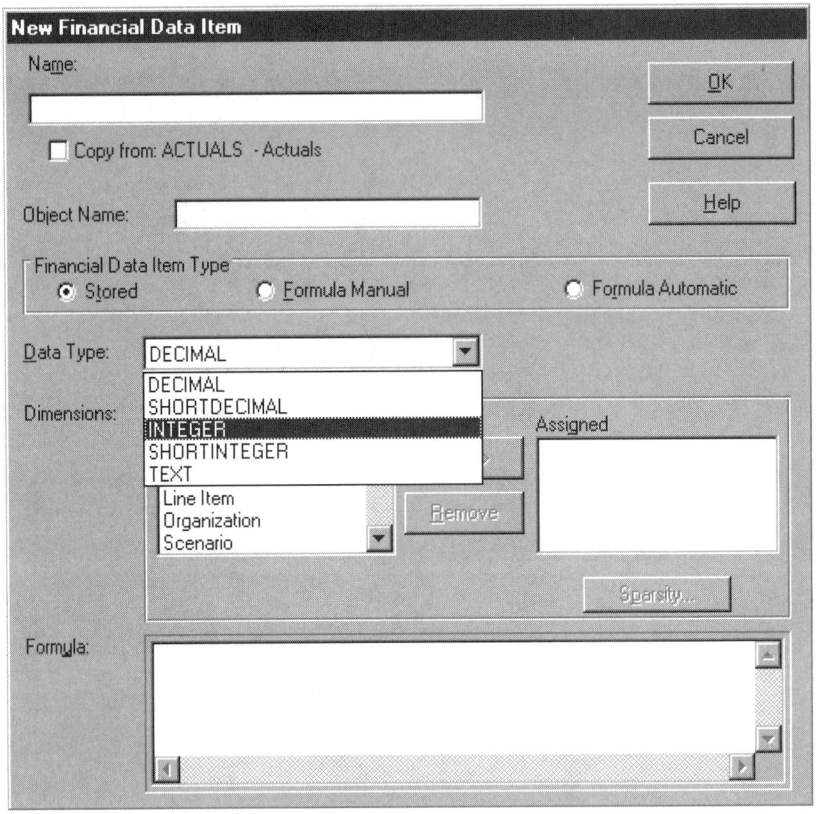

FIG 5.24   **Maintenance screen for Financial Data Items**

Each Solve (or Group Solve) is essentially a program, and hence can be defined in a form of pseudo-code, which can be given to the system builder to implement in the most efficient way he or she sees fit, as in the example below:

Create an attribute to link cost centre/account to cost pool

Create variables to carry source list of cost centre/accounts and target list of cost pools

Using these variables, limit the dimension values to the set required for calculations

For each cost pool, add up the many cost centre/accounts which relate to the cost pool.

The attribute will be created in Oracle Financial Analyzer front end

The selections for the variables will be created in Oracle Financial Analyzer front end

The limit and calculation process will be an SPL program, to be run from Oracle Financial Analyzer as a custom Solve

The programs are held in a custom Express database. For readability and maintenance, these programs should be commented within the code by the author, so that the need to further document the programs is restricted to a list describing the programs in the Technical Documentation. The format should follow programming conventions:

Header
    System Name
    Program Name
    Description/Purpose
    Creation Data
    Express Version
    Version Number
    Last Updated Date
    Arguments
    Programs Called
    Amendments History
Footer
    Error trap with error report showing program name/code/text

5.7.8 Documenting the reporting and analysis requirements

As discussed in Section 5.5, the design of the dimensionality of an OFA system is commonly influenced by the format of existing reports from formal systems such as GL or from the spreadsheet variants of these reports. Reporting requirements are met by the user exploring the dimensions of the data using the Selector, Rotate, etc., not by accessing pre-formatted fixed reports. Hence there is no need to document the reporting requirements with the precision required of fixed format reporting systems. Any particular requirements for certain reports can be achieved by marking up the existing reports as required to provide what the users would like to see in the new system.

The 'analysis' requirements may be more complex:

1. Does the user need simply to manipulate existing data by drill down, Select, Rotate etc.?

2. Or is there a need to generate new data and structures?

We have covered in Section 5.2 the need to have explicit business process modelling for the tasks performed by the user community. The business process models should provide all the documentation that is required to define what functionality is required for the analysis process.

5.8   ROLL-OUT AND CONTINUING CHANGE MANAGEMENT

We have discussed in the preceding sections a number of the 'front-end' issues, such as sponsorship and change management planning, which are as important to a successful OFA implementation as the software itself. They may be done well and on time, or late and badly. Thereafter, the software-focused activities of the design of the application architecture, database design and technical architecture may proceed to plan or slip, so impacting physical implementation of the Super Shared Database and procurement/configuration of the hardware.

The 'back-end' activities such as roll-out tend inevitably to be impacted by any issues with the preceding activities – from delay in commitment from the sponsor to failure to deliver all the designed functionality, or indeed hardware/network issues. However, until the Super Shared Database is in place and installed on the required technical architecture, the Manage menu activities of creating OFA users and then distributing structures and data cannot commence. With a tiered architecture, which requires a downward cascade of activity of creating Administrators, who then create users, the impact of delay will be more pronounced.

All of the preceding factors can impact the roll-out process. However, even if the preceding phases of activity have been done to specification and on time, an effective roll-out process is critically important for an OFA implementation.

5.8.1 Why is the roll-out process so important for OFA implementation?

We have already seen that explicit business process modelling is required if we are to fully understand 'as is' and 'to be' processes since they critically affect the application architecture, which then influences database design and infrastructure specification. For all users, be they Super Administrators, Administrators, or members of the end-user community (data submitters, planners, analysts, executives), the effect of adopting this approach should be a performant system – 'It does what I want and it does it fast enough'.

However, with a community of users as diverse as these, and the inherent complexity of the processes that OFA supports, unless their instructions and their knowledge of how the software works are adequate as the system becomes operational, we may well succeed in providing a performant system which is resisted or simply not used, on the basis that it is not 'user-friendly' because no one knows how to use it properly. We have discussed this earlier in the book, and will expand on the theme of both good and bad practice in this regard with some examples later.

5.8.2 Why is continuing change management important for OFA implementation?

Implementing OFA is about changing business processes. Change is difficult and best viewed as a transition, rather than an event. Hence the project manager should view roll-out as just a phase in continuing change management. We noted earlier the inherent dangers of using conference room pilots to verify functionality when there may be user resistance to the project's objectives. We could have a performant system, with knowledgeable users, but resistance can go on until the change process is complete.

5.8.3 Training

Generic training on OFA and Express

Generic training on OFA and Express is provided through Oracle University and is available in many media types, such as computer-based training (CBT). Public courses are run by Oracle for both end users and Administrators. The Administrator should attend an Express Fundamentals course before attending the OFA Administrator course. The Help screens for both OFA and Express are another important source of training material, as is the OFA User Manual. However, these courses must be supplemented by training which is application specific.

Training which is application specific

The typical OFA development team will be cross-functional: IT and the business, with the emphasis on IT skills in the early and middle stages. However, an OFA Super Administrator and alternate, plus any tiered architecture Sub Administrators and their alternates, should be appointed at project kick-off. OFA is a business application which should be run by the business, since very few tasks require a significant IT background during routine operations and routine maintenance. Instead it is vital that those running the system have a clear business view of the processes supported. Recall, for instance, that the Task Processor is simply a queuing device. The Administrator must be able to detect that the results of processing a Task on the Shared Database are sensible in business terms. For this reason, the Administrator role should be resourced from the business, rather than IT.

Skills transfer to the nominated Administrators (Super Administrator and alternate) must take place during the development phase so that:

- the Administrator can write the Administrator Manual and the User Manual;
- the Administrator can work with those managing the training and roll-out process from a commanding position of knowledge of how the system works.

Note: As development deadlines approach, skills transfer may take a lower priority than development, so very little time may be devoted to skills transfer. Strong project management on this issue is required.

End-user training

The 'train the trainer' concept is widely used in OFA roll-outs. By this we mean that at each location or node in a tiered architecture, the trainer trains local trainers to conduct the initial and subsequent training sessions. Users' needs will depend on how they have been classified into user groups and then mapped to OFA client types, thus:

Data submitters	(mapped to the DEF client)
Reporters	(mapped to the Web Analyst client)
Analysts	(mapped to the Budget Workstation client)

Training needs analysis for each user group can then proceed. The content is likely to cover:

- the concept of multidimensional data storage and retrieval;
- how the OFA structures meet business requirements (Dimensions, Dimension Values, Hierarchies, Attributes etc.);
- how to find the appropriate menu option in OFA;
- reach and range of the system; what data is in the system and at what depth of detail.

Users commonly find that OFA has an intuitive interface, once they understand the OFA structures. Getting them to draw cubes with the dimensionality of their environment assists in this process. A few demonstration reports are normally enough to get the users creating their own reports.

Where the application involves creating new structures and/or data, it is important to have a training environment which can be rolled back after the training is completed on each occasion. Anticipating the need for this will allow space on the server to be planned ahead of the requirement. It is important that the user gets the opportunity to consolidate knowledge by doing real work as soon as possible after being trained.

End-user feedback mechanisms

Ensuring that the trainers provide feedback from the courses is an obvious step. For Web OFA clients, clickstream analysis on log files to monitor actual interaction with the system over time would be an additional option, to track actual utilization after training and roll-out. In fact this approach can also be used in client/server mode.

5.8.4 Administrator Manual

The Administrator Manual will cover all the processes required to:

- create and scope the user community;
- load production data;

- gather data and know when the process is complete;
- perform the calculations and aggregations in the correct order;
- distribute structures and data to the scoped users for reporting and analysis;
- troubleshoot common problems, including using checklists;
- perform routine maintenance tasks, such as creating new structures in the OFA front end.

The objective of the Administrator Manual is to ensure that staff in the business are in a position to run the system and perform routine maintenance tasks. What is routine maintenance? One way of determining if the task is non-routine is to ask whether or not the task would require full system testing before use. When system enhancements are necessary, requiring non-routine maintenance, such as modifications to custom Express SPL programs, these will be conducted with a normal software development life cycle, including a formal system testing phase.

5.8.5 Technical documentation

Technical documentation will commence with the documents specified in Section 5.7, which focus on the design phase of a project – the 'to be' system:

- requirements document;
- prototype;
- business process models, possibly software-supported with documentation referenced from the process maps;
- cube maps;
- narrative supporting OFA structures in cube maps.

Technical documentation at roll-out stage should reflect the 'as built' system. For instance, the documents specified in Section 5.7 will need to be amended to reflect what was built and to cover the technical infrastructure on which the OFA implementation has been delivered. Documentation of the server and client hardware, as well as the network topology, is required. If the performance and reliability of the platform become an issue, a first port of call may be to check if it has been poorly configured. The troubleshooter should be able to quickly understand the particular choice made of operating systems/servers etc. to establish with Support whether OFA performs in a similar way on equivalent platforms at other sites. Other useful inputs to the technical documentation will be the test scripts used to test that the system is robust and mathematically correct, since these can be amended when system changes are made.

5.8.6 Use of Oracle Support Services

Oracle Support Services run a 24-hour service seven days a week on a global basis. They can provide support during roll-out and subsequently. Support can provide technical advice to the Administrator, who can log a Technical Assistance Request when the problem cannot be resolved immediately. However, since OFA is an application development framework, Oracle Support cannot be about the specific business process as implemented in OFA, or indeed any custom Express SPL programs which have been implemented. It is therefore important to set up a central support desk in-house to answer questions for the users. Where many custom Express SPL programs have been implemented, Oracle can provide a bespoke support service.

5.8.7 Roll-outs and pilots

Typically, any issues will be anticipated before the full roll-out process by running a pilot to:

1. test the effectiveness of the install and commission activity;
2. test the clarity of the operational instructions as set out in the Administrator Manual;
3. test the effectiveness of the training activity, materials and User Manual;
4. prove that the system is performant;
5. provide feedback as to the need for action on 1, 2, 3 and 4; and
6. alert management to any serious expectation gaps in functionality which have arisen because of the natural delay between requirement analysis and implementation.

We now consider two cases to bring the issues into sharper focus.

5.8.8 Case 1: Flat architecture, no data gathering, reporting application

The system concerned provided the real cost, on an activity basis, of providing over 500 intangible products in the financial services sector, in eight regions, through different outlet types. The business process supported was that of pricing the products. The structure of the roll-out looked like this:

1. Workshops
2. Business process modelling
3. Software development
4. Roll-out and training

1. Workshops

Each workshop:

- provided a statement about the difficulty of arriving at the true cost of delivering products to a customer, in one of eight regions, through different outlet types;
- asked for feedback about these difficulties;
- responded by proposing solutions to the difficulties;
- presented a vision about how much better it would be if, for pricing purposes, everyone knew what was the true cost of delivering products to a customer, in one of eight regions, through different outlet types.

Note that there was no detailed reference to the software which would be employed in addressing the issues raised; this was *why* we should do it, not *how*. It was clearly seen as a change process; it was unreasonable to expect users to welcome a system which might reveal inefficiency in a highly transparent way.

2. Business process modelling

This phase included the preparation on paper of the costing model, crucial to which was the identification of activities which needed to be costed so that they could be associated with the products that consumed them. Attributes were defined for these activities as below:

Value-added/Non-value-added
Discretionary/Non-discretionary
Fixed/Variable

The source of the Actuals was an ERP, while much of the volumetrics used to allocate costs came from formal time-keeping systems.

3. Software development

The results of the preceding phases were a good specification in business terms for what was required, and a technical design was produced relatively quickly, enabling a fast start to software development. As the software development neared completion, the preparation of documentation commenced, which, as discussed in Section 5.7, required:

- Administrator manual;
- User documentation;
- Technical documentation.

4. Roll-out and training

The user groups were a Head Office-based group and also the accountants involved in the costing process in each of the eight regions. Since many of the Head Office people were in the software development team, they were already aware of end-user functionality. Hence the focus of training was on the regional accountants, of whom there were 64. This was planned to occur over an eight-week period, comprising eight 3-day courses. Eight OFA Analyst Workstations were set up in a training environment, and the Administrator distributed the required structures and data to these users.

The training materials were designed to:

a) introduce the user to multidimensional reporting by reference to their own structures;

b) encourage them to create their own reports immediately;

c) understand the reach and range of the system to pre-handle functionality gap objections.

With hindsight, training objective (c) was very important. The workshops discussed product profitability, for which there is a need for product revenues, not just product cost information. However, product revenues did not exist in the system and were not planned to exist. While the courses were well received and participants believed that they achieved their training objectives, there was considerable feedback on the fact that cost analysis, but not profitability analysis, was enabled by the system.

Review of perceived success of the roll-out relative to the complexity of the system

The example above involved a reduced OFA generic process model, in that no use was made of Worksheets to gather data, as in Figure 5.25.

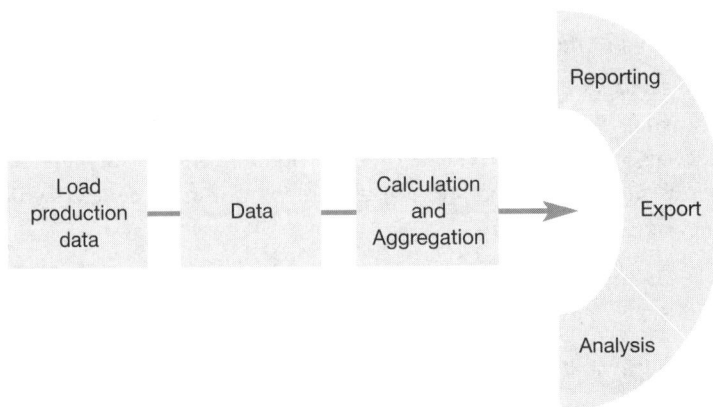

FIG 5.25   **No use made of OFA Worksheets to gather data**

The data required for allocation processes was initially captured by paper returns which were keyed into a bespoke system, written in Express. When the system is upgraded, the opportunity to replace this process with OFA Worksheets can be taken and an ultimate upgrade to OFA 11i will offer the opportunity to migrate to the Data Entry Form, with potentially much greater ease of deployment. However, in the interim, the consequence of leaving some data capture outside the OFA system boundary means that control via the Task Processor is lost. The cost of such manual processes will continue to be borne in the interim period, and there may be no way of assessing this cost.

There was no complexity introduced by data gathering in this example and no distributed architecture, simply Analyst Workstations on a single Super Shared Database.

At the other end of the spectrum, we now consider an implementation consisting of a tiered architecture with four layers of Administrator users and ultimately over 400 end users.

5.8.9 Case 2: Tiered architecture, data gathering using OFA, a planning, budgeting and reporting application

The business was again in financial services, but this time there was a tiered architecture with four layers and gathering of data from people. A number of issues had emerged after roll-out which can be classified into **functionality** and **performance**. It was therefore decided that they should be addressed under the following headings:

- Database design review
- Application architecture review
- Performance review, possibly involving simulation of concurrent usage and volume testing
- Performance tuning
- Knowledge transfer to users

The four layers of user clearly had presented challenges in ensuring an orderly flow of structures and data downwards and of data upwards. It was acknowledged that not enough hands-on training when the system went to production had been a factor. One approach would be to repeat the training process, another to reduce the number of tiers and leave the lower layers in spreadsheet mode. To regain project momentum, it was decided that reduction in the complexity by removing some of the tiers, namely 3 and 4, was the best option. The perceived benefits were not just confined to reduced complexity, since other issues had to be dealt with, namely:

- reduced space requirements;
- faster roll-up time.

The consequences of regressing to a different application architecture are non-trivial. There are two possible approaches:

- Option 1: Delete all layer 3 and 4 users, re-creating users at layer 2.
- Option 2: Delete all DBAs at the layer 1 level below the Super Shared Database, re-creating users at layer 2 level.

Either option requires that data is submitted back up to the Super Shared Database, Solves run to consolidate the data and a backup taken. The users need then to be created at the layer 2 level, whereafter the process involves:

- redistribution of structures and data;
- re-creating personal database structures;
- amending user status in the operating system;
- testing the new architecture;
- re-training the users.

The consequences of :

1. not addressing training needs, and
2. not benchmarking performance for a large user community

are obvious. Roll-out and continuing change management are clearly non-trivial issues.

5.9 BACKUPS, DATABASE REORGANIZATIONS AND DATA ARCHIVING

ROAD MAP

This section deals with the backup procedures required for an OFA installation. It identifies some of the common causes of corruption in Express databases, and how the database can subsequently be recovered. Secondly, it covers how to reorganize an OFA database to maximize its efficiency. Finally, it offers some ideas for archiving historic data that is no longer needed in the live OFA installation.

5.9.1 Files to back up

Backups of all the data databases should be performed on a regular basis, ideally every night if a backup window exists.

In OFA6.3 and 11i the essential files to be backed up are those containing moving data. These files will be the following:

⬚ all databases in the Super Shared directory;

⬚ all databases in any Sub Shared directories;

⬚ all user Personal Databases, including the SuperDBA and any SubDBA databases.

Other files, such as the OFA code databases in the code subdirectory, need to be backed up only once as they do not change after installation. They can be recovered from other sources if necessary, such as the OFA CD (don't forget to re-apply any OFA patches if you use this recovery method). These files, however, are not very big. The simplest solution is to back up the whole OFA file structure each night.

5.9.2 Stopping Express

The Express instance used to run the OFA application should be stopped whilst the backup is performed. This ensures that no users, including the Task Processor, are accessing the system during the backup. If the database is inadvertently updated during the backup, the backup is invalidated.

Stopping Express every day has the added benefit of removing any hung users and clearing the memory page buffer. Express will generally perform more quickly and reliably if it is stopped and restarted on a regular basis.

To stop an Express instance using a script, before a backup is taken, the 'oesmgr' function can be used. This is found in different locations depending on your operating system. For a UNIX installation it can be found in the OLAP_HOME/bin directory. For an NT OFA 6.3 installation it is in the OLAP_HOME/oes630/tools directory. The script will be something like this:

```
OLAP_HOME/bin/oesmgr stop Instancename
```

where Instancename is the name of the Express instance (e.g ExpSrv630). The exact name can be found in Instance Manager. This script will, by default, time out after 120 seconds if it has not successfully completed, leaving the Express instance still running. To extend this timeout limit you must use an additional parameter in the script:

```
OLAP_HOME/bin/oesmgr -t 600 stop Instancename
```

where 600 is the number of seconds before timeout. A timeout parameter of –1 will disable timeout altogether.

In a UNIX installation the library path must include the ORACLE_HOME/lib directory before oesmgr will function. The *Oracle Express Server Installation and Configuration Guide* gives more details on the components of oesmgr.

Again on a UNIX platform, stopping the instance using oesmgr may not always be successful. It sometimes times out before completing, even with a long timeout parameter setting. (For this reason it is not a good idea to use the –1 timeout parameter.) If this happens, Express will still be running when the script finishes. Oracle often recommend stopping the Express service entirely before performing the backup. Runing the following UNIX script with root access will do this:

OLAP_HOME/bin/express stop

This is sometimes not an option if there is more than one instance on the box with different backup windows. Stopping the entire service will stop all Express instances. However, even this is not always successful in removing all Express processes. A rogue instance is possible, so the backup script should take the precaution of looking for, and killing, any remaining Express processes after the 'express stop' command has been issued and finished. If a rogue process does exist, the instance concerned will not restart. A port number error stating that the RO Listen Port is already in use may appear.

5.9.3 Task Processor running in background mode

We have said that Express should be stopped before the backup commences, and restarted when it has completed, ready for the users in the morning. On restarting Express, if the Task Processor was running in background mode when Express was stopped, it will automatically restart in background mode. This feature can be used to schedule significant overnight processing after the backup has finished. If the time required for the overnight processing is uncertain, we do not want to begin the task before the backup commences because if the process has not completed before the allotted backup time, Express will stop as part of the backup initialization procedure, killing the current task. A better strategy might be to:

- schedule the backup as early as possible in the evening, after working hours;
- use the OFA Task Processor scheduling facilities to schedule the OFA task for a time after the scheduled backup start time;
- run the Task Processor in background mode;
- when Express restarts after the backup has completed, the Task Processor will restart (again in the background) and begin processing the scheduled tasks. These tasks will then run uninterrupted until completion.

5.9.4 Providing a 24-hour service

If there is not a sufficient time window to perform a backup every day, for example when the system needs to be available to the users 24 hours a day, then an alternative method of performing a backup is to use Express itself to export a copy of the database. This uses the EXPORT Express function. Express can export the Shared Database, attached in read-only mode, whilst the users continue to use and update the database (via the Task Processor). The export is usually slower than a traditional backup to tape because Express reorganizes the data on export. This produces a clean eif file, which imports quickly. It can therefore take several hours if the database is large, especially if the export process is competing for CPU and memory resources with other OFA tasks.

The restore of the database using the eif file method is slightly more complicated than a restore of the database file from tape. The database must be re-created and the eif file imported and updated using the Express command line. It is advisable at least to create an Express script to do this, so that it can be performed by anyone with access to adequate documentation.

A more efficient eif file backup method, in terms of the time taken to perform the export, would be to export only the minimum data needed to rebuild the database. This would typically be just the data at base levels in all of the dimension hierarchies. The obvious disadvantage of this method is the effort and time involved in rebuilding the database during a restore. It not only has to be imported, but also re-aggregated before the database is fully restored. See Section 5.9.8 on reorganisation of the database for techniques for exporting and importing databases. The eif files created by this method of backup should be moved off the server immediately, and off-site regularly, as you would do with a normal backup tape.

It is advisable to perform a traditional backup whenever possible. The performance benefits Express receives when stopped and restarted should also not be overlooked when a 24-hour service is being provided. If it is not included in the backup procedures, it is advisable to try to impose 20 minutes of downtime per day to stop and restart Express.

5.9.5 Corruption of Express databases

Express databases are not immune from data corruption. They can, in exceptional circumstances, become unreadable after apparently normal data processing.

DATABASE VALIDATE is an Express command that will examine a database for page allocation errors. It returns a list of pages that are allocated more than once, pages that are actually in use but not marked as allocated, and allocated pages that are not actually in use. It will return nothing if there are no paging errors. The database must be attached read/write, and the command should be run immediately after attaching the database, before any other operation, otherwise it is unreliable.

If DATABASE VALIDATE indicates that there are pages that are allocated more than once, this means that more than one logical record in the database is mapped to the same physical page, i.e. a corruption in the database. The database may export and import successfully, and if possible this is the best course of action. If a restore is required, steps should be taken to ensure that the restored database does not suffer from the same terminal condition.

If DATABASE VALIDATE indicates that there are pages that are actually in use but not marked as allocated, the potential for allocating pages more than once exists in the database. When a page is not marked as allocated although already in use, Express may allocate the page again. Because of this potential situation, it is advisable to export and import the database as soon as possible before the database actually corrupts.

If DATABASE VALIDATE indicates that there are allocated pages that are not actually in use, then these pages are simply wasted space. This can be corrected by exporting and importing the database, but there is no imminent danger of corruption.

In some circumstances the corruption may be isolated to a single object in the database. The database can possibly be recovered, without recourse to a backup, by deleting and redefining the affected object. This type of corruption becomes apparent because the Express session crashes when the object is referenced by OFA. An export of the database to an eif file will also fail when it tries to export the affected object. It may not even be possible to describe the object at the Express command line, although this is not always the case. To use the eif method to identify which object is corrupt it is necessary to export the database one object at a time, i.e. looping over the name dimension and exporting each object in turn, in an Express custom program. Text variables are particularly susceptible to corruption, so these should be checked first. See Section 5.9.6 below for a possible remedy to the problem. The data contained in a corrupt variable is of course lost with the deletion and redefinition of the object, so if it is a large data item that cannot easily be reproduced, reverting to a backup copy may be the only way of recovering the lost data. Redefining the object is therefore only an option if it is small or contains static data that can be reloaded or re-entered.

In some cases it is not the whole object that is corrupted, but only a sector of its data. This is typically a result of a physical disk corruption, and an integrity check on the disks used by the database should be part of the recovery procedure. Some of the data in the corrupt data item can be recovered by exporting the data item, with the status of its dimensions appropriately set to exclude the corrupt section. Unfortunately this corrupt section can only be identified on a trial and error basis. If it is time-series data, try exporting one time period at a time, with the other dimensions limited to all values. This can be a time-consuming process, but with a high chance of retrieving most of the data from the object. A restore of a backup copy of the database may still be necessary to recover the lost segment, but the retrieved data, in eif format, can be imported over the restored data, to bring the database back to a near pre-corruption state.

5.9.6 Corrupt text variables

Text Financial Data Items are prone to corruption in some versions of Express Server. Once identified, they can usually be deleted and redefined, as they typically hold static data that can easily be reproduced. To protect text variables from corruption they can be redefined with the OWNSPACE parameter. OWNSPACE specifies that the data will be stored in one or more private page spaces that are associated with the variable rather than in the database's global page space. OFA does not provide any front-end means of defining objects in this way. It must therefore be done at the Express command line in the following way:

Suppose we have defined a new text in the OFA Administrator GUI, called PRODUCT.TEXT, dimensioned by the PRODUCT and TIME dimensions. If we describe this object in Express Monitor, its definition will be

```
PRODUCT.TEXT TEXT <PRODUCT TIME>
```

Before this object is distributed to the Shared Database, go to Express Monitor in the DBA and type the following:

```
Delete product.text

Define product.text variable text <product time> ownspace
```

The object has been redefined and can now be distributed in the normal way.

5.9.7 Restoring databases from backup

Because of the tiered architecture options offered by OFA, the restore of a corrupt database will need to be considered in light of its relationship with other databases in the tiered architecture. If a single database is restored from a backup copy it may not integrate smoothly into the whole, because of changes made to the system since the backup was made.

The implications of these selective restores on the different OFA databases are summarized in Table 5.11.

The actions required to bring the restored database back into alignment with the rest of the system are summarized in Table 5.12.

5.9.8 Reorganization of the database

Why is a reorganization needed?

As structures are incrementally added to and deleted from a database, the internal storage becomes increasing fragmented. New dimension values are necessarily added to the end of the internal organization, not in their most logical position. Deleted dimension values continue to exist within the internal organization. In short, the physical storage diverges more and more from the logical storage. As the data within these structures is recalculated and re-aggregated, it expands the file size of the database to create temporary storage space. An export and import of the database will remove fragmentation and unused space from the database, making it meaner and leaner. The database will, to some degree, certainly perform quicker and use less disk space after a reorganization. The improvement will depend on the nature of the data in the database, and how often the reorganization is performed.

TABLE 5.11   The implications of selective restores on the different OFA databases of a typical multi-tiered OFA implementation

	Distribute structures	Distribute data	Submission	Refresh
DBA Personal Database	Structural changes are lost. UADs are behind the Shared Database.	Data is 'lost' from the Personal db, but Shared Database has a copy.	In workstation mode, may have lost some of the audit trail supporting a submission to a Shared db. In administrator mode, no direct effect.	In workstation mode, refreshed data lost. In administrator mode, no direct effect.
Shared Database	UADs are behind the DBA's Personal Database. Subordinates may have already refreshed structures, and will be ahead of the Shared Database	Record of who should receive data is lost. Data itself may or may not be lost.	Sub Shared may have lost some of the audit trail supporting a submission to a superior level.	Shared data is lost, but can be refreshed.
Task Processor Database [tasks waiting at time of failure]	Tasks are lost. Orphaned files left in Task Queue.	Tasks are lost. Orphaned files left in Task Queue.	Tasks are lost. Orphaned files left in Task Queue.	Not applicable
Task Processor Database [no tasks waiting at time of failure]	Task log is lost. Record of who has what distributions is lost.	Task log is lost. Record of who has what distributions is lost.	Task log is lost.	Not applicable
Budget Workstation Database	Personal data and reports are lost. Refreshes of structure also lost.	Personal data lost.	May have lost some of the audit trail supporting a submission to a Shared db.	Data is lost, but can be refreshed.
Analyst Workstation Database	Personal reports are lost. Refreshes of structure also lost.	Not applicable	Not applicable	Not applicable

(reproduced courtesy of Matthew Shaw)

How often is it needed?

Shared databases cannot be reorganized too often. The process may take several hours to execute, so the window of opportunity will dictate the frequency of its execution. Because the database is completely rebuilt, obviously there can be no users accessing the system, at least during the rebuilding (import) process. Neither can the database be updated at any stage. Within these constraints, for each Shared Database we recommend that it is reorganized as frequently as possible.

The DBA and SubDBA personal databases also become disorganized over time. Whilst there is not normally any significant data within these databases, the

TABLE 5.12   The recovery activities required on the different OFA databases of a typical multi-tiered OFA implementation

	Distribute structures	Distribute data	Submission	Refresh
DBA Personal Database	Structural changes re-created and redistributed. Users will have to be discarded and re-created.	Data can be refreshed from Shared db back to Personal db.	In workstation mode, results may be refreshed back from Shared db, but supporting data may have to be re-created. In administrator mode, no action required.	In workstation mode results may be refreshed again from Shared db. In administrator mode no action required.
Shared Database	DBA repeats distributions, based on task log.	Data may need to be re-created. Data distributions will have to be re-created by DBA.	Results may be refreshed back from superior db. Sub Shared may need to re-create supporting audit trail by getting its satellites to resubmit.	Results may be refreshed again from superior db.
Task Processor Database [tasks waiting at time of failure]	DBA must redistribute structures. Orphaned files should be deleted from Task Queue – not urgent.	DBA must redistribute data. Orphaned files should be deleted from Task Queue – not urgent.	Users must resubmit. Orphaned files should be deleted from Task Queue – some files may be large, so this should be done promptly.	Not applicable
Task Processor Database [no tasks waiting at time of failure]	Tasl log is not recoverable. Users will automatically receive some distributions they have already had.	Task log is not recoverable. No other effect.	Task log is not recoverable. No other effect.	Not applicable
Budget Workstation Database	Personal data must be rekeyed and reports redone. Lost distributions must be re-sent by DBA (or the TK.L.DIST.R flag in the Task Processor can be manually rolled back at the Express command line).	Data must be redistributed by DBA.	Results may be refreshed from Shared db, but supporting data may have to be re-created.	Results may be refreshed again from Shared db.
Analyst Workstation Database	Personal reports must be redone. Lost distributions must be re-sent by DBA (or the TK.L.DIST.R flag in the Task Processor can be manually rolled back at the Express command line).	Not applicable	Not applicable	Not applicable

(reproduced courtesy of Matthew Shaw)

structures are constantly being amended. A reorganization is not required so frequently, but a noticeable performance improvement within the DBA can be achieved with a regular reorganization of this database. The same argument applies to Budget Workstations.

Why is it missing from OFA?

It does seem strange that such an essential administrative task to maintain an efficient database is not included as part of the OFA DBA functionality. At the time of writing, there are no known plans to include it, so each installation must decide how best to tackle the problem for themselves. See Sections 5.9.9 and 5.9.10 below for some ideas for your system.

5.9.9 Export techniques

The export and import functionality is all within the Express SPL. The SPL must therefore be used, either manually at the command line or through a custom program, to execute the reorganization. The manual option, in its simplest form, is the following;

1. All users should be off the system, and the Task Processor turned off.

2. Attach the Shared Database.

    Export all to eif file '../../ofas.eif'

3. Detach the Shared Database.

4. Create a new database.

    Import all from eif file '../../ofas.eif'

    Update

5. Rename the old Shared Database, and replace it with the new database.

The logic above can be included in an Express program. Some controls need to be included to pick up failures at each significant point, so now we need to know the Express SPL syntax well. Other subtleties that can be incorporated into the program are:

- Check that there are no users on the system.

- Disable the Task Processor.

- Compress the old database after exporting it to release disk space for the rebuild.

- Split the export into several files to improve performance.

It is the export routine that does most of the reorganizational work on the structures. A large OFA Shared Database typically takes three or four times longer to export than it does to subsequently import. There is some scope to influence how long the export takes by splitting the structures into separate export files. The relationship between the size of individual Financial Data Items in the database and the amount of memory on your machine that Express can use will dramatically affect the performance of the export routine. When exporting, Express will need to read the whole data item into the memory buffer (this is the PageBufferCount setting in the Express DatabasePagingManagement configuration – see the help facility in Oracle Express Instance Manager for more details of this setting). If the data item is bigger than the memory buffer available, Express will have to page the data, which will reduce the performance of the export. The bigger the differential, the worse the performance will be. Exporting large data items separately from the rest of the database will make efficient use of the available memory buffer. Splitting the cube into more memory-friendly chunks, e.g. looping over the time dimension, may increase performance further.

To determine the size of individual data items within the Shared Database, use the Express OBJ function in the following way from the Express command line:

    Show obj(disksize 'FDI')

where FDI is the object name of a stored Financial Data Item.

This returns the total number of pages used by the data item. Multiply it by the page size (4 for a 32-bit installation, 8 for a 64-bit installation) to calculate the number of bytes, e.g.

    Show obj(disksize 'ACTUALS') * 4/1000

This returns the size of the ACTUALS data item in Mbytes, on an NT platform.

To a certain extent there is a trial and error element to the performance improvement. You will need to test your particular database using different techniques to achieve the most efficient performance.

One point to remember when rebuilding your database is that any SEGWIDTH changes you have made to your Financial Data Items will be lost. The resetting of SEGWIDTH should be included in the IMPORT routine. See the Oracle Technical Note 'Optimizing Oracle Financial Analyzer: Performance and Architecture' for more information on SEGWIDTH in an OFA context.

5.9.10 Methods of executing the reorganization program

As discussed earlier, the easiest way to perform a reorganization is simply to run it manually from the Express command line. This will require manual monitoring of the process by the DBA, which will certainly be inconvenient if the export is run every week, on a Sunday morning.

The program can be scripted to run automatically, using the 'oescmd' functionality provided by the Express installation. See the *Oracle Express Server Installation and Configuration Guide* for more details on oescmd.

A nice enhancement is to run the program through the Task Processor. This allows the DBA to schedule the routine like any other OFA task, effectively stopping the database being updated whilst the task is running. It also fits the reorganization process into the backup procedures as described in the discussion above when running the Task Processor in background mode.

To hook the program into an OFA task requires the creation of a custom task. This is described in detail in the *Application Programming Interface: Structure and Supporting Meta Data Guide* that is supplied with the OFA client CD, or on MetaLink.

5.9.11 Archiving data in OFA

A live OFA database will expand over time as more dimension values are added. Product ranges grow and change, customers come and go, and new years are added. The historic data may become less and less relevant to users. If this position is reached it may be time to remove the earliest year of data from OFA.

The reason for removing this old, infrequently used, data is to ensure that the size and thus the performance of the database are not compromised by storing unnecessary data. There may be a disk space constraint to consider, but the primary reason is likely to be aggregation and calculation times for historic data and the impact of large cubes on the performance of current data calculations.

If the old data must be retained in some form just in case it is needed in the future, we have several options available to archive this data before it is deleted from OFA.

Separate Financial Data Item

Copy the data into another Financial Data Item. This will remove it from the live data item, which may improve the performance of the live cube. The data is still immediately available in OFA so there is no disk space saving. A new archive time dimension is needed with the same values as those time values to be deleted, so that the original time dimension values can be deleted. An attribute linking the two dimensions together will allow you to use the 'Copy Data' functionality to populate the archive data item, before deleting the original data. This method is only really appropriate if the archived data is no longer going to be processed, i.e. not re-aggregated to reflect hierarchy changes. If it is going to be updated there is no benefit to be gained by moving the data.

Budget Workstation

Copy the data into a Budget Workstation, then remove it from the rest of the system. This provides single user access to the archived data through the OFA client. Multiuser access can be provided with use of the Speadsheet Add-In to interrogate the data. The Budget Workstation should be disconnected from the live system to avoid the system deletion of the dimension values removing the archived data as well.

SubDBA system

If true multi-user access to the archived data is required, the data can be moved to the Shared Database of a subDBA. The full range of client types can then access the archived data.

Eif archive

Remove the data entirely from the OFA environment by exporting it to an eif file. The data is not then readily available to the users but can be recovered quickly if it is required. Perhaps a summary level of the data could be downloaded to a spreadsheet, or some other reporting mechanism, to provide users with immediate access to all but the finest detail of the archived data.

6 Case study in the consumer packaged goods (CPG) industry

ROAD MAP

The chapter provides a detailed examination of an existing project in the CPG industry. It explains the objectives of the system, and how some of the project principles described in Chapter 5 have been applied. On the subject of database design we pick some of the fundamental issues that needed to be addressed and explain in some detail the solution that was implemented.

6.1 COMPANY OVERVIEW

The company used in this case study operates across Europe in the CPG industry. It is a subsidiary of a large multinational company, operating primarily in the same industry. The company manufactures its own products and supplies them to retailers to the general public. It maintains several well-known product brands.

The company has been using OFA for several years. The application of OFA has evolved over time from a specific requirement in the UK to a pan-European application that encompasses most of the volume and financial reporting requirements of the finance, marketing and sales departments.

6.2 THE REQUIREMENTS OF THE OFA SYSTEM

6.2.1 Summary

The basic requirement of the system is to produce product and customer profitability, for actual, budget and forecast scenarios. The P&L structure is that of a fast-moving consumer goods manufacturer, split into volumes, revenue, sales support costs (costs of supporting customers), manufacture and distribution costs, and brand support costs (costs of promoting and developing the company's brands). It looks something like this:

Volumes
> Sales Volume Cases
> Sales Volume Weight
> Consumer Units

Turnover
> Turnover 000's
> Gross Invoice Value

On-Invoice Discounts
> Order discounts
> …

Net Invoice Value

Off-Invoice discounts
> Long-term Sales agreement discounts
> …

Net Proceeds of Sale

Sales Support Costs
> Temporary Price Promotions
> Advertising
> …

Cost of Goods
> Raw Materials @ Std
> Packaging @ Std
> Variable Manufacture cost
> …

Total COGS

Other Variable Costs
> Royalties
> …

Total Variable Cost of Sales

Total Variable Costs

Marginal Contribution

Brand Support Costs
    Media
    Promotions
    Market Research
    …

Other Fixed Costs
    Fixed Manufacturing Costs
    Overheads
    Operational
    Fixed Distribution
    Marketing General Expenses
    Bad Debts
    …

Integrated Operating Profit/Loss

    Manufacture Margin Op P/L
    Variance: Manufacturer's Margin

Operating Profit/Loss

    Operational taxes

NET OPERATING PROFIT/LOSS

The P&L is the basis of most of the reporting requirements. We discuss reporting in more detail in Section 6.6 on Database design.

The lowest level of product is the stock-keeping unit (SKU), with several hierarchies aggregating into brand, product size and product format categories. Customers at the lowest level represent the delivery points of the retailers, who sell the products on to the general public. These delivery points are aggregated into retailers in one hierarchy, and into salesperson territories in a second.

The requirement exists in the 10 primary European markets of the business, with the prospect of rolling out to several secondary markets in the near future. All of the countries operate autonomously, with their own local DBAs. There is no requirement for a full consolidation of all of these markets. Only summarized product data needs to be aggregated at the group level.

How does the application fit into the generic OFA process model that we defined in Chapter 1, as in Figure 6.1?

6.2.2 Load production data

Product and customer dimension values are loaded from the sales order processing system (SOP) system. Lower levels of the hierarchies are also loaded, along with

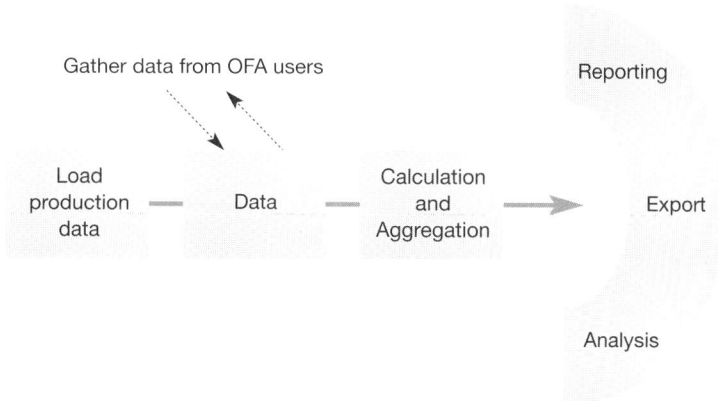

FIG 6.1   **The generic OFA process model**

product definition data, such as product weight and the number of units per case. The only fundamental data loaded from an external source is the weekly invoice data, also from the SOP system. This provides the sales volumes and on-invoice discounts offered to customers. The load is on an incremental weekly basis.

6.2.3 Gather data from OFA users

Forecast volumes are produced externally, using a manufacturing forecast package, and loaded into OFA. The rest of the P&L, in actual, budget and forecast scenarios, is gathered from OFA users or modelled in OFA directly.

6.2.4 Export to external systems

Each local OFA system is the feeder for other related systems, such as:

▪ Group Company consolidation of summary data;

▪ Head Office consolidation of summary data;

▪ volume forecasting.

The volume forecasting interface provides an example of the two-way communication between OFA and an external system. OFA feeds actual volumes to the volume forecasting application. This aids the creation of the forecast in the forecasting application, which is primarily prepared for factory planning purposes. The volume forecast is then loaded back into OFA, where the financial forecast is prepared from these volumes. Hence the actual process model looks more like Figure 6.2.

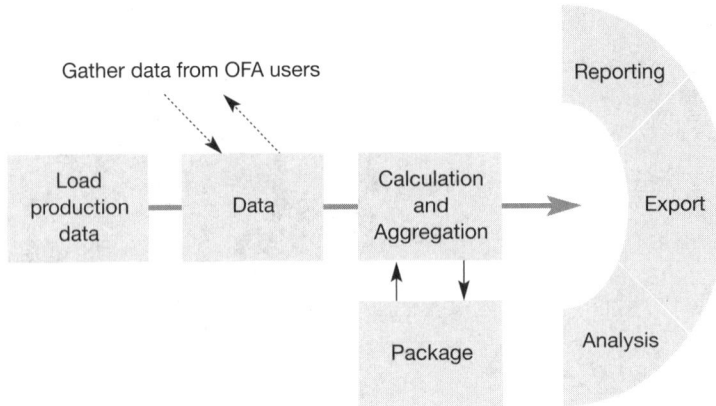

FIG 6.2 **Two-way communication between OFA and an external system**

6.3   SPONSORSHIP AND CHANGE MANAGEMENT

The project has been very much driven from Head Office in the UK. Although the application is intended primarily for local management use, and not as a feeder system to provide a central consolidation, gaining local support for the project was not easy in some countries. We discuss later in the case study the project's objective of developing a common design for all European countries using OFA for management reporting. This produces its own peculiar roll-out issues with regard to local requirements.

One European country was chosen as a pilot implementation. This then became the basis for generating a generic product that could be rolled out around the rest of Europe. There was a great deal of discussion with representatives from each country to establish the core requirements and hence design of the application. Business owners in each country were therefore made to feel fully part of the requirements gathering process. There was a degree of inflexibility in the design, because of the work done on the initial pilot project. This had established all of the fundamental principles of the design, but there was still plenty of scope for defining the working European-wide processes and procedures. There can sometimes be too much discussion on local requirements. As the finer detail of each country's procedures highlights differences at the local level, it is sometimes difficult to identify what is an essential specific local requirement and what is just an historic way of working that can be changed without disrupting the business process. A line needs to be drawn to enforce a common standard on everyone. This requires a strong directive from the management. The executive sponsor, in this case a group board member, provided the project with this. However, because all the countries have a great deal on autonomy in their own marketplace, it was necessary to have a strong local sponsor, usually the local finance director. If the local sponsor could be convinced of the long-term benefits of the solution, then the implementation went much more smoothly.

Another contributory factor to a smooth implementation was a local project manager who had the commitment and support to dedicate a significant proportion of his or her time to the detailed management of the project.

There was a lot of disruption required to implement a common solution, and care was needed from the central team not to appear inflexible to local needs. But if an exception to the established common rules is identified, it has to be for the country concerned to prove its necessity. If this is done then the exception needs to be evaluated. Should it be included in the overall design, or remain a local customization? One example of this was the complicated nature of one country's sales discount structure with its customers. The sales discounts provided to customers were far more numerous and detailed than any other country. As a result, a data capture and reporting module was developed specifically for the local requirement, outside the common product. This placated the country concerned because their requirements were met in full, but it did mean a divergence from the fundamental principle of a common OFA product for all, and the associated support implications of this.

6.4   BUSINESS PROCESS MODELLING

All of the business analysis was performed in-house. The project adopted the conference room pilot (CRP) principles, learnt from the management consultancies.

The project definition was split into four discrete sections, which reflected the implementation strategy. They were:

- Actual sales invoice data
- Actual customer profitability
- Full Actual profit statement
- Budgeting and forecasting.

For each section a 'model definition' was created by each country's project manager. A model definition is a generic definition of all the reporting lines in the application. It specifies by P&L line the following:

- Identify if the line is loaded externally, entered manually through worksheet, or calculated by a model.
- If a data entry line, then
  - Customer level of data entry (e.g. at customer group)
  - Product level of data entry (e.g. at brand level)

- Time level of data entry (e.g. monthly)
- Rate or absolute amount
- Basis of spreading, or basis of rate calculation, to base level product and customer (e.g. spread down based on tonnage, or a rate calculation based on gross sales value).

■ If calculated, then the definition of the calculation.

A model definition was necessary by country because of the detailed P&L lines unique to each country, and helped highlight special local requirements. It often involved much work by the local team, but it helped them to concentrate on the core requirements of the system, and understand the data processing in an OFA context. With this information completed, it was possible to design most of the aggregations and OFA models, and understand the data process flow.

6.5   DESIGN OF THE APPLICATION ARCHITECTURE

Because there is no requirement for a detailed consolidation of each European market at a Head Office level, the design of the OFA architecture is a flat structure. Each country has a separate installation of OFA, with their own SuperDBA (this is option 4 in the examples given in Section 5.4). Although the definitions of all of the OFA structures are common for each country, the design does not incorporate any SubDBAs. This decision was taken to keep the architecture as simple as possible. Generally, none of the fundamental structures will have common values across the countries. Customer and product values, and their hierarchies, are not common across markets, or at least only at a very high level. It is only at this high summary level, for some key P&L lines, that a central consolidation is required at the group level. This is dealt with as a separate OFA application, with an extract created from each country's local system.

The creation of any new structures required by all the countries cannot therefore simply be distributed using the OFA distribution functionality. Changes are regarded as upgrades to the application. This requires the creation of an upgrade file and upgrade procedure. This is not really an issue, because the majority of the changes resulting from an upgrade are custom programs. This would require an upgrade process whether there was a SubDBA architecture or not.

Access to the Shared Database by the users is exclusively through OFA Analyst Reporters. There is no requirement for individual users to model and consolidate data themselves in Budget Workstations. There was also a strong feeling that there should only be 'one version of the truth' – one source for the financial data. As a result, user manipulation of the data outside the main application was discouraged.

DATABASE DESIGN

6.6.1 Cube design

The P&L lines have common summary headings across all countries, although the detail within these common headings can vary. The full P&L can have over 200 lines in any single country. The level of revenue and cost detail required changes as we move up the customer hierarchy. For delivery points, at the bottom, users are only interested in sales invoice data, i.e. volumes sold, gross sales value, and any on-invoice discounts given. At the retailer level, users require a fuller P&L, but only to the level that can meaningfully be allocated to customer. At a channel level, the full P&L is appropriate.The philosophy of the cube design is of reducing customers and increasing lines (Figure 6.3).

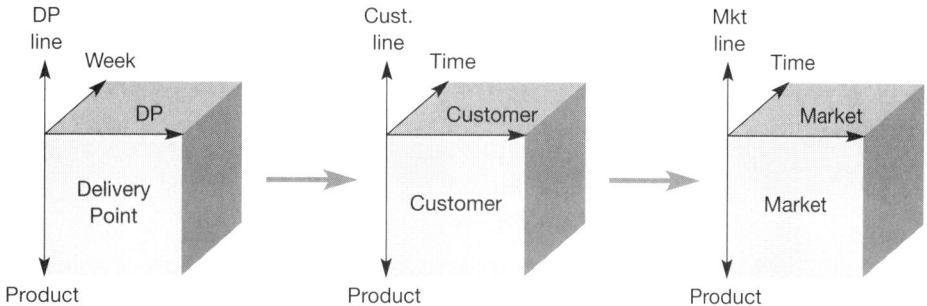

FIG 6.3   Cube detail

The Delivery Point Cube, since it is fed from invoice-level detail, has the highest level of customer detail on the DP dimension and the lowest level of detail on the Line Item dimension. This cube is the only cube that contains weekly data.

The Customer Cube has a lower detail on customers (major accounts instead of delivery points), but it has more detailed line items. The data in the Customer Cube is monthly. The Market Cube has the lowest detail on customers (channels), but the highest line detail. The data in the Market Cube is also monthly. All of the cubes are dimensioned by product.

This design controls the sparsity of the data to a certain extent, even before introducing composites. It keeps Solve times to a minimum, but it does complicate the Solve procedures. All the cubes need to be processed together, and they need to be consistent.

Each set of cube structures can be duplicated for budget and forecast scenarios, for each country. In practice nobody budgets or forecasts at delivery point level, so this cube in unnecessary. Indeed, some countries do not even require a budget at the Customer Cube level, so only a Market Cube is needed.

Adjustments

Revenue and costs are loaded into, and calculated in, the appropriate cubes. These figures may then need manual adjustment. An adjustment facility was required to store and report the adjustments separately from the calculated figures (Figure 6.4). Adjustments can be made to both the customer-based actuals and the market-based actuals. But adjustments made to the customer actuals will flow through to the market actuals.

The data entry for the adjustments is made into a text financial data item that tries to emulate a journal-type data entry screen. It also allows the user to select any level of product and customer for adjustment on a single line dimension value. The user selects the method to be used to spread this adjustment down to the lowest levels of product and customer. This spreading of the adjustment is integrated into the general spreading mechanism built into the application. This is discussed in more detail in Section 6.6.7, 'Spreading and rate calculations', a little later in the case study.

A limitation of this text worksheet is that the product, customer and line codes must be entered as codes rather than descriptions. There is no access to the Selector to allow user-friendly selection of each of these adjustment properties. Because the finance users who prepare the adjustments are familiar with the product, customer and line codes, this was an acceptable restriction.

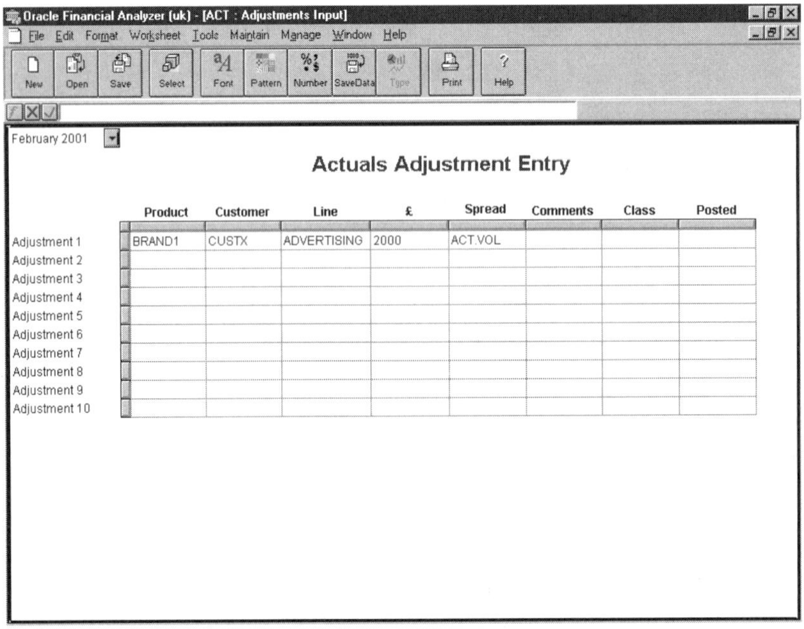

FIG 6.4   Adjustments screen

After the adjustment calculation (Figure 6.5) has been run, the Adjustment Entry screen will show the status of each adjustment in the 'Posted' column, indicating that the entry has been added to the appropriate adjustment cube, or reasons for its failure to do so.

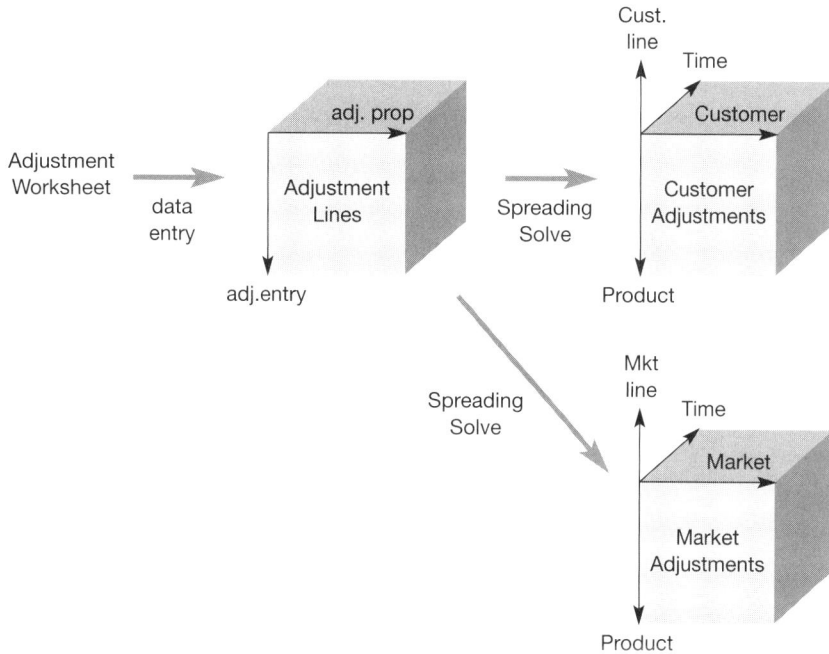

FIG 6.5   Adjustments calculation

A reporting formula adds the unadjusted and adjustment cubes together to get the adjusted figures (Figure 6.6).

Cube summary

We therefore have stored data in data entry cubes, we have resulting cost cubes, adjustment cubes... . Diagramatically, it looks as shown in Figure 6.7. The reporting cubes then reference these stored cubes for the appropriate scenarios.

6.6.2 Configuration catalogs

In Section 3.1, we discussed how two-dimensional Express cubes called catalogs are populated during implementation, mostly through the OFA 'front end', to reflect the specific features of the implementation. Just like OFA itself, configuration catalogs are used extensively in the application. The design mirrors the techniques

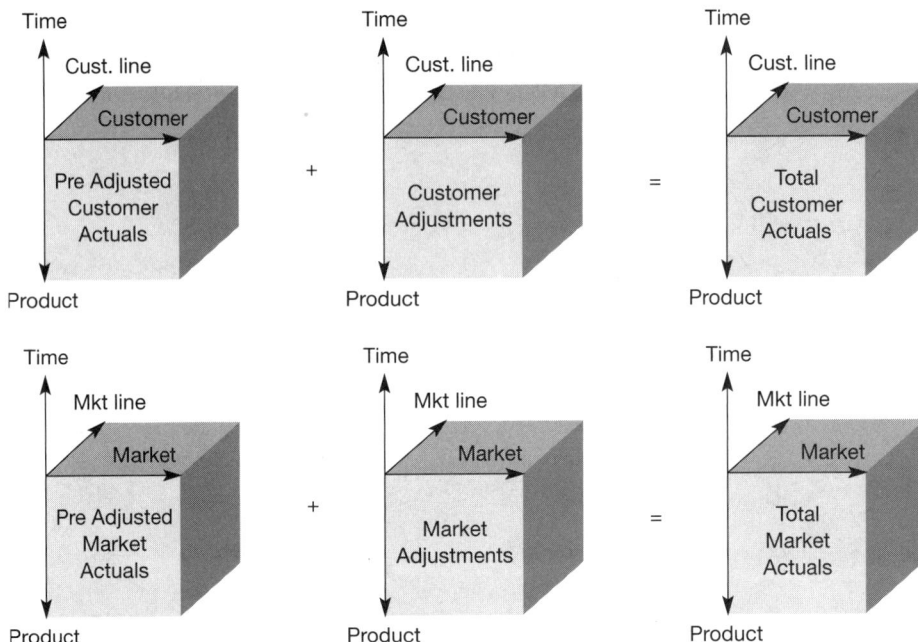

FIG 6.6   **A reporting formula adds the unadjusted and adjustment cubes together to get the adjusted figures**

used by the standard OFA code. The catalogs are used to record file and structural information that may change from market to market. All customized programs refer to the relevant catalog entries rather than hard-coding the value within the programs. The use of catalogs offers system flexibility and easier roll-out of the central application:

- *Flexibility*: Any change required to the values within a catalog will need to be changed in one place only. All references to the catalog value are automatically updated.

- *Easier roll-out*: Implementing the application in a new market requires no custom program review, only the configuration of the catalogs.

The catalogs themselves are just one-dimensional text financial data items, maintained in the DBA user, and distributed to the Shared Database only. The application has two major catalogs, recording interface file information and OFA structural values.

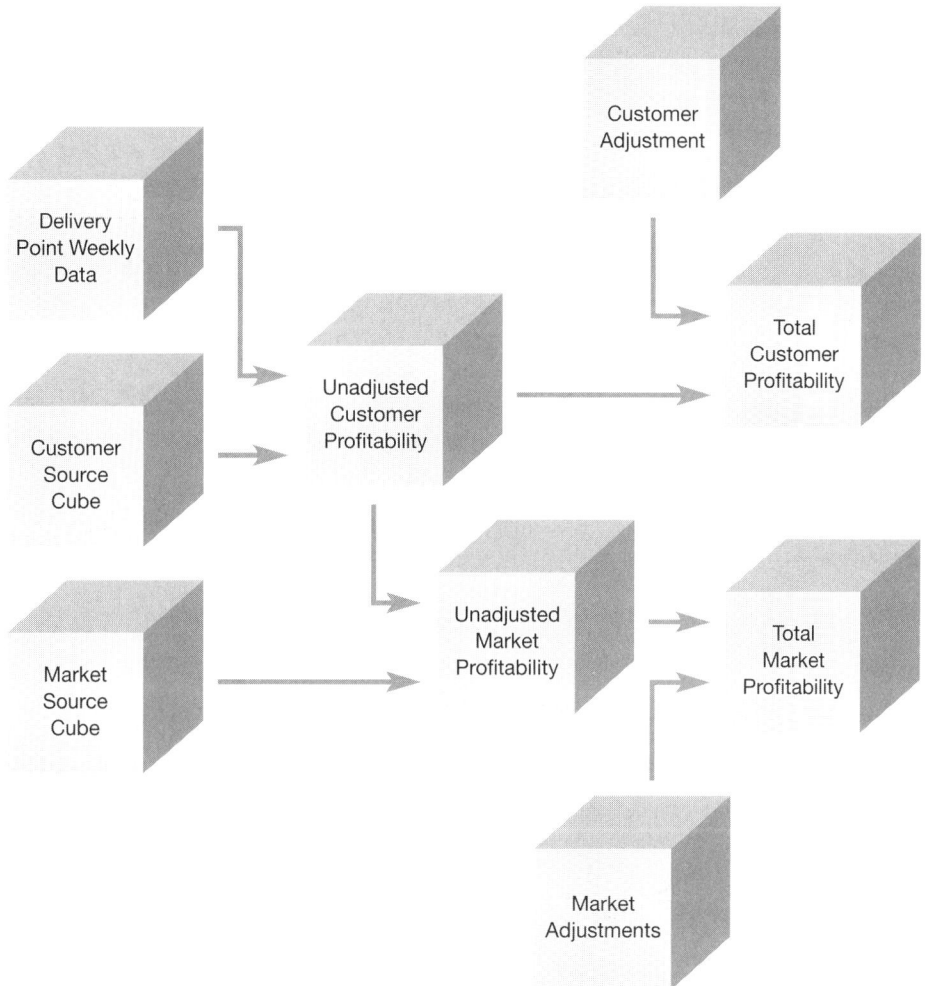

FIG 6.7   High-level cubes structure

Interface file catalog

Data loading, process and error logging, and integrity reporting all require file and path information that may differ from market to market. This catalog contains the following entries:

- Actual Data Files Directory
- Read Data Files Directory
- Data File Error Directory
- Product Filename

- Customer Filename

- Weekly Data File

- Main logs Directory

- Name of the Main OFA Log File

- Name of the Automatic Structures Maintenance Log File

- Budget Data File Directory

- Budget Data Read Directory

- Budget Data Error Directory

- Integrity Reports Log File

- Forecast Data File Directory

- Forecast Data Read Directory

- Forecast Data Error Directory

- Directory for Automatic Structures Maintenance Log File

- Directory for Integrity Reports Log File

- PC Directory for FTP transfer from Unix

- Archive Log File

- Directory for Export Files

- Directory for Compressed Shared Database

OFA structure catalog

In many of the custom data processing and maintenance routines reference is made to OFA structures that may change or differ across markets. This primarily refers to the internal hierarchy codes generated by OFA. Many of the custom routines reference the standard product and customer hierarchies for such things as data spreading or attribute inheritance.

Another example of the use of this catalog would be the dimension value of the top node in a hierarchy. The full list of entries in this catalog is as follows:

- Standard Product Hierarchy

- Standard Delivery Point Customer Hierarchy

- Standard Weekly Time Hierarchy

- Standard Time Hierarchy

- Product Hierarchies for Detailed Actuals

- Customer Hierarchies for Detailed Actuals

- Weekly Time Hierarchies for Detailed Actuals

- Lowest level in the All Customer Dimension

- Lowest level in the Product Dimension
- Parent for Unallocated Products in the Standard Product Hierarchy
- Parent for Unallocated Customers in the Standard All Customer Hierarchy
- Standard Customer Hierarchy
- Standard Market Hierarchy
- Total Product Node
- Total Delivery Point Node

6.6.3 DBA maintenance routines

A secondary objective of the project was to make the life of the DBAs as easy as possible. The solution to this was twofold: firstly, to automate the maintenance of OFA structures as much as possible, and secondly, to provide integrity reports that highlight any structural or data anomalies to the DBA before the users themselves discover them.

Automatic maintenance

A custom Express routine maintains as many of the OFA structures as possible. The DBA runs this routine from a custom tools menu option, and includes it in his or her weekly procedures. There are many interrelated structures in the system. This allows many objects to be maintained automatically based on an original master. The DBA therefore only needs to maintain manually the masters that provide the source information for all the other related structures. These routines are again driven by catalogs. This facilitates their easy implementation into the markets with different structural relationships.

6.6.4 Hierarchy inheritance

A market will often have several hierarchies on each of the product and customer dimensions. However, many of the levels in these hierarchies are common, especially at the lowest levels, where, for example, SKU codes are children of their base pack. The product and customer dimensions all have a level attribute that identifies the generic level of a dimension value. The level attributes identify the different levels within the hierarchy of the dimension. Examples of the product levels are:

SKU: Stock-keeping unit, usually the lowest level in the product hierarchies
BRAND: Brands familiar to the consumer
PRODUCT GROUP: A high-level grouping of brands
TOTAL PRODUCT: A treetop in a product hierarchy

TABLE 6.1   **Catalog for hierarchy inheritance**

Catalog properties	Customer example	Description
Source Dimension	Customer	Dimension name of the source
Target Dimension	Market	Dimension name of the target. This may or may not be the same as the source dimension. If it is different, as in the example, there is an implied relationship between the two dimensions. In this case, Market is a subset of Customer.
Source Hierarchy Code	HI.AA98765	The OFA internal code
Target Hierarchy Code	HI.AA8754	The OFA internal code
Maintain New Dimension Values	YES	Boolean to indicate whether new values should be automatically added to the target dimension if they do not already exist
Level Attribute	CUSTOMER.CLEVEL	The Express name of the attribute used to identify the levels.
Levels to Copy	TOTCUST MARKET CHANNEL	The values of the level attribute that will be inherited by the target hierarchy from the source.

These level attributes are a critical driver in much of the automated maintenance, as they provide an easy way of categorizing the dimension values quickly.

The catalog driving the routine looks like Table 6.1, each inheritance having a single column.

6.6.5 Attribute inheritance

This is a similar concept to the hierarchy inheritance above, but applied to OFA attributes. Its use is more specific than that of the hierarchy inheritance. This facility copies an attribute in one base dimension to another attribute in a different base dimension, with the same grouping dimension. There is therefore a strong relationship between the two base dimensions, the target usually being a subset of the source.

The catalog looks like Table 6.2.

Inheriting attribute values within a single attribute

There is often a strong relationship between an attribute's value and a hierarchy built on the same dimension. The attribute value is populated based on which branch of the hierarchy the dimension value falls in. For example, a brand attribute built on the product dimension will have the same brand attribute value for all products that are descendants of the brand. This can be a painful attribute to maintain manually when the hierarchy is constantly evolving.

TABLE 6.2   **Catalog for attribute inheritance**

Catalog properties	Customer example	Description
Source Dimension	Customer	Dimension name of the source base dimension
Target Dimension	Market	Dimension name of the target base dimension. This is expected to be different from the source dimension.
Source Attribute Code	CUSTOMER.CLEVEL	The OFA internal code
Target Attribute Code	MARKET.CLEVEL	The OFA internal code

TABLE 6.3   **Catalog for inheriting attribute values within a single attribute**

Catalog properties	Product example	Description
Base Dimension	Product	Dimension name of the source base dimension
Attribute Code	PRODUCT.BRAND	OFA code for the attribute
Level Attribute	PRODUCT.PLEVEL	The attribute used to identify the input level
Input Level	BRAND	The value of the level attribute at which the new attribute is manually maintained.
Hierarchy Code	HI.AA67491	The OFA internal code of the hierarchy used to identify ancestors of the input level. If more than one hierarchy is required, then a second column entry should be created.

This maintenance routine allows the attribute to be maintained at a single level (this level attribute again being a significant factor), and ripples down the value to all descendants. Hence in our brand example, the manual DBA maintenance is only done at the brand level; this is a very static level with few new brands requiring only infrequent manual update, and with all ancestors automatically receiving the brand value when the maintenance routine is run. Therefore, even with a rapidly changing dimension and hierarchy, the attribute requires little or no DBA intervention.

Again, there is a controlling catalog, as in Table 6.3.

6.6.6 Managing structural and data integrity

The DBA is responsible for the quality of the OFA structures and the integrity of the data within the Shared Database. If users discover flaws in either of these areas, it affects the acceptance and reputation of the system. It is therefore imperative that the DBA discovers and rectifies them first. Integrity checks on the Shared Database and the DBA's own Personal Database provide a report of integrity failures. The structural and data checks are split because the nature of the checking is different.

Structural integrity

The automatic maintenance routines described above are a big help in ensuring structural integrity because they minimize manual intervention. The checks performed by this custom routine therefore concentrate on the areas of manual maintenance. The program itself is run from the Tools menu, and is performed on both the DBA's Personal Database and the Shared Database.

The routine asks and reports on the following questions:

- Do all products have a product level?
- Does every base-level product have a net weight?
- Does every base-level product have a conversion factor?
- Are all base-level products in the Standard Product Hierarchy?
- Do all Delivery Points have a customer level?
- Are all base-level Delivery Points in the Standard Delivery Point Hierarchy?
- Do all base-level products have a Brand?
- Do all Customers have a customer level?
- Do all Markets have a customer level?
- Do all base-level products belonging to one pack have the same brand?
- Do all base-level products have a manufacturing plant?
- Do all base-level Delivery Points have a salesperson?
- Do all common hierarchy levels have the same last descendants?

Data integrity

If all of the structural tests above are successful it does not guarantee that the resulting data will also be free of inconsistencies. A typical example would be that the hierarchies have changed to a new, structurally sound, state, but the data has not been re-aggregated. All the parents are not the sum of their children – a particularly visible data integrity problem for the users to find.

Ensuring hierarchy roll-ups

An obvious control here is for the DBA to ensure that all of the historic data is reconsolidated every time a hierarchy changes. In some ways the automatic structural maintenance discussed earlier can be a handicap here, because the DBA does not necessarily know that the hierarchy has, in fact, altered. This implies that the historic data should be re-aggregated as part of the weekly procedures to ensure that the data reflects hierarchy changes. Whilst for some of the markets this is the approach they take, for the bigger databases this is a very time-consuming calculation.

An alternative approach to re-aggregation is to check that parents add to the sum of their children. There is little benefit in checking every level of every dimension, as this will be as slow as actually consolidating the data. The checking must be done at relevant, importantly perceived, levels in the hierarchies only. In order to provide the level of detail required by individual countries, the level of detail checked by this report is configurable using another catalog.

FDI integrity

The purpose of this integrity check is to ensure that all cubes with common data agree, e.g that the Customer Cube equals the Market Cube. If the hierarchy roll-up integrity checks are successful, this is an easy test to make to ensure that all the reporting cubes tell a consistent story. Once more, a catalog configures the parameters of the test.

6.6.7 Spreading and rate calculations

Each market needs to spread fixed costs from high-level products and/or customers down to the base level. They all also need to enter a rate, also at a high level, and generate a cost based on another P&L line, at the lowest level. These calculations are needed for actual, budget and forecast scenarios, each using potentially a different set of rules for the calculations. The types of costs, the basis for spreading and rate calculations, and the scenarios for which they are required, differ from one market to the next.

Each market could have generated its own custom code to perform its own version of spreading and rate calculations. However, in keeping with the overall project strategy of generating a generic system, the core characteristics of the spreading requirements were analyzed, and a module developed to provide a single solution for all markets.

What are the core characteristics?

1. Data entry, through OFA worksheets, of rates and fixed costs at any level of product and 'customer'. The 'customer' dimension here is a floating concept. It could be delivery point, customer or market.

2. The basis of the spread or rate calculation is dependent on the P&L line. A P&L line will only be a rate or a fixed cost, never both.

3. Calculations are needed for the Customer and Market Cubes, for Actuals, Budgets and Forecasts.

This led, in summary, to a design with two Financial Data Items, a Data Entry Cube and a resulting Cost Cube. The dimensions of these two cubes are identical. A text

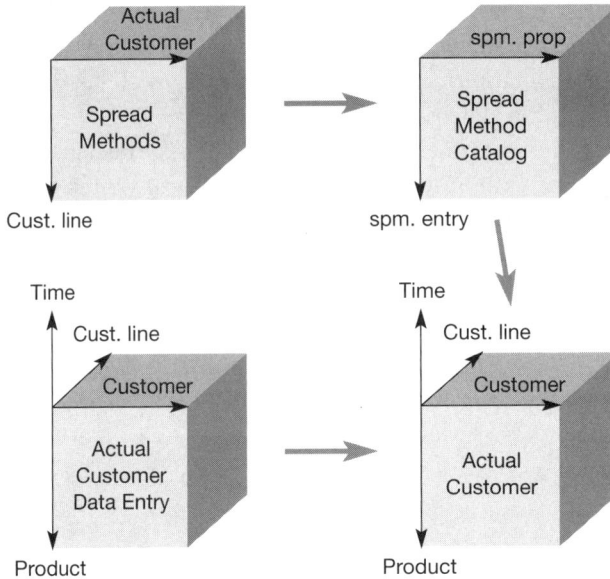

FIG 6.8   **Customer Actuals**

Financial Data Item, built on the line dimension, indicates which spread method to use, which in turn is used as a lookup in a configuration catalog. This identifies whether it is a rate or a fixed cost and the basis of the calculation.

The generic program is passed all this information as arguments and processes the Cost Cube, controlled by an OFA Solve Definition, with the DBA making selections for the Solve in the normal way. Each scenario (Actual, Budget, Forecast) and cube (Customer or Market) within the scenario has its own set of two cubes and spread method text variable. See Figure 6.8.

The program is relatively complex, because it is so generic. It uses dynamic programming techniques to ensure adequate performance. But the end result for the overall project is that each market can produce its own personal cost calculations, configuring data entry to the exact levels that its users require, whilst still using a centrally developed, maintained and supported routine.

6.6.8 Reporting and analysis

There are three reporting cubes, reflecting the three levels of detail at which the data is stored: Delivery Point invoice data, Customer data and Market data. Each cube is a Financial Data Item formula that calls a program function. This function has been dynamically created from reporting configuration catalogs giving the express syntax for each cell.

Each reporting cube has a scenario dimension that encompasses all variants of the basic scenarios: Actual, Budget and Forecast. Examples of the scenario dimension are given in Table 6.4.

TABLE 6.4   **Examples of the scenario dimension**

Dimension value	Description
ACJ.MN.LY	Adjusted Actuals (LY) Monthly
ACJ.YD.LY	Adjusted Actuals (LY) YTD
ACJ.MN.TY.LY	Adjusted Actuals (TY – LY) Monthly
ACJ.YD.TY.LY	Adjusted Actuals (TY – LY) YTD
ACJ.MN.TY.LY.P	Adjusted Actuals % (TY – LY) Monthly
ACJ.YD.TY.LY.P	Adjusted Actuals % (TY – LY) YTD
AC.MD	Actuals Weekly Month to Date
AC.WK.AVG	Actuals Weekly Average This Yr
AC.MN	Actuals
AC.YD	Actuals YTD
ACF.MN.LY	Actuals (LY)
ACF.YD.LY	Actuals (LY) YTD
ACF.MN.TY.LY	Actuals (TY – LY)
ACF.YD.TY.LY	Actuals (TY – LY) YTD
ACF.MN.TY.LY.P	Actuals % (TY – LY)
ACF.YD.TY.LY.P	Actuals % (TY – LY) YTD
ACJ.YD	Actuals Adjustments YTD
ACJD.MN	Adjusted Actuals
ACJD.YD	Adjusted Actuals YTD
G.AC.UNADJ	Actuals: Unadjusted Scenarios
G.AC.ADJ	Actuals: Adjusted Scenarios
G.ACJ	Actuals: Adjustments Scenarios
AC.PC.MN	Adj Act – Rates Per Actual Case
AC.PC.YD	Adj Act – Rates Per Actual Case YTD
AC.PT.MN	Adj Act – Rates Per Actual Tonne
AC.PT.YD	Adj Act – Rates Per Actual Tonne YTD
BD.MN	Budget – Bef Phasing Adj
BD.YD	Budget YTD
BD.MD	Budget MTD
BD.PT.MN	Rates Per Budget Tonne
BD.PT.YD	Rates Per Budget Tonne YTD

Dimension value	Description
ACT_TON_CASE	Adjusted Actuals: Rates Scenarios
BUD_TON_CASE	Budget: Rates Scenarios
G.BUD.UNADJ	Budget Scenarios
G.FC	Forecast Scenarios
LF.MN	Forecast Latest
LF.MD	Forecast MTD
ACJ.MAV.12	Adjusted Actuals Moving Avg (12 Mn)
ACJ.MAV.6	Adjusted Actuals Moving Avg (6 Mn)
ACJ.MAV.4	Adjusted Actuals Moving Avg (4 Mn)
ACJ.MAV.3	Adjusted Actuals Moving Avg (3 Mn)
LF.YD	Forecast Latest YTD
ACLF.MN	Actuals – Latest Forecast
ACLF.YD	Actuals – Latest Forecast MTD
ACBD.MN	Actuals – Budget
ACBD.YD	Actuals – Budget YTD
LE.MN	Latest Estimate
LE.YD	Latest Estimate YTD
ABCD.YD.P	Actuals – Budget YTD %
ABCD.MN.P	Actuals – Budget %
LFBD.YD	Forecast Latest YTD – Budget YTD
LFBD.YD.P	Forecast Latest YTD – Budget YTD %
ST.MN	Salesperson Target
ST.YD	Salesperson Target YTD
ACST.MN	Actuals – Salesperson Target
ACST.YD	Actuals – Salesperson Target YTD
ACST.MN.P	Actuals – Salesperson Target %
ACST.YD.P	Actuals – Salesperson Target YTD %
ACJBD.YD	Adjusted Actuals – Budget YTD
ACJBD.YD.P	Adjusted Actuals – Budget YTD %
ACJBD.MN	Adjusted Actuals – Budget
ACJBD.MN.P	Adjusted Actuals – Budget %
BD.FY	Budget Total Yr
LF.CP	Forecast Latest (Current Period)
LE.YR	Latest Estimate (Rem Yr)
ACLMN	Actuals Adjustments
ACJ.MN.LY.FY	Actuals (LY) – Total Year

These scenarios can be split into two groups: the first is a base level scenario, created from stored data, e.g. Monthly Actuals; the second is a scenario created from other scenarios, e.g. Adjusted Actuals – Budget YTD %.

The second example can be created from two other scenarios, which in turn are themselves made up of other scenarios. Eventually a scenario that must refer to basic stored data is reached.

Creating complex scenarios from other scenarios

The two categories of scenario are controlled by their own catalogs. The simpler conceptually of the two is the second, scenario-based group, called complex scenarios here (complex only in that they are made up of combinations of 'simpler' basic scenarios). The syntax for these calculations is stored in a catalog dimensioned by reporting scenario and cube type (Delivery Point, Customer and Market). The dynamic custom routine produces the functions from this catalog, creating an Express case statement for each scenario, in each of the cube's functions.

An example of the resulting Express code looks like this:

```
DEFINE P.CUSTOMER.CUBE PROGRAM
PROGRAM
"Formula program dynamically generated from cube.catalog
"Program for formula CUSTOMER.CUBE – Customer

variable _SCN.ENTRY text
_SCN.ENTRY = SCN.ENTRY
switch _SCN.ENTRY
  do
  CASE 'ACJ.MN.LY':
   return –
lag(CUSTOMER.CUBE(SCN.ENTRY'ACJD.MN'), TIME.LAG.YAG, TIME)
   break
  CASE'ACJ.YD.LY':
   return –
if time.period eq 'MONTH'–
then lag(movingtotal(CUSTOMER.CUBE(SCN.ENTRY'ACJD.MN'),
1-month.number, 0, 1, time), time.lag.yag, time) – else na
   break
  CASE'ACJ.MN.TY.LY':
   return –
CUSTOMER.CUBE(SCN.ENTRY'ACJD.MN') –
CUSTOMER.CUBE(SCN.ENTRY'ACJ.MN.LY')
   break
```

```
CASE'ACJ.YD.TY.LY':
 return –
CUSTOMER.CUBE(SCN.ENTRY'ACJD.YD') –
CUSTOMER.CUBE(SCN.ENTRY'ACJ.YD.LY')
 break
CASE'ACJ.MN.TY.LY.P':
 return –
((CUSTOMER.CUBE(SCN.ENTRY'ACJD.MN') –
CUSTOMER.CUBE(SCN.ENTRY'ACJ.MN.LY))/ –
CUSTOMER.CUBE(SCN.ENTRY'ACJ.MN.LY')) * 100
 break

etc. ...
```

The catalog also identifies which scenarios are basic scenarios, not able to be calculated using this simple approach. This information is then used for the first group of scenarios.

Creating basic scenarios

The basic scenario must reference a stored data cube. However, the on-the-fly element here transfers away from the scenario dimension to the line dimension. All the basic revenue and cost data is stored, but the simple subtotalling and ratio calculations can be performed on the fly, without any reduction in performance to the reporting user. The configuration catalog for these scenarios is therefore dimensioned by Reporting Line, Scenario and Cube Type. The syntax is usually simpler than the earlier catalog, because it is line based. The system can even be configured to allow the DBA to enter these calculations in a front-end OFA model. This model becomes the source for the catalog, which in turn populates the function. This function provides the calculations of line subtotals for one of the basic scenarios. Each basic scenario will have its own function, generated from the single catalog (dimensioned by scenario, remember).

To recap, the basic scenarios reference stored data, but produce line subtotalling at run time ('on the fly'). These scenarios can then be built into more complex scenarios, in combination. The complex scenarios will inherit any of the on-the-fly subtotalling.

6.7   ROLL-OUT

The initial implementation was performed in a single market. This implementation was used to iron out the requirements for the European-wide application. Roll-outs to subsequent markets were done in parallel. Because OFA was new to the users the implementation was done in a stepped manner. Users were given limited functionality, the system was allowed to bed in, then the functionality would be extended further. This stepped approach consisted of four fundamental phases:

- Sales invoice data
- Customer contribution profitability
- Full profitability
- Budgeting and forecasting

The use of configuration catalogs certainly eased the roll-out process, because to a certain extent it turned a roll-out into a configuration exercise. It did not, however, remove all of the complications of a local roll-out. Implementation in a local site always highlighted difficulties in imposing a common model.

6.7.1 Training

The user population varies across countries from a dozen or so in the smaller markets, to over a hundred in the larger ones. A 'train the trainers' approach was taken to the training of these users. Key power users were identified in each country. These people were trained by the central development team, in advance of the implementation in their country. They were the first users of the system, and they then provided the training for their own local users.

| 6.8 | **CONTINUING CHANGE MANAGEMENT**

There is an ongoing programme of increasing the functionality within the European application. This primarily involves the development of new custom routines and the amendment of existing ones. This work is done by the central development team, based in the UK. These changes then need to be applied across Europe. This is done using an upgrade routine built into the application. An upgrade file and procedure is produced which is applied to each site, just like any other software product upgrade. Detailed versioning of each custom program and database is maintained to help with the support of the application from the UK.

7 Case study in the financial services industry

ROAD MAP

ROAD MAP

The chapter provides a detailed examination of an existing project in the financial services industry. It explains the objectives of the system, and how some of the project principles described in Chapter 5 have been applied.

7.1 COMPANY OVERVIEW

The company used in this case study operates worldwide in the financial services industry and is part of a large US conglomerate. It has around 20 businesses operating in separate countries across Europe, Asia and Australia with the headquarters in North America.

All businesses provide consumer finance and there is a large degree of overlap in the products and markets in which the different businesses operate, although no two businesses are identical.

The businesses are relatively autonomous, and are managed primarily by measurement of their net income and return on average net investment. The company has grown significantly over the past few years, primarily due to acquisition.

7.2 THE REQUIREMENTS OF THE OFA SYSTEM

The basic requirement of the system is to fulfil three main application areas:

▪ management reporting;

- budgeting and forecasting;
- product and client profitability.

In all three areas, there is a good fit with our generic OFA process model (Figure 7.1). This is to complement the implementation of Oracle General Ledger which has recently been implemented. Whilst the businesses are autonomous, there is a significant amount of functionality that is common to all businesses, and these form the core requirements. On top of these, the businesses require the flexibility to satisfy their own requirements. Both the core and local requirements are discussed later.

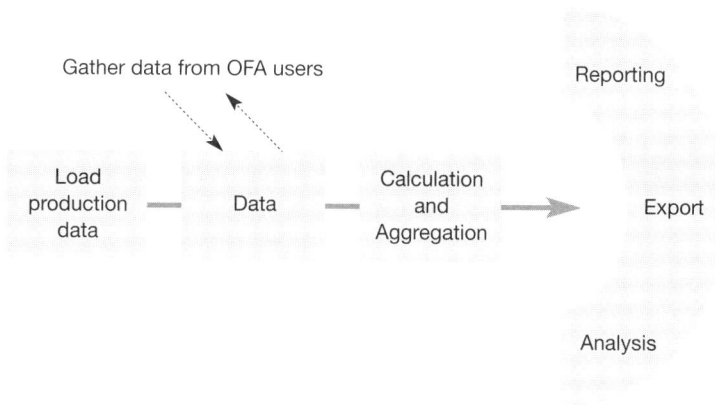

FIG 7.1   **The generic OFA process model**

ROLL-OUT

The system has been implemented in:

- the headquarters in North America, for management reporting and budgeting and forecasting at a consolidated level;
- the regional headquarters in Scandinavia, for management reporting and budgeting and forecasting – this is at a consolidated level of detail, albeit more detailed than the US headquarters;
- several businesses across Europe for management reporting, budgeting and forecasting, and product/client profitability at a detailed level.

The system is currently being implemented in:

- Asia regional headquarters for management reporting and budgeting and forecasting – this is at the same level of detail as the US headquarters;

■ several of the Asian businesses for management reporting and budgeting and forecasting.

The system is due to be implemented in further businesses in Europe, Asia and Australia.

7.4   SPONSORSHIP

As mentioned earlier, the OFA implementation started after Oracle General Ledger had been implemented in a number of businesses in Europe. The implementation of Oracle General Ledger was initiated and sponsored by the group financial controller in US headquarters, with the objective of radically improving the efficiency and control of the financial processes, particularly the month-end close, across the whole company. The GL project was implemented in partnership with a Big 5 management consultancy practice, and required significant business process re-engineering and change management to improve the month-end close. The GL project was therefore a serious undertaking, requiring senior management buy-in and sponsorship.

The OFA project was initiated by the same sponsor under the same programme as the GL implementation, but the objectives involved far less business process re-engineering and change management. The objectives were primarily to complement and enhance the functionality already provided by GL, by providing improved reporting and budgeting functionality. Consequently, the OFA project was generally a lower profile project than GL, requiring less input from the central sponsor.

This had an effect on the implementation in the headquarters, where permanent headcount was kept to a minimum, supplemented with temporary staff. This meant that it was frequently difficult to obtain appropriate business resources to specify requirements etc., as the temporary staff available did not have a detailed knowledge of the business. The knock-on effect of this was an increase in the change requests raised during user testing, as new requirements came out, and this delayed the final go-live. The lesson learnt is that regardless of the level of process re-engineering being performed, an OFA implementation still needs an active sponsor who can ensure that OFA is given sufficient priority.

This was less of a problem in the business implementations. The businesses were expected to fund their own OFA implementations, and so at the project initiation workshop, the local senior finance manager would be involved to understand the potential benefits of OFA, together with the likely costs and resource requirements. At this level, therefore, the projects had a higher profile, particularly when they were delivering significant value over and above General Ledger, e.g. when product and client profitability were implemented. The lesson learnt here was the benefit of involving senior finance and business managers in the early presentation workshops, and the significant benefit that profitability management gives to finance and business managers.

7.5   CHANGE MANAGEMENT

As described above, in general the OFA implementation did not require significant process re-engineering, as the objective was to enhance existing functionality. This was also because the OFA functionality was not being rolled out to a significantly large user population. Typically it was rolled out to the finance function, and to selected users outside of this. The main driver for the limited roll-out was that some of the GL and OFA project overhead costs were allocated on a per-user basis, and this created a per-user cost significantly greater than the OFA licence cost. The charging algorithm is currently being reviewed with a view to encouraging 'light' users of OFA or other clients, to encourage the business to derive maximum benefit from their investment in OFA.

The exception to this is where one of the headquarters objectives was to streamline the process whereby pre-close financial information was submitted to and reviewed by the US headquarters. This was achieved by replacing a GL consolidation with an OFA system, and in this case, the sponsor took an active part in communicating the change in business process and responsibilities to the businesses. The emphasis given to the new process by the senior management was clear to see during the first processing cycle, with all businesses submitting well before the deadline – an unusual occurrence!

7.6   REQUIREMENTS

The core and local requirements for the different application areas are described below.

7.6.1 Management reporting – core

All the businesses that used General Ledger use the same chart of accounts segments:

Company	Standard values across company
Cost Centre	Different values for each business
Account	Standard values across company
Sub Account	Different values for each business – dependent on account
Product	Different values for each business
Client	Different values for each business

For Cost Centre and Product, there is a standard definition across the company of Cost Centre Group and Product Group.

The following mappings exist:

- Cost Centre to Cost Centre Group, e.g. Cost Centre 8100 Systems Development maps to Cost Centre Group 8XXX;

- Product to Product Group, e.g. Product 1100 Store Card maps to Product Group 1XX Sales Finance.

These mappings are stored in GL as descriptive flexfields against the segment value.

At the Consolidated Level in the US headquarters, the following segments are therefore required for reporting:

Company
Cost Centre Group
Account
Product Group

Data

■ Data is to be extracted from Oracle GL in functional and USX currencies.

■ Where data is extracted from GL, the same extract file should be used to populate both the business and HQ view of data, to avoid data integrity issues.

■ Data is to be extracted by the business to be loaded into the HQ view of data to enable 'pre-close' reporting, effectively to assess how close a business is to its net income targets before closing its books. This data needs to be loaded and rolled up automatically to enable businesses working outside the Eastern Standard time zone to check that their numbers have been loaded successfully.

■ Existing Budget data will initially be loaded (one off) from ASCII files.

■ There will be multiple versions of budgets.

See Sections 7.6.3 and 7.6.4, 'Budgeting and Forecasting', for more detail on how budgets are created.

Reporting and ratios

■ Company-wide standard hierarchies on Company and Account are to be shared across the group.

■ Typical comparatives between actual and budget, actual and last year are required.

■ Company-wide standard calculations are to be performed to enable reporting of key measures and ratios.

■ Measures and ratios will be available on a periodic or Year to Date basis.

7.6.2 Management reporting – sample local requirements

■ Local hierarchies and ratios are required for most businesses.

■ One business merges two segments together, and creates a hierarchy on this combined dimension for reporting.

■ Scandinavia sub consolidation requires to report on the first digit of the sub account, in addition to the US headquarters dimensions (Company, Cost Centre Group, Account, Product Group).

7.6.3 Budgeting and forecasting – core

■ Pre-population of formatted spreadsheet templates with Actuals data.

■ Collection of spreadsheet templates by Company, by Cost Centre or by Full Account Key.

■ Automated load of returned templates into OFA.

■ Local preparation and submission of budget data from business to sub consolidation or US headquarters.

7.6.4 Budgeting and forecasting – sample local requirements

■ Currency conversion of budgets.

■ Automatic calculation of budget using calculation models, e.g. payroll models, income models.

■ Scandinavian businesses have additional time dimension values for statutory reporting.

■ Some businesses also required to load budgets and statistics from GL.

7.6.5 Product and client profitability – core

■ Extraction of General Ledger data into Cost Pools.

■ Data Collection of Cost Drivers.

■ Generation of some Cost Drivers from GL.

■ Association of Cost Pools with Cost Drivers.

■ Allocation of Costs to products and clients.

■ Resultant Profitability reporting.

7.6.6 Product and client profitability – local

■ Separate administration of cost allocation and profitability reporting.

■ Transfer of costs between cost centres (cascaded) before allocation to products and clients.

7.7   DESIGN OF THE APPLICATION ARCHITECTURE

In reviewing the possible application architectures (as described in Section 5.4) there were some options that were felt not to be workable or that would put a major constraint on the system.

Option 1 – 'SuperDBA and no SubDBAs' – was felt to be too restrictive on the flexibility of the businesses. There is a different level of detail in the businesses, with different segment values, hierarchies and calculation models within each business. Each business had identified their own administrator to look after their OFA application, and the single SuperDBA and Task Queue would present a significant bottleneck. To try to squeeze all this functionality into one SuperDBA was felt to be very inappropriate.

Option 4 – 'Multiple SuperDBAs' – was also discounted owing to the number of shared structures between the headquarters and the businesses, and the ease with which these can be shared within a tiered architecture. As described in the requirements, there were standard hierarchies on the company and account dimensions, which were impractical and undesirable to maintain in more than one place. There were also sophisticated calculation models to calculate average net investment, return on investment and other key measures and ratios, and it was important to share these model definitions for efficiency of set-up and consistency of calculation. The requirements also specified the ability for budget data to be prepared locally and easily transferred back up to the higher levels in the organization for consolidation (Scandinavia headquarters, US headquarters, Asia headquarters).

This left options 2 and 3, both variations of the tiered architecture. The additional administration required in option 3 led to option 2 being generally recommended as a rule. However, there were some exceptions to this rule:

- In one business, profitability was required to be administered separately from the main reporting and budgeting. This was because a number of maintenance activities were required for profitability: maintenance of attributes linking cost pools to cost drivers, running Tasks in the Task Queue to load cost driver data from an external file, initiation of Solve Definitions to perform the processing. Also, the users of profitability needed an area to work in finalizing the cost allocation processing and resultant profitability before publishing the results to the larger user community.

- In two cases, there were sub consolidations of businesses, e.g. Scandinavia, effectively a layer of management between the business and headquarters. When it was attempted to fit this into a two-tier architecture, neither option was appropriate. Forcing the Scandinavia system into the US headquarters tier meant that Scandinavia could not review their budget before the US headquarters could review it. Forcing Scandinavia into the business tier would mean putting all these businesses into one Shared Database with one SubDBA, with the associated problems identified in option 1.

The application architecture is shown in Figure 7.2. DBA Personal Databases have not been shown to make the diagram more readable.

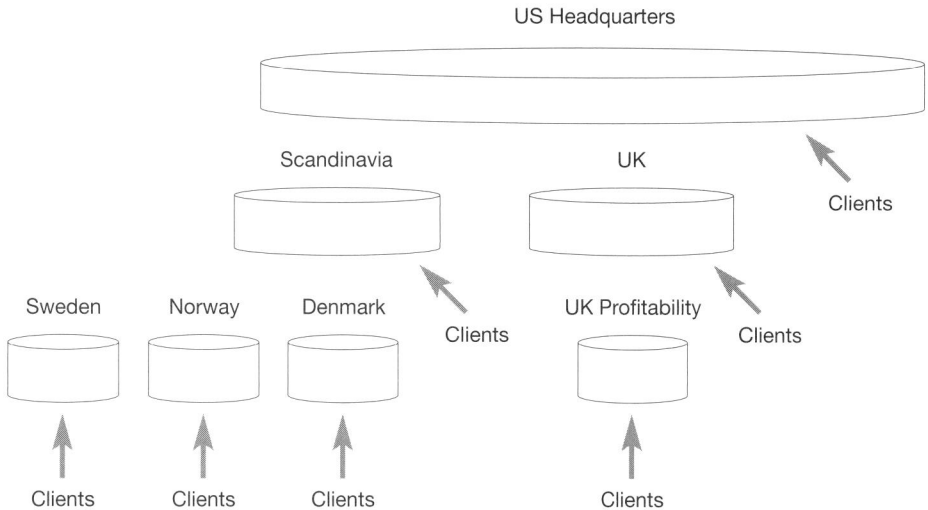

FIG 7.2   **The application architecture**

DATABASE DESIGN: MANAGEMENT REPORTING

7.8.1 Identifying the dimensions

As discussed earlier, a standard chart of accounts structure is used across the company, and this had been recently implemented. In general, the dimensions required for reporting were in line with the GL segments.

Bearing in mind that the sub account was a dependent segment on account, these two segments were to be joined together to form one dimension with a hierarchy linking GL account to its sub accounts.

For example:

GL Account 8100 Postage has four sub accounts: 100 Royal Mail, 200 DHL, 300 UPS, 400 Internal Mail.
GL Account 8200 Travel has three sub accounts: 100 Planes, 200 Trains, 300 Automobiles.

Then the OFA dimension values, shown indented to show the hierarchical format, would be:

A8100 Postage
    A8100.100 Postage – Royal Mail
    A8100.200 Postage – DHL
    A8100.300 Postage – UPS
    A8100.400 Postage – Internal Mail

A8200 Travel
    A8200.100 Travel – Planes
    A8200.200 Travel – Trains
    A8200.300 Travel – Automobiles

US headquarters

Company – Cost Centre Group – Account – Product Group – Time

Business

Company – Cost Centre – Account + Sub Account – Product – Client – Time

At the business level, the cost centre and product dimensions would also contain the cost centre group and product group values, with a hierarchy linking them to enable drilldown. This would enable queries from the headquarters at the cost centre group and product group level to be easily analyzed, with drilldown to the business detail if required.

Two exceptions to this rule were:

1. One business required to merge product and client together to form a 'hybrid' dimension, with a hierarchy grouping together combinations of client and product. This had come about primarily due to the difficulty of interfacing the source operational systems. Ideally, the segment values in GL would have truly reflected the management view of the business, but this had not been possible in the time of the GL implementation.

2. The company segment was actually made up of two dimensions – business and legal entity – and a small number of users requested to see these as separate dimensions. This was achieved using a reporting cube as described in Section 5.5.

Additional dimensions identified were:

- Currency, i.e. USD/Functional.
- Format, i.e. show P&L data as Monthly movement or YTD.
- Budget Version – with three standard versions – Session 1, Session 2, Operating Plan.

Reporting of the following data types was also required:

Actuals
Session 1 Budget
Session 2 Budget
Operating Plan
Actuals vs. Session 1
Actuals vs. Session 2
Session 1 vs. Session 2

7.8.2 Cube design

Owing to the number of dimensions in the system, and the likely number of hierarchies in the system, the primary concern was the batch performance, particularly when it had been estimated that 10 businesses would be rolled out OFA and they would all want to load and roll up overnight at month end. This led to a design that optimized the batch performance by minimizing the number of dimensions on the stored cubes, and therefore the number of code combinations generated during roll-up. Of the dimensions described above, the following needed to be part of the stored cubes:

Company
Cost Centre (incl. Groups)
Account + Sub Account
Product (incl. Groups)
Client
Ctime

The remaining dimensions were managed as follows:

- Currency: As there were only two currencies, USD and Functional, it was decided that this could be handled using two minicubes, which could be joined together in a reporting cube.

- Month/YTD: To avoid excessive batch processing, it was decided that one of these would be stored, with the other calculated – this is described in detail below.

- Budget Version: As the number of versions would be at least six (to allow for current and previous versions), with businesses adding versions for their own use, it was decided that this should be a dimension on the stored budget cube.

Month/YTD

- To give optimal YTD reporting performance, Actuals were stored as YTD with a formula cube to give the monthly view.

- To enable worksheet data entry and data entry forms, Budget was stored as Monthly with a formula to give the YTD view.

See Section 7.8.4 to see how the requirement to report ratios on a month and YTD basis was satisfied.

Sparsity

Owing to the number of dimensions, sparsity needed to be managed using composites.

All the GL dimensions had a significant number of dimension values in them, so there was no candidate for having one of the dimensions outside of the composite.

The only possible short dense dimensions were time and budget version (budget only). So the cubes were defined as:

Actuals   <ctime <Composite>>
Budget   <ctime <Composite> Version>

Composites were defined and shared in line with the recommended guidelines.

Data type

Cubes were defined as decimal owing to the size of the numbers involved (more than 10 significant digits) and the preference from the users to see a balanced balance sheet without rounding differences.

7.8.3 Data storage

To ensure that the batch performance would be satisfactory, a proof of concept was initiated, primarily to do volume testing on the batch load and roll-up, but also to give an environment where the features and benefits of OFA could be demonstrated based on real company data.

At the start of the proof of concept, it had been envisaged that all the code combinations of the cube dimensions would be stored, but with the fallback that certain combinations or levels would not be stored, but instead calculated on the fly. When data was loaded for one of the larger businesses, roll-up times of 4–5 hours were seen for one currency for actuals data – extrapolating this for 10 businesses for two currencies and allowing for budget roll-ups (albeit smaller), it was clear that this would not fit into the overnight window.

Various options were considered for the data that would be calculated on the fly, but the preferred choice was to calculate the sub account level on the fly. This was because, in many cases, there was only one sub account for the main account, meaning that the sub account could pick up the main account figure using a formula, and because the sub account level was generally used for ad-hoc drilling rather than for large sub account reports.

This reduced the roll-up time to approximately 0.5 hour for one currency for actuals. This was because the number of code combinations was significantly reduced, although the ratio of parents to base combinations is still high (1,000,000 parents from 30,000 base-level combinations). Based on a multiprocessor environment, with the roll-ups being performed in separate databases, it was felt that this would fit into the overnight window, and this has been the case to date.

Calculation of cells on the fly works at approximately 10 cells per second. So if a user has six time selections across the page, and drills from an account to five sub accounts, the response time is approximately 3 seconds, which is generally seen as acceptable.

7.8.4 Ratios

As described above, ratios were required on a month and YTD basis. This could have been achieved by storing one set of ratios and calculating the other set on the fly. However, the calculations were complex and interdependent so it was decided to store both month and YTD versions of the ratios. This was because the performance of the resultant calculation on the fly was expected to be unacceptably slow, and the development, support and maintenance time was expected to be high.

An additional stored measures cube was created which included the additional month/YTD dimension, with custom Solves flowing those accounts required for calculation (Figure 7.3). The calculation models were then applied to this cube. The Reporting cubes then joined the resultant measures cube with the original stored cubes.

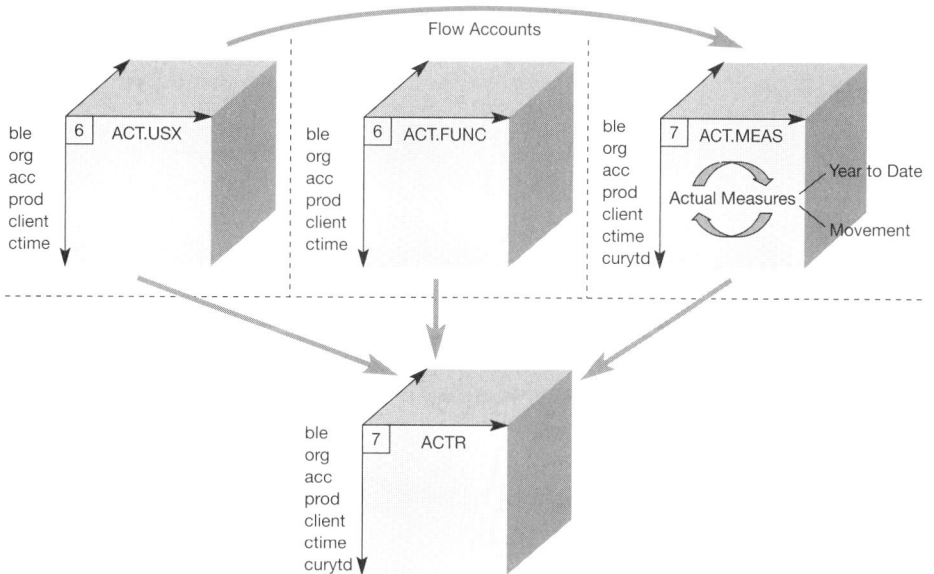

FIG 7.3   **GL Actuals Cubes design**

7.9   # INTERFACE DESIGN: MANAGEMENT REPORTING

The detail requirements of the interface from GL to OFA were:

1. Load GL segment values, descriptions and mappings (e.g. cost centre to cost centre group) on an ad-hoc basis, and whenever balances are loaded.

2. Load and roll-up GL balances into the Super Shared Database on an automatic basis, to enable businesses to check and reconcile their data without waiting for

manual intervention. This is particularly important for businesses submitting outside of working hours in the Eastern Standard time zone, when the US administrators would be unavailable.

3. Load and roll-up the same extracted GL balances into the Sub Shared Database on a scheduled basis. As the load and roll-up may take 1–1.5 hours' CPU per business, it is important that this is performed on an overnight basis, so that normal daytime response time is unaffected.

At the time of implementation the GL interface did not support:

- multiple chart of accounts;
- dependent segments;
- automated/scheduled loads into Super/Sub Shared Databases.

As these were essential features, a custom interface was designed. This interface was designed to meet the requirements in the following way.

7.9.1 Load GL segment values

On an ad-hoc basis, the business could run an extract of segment values and mappings. These files would then be automatically transferred from the GL platform to the OFA platform. The OFA administrator would then use a Tools menu option to initiate a Task in the Task Queue, which would import these files and create the hierarchies from the mapping files. A separate Tools menu option would transfer the dimension values and hierarchies to the SubDBA Personal Database by exporting and then importing the appropriate structures – the transfer of these structures into the DBA was specifically built as a Tools menu option as this was the only way of guaranteeing read/write access to the SubDBA Personal Database.

The segment values were always extracted with the balances in case a new segment value had been added. The balance load process would include an import of the segment values prior to the balances. Any new segment values would then need to be added into any manually maintained hierarchies. However, this was unlikely to be the case as the month end close process dictated the final date that segment values could be added, and the OFA administrator could initiate a structure load after this date prior to the month end.

7.9.2 Automatic load and roll-up into Super Shared Database

One of the design concepts behind the automatic load was that of a repetitive Task that would run periodically and resubmit itself to the Task Queue at the end. This would be an OFA Task that the administrator could initiate, monitor and delete through the Task Queue. More importantly, when the repetitive Task was waiting to run again, the Task Processor would be free to process distributions and data sub-missions. A utility program was developed to attach the Task database (allowing for other users temporarily attaching it) and create a new Task to run in a predefined number of minutes. The number of minutes delay was parameterized by being stored in a catalog and so could be modified by the administrator.

One of the other design concepts was the design of the file system to allow a 'staging' directory for each business. This would allow the automatic load to take place into the Super Shared Database, but leave a copy of the files processed in a staging directory for processing on the next scheduled load. This formed an essen-tial part of the data integrity design, ensuring that the same set of balances were being reviewed by both headquarters and the businesses. As the data being loaded into the Super Shared and Sub Shared Databases were at a different level of detail, the standard function of Refresh data was inappropriate.

A catalog stored unique details for each business, which would be matched to the header of the file to identify the business to be processed. The file could then be copied to the appropriate staging directory. Figure 7.4 shows the processing schematic.

The overall process flow for the repetitive Task would then be as follows:

1. Move the GL files from the inbound transfer directory to the headquarters staging area.

2. Copy the file to the appropriate staging directory by identifying the business from the header.

3. Build a list of files to be processed, and sort the files into order using the file type in the header (segment value extracts first, then balances).

4. Call the sub program to process each file appropriately according to its file type.

   4.1 For segment value extracts, store the individual segment value and its mapping to the HQ value.

   4.2 For balance extracts, accumulate the balance to the HQ level of detail using the mappings previously stored.

   4.3 Move the file to a processed directory when complete.

5. Initiate the group Solve Definition identified in the catalogs, for the businesses where data has changed.

6. Check whether there are any scheduled Tasks to be run and, if so, initiate the Task in the Sub Shared Database (see Section 7.9.3 for more detail).

7. Resubmit the repetitive Task for N minutes time.

On average, this process would take approximately 10 minutes per business (includ-ing the group Solve) and pre-close loads into the Super Shared Database were possible. The speed of the load was due to US headquarters using fewer dimensions, with fewer dimension values and fewer levels in the hierarchies. This meant that far

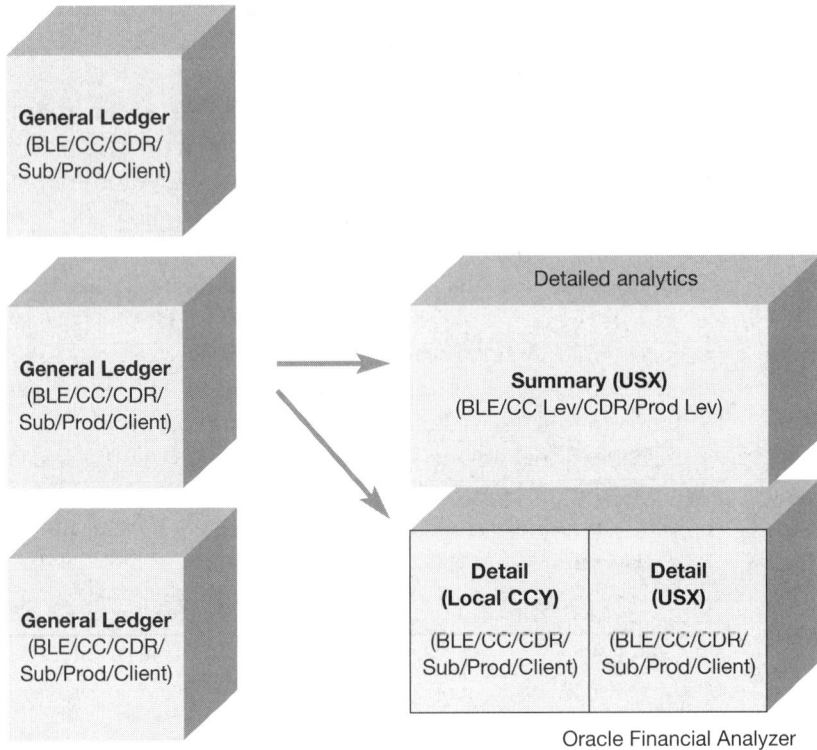

FIG 7.4   The processing schematic

fewer summary combinations were created. For a typical business with 30,000 base-level combinations, the number of combinations stored in the Super Shared Database for that business was 50,000.

This performance gave the US headquarters the opportunity to preview the results and raise any adjustments if necessary, before the local books were finally closed, leading to a more informed and manageable close.

7.9.3 Scheduled load and roll-up into Sub Shared Database

The main concept behind the scheduled load was the scheduled Task catalog. As the requirement was that the overnight loads should be centrally controlled to avoid contention, a catalog was created that would specify when each business load was to be initiated. The repetitive Task would then check this catalog (as described above) and initiate a Task in the Sub Shared Database. A similar sub program was used to initiate the Task in the Sub Shared Task Database, and the business catalog stored the path to the Task Database.

As the files in the staging directory for that business had already been confirmed as belonging to that business, the overall process flow was as follows:

1. Build a list of files to be processed, and sort the files into order using the file type in the header (segment value extracts first, then balances).

2. Call the sub program to process each file appropriately according to its file type.

    2.1 For balance files, load the data into account level.

3. Move the file to a processed directory when complete.

    Initiate the Group Solve Definition identified in the catalogs, for the businesses where data has changed.

Due to the overnight scheduled processing, businesses were able to use an overnight window of 2 hours' processing per business to roll up and process the core cubes, together with their own hierarchies and cubes. As the roll-up of the main cubes and hierarchies took approximately 1 hour, this gave them significant flexibility to perform their own processing.

7.10   DATABASE DESIGN: BUDGETING

7.10.1 Cube design

The cube required for Budgeting has the same dimensions as for Actuals, with the additional version as described in the management reporting cube design. This reflected the dimensionality of the target cube, i.e. the cube that users were required to populate for budgeting.

The main design difference with budgeting was that data was stored at all levels, including sub account. This was in contrast to the Actuals cube, where only data above sub account level was stored, and a formula was used to calculate sub accounts on the fly. As some users were using worksheets to input their data and as a worksheet needs to refer to a stored variable as opposed to a formula, it was decided that the budget would be stored at all levels. The roll-up of budget data did not take a significant amount of time as the number of code combinations was significantly less than for Actuals.

Users chose to populate their budget in one of two ways:

▪ Copy and paste from a source system – typically a spreadsheet. This made use of partial roll-up when the data was saved to the Task Queue, so users had quick access to summarized budget data.

▪ Load data from an Excel template, which might have been pre-populated. This is discussed in detail below.

Most businesses have considered developing OFA models to support their budgeting process, and in the medium term it is likely that these businesses will implement these. In the short term, the roll-out cost per user is prohibitively high, so calculation logic would need to be replicated in Excel. This removes many of the benefits of implementing using OFA, as an Excel model would still need to be maintained and supported.

7.10.2 Pre-population and data collection of Excel templates

Owing to the high roll-out cost per user, most businesses implemented an Excel data collection mechanism. The Data Collection Toolkit was considered for this, but rejected as it needed an Express licence and a connection to the server. The templates were to be user friendly, with formatting and calculations within the template, and containing pre-populated Actuals data where appropriate.

For pre-population, a two-stage approach was designed. Temporary WK1 files were produced containing the Actuals data. WK1 format was used as it is a native spreadsheet format, although CSV format would probably have worked just as well. One WK1 file would be produced for each cost centre – catalogs were used to store the selection of cost centres to be produced, together with the selection of rows and columns. These were effectively raw files without formatting and calculation. Control files were also exported, e.g. a file containing the list of cost centres was produced. An Excel macro then loaded a template master file containing the appropriate formatting and calculations. It then imported the control file listing the cost centres, and looped over the list of cost centres producing a separate file for input. These would then be located on a file server for users to collect and fill out.

For data loading, the reverse of the above process was designed. An Excel macro would export the relevant data area to a WK1 file. A Tools menu option would then initiate a Task to import any files waiting in a certain directory. This data load would store process information in a catalog for each cost centre such as:

- date and time of last read;
- number of valid rows and columns read;
- any invalid accounts within the WK1 file;
- any invalid time periods within the WK1 file.

The data load would also populate an attribute to indicate that this cost centre had changed, which could then be used in a Solve Definition to perform partial processing, recalculating only those cells impacted by the change.

DATABASE DESIGN: PROFITABILITY

The objective of the profitability design was to achieve a profit and loss statement (down to net contribution) by product, client and time for Actuals and Budget data. Some of the profit and loss lines were already analyzed by product and/or client, and others needed to be allocated. The resultant profit and loss was also at a summarized account level.

The processing requirements were therefore as follows:

▪ For those profit and loss lines already analyzed by product and client, extract this information from the GL cubes and transfer them to the profitability cube. An example of this type of profit and loss line was financing income, fed into GL from the source operational systems by product and client.

▪ For those profit and loss lines already analyzed by product but not client, extract this information from the GL cubes, allocate across client and transfer the result to the profitability cube. An example of this type of profit and loss line was marketing and promotional cost, which was posted to GL by product, but was allocated to client based on net receivables.

▪ For those profit and loss lines already analyzed by client but not product, extract this information from the GL cubes, allocate across product and transfer the result to the profitability cube. An example of this type of profit and loss line was direct sales costs for a client, which was posted to GL by client, but was allocated to product based on net receivables.

▪ For those profit and loss lines not analyzed by product or client, extract this information from the GL cubes, allocate across product and client and transfer the result to the profitability cube. An example of this type of profit and loss line was call centre costs, which would be allocated based on call volume.

The process seemed naturally to fall into three stages:

1. Extract the data from GL, keeping the product and client detail where applicable, and grouping similar costs into cost pools.
2. Allocate the data that needs allocating.
3. Report on the result.

The identified dimensions in this process were therefore:

▪ A cost pool dimension to group costs that shared a cost driver, which could then be allocated using that driver. Examples of drivers used were number of calls received at the call centre, which would be used to allocate call centre costs to products and clients.

▪ A profit line dimension to hold the resultant summary profit and loss.

On closer examination of these dimensions, it appeared that the profit lines reported were groupings of cost pools, and that the users would benefit from drilling from the profit loss line to view the source costs.

The main design concept was therefore to create one new dimension called profitability line which would be used for both purposes.

For the extraction from GL, a catalog dimensioned by profitability line would include the ranges of accounts, sub accounts and cost centres to be grouped together. The company dimension was not included in this catalog as this was not required in the profitability reports. Ranges were used in the catalog as this would reduce catalog maintenance when segment values were added in GL.

For the allocation to product and client, the same catalog dimensioned by profitability line would indicate the cost driver to be used, if one was required.

The cube map shown in Figure 7.5 was designed to meet these requirements and this process flow.

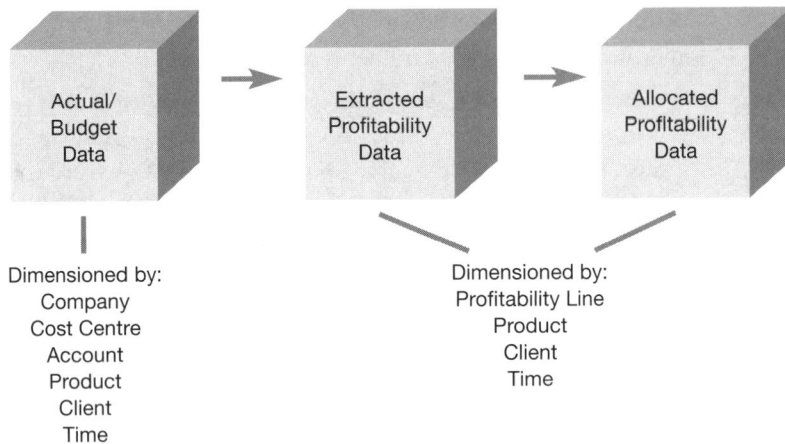

FIG 7.5　　The cube map

The profitability line dimension values were as shown in Table 7.1. From these lines, the product P&L report was produced.

TABLE 7.1　　Profitability line dimension values

Profitability Line
Financing Income
Late / Delinquency Interest
Legal Collection Interest
Other Interest

Profitability Line
Commission Received
Cash Fees
Statement Fees
Delinquency Fees
PPI/CFI
Start-up Fees
Limit Fees
Other Fees
Commission Paid to Affiliates
Other Sundry Income
Total Funding Cost
Finance
Business Dev.
Risk
HR
Professional Development
Training
Systems – Other
Systems – Maintenance
Systems – Development
Facilities
Quality
Marketing
Telecom
Operations
Finance
Risk
Facilities
Quality
Facilities
Sales
Marketing
Statements
Marketing Expense
External Call Centre
Cash Fee New Accounts

7.12   INFRASTRUCTURE SPECIFICATION

For the European and US headquarters implementations, one physical server was used, based in the data centre in the UK. This housed the Super and Sub Shared Databases for the European businesses and the US headquarters. The Express environment was set up with one service per country, to enable CPUs and memory to be allocated to a particular country. The data layout on the disks was also managed so that each country had its own disks and disk controller, and this minimized the contention between the countries.

Initially, the service was shared between countries, and so the CPUs, memory and disk were all shared between the countries. For the month-end scheduled loads, this was not an issue as these could be scheduled so as not to conflict with each other. However, for ad-hoc processing, such as restatement of prior years following a significant hierarchy change, we found that processing on one country's system could significantly affect the performance of another. As the countries were rarely aware of each other's activities, this effect was undesirable, as it meant that responses times were variable.

The multiple service environment was put in place to reduce this and this was achieved using the cluster mechanism of OFA, albeit on one physical device. As a database can be attached by only one service, and as a SubDBA needs to attach the Task and Shared Databases for the tier above to check for distributions, the cluster mechanism uses XCA to connect to the other service and attaches the database through that service. XCA stands for Express Communications Architecture and is the communication protocol supported for server-to-server communications, whereas SNAPI is for client-to-server communications. The cluster mechanism is generally used to link SubDBAs on one physical server to a SuperDBA on another physical server, but can be used across multiple services on one physical server.

The Asia implementations will be implemented on a local server, and this will connect through to the Super Shared Database on the European server, again via the cluster mechanism.

8 Case studies in activity-based management

ROAD MAP

We first review activity-based management (ABM) principles to provide an overview of the issues for those less familiar with activity-based management. We then review at a high level some cases across three vertical markets – CPG, public sector, and financial services, considering project planning and critical success factors.

There are numerous ways of implementing ABM. So why was Oracle Financial Analyzer applied to ABM in the past? By referring to key functions of Oracle Financial Analyzer applied in ABM projects, the analyst is provided with an outline checklist for the questions which need to be asked when considering software options for implementing ABM. Current developments in the ABM package market may deliver some or all of these functions, offering a total solution or a hybrid approach within an OFA architecture, as discussed in Chapter 2 and later in this chapter.

We then consider Oracle Financial Analyzer and activity-based planning and budgeting. Activity-based planning and budgeting has been a prime driver for the use of Oracle Financial Analyzer in the public sector in the UK; we abstract from a number of public sector implementations to cover this topic.

We then move from the developer's view to the perspective of those using the built system, such as gathering driver data, activity analysis and 'what-if' analysis (including the issue of constraints).

More granular ABM, sizing issues and solution architectures which go beyond just OFA are then considered. If the spectrum of requirements ranges from 'simple' cost allocation, through <Product Channel Time>, to <Customer Product Channel Time>, how does the system architect propose a scalable and extensible technical architecture which might require:

- Oracle RDBMS?

- Oracle Financial Analyzer?

- An activity-based costing package such as Oracle ABM?

- and a 'black box' high volume cost allocation engine?

We then follow the generic ABC process model from logical definition of the requirements, through cube maps documenting structures and process flows, down to high-level program definitions. The reader will note how the generic ABC business process model is mapped in detail to OFA functionality, understand the importance of the use of Attributes and the need for Express SPL programs to perform the required cost allocations.

8.1   ACTIVITY-BASED COSTING: THE PRINCIPLES

Activity-based management uses the techniques of activity-based costing to deliver an activity-based management approach to running the business. The techniques of activity-based costing are based on a premise that it is business activities that give rise to the need for resource costs, not the products or services produced (often called outputs or cost objects). The process can be summarized into two steps, as in Figure 8.1:

1. Allocate cost of resources to activities.

2. Allocate the activity costs to products (cost objects) which consume those activities.

Resources → Activities → Cost Objects

FIG 8.1   **The generic ABC process model**

There may be many intermediate steps, for instance the need to re-allocate resource costs or activity costs and to aggregate many cost objects to generate final product costs, as discussed later. However, the model above is essentially the core of activity-based costing.

In the simple example shown in Figure 8.2, the ledger produces costs of 100, split between cost centres 1 and 2. Each cost centre manager will provide the basis of driving the resource costs to activities, known as resource drivers. This results in activity costs of 30, 20 and 50 for the three activities, A1, A2, A3. The product managers will negotiate with the process managers an appropriate basis for driving the activity costs to the products, known as cost drivers. This results in the products being allocated activity costs of 15, 35 and 50 respectively.

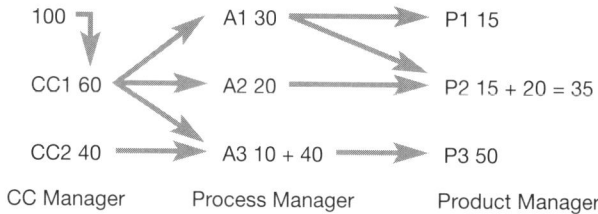

FIG 8.2   The generic ABC process model applied

Cost allocation for ABC is focused more directly on the cost of processes, unlike the cost allocations discussed earlier in the book. Activities are only one tier in a Task–Activity–Business Process hierarchy. There has been much use made within the large consultancies of ABC in programmes for business re-engineering (or business process redesign). For example, business process re-engineering uses ABC to review the cost of processes.

Some business processes are involved neither directly in production nor in supporting production activities. It is often therefore inappropriate to try to allocate these costs to products – these are called business sustaining costs. However, those concerned with the supply chain, such as distribution, selling and advertising, can be traced to specific customers, channels or market sectors for improved customer account profitability analysis, whether the product is intangible or not. Hence ABC techniques are of importance to both manufacturing and service-based industries.

8.1.1 ABM and re-engineering business processes

ABM is about using the techniques of ABC to re-engineer the business for efficiency, and by extension, profitability. Figure 8.3 below demonstrates the range of options.

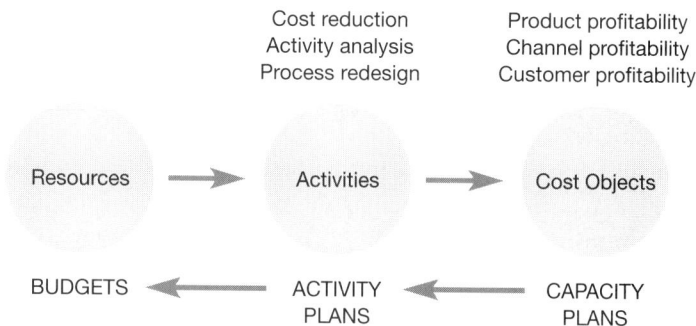

FIG 8.3   Using ABC for activity-based management

For example, in activity analysis, each task or activity can carry an attribute, such as:

- non-value-added vs. value-added;
- discretionary vs. non-discretionary;
- outsourced activities vs. internally supplied.

Companies in the same – or different – sectors can use activity analysis for benchmarking their efficiency against others. It can also be used to calculate the level of activities and hence resources to support capacity planning.

In the example below of activity analysis from the utilities sector, domestic call-outs were attracting huge costs, £160,000 in the period considered. When subjected to activity-based allocation, the costs of activities were as follows:

	£
Ineffective call-out – caller not in	29,000
Ineffective call-out – caller fixed problem	39,000
Ineffective call-out – fault not corrected because no parts	56,000
Effective call-out – fault corrected	36,000

The need to gather much more information from customers when they phoned to ask for help was evident, leading to process improvement in the call centre processes.

Such business change programmes normally suggest that evolution, not revolution, is the best approach; the organization can be progressively managed by an incremental move to the use of activity-based information. Furthermore, different levels of the business have different information needs. Hence a bottom-up approach is important, because unless the results are relevant to operational users, whilst still meeting company-level needs, getting participation in the data capture process will be difficult.

As discussed in Chapter 2, 'black box' cost allocation engines and ABC packages exist, and we shall refer to them later. ABC projects often commence with prototyping tools, such as PC packages, spreadsheets and sometimes paper. These initiatives may be remote from enterprise operational systems, and conducted in a specialist costing department. However, as we will see later, major change programmes across the enterprise have involved OFA in delivering enterprise solutions, as well as for the costing department.

Finally, with ABC, starting in the right place is important. How good are current systems at data collection, managing many versions of the data, sharing information, reporting and modelling, performing top-down as well as bottom-up budgeting? As we will note later, an OFA ABC project often delivers quick wins on the way towards full ABC.

8.1.2 Some cases in OFA ABC

Typically, Oracle Financial Analyzer manages the soft data gathering process, and, using actuals data loaded from the ledger, harnesses SPL routines written in Express to provide the required calculations, reporting and analysis facilities. Typically, there are no changes required to the ledger. All of the features of the generic OFA requirements architecture, as shown in Figure 8.4, are present.

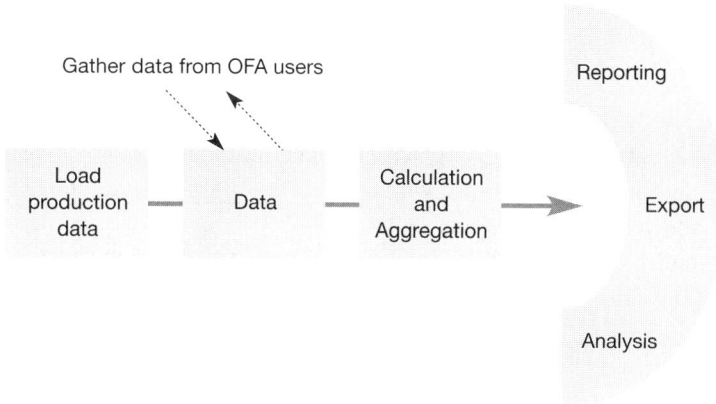

FIG 8.4   **The generic OFA process model**

OFA has been used to implement ABC in a number of industries, including the following.

CPG

A multinational CPG has been using an Express/Oracle Financial Analyzer solution for factory-based ABC, rolled out to food factories across Europe. Every site has different feeder systems, with SAP an important source of Actuals, so the implementation is locally configurable. There is a separate system which consolidates the information from the local implementations, also based on Oracle Financial Analyzer, to support pan-European benchmarking of ABC data. This has been used to help rationalize the supply chain.

Public sector

In the UK public sector, there are a number of sophisticated ABC systems within major government agencies, typically developed by Oracle working with the large consultancies. One UK government department responsible for collecting indirect taxes uses Oracle Financial Analyzer to provide for funding based on a fixed unit cost for supply. The system uses Oracle Financial Analyzer linked to Oracle GL, with all the activity and product costing done in Oracle Financial Analyzer. Another government agency, having implemented accruals accounting with Oracle GL, then delivered an activity-based planning and budgeting framework, based on Oracle Financial Analyzer and Express, to an initial user group of over 700 users. The aim was to establish a planning and budgeting framework through the levels within the agency:

The Agency
14 top-level groups
128 mid-level groups
800 bottom-level groups

Budget assumptions/guidelines flow down from the top (SuperDBA) through the top-level groups (subDBAs) to mid-level (Sub SubDBAs), and finally to the client Budget Workstations from which the data is then aggregated back up into a consolidated enterprise budget. At each level, there is an opportunity to extend and enhance the core Oracle Financial Analyzer enterprise model to meet local business needs. In another case, the ABC system brings together financial data from SAP and operational data from various sources into Oracle Financial Analyzer, and calculates costs of activities and products for the purpose of setting prices and remunerating operators of franchised distribution outlets. For this purpose, costs objects are dimensioned by <Product Activity Region Outlet_Type Time> and in this regard show similarities with implementations in the financial services sector, where <Product Activity Channel Time> is common.

Financial services

Case studies in the financial sector have been smaller in terms of users, but are significant in terms of the business driver for ABC. As noted above, the need to understand how costs vary by <Product Activity Channel Time> is critical to providers of intangible products such as mortgage, pension and insurance products. With the introduction of new Web-based channels, and competition from clicks and mortar types, as opposed to bricks and mortar types, of product providers, such implementations assume an even greater importance in delivering meaningful costings for pricing and output decisions.

8.1.3 Project planning

Implemented projects indicate high degrees of commonality in approach, whether the industry is financial services, manufacturing, public sector or utility. The stages of an OFA implementation which are particularly important for an ABC implementation are italicized in the project life cycle set out below:

Project sponsorship
Pilot or proof of concept
Team formation/authorization – go ahead

Business process modelling:

    Ledger summarization to cost pool
    Task/activity/process hierarchy and resource driver definition
    Cost driver definition and cost object modelling

Change management planning

    Cost centre managers
    Product managers

Software and related activities

    Implementation – development phase
       Design, using prototyping
       Source data analysis
       Build and populate structures
       Report
       Training of DBA/SubDBAs
       Acceptance test
       Documentation

Implementation – roll-out phase

    Install remote workstations
    End user training

Project resourcing and skill sets

It could be argued that the most significant contributor to project success in delivering ABC generally and OFA ABC in particular is the availability of people with the appropriate mix of business, financial and technical skills. As activity-based costing (and activity-based management) does not yet use a standard terminology or methodology, implementers need to work proactively with business people, overcoming terminology difficulties in clarifying business model issues as well as technical issues as they go. This may be particularly important where an ABC project is being driven by business process re-engineering or involves extensive activity analysis.

However, it is very important not to relegate critical business process decisions to 'clarification' during implementation; if important design decisions need to be made at the logical level, the project plan needs to reflect this.

Duration of implemented projects

Projects have been implemented over timescales ranging from three months to four years, with resources of a few person-months to many person-years, on a 'big-bang' or a phased deliverable basis. The maturity and duration of the OFA ABC-specific project phases are obviously a significant factor.

8.1.4 Business process modelling

The duration of the business modelling phase of implemented OFA ABC projects depends critically on the degree of completeness of the ABC modelling itself at the date of project sponsorship. ABC proof of concept modelling is often accomplished by spreadsheets or on a single-user ABC package. However, the business modelling may not even be started, under revision or incomplete, or fully represented within spreadsheets or a de-facto prototype built in a package. Estimating the duration of this phase is crucial, as it is on the critical path. There are extremes, with one project consuming 200 person-days of large consultancy time on business modelling alone, and another where the whole project was delivered in nine days.

8.1.5 Change management planning

The change management process itself may absorb significant resources; a road show to all the field units in one implementation took place over four months, reflecting the national spread of data submitters, and report users, prior to the system build. Again, there are extremes. If the move to ABM involves substantial organizational change in an organization which is unused to change, the time absorbed can be considerable. One organization in the public sector claimed that 30 person-years were spent in communicating the vision and gaining buy-in from the top to the bottom of the organization. It is equally clear that the impact of price competitiveness stimulated by new business models such as e-procurement and e-exchanges will make change necessary for business-to-consumer and business-to-business operations alike. Where price competition was severe in one implementation of OFA ABC in the CPG sector, there was no change management necessary at the factory level; everyone knew the consequences of not pricing competitively and avoiding loss-making supply to market segments where the competition was too severe. A practical rule: if no change management is planned to take place, a risk factor should be introduced when assessing project risk until the issue is addressed and either dismissed or acknowledged.

8.1.6 Design, prototyping and documentation

The OFA ABC projects typically commence with a design workshop to define the ABC calculation processes and how they are to be delivered within the organizational structure in terms of data gathering, processing and ultimate utilization. As discussed in Section 5.5, the ease with which a prototype can be built offers the option of using prototyping to define the requirement. This may take place in parallel with documenting the logical system requirement, leaving requirement detailing to screen shots/the prototype software itself where appropriate. The next step will be a technical specification, and then the commencement of the build. As the build proceeds, the technical specification can be detailed and moved towards being 'as-built' technical documentation. In parallel with this, those charged with change management and training can use both the logical and technical specification to design:

▪ Super Administrator/Administrator manuals;

▪ the user documentation;

▪ any other documentation required to support the roll-out phase.

The logical system requirement covers the functional requirements to meet the ABC calculation process. It identifies the structures required: cost pools, resource drivers, activities, cost drivers, products, with their attributes (cost driver to activity, direct, indirect, etc.) and hierarchies (activity, product, etc.), and the allocation processes themselves. It will also cover the roles of the user within the system boundary (providing data, running the system, using the output) and their location.

The technical specification translates the logical system requirement into the OFA structures, the Dimensions (cost pools, activities, products, etc.), Financial Data Items (activity costs, product costs, etc.), Attributes and Hierarchies, and defines them with sufficient precision for the system implementer to use them directly during set-up. The ABC calculation process is defined as a cube map(s) and will provide the system implementer with:

▪ sufficient information to commence the build, and

▪ a basis of clarifying the allocation processes with the business users concerned with the ABC processes themselves, and

▪ a basis of clarifying the output requirements with the business users concerned with using the results of the ABC processes.

The technical specification documents will be detailed by the implementer as the development proceeds. The result will be that all structures, allocation processes and reporting requirements are fully documented within the technical specification as the 'as-built' system:

▪ Dimensions definition

▪ Attribute definitions

▪ Financial Data Item definitions

▪ Model definitions

▪ Solve definitions

- Custom program definitions
- The cube maps, showing process flow
- Platform specification for both the development and roll-out (file locations, operating system, network environment).

OFA ABC projects gain from the logical system requirement and the technical specification documents throughout the development phase and into roll-out. In the transition from development to roll-out, their existence has assisted in preparation of the Super Administrator/Administrator Manuals and the User Documentation, which themselves are vital in transferring the system from the developer to the business owner.

A common requirement is to allow the interested parties in the system to be able to audit the calculations performed by the system, tracing the cost/driver data input through activity cost to product cost:

- **managers**, who have to justify the decisions based upon the system;
- **administrators**, who have to field queries on 'how we got to this figure';
- **internal and external auditors**, who need to prove that the process is working to signed-off specification.

Explaining the processes should be aided by the transparency of cube maps showing process flow, combined with the intuitive multidimensional structures in the software. Since the documentation is of the 'as-built' system, driven from the logical and technical specification documentation, there should be no gaps between documentation and actual functionality.

8.1.7 Software and related activities

The titles in an OFA ABC project progress report in Table 8.1 show typical software implementation activities: note that it excludes the business process modelling and the pre-implementation change management activities.

TABLE 8.1 Interim deliverables and project planning

Task
1. Analysis and Design
2. Install OFA Software
3. Write data readers
Actuals NL
Actuals sales system
Actuals production system
Dimensions
Budgets

Task

4. Build structures

> Dimensions
> Dimension values
> Financial data items (FDI)
> Attributes
> Models
> Solves
> Custom programs
> Users
> Hierarchies
> Budget entry worksheets
> Allocation adjustment worksheets

5. Load data

> Actuals NL
> Budget NL
> Mapping GL to CCACC
> Mapping CCACC to cost pool
> Primary allocation
> Secondary allocation
> Material allocation
> Packaging allocation
> Distribution allocation

6. Set up OFA reports

GL reports
Production costing
Customer profitability
Budgeting
Allocation review

7. Reconcile with existing system

Confirm production costing
Confirm distribution costing
Confirm GL data
Transfer to contingency
Confirm budget results

8. Train users

> Train SDBA
> Train SubDBA
> Train accountant users
> Train directors
> Train activity managers
> Train sales representatives
> Transfer to contingency

Task

---

9. Rollout

Install software
Check GL codes
Arrange data sources

---

10. Documentation

System documentation overview
Technical documentation
User documentation

---

11. Project Management

Planning and control
Meetings
Time and progress report

The first stage in all ABC projects is the loading of Actuals to Oracle Financial Analyzer. In one project, the benefit of being able to simply slice and dice the Actuals gave a quick win on the project, as the GL report writer had been notoriously hard to use for ad-hoc analysis. In another, the use of the Oracle Financial Analyzer Worksheet for capturing driver data for ABC purposes prompted the customer to use Oracle Financial Analyzer to refine the budget process as an interim deliverable preceding full ABC. In this case the budget cycle was three months long, and was reduced to two weeks. Then within the ABC project itself, the full functionality could be delivered in a phased approach over time, as below:

Pilot (with small Head Office group)

- Traditional fixed and variable cost analysis
- Value-added/non-value-added activity analysis
- Reporting of the results of both to a wider conununity

    Roll-out of above pilot functionality as Phase 1

Pilot (with a larger group in Head Office)

- Activity-based budgeting

    Roll-out of above pilot functionality as Phase 2

Pilot (with a larger group across the organization)

- Capacity planning and analysis

    Roll-out of above pilot functionality as Phase 3

8.1.8 OFA ABC implementation – critical success factors

Setting up the calculations in OFA is typically only a small part of a project. The investment in the software implementation for ABM systems is often very modest compared to the required investment in change management, activity analysis, consultancy and design, which may not have been made. An ABM project can easily get going and appear to be progressing well as software development issues are addressed, whilst the more difficult job of selling ABM internally is neglected. The correct approach to planning and executing the OFA implementation can help, but is only one of the critical success factors.

8.1.9 Why was Oracle Financial Analyzer chosen to deliver ABM?

In Chapter 2, we discussed how the business analyst must carefully describe any business process which involves cost allocation. Such careful analysis must determine:

1. the nature of the cost allocation process; for example, simple/cascade or complex/iterative;

2. whether there is a need for the costs of activities to be calculated to support activity cost analysis itself, rather than ultimate cost object costing;

3. the volumetrics, as in number of source cost pools and number of target cost pools, number of dimension values, etc.

The results of the analysis may exclude OFA from consideration as a potential implementation tool. This could be on the grounds of volumetrics, or OFA may offer no advantages over an alternative approach (where, for example, a 'black box' calculation engine is all that is required). Furthermore, the technology to deliver the business process may already be in place – most GL packages (including Oracle) offer cost allocation functionality, which would be sufficient if only static/simple cost allocations are required. Finally, packages exist for cost allocation, in particular activity-based costing. We have discussed how they may be harnessed within an OFA architecture in Chapter 2.

There is an obvious need for the business analyst to proceed with caution when deciding to apply OFA to ABM projects. So, why was OFA chosen in the cases we have discussed?

■ ABM Packages (and ABC functionality within GL) did not, at the time, offer integrated multidimensional data handling; in contrast, the Express multidimensional structures which underpin data gathering, modelling, reporting and further analysis were already in place with OFA.

Activity-based applications are about multidimensionality – looking at costs by <Product Region Activity Time> – and this applies to all functions of the system, be they data gathering, modelling, reporting or further analysis, perhaps involving 'what-if'. Oracle Financial Analyzer Worksheets collect data in multidimensional form naturally, cube arithmetic makes the calculation rules easily readable, the report user can easily slice the cubes to get the desired view. If, for instance, we seek to collect cost driver data to allocate activity costs to products distributed for different time periods and different regions, we have four-dimensional data to collect. One OFA Worksheet dimensioned by <Product Region Activity Time> provides a means of easily inputting the data, simply paging through the appropriate dimensions to replicate what would be very many spreadsheets or data capture screens.

- ABM packages tended to deliver single-user facilities; Oracle Financial Analyzer allowed ABM to be a shared distributed application across the enterprise.

  Although ABC applications are likely to be in the control of the finance professional, the results may be useful to operational and sales and marketing staff. Through client/server or Internet architecture, a central Super Shared Database provides a range of different users with access to the relevant subset of data they are allowed to see and/or change. By careful use of the appropriate OFA client type, appropriate functionality is available to each of these users so they can review, report, input and model the data in the manner most appropriate to their needs.

- ABM packages were commonly used for the prototyping phase in large projects, but constraints were perceived on moving from prototype to enterprise delivery; the flexibility of Oracle Financial Analyzer enabled moving from prototyping to production system.

  ABM packages must necessarily impose constraints in seeking to meet core requirements of the majority of the user community. The gap analysis between functional requirements and alternative packages can take months. In this period, it might be better simply to prototype the required functionality in Oracle Financial Analyzer and then transition to a full production system. This approach generates momentum and ensures a positive and responsive interaction during the prototyping stages, when it is important to win the hearts and minds of users.

- ABM packages delivered one model to a small group of users, with no facilities to allow different parts of the organization to model their own particular environment; the Oracle Financial Analyzer distributed architecture supports more detailed structures, such as activities, for particular business units.

  Organizations with diverse businesses may well require more detailed structures, such as local sub-activities, to capture local business processes and reflect the peculiarities of different parts of the business. OFA allows this through the tiered architecture, while ensuring that top-level structures continue to provide the enterprise view. Being able to deliver separate structures for each business unit eases the process of rolling out applications to divisions or departments. Then at each level in the hierarchy of Administrators, users with the appropriate responsibilities can copy both the shared data and the structures. They then create their own detailed structures to manipulate and model the data. Each business unit can:

- modify/create new aggregation hierarchies;
- define alternative ABC models;
- perform what-if? via the Oracle Financial Analyzer Worksheet, applying their own models;
- create their own reports with ad-hoc calculations.

■ ABC packages were not all based upon the RDBMS model and hence were not open to efficient data handling; the underlying Express Database is open to source data and to other applications, allowing the application to:

- read flat files;
- retrieve and write data to operational relational databases via embedded SQL;
- push data to or pull data from another ABM package or application.

■ ABM packages, largely because they were single user, could not be migrated from prototype to production system; Oracle Financial Analyzer could provide a smooth development and roll-out path.

If required, stand-alone prototyping in NT could be undertaken before migrating to UNIX, providing the performance and capacity for enhanced database size and complexity, and the support for a wider number of users as the activity-based management system is rolled out across the enterprise.

■ ABC is about relationships between structures. Both structures and the relationship between them may change; maintaining structures and the relationships between them was supported by the OFA Attribute function.

Being able to create and change the many relationships between structures is very important while developing the prototype, as well as when maintaining an operational system, in ABC:

1. There may be changes in how actual costs are aggregated during the ABC process. The majority of the financial data will be sourced from the General Ledger, which may be structured by account and by cost centre. One approach is to allocate each account balance to activities. While accounts can be mapped directly to activities in this way, it is a common practice to try to keep to a manageable number of rules in tracing costs to activities. For this reason, cost centre/account balances are often

aggregated into cost pools which share an allocation rule. The almost inevitable changes to cost centres and accounts which may be made within the GL can be remapped to the correct cost pools in the OFA Maintain menu using the Attribute function, as in Figure 8.5.

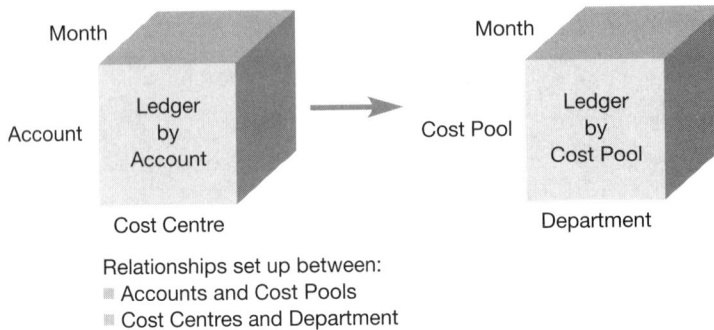

Relationships set up between:
- Accounts and Cost Pools
- Cost Centres and Department

FIG 8.5   Using OFA Attributes to maintain relationships

2. Activities and cost drivers will often need to be changed to reflect changes in business processes; review of process efficiency is, after all, one of the objectives of ABM and hence will naturally lead to changes in activities.

3. The organizational structure itself may change. It may be decided not to aggregate ACC with CC, to facilitate conventional analysis by department. By maintaining the relationship between cost centre and department in an OFA Attribute, re-mapping of cost centre to department may be easily achieved.

The use of Attributes will be expanded upon considerably in Section 8.3.

- ABC packages assumed that the required data exists, whereas it may need to be calculated; Oracle Financial Analyzer provided facilities through the Model for *calculating* driver volumes for use in ABM.

Driver volumes may not always be simply *gathered* from people or *loaded* from production systems. In certain situations, they may need to be *calculated*, since while some driver data may be static (such as floor area) others drivers are variable over time, depending upon the production volumes for the period. The number of hours a particular product takes to be packaged would be dependent on the production volume of that product, which is dependent on the number in a pack for that particular packaging option, and the throughput of the packing line. An OFA Model can be used to compute the amount of each cost driver in such circumstances, as in Figure 8.6.

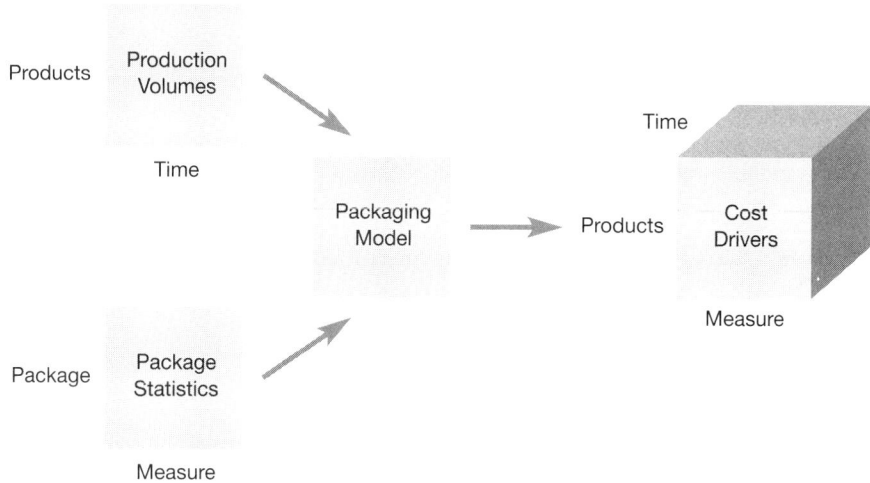

FIG 8.6   **Using an OFA Model to calculate cost drivers**

■ Clarifying the calculation process, mapping the calculations into software and then checking with the users that the system is correctly configured were separate processes in most approaches to ABM; visualization of the calculation processes using the cube maps within Oracle Financial Analyzer makes it easy to discuss the requirement between technical and non-technical people.

For example, the calculation of unit costs is an important step in ABC, often for benchmarking purposes. Oracle Financial Analyzer cubes and the cube arithmetic give a high level of transparency to the user when discussing the calculation of unit costs, as below. Unit costs for each activity are calculated by dividing the total activity cost of a particular activity for all cost pools by the total volume of the appropriate cost driver for that activity, as in Figure 8.7.

Transparency is maintained as unit activity costs associated with a particular product are applied to generate the cost of each activity consumed in producing a product. In this case, an Oracle Financial Analyzer Attribute limits the cost driver data cube to the appropriate cost driver for an activity to the product as the program loops over the calculation, as in Figure 8.8.

■ Many organizations feel that their ABC processes have unique features; Oracle Financial Analyzer, through Express SPL programs, provided the mechanism for delivering the required allocations and re-allocations unconstrained by the functionality of a package.

ABC often requires fairly complex allocation and re-allocation rules to be applied. Cascade allocations, in which costs are allocated down a hierarchy, are much simpler than the more complex, often iterative, cost allocations which are typical of many ABC implementations. Resources are frequently

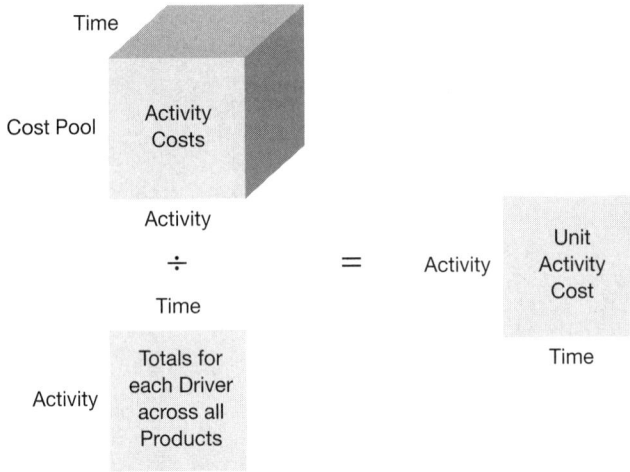

FIG 8.7   **Cube arithmetic in calculating product costs**

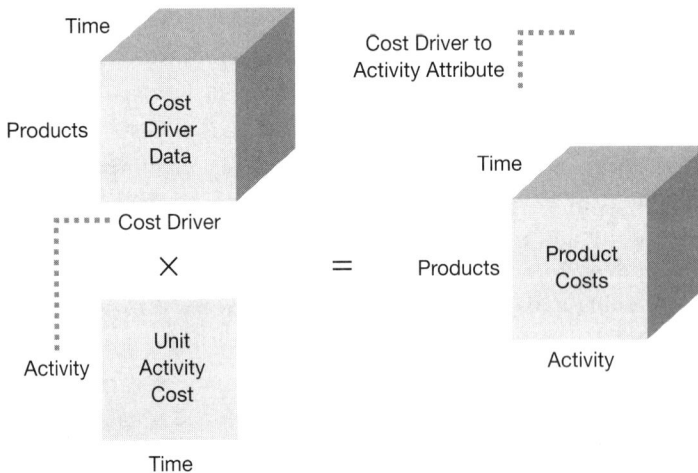

FIG 8.8   **Cube arithmetic in calculating product costs**

re-allocated, even before allocation to activities are considered. This is because general ledgers are usually set up to support the responsibility for paying bills, not who consumes the resource. So, for example, to arrive at total staff costs it may be necessary for staff pension costs to be apportioned from a central payroll cost centre to the cost centres employing the staff. The need for more complex allocation processes also occurs because not all activities are directly involved in making a product or service. Some are support services, such as staff restaurants, whose costs cannot be traced to products but instead to other activities. Even production activities may support other activities, such as tool-making in manufacturing processes. Firstly, a suitable basis for charging these services needs to be established – for example, the number of staff engaged in an activity may be the basis for allocating canteen costs, thus headcount becomes the cost driver for allocating canteen costs. However, canteen costs may be allocated some other support costs, such as buildings maintenance. Allocations must be done sequentially, preventing a single phase of allocation to clear the 'support' activities. An iterative calculation may be required. Express SPL programs have typically been written to define the rules required to perform such iterations, as well as simpler allocation processes, such as cascade allocations. The Express SPL programs enable Oracle Financial Analyzer to provide the functionality to meet specific allocation requirements and also to give flexibility when the underlying structures or processes need to change.

■ Reporting facilities in ABM packages had only just embraced the multidimensional OLAP model; Oracle Financial Analyzer already had those facilities.

Thus, Oracle Financial Analyzer enabled the data held in the account, cost pool, activity or product dimensions to be aggregated in many different ways, since there can be multiple hierarchies on any dimension.

For example, activity costs can be aggregated by process and by organization, depending on the view required, as in Figure 8.9.

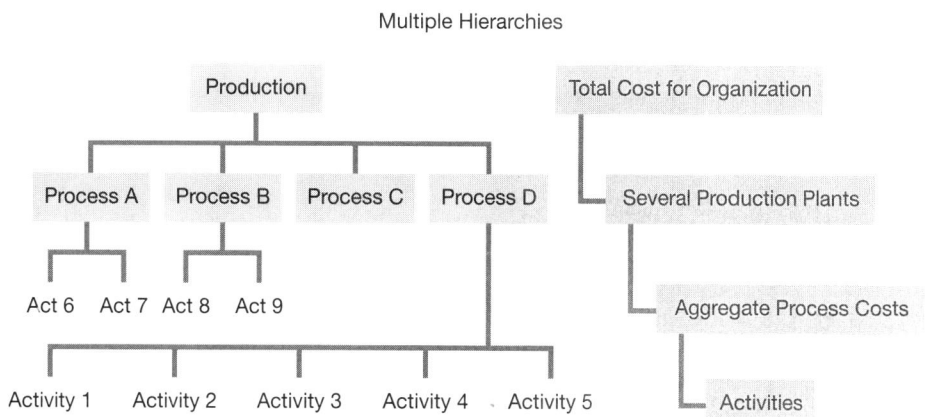

FIG 8.9   **Activity costs aggregated across multiple hierarchies**

8.1.10 So why choose Oracle Financial Analyzer to deliver ABM now, rather than a package?

In summary, OFA was used to deliver ABM because the specific features outlined above supported the actual requirement. The ABM package market has evolved considerably over time, providing:

1. open data structures, primarily by using RDBMS (and often Oracle RDBMS) to store the data;

2. better reporting facilities through a multidimensional reporting front-end.

There has also been a move towards multi-user architectures and facilities to provide local models which aggregate to a corporate model.

The logical approach should be to refer to key functions of Oracle Financial Analyzer applied in ABM projects in the past as an outline checklist for the questions which need to be asked when considering software options for implementing ABM now. Current developments in the ABM package market may deliver some or all of these functions, offering a total solution or a hybrid approach within an OFA architecture, as discussed in Chapter 2 and later in this chapter. For large tiered enterprises, such issues as gathering the data in a robust enterprise way, scoping the rights of a large tiered user community to access the results of ABC modelling while enabling local modelling within an enterprise framework, may continue to influence the use of OFA for ABM.

8.2 ORACLE FINANCIAL ANALYZER AND ACTIVITY-BASED PLANNING AND BUDGETING

In the UK, activity-based planning and budgeting has been a prime driver in the use of Oracle Financial Analyzer in the public sector. The public sector spends a large part of the UK's gross domestic product. Although a significant part of this is the payment of social security benefits to individuals, more than half is its own capital and current spending, so there is pressure to contain current spending while ensuring that adequate infrastructure investment is maintained. Structurally, the public sector comprises central government departments such as the Department of Trade and Industry, their subordinate Executive Agencies such as the Highways Agency, as well as various non-departmental public bodies and a wide variety of local authorities. It is the Departments that concern us, and their Executive Agencies.

8.2.1 The UK public expenditure budgeting process

Each year, the UK Treasury undertakes a Public Expenditure Survey (PES), during which the Departments 'bid' for resources, to be spent through their Agencies. This is essentially a resource allocation or budgeting exercise. For many years, most public entities had traditionally used cash accounting, rather than accruals accounting, to account for resources spent, which broadly meant that funds allocated for a year must not only be committed but actually be spent in-year, since no carry-over was permitted. This was felt to encourage year-end spending which might otherwise have been avoided. Furthermore, current and capital spending were not distinguished, providing little incentive to contain current spending in order to invest in infrastructure, where the benefits could be enjoyed over a longer timescale. The private sector, of course, had long since moved to resources being monitored on an accruals accounting basis, with budgeting being conducted on more rational bases, sometimes on an activity cost/output costing basis.

In an effort to bring the UK public sector more in line with long-accepted private sector practice, the UK government published a White Paper in 1994, called 'Better Accounting for the Taxpayers' Money' (Her Majesty's Stationery Office, UK) and widely known, by those affected, by the acronym RAB, standing for Resource Accounting and Budgeting.

Resource Accounting and Budgeting has two features:

■ Resource **Accounting** is the replacement of cash accounting with accruals accounting.

■ Resource **Budgeting** is the allocation of funds as part of a contract between the Treasury and the Department to deliver agreed outputs.

Accruals accounting has been largely achieved with various ledger enhancements and replacements, and as far as resource budgeting is concerned, the UK Treasury now expects to make allocations on an outputs basis. The processes can be summarized as shown in Figure 8.10.

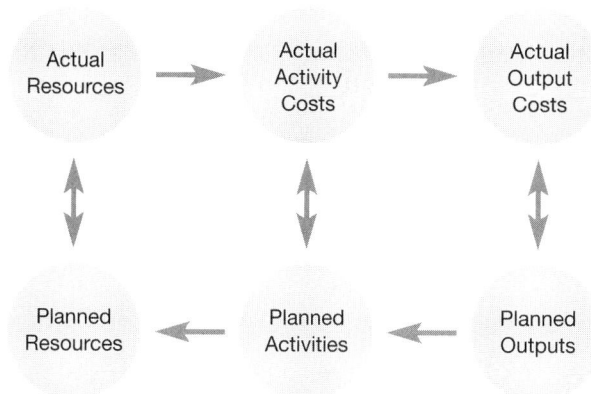

FIG 8.10   The Resource Budgeting process

The logical process flows are:

Actuals Costing	left to right in the diagram
Planning	right to left in the diagram
Monitoring	the vertical arrows indicate comparison of Actuals vs. Plan

As can be seen, resource 'budgeting' is too narrow a definition of the process. All budgeting systems need to be accompanied by a reporting system which delivers feedback – Actuals versus Budget, Plan or Forecast. The concept might be better described as resource management, and can then be viewed as falling into three strands:

- planning, in volume as well as cost terms, for resources, activities and outputs through all levels in the organization;

- recording Actuals in terms of volumes as well as cost terms, resource usage, work done (activities) and results achieved (outputs);

- in-year monitoring, i.e. comparing Actuals with Plans and current Forecasts accordingly.

8.2.2 General features of the implementations

They are large

The key feature of the implementations is that they are large – large in terms of numbers of users and large in terms of the Super Shared Database. In one implementation, over 700 users participate in a bottom-up and top-down planning and budgeting process. In terms of the number of structures in the Super Shared Database, indicative metrics are as shown in the table below.

The size of the RAB Super Shared Database does not give an unambiguous indicative metric since best practice in the design of the Super Shared Database in a tiered environment should normally be to restrict the structures to a summary level, as discussed in Section 5.5. However, not all of the implementations have followed this best practice recommendation, with the result that figures of between 7 and 99 Gigabytes have been predicted at the point where the implementations are loaded with some years of data.

	RAB project	Large financial service	Small financial service
Attributes	41	34	7
FDIs	88	20	15
Models	0	10	4
Solves	108	16	7
Custom Program	85	38	16

RAB means tiered architectures

The principles of RAB are those of activity-based management. Outputs require work to be done (activities) and it is the activities that consume the resources. However, these processes take place at all levels in what are very large organizations, with a tiered and geographically distributed structure. The top of the hierarchy is the national level, with the next level being the regions, within which there are individual locations. In some agencies, there are cost centres within the locations. Hence for our purposes one can consider the generic hierarchy as:

> National
> > Regional
> > > Location
> > > > Cost Centre

Three issues related to the tiered architectures need consideration:

- Top-down planning and bottom-up planning have to coexist in such an environment, and OFA offers a mechanism for reaching agreement on the final version.
- 'What-if' scenario planning support at all levels in the organizational hierarchy is essential, because it is necessary to test the impact of various policy changes, some of which can only be assessed locally.
- Capture of Actuals on the volumetrics – work done and outputs achieved – is done at the front line and must flow upwards in an orderly way.

The challenge is for regional variations to be accommodated if government is to escape the charge of obsession with central control, permitting local activities to be modelled, while winning commitment across a large organization to the upwards flow of data.

RAB requires human resources planning

Since the major element of the cost structure of a government agency is payroll cost, a critical component of both the actuals costing and the planning process is human resources planning. UK government agencies embraced human resources planning with a degree of commitment long before RAB, since it is critical to the provision of services such as defence, policing, public health, etc. The agency will typically have a strategy, within which tactical objectives are stated, and from which operational plans are prepared. Process decomposition from these operational plans provides the activities required to deliver operational capability. The human resources planning process calculates the average time taken to perform each activity, looks at planned activity levels and computes the headcount required.

From an OFA point of view, this information allows the calculation of the cost of activities. Each grade of public servant will provide a number of activities, hence the resource driver cube is logically dimensioned by <Location Activity Pay_grade Time> which can reference for the staff grade performing the particular activity, the appropriate pay rate dimensioned <Pay_grade Pay_rate Time>. This information should be shared across the tiered architecture, and hence first loaded into the Super Shared Database before distribution to the Sub Shared Databases. Note that the granularity of the human resources planning is at headcount for a particular grade, not by individual.

We now describe the processes implemented in OFA in more detail, commencing with the left to right process, Actuals Costing.

8.2.3 Actuals Costing

Note that many ABC implementations are largely 'Head Office' systems. Although the costs of the functions operated within the local network of these organizations are allocated along with Head Office costs, the primary focus is not on cost efficiency in the local network, but instead that of establishing costs for the type of decisions made at Head Office, such as:

- pricing decisions;
- channel to market decisions.

In contrast, the UK government agencies are concerned with cost efficiency, and, since the outputs provided are, by and large, delivered locally within the local network, the primary focus is of cost efficiency in delivering local services at the location itself. Accordingly, the left to right process of Actuals Costing commences with what happens at the location, to which are allocated costs incurred at the region and national level. Such costs, and the activities to which they relate, are referred to as indirect, in that they are not incurred in directly providing outputs. Note, however, that indirect activities and hence indirect costs can also occur at the location, where they will be incurred in support cost centres.

Unit costing of outputs in Actuals Costing

Unit costing of outputs is the core RAB component, critical, as with all ABM applications, for benchmarking purposes across a regionalized organization. The sub-processes are as in Figure 8.11.

As noted above, both direct and indirect activities are involved, so the actual steps for preparing unit output costs are:

1. Load costs from GL into OFA.
2. Allocate these costs to direct and indirect activities.
3. Re-allocate the indirect activity costs to direct activities.
4. Divide the direct activity cost by output volumes to arrive at unit output cost.

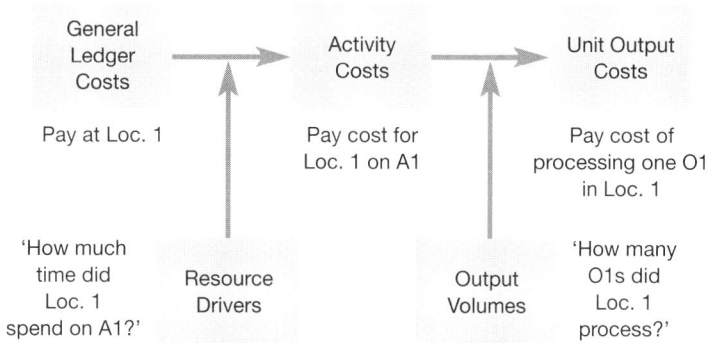

FIG 8.11   Actuals costing: unit costing of outputs

A large element of the cost of resources is payroll. Typically, there is a staff grade system with appropriate rates for each grade. The costs for each direct cost centre at each location will be exported from GL, and aggregated to location level, ready for allocation to activities. The costs for support cost centres at the location will be loaded and allocated separately.

The resource driver data for direct cost centres will typically be dimensioned as:

<Driver Pay_grade Activity Time>

to allow the staff of a particular grade to allocate their time to activity.

So far, we have ignored:

1. activities conducted at regional and national level by support cost centres;

2. support cost centres cost at the location.

Support cost centres (SCC) activities conducted at the local, regional and national level require those units to provide driver data for allocation, dimensioned by:

<SCC driver Activity Time>

The SCC indirect activity cost will then require re-allocation to direct activities before aggregation to provide direct activity cost, dimensioned by:

<Location Pay_band Activity Time>

in which Activity = direct activities. The activity costs are then divided by output volumes to calculate unit output costs.

Using unit costs of outputs to provide aggregate output costs

Recall that the Treasury instigated Resource Budgeting to provide for allocation of funds as part of a contract between the Treasury and the Department to deliver agreed outputs. So far, all we have is unit output costs. Multiplying by *actual* output volumes will give the total cost, in activity-based terms, of the actual outputs delivered in the period just closed. Multiplying by *planned* output volumes will give the total cost, in activity-based terms, of the outputs planned for the period ahead, as we will discuss later. The UK Treasury will normally require a much more aggregate view of the outputs, which of course is no problem with OFA. For example, one agency has eight key outputs, arrived at by aggregating the hundreds of more granular outputs produced by the OFA ABC model.

8.2.4 The planning process

So far we have dealt only with how actual costs are applied to outputs in order to monitor the actual cost of delivery of the outputs actually delivered in the year, for the purposes of in-year monitoring. The Planning process looks forward to future years and enables annual plans of output volumes, staff activity, staff cost and other costs to be created. It provides the means to distribute the plans between Head Office and the regions, and to reach an eventual compromise between regions and locations by allowing the flexing of inputs to meet assumptions of the plan. Looking at the planning process business process model in more detail:

1. At national level, the historical output volumes are reviewed and revised in light of projected future constraints, and the data set provided to the regions as:

    <Output   Organization   Time>

2. The regions compute the time required in person-hours to deliver the required activity level, using the relationship between direct activities and outputs determined at the national level as a result of the manpower planning exercise described earlier. The calculation is:

    output volumes × average time taken for each activity

3. The regions apply the planned average hourly salary for each pay grade to the time required in person-hours. This produces a data set dimensioned by:

    <Activity   Pay_grade   Time>

4. Using appropriate uplift %, the accommodation and other overheads are added to the costs derived from step 3.

5. The regions submit the plan to national level.

8.2.5 What were the issues in implementing the business process model in OFA?

Iterative planning and procedures to protect versions

It is essentially an iterative planning process which allows regions to amend local plans, to amend the regional plan and then to submit it to Head Office, with Head

Office being able to amend the plans and redistribute them to the regions. The Task Processor is a device to control a queue of tasks; strict procedures are required outside OFA so that regional plans are not overwritten by Head Office. Procedures to protect versions were documented in the OFA User Manuals and communicated as part of the roll-out training.

Local activity modelling

A connected issue was the ability of the regions or locations to extend the list of outputs and activities to permit local modelling which will only apply to the region or location. (Note that if an output or activity is to be added across the system, it must be added by the system administrator at Head Office who will then distribute it to all regions, a constraint to perceived 'ease of use'.) This allows the 'what-if' analysis to be performed. For example, if a region has submitted a plan to Head Office which Head Office has then amended for certain constraints, then when Head Office distributes this back down to the region, the region can use 'what-if' analysis on local activities to converge the local plans to use the reduced resources.

Number of versions of the plans

Both Head Office and the regions may store more than one version of the plans. This will enable, for example, a region to prepare its plan, submit it to Head Office, and then keep its original when Head Office sends down the revised version. As noted in Section 5.5, a critical issue is the number of versions for database sizing. In one implementation, the number of versions became a critical factor in influencing database size. Setting an arbitrary limit on the maximum number of stored versions for each region and for Head Office may be a pragmatic approach to containing database explosion.

Profiling the plans

If the plans have been prepared on a year-by-year basis, there is a need for a profiling process which will allow in-year tracking of actual progress against plan by spreading forecasting of the annual budget across the year to enable ongoing monitoring of actual results against planned results. It enables Head Office to provide monthly profiles to regions, and lets regions prepare monthly plans for local offices if required. While the actuals costing process moves resource costs to activities to outputs, the profiling process works in reverse. Standard timings were used to profile direct activities. Indirect activity time and costs proved challenging; in one case, the precise method for this was investigated further at a conference room pilot which had the interesting side-effect of securing local buy-in to the project as a whole.

The monitoring process

The monitoring process, the reporting deliverable of an Oracle Financial Analyzer ABC implementation, allows the comparison of actual results during the year with profiled plans and updated forecasts. A number of predefined reports, to form the enterprise core reporting pack, are common to OFA RAB applications (and indeed to all Oracle Financial Analyzer projects). Typically they will show the data for the current month, cumulative year to date, current month prior year and cumulative year to date for the prior year.

The level of detail required for reporting purposes and implications for the number of stored Financial Data items

For RAB projects, the reports will typically include:

1. actual output volumes vs. planned/forecast output volumes;
2. actual unit output costs vs. planned/forecast unit output costs;
3. actual activity time vs. planned/forecast activity time (split by direct and indirect activities);
4. actual activity costs vs. planned/forecast activity costs;
5. actual GL costs vs. planned/forecast GL costs.

These reports will contain the data for national level, and/or regional level, and/or location level.

When the packs are prepared for locations, reports 2 and 3 above may have the following options:

- the location's own costs, analyzed by appropriate cost category;
- as above, but including amounts allocated to it from the location support cost centres;
- both the above, but including amounts allocated to it from its region;
- all three of the above, but including amounts allocated to it from regional support cost centres;
- all four of the above, but including amounts allocated to it from Head Office cost centres.

Each cost category element of unit cost can thus be identified, as well as the total unit cost of each output. However, the need to provide this level of detail in reporting means that many more stored Financial Data Items than otherwise might be the case are required. Recall the indicative volumetrics we considered earlier, noting 88 Financial Data Items for the RAB project:

	RAB project	Large financial service	Small financial service
Attributes	41	34	7
FDIs	88	20	15
Models	0*	10	4
Solves	108	16	7
Custom Program	85	38	16

* from Super Shared Database containing the cost allocation logic,
but prior to creating reporting structures, which often use Models.
This indicates the irrelevance of Models to the cost allocation process itself.

The role of conference pilots in the business requirement and change process

As we noted in Section 5.7, the functional specification in Oracle Financial Analyzer projects at commencement of implementation is commonly less detailed than those prepared for RDBMS-based projects. There is extensive use of rapid application development techniques such as prototyping and conference room pilots. Some of the RAB projects followed this pattern, with, at each stage of the detailing of the requirement, conference room pilots being held to allow a subset of potential users to examine each module for functionality. The modules incorporated all the requirements detailed so far in the functional specifications. Each CRP delivered a wish list of enhancements and changes to the modules, which, as in the project approach described earlier, were incorporated both into the modules and into the documentation, so developing the 'as built' specification and supporting 'how to use the system'.

Change management

There are three issues for consideration, one an ABM issue in which OFA is irrelevant, and two which touch OFA:

1. In most Departments, resource budgeting brings together money, work done and results achieved perhaps for the first time, in a manner which reveals the position at national, regional and location level. There are obviously many reasons why such transparency might be resisted. This is a generic ABM issue in which OFA is irrelevant.

2. Unlike most commercial organizations, the outputs of the public sector are subject to policy changes outside a Department's control. A well-designed OFA ABC system should be able to handle change, as discussed in the first part of this chapter.

3. With budgetary responsibility effectively delegated across a tiered architecture to front-line managers, there must be serious commitment to training and roll-out issues.

In one implementation, administrative complexity was felt to exist when there are any Budget Workstations in the architecture, on the basis that the Budget Workstation user has to remember to submit to the Shared Database, whereas the Worksheet user is prompted to Save on exit. The other issue was that the Sub Administrators had not been effectively trained to manage their Sub Shared Databases. The application architecture was redesigned and the project relaunched with the end users as Analyst Workstations on one Super Shared Database. There were other issues in this case; apart from reducing the amount of regional involvement in system administration, simplifying the architecture in this case also involved reducing the server requirement from many to one.

Sourcing the data

The data warehouse

In one instance, a data warehousing system was already in existence to merge and cleanse data from hitherto free-standing legacy and operational systems, hence sourcing production data was not a problem. The existence of a legacy data capture system for activity information at the locations meant that a great deal of the data to be gathered from people was already being fed into the data warehouse. Despite the philosophy that that all enterprise data should be sourced from the enterprise data warehouse, there were still exceptions made where manual data entry was required because no system exists to source the data warehouse with some of the required data. Hence the OFA data gathering facilities were crucial.

Potentially very large data submitter communities

If no data warehouse or in-place data capture system had been in place, there would have been a generic requirement for potentially very large data submitter communities. In the UK public sector, data submitter communities may range up to 5,000 users involved in providing the resource management system with the range of data necessary to support the RAB-type project.

Technical infrastructure issues

Security is obviously paramount with public sector agencies, and physical security paramount in the agencies concerned with defence. In the UK RAB projects, both ends of the spectrum of possibilities in regard to the number of servers were used. In one case the logical tiered architecture is spread over 70 servers. In another case, one server and a mirror host the whole distributed system.

Leap to the Web delivery model

The implementation, training and cultural change processes required to deliver an integrated solution across a government agency are substantial; in the UK, many agencies have transacted business for more than a hundred years. However, the very fact that there may be a long overdue need to replace ageing systems/ageing MIS encourages the leap from the old systems to the new Web delivery model enabled by OFA.

Think big, start small: the data mart approach

Resource budgeting clearly benefits from a data *warehouse* approach to marshalling the required enterprise data set. However, it was sufficiently urgent to drive the data *mart* approach in some Departments, in advance of a full warehouse. Oracle Financial Analyzer delivered a solution sufficiently flexible to adapt to what were emerging, rather than fixed, requirements, with a prototype to pilot the production system phase approach, rather than the traditional software development cycle. However, it was credible as a strategic solution, since, from the Express data mart, it delivers the required functionality to the end user in advance of any data warehouse implementation. When the enterprise data warehouse appears, OFA can move to being a client application of the enterprise data warehouse, with little or no disruption to the end user, as discussed in Section 4.4.

This concludes the discussion on activity-based planning and budgeting. Using implemented cases where appropriate, we have moved through:

- why OFA was used for ABC;
- activity-based planning and budgeting with OFA.

The focus so far has been on implementing OFA ABC systems. We now move to issues relating to how the user actually uses the built systems.

8.2.6 Using the built system

The OFA generic process model allows data gathering, analysis and reporting facilities to be exploited by the user in a highly flexible way.

Gathering cost driver data

Oracle Financial Analyzer functionality for informal data gathering is often key to ABC. A typical driver for allocation, for example, is time sheet information, often translated into Full Time Equivalents, or FTE. Such information may come from production systems, such as HR, with a file reader. It could also be gathered from people in an orderly way using Oracle Financial Analyzer Worksheets or Data Entry

Forms. The data capture mechanism will obviously depend on whether formal systems exist; a benefit of the use of OFA is that the tiered architecture and Task Processor provide a means of review, not just validation, during data capture.

Activity analysis

We have already considered how users perform analysis simply at the level of activity cost information – the cost of value-added versus non-value-added activities, for example. We now consider the uses made of unit activity costs.

The activity cost in total for an activity is calculated by allocating resource costs based upon the appropriate activity allocation driver. This total activity cost must be divided by the volume of activity performed during the period, the cost (object) driver. Let us assume that a driver is telephone calls. The volume of telephone calls performed by the marketing department in Q2 is 1,500. There are many products requiring marketing and they are distributed through many regions. We divide the total marketing cost of £150,000 by 15,000 and produce a unit cost of £10 per telephone call for that activity. This is a useful measure for benchmarking efficiency; companies in the same industry might usefully all agree to contribute such statistics to an independent third party on a 'blind' basis, to which all have access, so that each contributor can see comparatively how cost efficient they are in providing marketing services.

The user must consider the problem of handling wasteful effort, in the metric which measures activity level, volume of activity. Readers should refer to a textbook on ABC if unfamiliar with the issues, but, in essence, either we use a metric that measures the actual activity level and ignore wasteful effort, or we separate productive effort from unproductive effort by reducing the divisor in the unit costing calculation to productive effort, thus:

Activity Cost of providing Activity A	£10,000
Total Cost driver volume	5,000 units
Productive activity	4,000 units
Unproductive activity	1,000 units
Basis A	10,000/5,000 = £2 per unit
Basis B	10,000/4,000 = £2.50 per unit to be used in costing output

If Basis B is applied, the actual productive activity level, 4,000 units, will be charged to the products/outputs and result in a cost of production of £10,000. If Basis A is applied, the unit rate of £2 per unit will be applied to the products/outputs and result in a charge of £8,000 for the period, the balance of unproductive units being reported at a cost of £2,000 in the period.

'What-if' analysis

'What-if' analysis in OFA ABC projects can be many things:

1. the ability simply to view the data generated by the current ABC model, from *different perspectives using the Selector,* for example by using multiple hierarchies on outputs/products, activities or resources; and/or

2. the ability to make *changes in the structure* of the ABC model using the Maintain menu; and/or

3. the ability to make *changes to the data* processed in the ABC model, by inputting new data at the keyboard using the Worksheet/Data Entry Form or by loading new data using Express Administrator or a file reader or by using Copydata to create new versions of the data already loaded; and/or

4. the ability to compare one ABC model to another model, by creating entirely separate Super Databases, creating Reports to compare results; and/or

5. the ability to compare one period to another, easily done by using the Selector to apply the same data to different Time period; and/or

6. the ability to model a particular business unit's processes and compare them on the same basis to another business unit, by using a tiered architecture so that the Sub Shared Database for each business unit can have an ABC model with an extended hierarchy of activities more specific to local business unit processes, but still within more aggregate activities defined at the Super Shared level which will permit comparison.

Activity-based budgeting or 'back flushing' is often seen as important in ABC implementations, understood as changing output, calculation of the required activity levels and hence the resources required. 'Back flushing' is in fact just another 'what-if' exercise, and has largely been covered in our discussion on the UK RAB implementations.

Resource constraints when modelling output levels

Another set of user issues relate to the need to consider resource constraints when modelling output levels. The objective here is sensitivity analysis, where cost object volumes are varied, for example, to assess the effect on costs of a 10 per cent increase in production. To perform sensitivity analysis, the user creates a baseline FDI, probably based on Actuals and a what-if version so that the results can be stored and compared with the baseline. New cost object volume figures are then entered against this what-if version. However, planned output levels may not be possible because the 'back flushed' activity levels or resources may simply not be available at all at the planned levels or because of the problem of handling fixed, semi-fixed/variable and variable cost relationships.

It is important for the user to be able to make judgements on how activity volumes will vary with changes in cost object volumes and how resource costs would vary with activity volumes. The system should enable the user to input:

- *an activity volume elasticity factor*
  The user makes a judgement on the % by which each activity's volume might change for a given change in output volume.

  For example, in a production environment, the activity line processing is probably around 100 per cent variable (a 10 per cent increase in output volume will require the line to run 10 per cent longer) whereas the activity line changeovers may be only 20 per cent variable (a 10 per cent increase in volume will only increase the changeover time by 2 per cent i.e.10% × 20%). The system uses these factors to generate what-if activity volumes, relying on the baseline. It was assumed for this type of simulation that support activity levels are not affected, although in reality there might be small changes.

- *a cost pool or cost item elasticity factor*
  The user makes a judgement on how the costs of activities behave with new activity volumes. For example, an energy cost item is more variable (perhaps 80 per cent) than Depreciation (perhaps 0 per cent).

In practice, step changes, particularly in activity volumes, become an issue as the two versions of the output FDI diverge, because capacity levels are breached. Furthermore, the capacity of each activity will probably be utilized unevenly, with certain activities emerging as bottlenecks as the user progressively increases throughput in a 'what-if' scenario. Functionality can be set up to address the issue in a pragmatic way.

Capacity levels

To set up the capacity monitoring facility, the user first defines the capacity levels. These might range from single-shift working, with stoppages for unproductive tasks and no overtime, up to a theoretical maximum of 24-hour working per day, 365 days a year.

Capacity warnings

Routines are created to monitor capacity utilization and to warn when levels are being breached. This is an important aid in assessing the viability of 'what-if' scenarios encompassing many hundreds of activities.

Capacity reporting

The object cost calculations generate the cost driver volumes consumed by each activity. This volume could be compared with the capacity levels entered by the user, and the result viewed in a report as a utilization percentage. Analysis by using the Exception tool in the Selector permits the user to extract those activities where the capacity utilization is over 100 per cent, sort them into order and decide appropriately on the course of action required.

8.2.7 Sizing issues, more granular ABM and solution architectures that go beyond just OFA

Sizing issues

In Section 5.4, we discussed the value of tiered architectures in allowing local modelling while supporting roll-up to a common reporting structure. A tiered hierarchy of Oracle Financial Analyzer Sub Shared Databases allows the size and complexity of the top-level structures in the Super Shared Database to be reduced, while permitting greater autonomy and control at lower-level and remote sites. As discussed in Section 5.5, size impacts performance and is an issue for both the Administrator and the user in all Oracle Financial Analyzer systems. The size of the database at the top of the tiered architecture need not be very large, as the detail is kept at the appropriate level. By harnessing the tiered architecture, local Oracle Financial Analyzer ABM modelling can occur within the business units, with only the more aggregate – and, at that level, perhaps more meaningful – views being available from the Super Shared Database.

More granular ABM

The OFA system designer often encounters the issue of granularity when analyzing ABM requirements; how many Dimension Values are required on each dimension to model the activity-based costing process correctly? More granular ABM approaches can have implications for database size. Dimensionality such as <Activity Product Channel Time> is common in Oracle Financial Analyzer ABM implementations, but the number of dimension values on these dimensions will be modest.

However, customer profitability analysis, for example, can present challenges as a result of database growth. Logically customer profitability can be monitored by adding a customer dimension to the Oracle Financial Analyzer ABM model structures – this time with activities related to customers, as well as products, to be analyzed and costed. Customer Profit and Loss statements can then take into account promotional, distribution, finance and selling costs to reveal the net customer contribution. Product Profit and Loss statements can still be drawn together using standard product costs with 'factory' overheads allocated or apportioned by relevant activities, with unattributable overheads identified as business sustaining costs. Aggregating on the appropriate dimensions will allow companies to monitor profitability at several levels.

However, a customer dimension, even with customers segmented by demographics or otherwise, may potentially carry hundreds of thousands of dimension values. This will impact both data loading and calculation and aggregation durations. Furthermore, there is a soft limit of 100,000 values above which the Selector in Oracle Financial Analyzer will not operate efficiently, even if the calculation and aggregation process executes in acceptable timescales. There is a need to consider solution architectures that go beyond just OFA.

Solution architectures that go beyond just OFA

In Chapter 6, we have seen cost allocation to arrive at product and customer profitability. This is typical of the CPG industry, where, although there may be thousands of products at the SKU level, there may only be tens of customers. Thus, a CPG manufacturer selling to the multiple chain store market may have only the main chain stores such as Walmart, Tesco, Safeway, Waitrose etc. as customers, as well as the larger wholesalers who then service the small retailers. However, certain vertical markets typically have millions of customers, for example telecommunications companies, financial services, utilities and large retailers. With the move to loyalty cards in the retail sector, for example, the actual customer is known. In the financial services sector, most large operators are moving from a product view of sales to an **individual customer** view of sales. However, we need to allocate costs to an **individual customer** if one seeks a customer *profitability* view.

Allocating a modest number of cost pools, using volume drivers such as number of ATM transactions, quotations etc. to millions of customers is a black box process; only the calculation results are interesting. This is not ABM. With ABM, we are interested in the processes undertaken to service the customer, and a much more modest number of targets for cost allocation will be required. Furthermore, with ABM, the allocation process is not black box. Both the process and the costing results are of interest since we seek to change processes as a result of doing the calculations and interpreting them. We cannot change the process of paying cash out through an ATM; we simply need to know how many times a customer does it and allocate cost appropriately. Hence for ABM, we need aggregate ABC costing, for individual customer profitability, granular black box cost allocations. OFA can provide the first but, used as a 'black box' calculation engine, most of OFA's features are redundant. With careful use of the Aggregate command, performance is less of an issue with long dimension value lists, but there it may be that other technology should be used because ultimately the scalability of the Oracle relational database is required. The discussion commenced in Section 4.4 should be recalled at this point. The Oracle product stack can provide a scalable solution, using an Oracle relational database for storing the granular data and Express for the aggregate view and to store driver data not already captured as production data.

A case may draw out some of the issues. An approach to improving the current infrastructure involved taking data from all relevant source systems into a 'staging area'. The staging area would feed a number of systems, including a finance and sales data mart. An incremental approach, to achieve proof points and risk-containment, was to be used, conceived as comprising:

- a definition phase to win sponsorship of the overall programme and precise definition of Phase 1 of the 'think big, start small' project, in which there were a number of phases:
  - Phase 1: product profitability at an aggregate level by allocating actual operating expenses against product groups;
  - Phase 2: expense management through business process review utilizing ABC techniques;
  - Phase 3: customer profitability.

It was clear that Phase 1 was part of an evolutionary approach to improving management information, focusing initially on product profitability, but not ABC. Phase 1 simply involved reporting, by product group, the account headings such as contribution, income, and simple allocations of overhead costs. However, the supporting technical architecture had to:

- support the Phase 1 'quick win' deliverables;
- support subsequent phases.

The objective was to accommodate the planning process underpinning the provision of management information and, ultimately, customer-level profitability in Phase 3.

It is clear that a scalable and extensible technical architecture might involve:

- Oracle RDBMS;
- Oracle Financial Analyzer;
- an activity-based costing package;
- a cost allocation engine.

The results of the analysis

IT had a clear ETL (Extract, Transform, Load) view of the required technical architecture. However, the business people had a clear view of the need to support planning, budgeting and ABC with a robust mechanism for gathering data from people to support such processes. A compromise was reached in the architecture, agreed as shown in Figure 8.12.

The technical architecture provides for the merging of data gathered from people in a robust way, using OFA, with production data from the RDBMS, to provide for calculations and aggregations to cover:

- planning;
- budgeting;
- cost allocations of an appropriate nature to OFA;
- transfer back to the RDBMS of the results;
- reporting export and analysis using the OFA clients in the normal way.

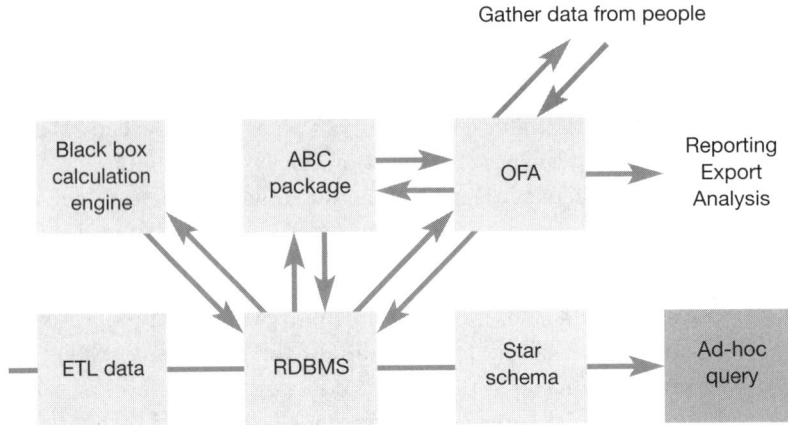

FIG 8.12   **Scalable and extensible technical architecture**

As far as the activity-based costing is concerned, OFA can feed the ABC package with data which has not been captured into the RDBMS by ETL from production systems. OFA can import useful data from the ABC package, such as unit costs, inheriting the benefits of the package solution without the overhead of setting up the appropriate structures in OFA.

The black box cost allocation engine can be an RDBMS-based package dedicated to highly granular cost allocation for customer-level profitability. The output will be fed back into the main RDBMS. Granular ad-hoc queries of a type appropriate to customer-level profitability can be conducted using the appropriate canned SQL tool against the star schema fed from the RDBMS.

8.3   A MORE DETAILED LOOK AT THE GENERIC ABC BUSINESS PROCESS MODEL AND OFA

We now move to a deeper level of detail. Using cube map extracts, we will expand upon the processes, detail the required OFA functions, represent the Express SPL programs as pseudo-code, and seek to assist the reader by providing some representative calculations and screen shots along the way.

The simple generic ABC business process model we started with is set out in Figure 8.13. However, we noted earlier in this chapter the generic need across many projects to deal with indirect costs and support activities. We need to expand the model to six generic processes, not just two, some or all of which will require to be set up in OFA for a particular implementation, as set out in Figure 8.14.

FIG 8.13   The generic ABC process model

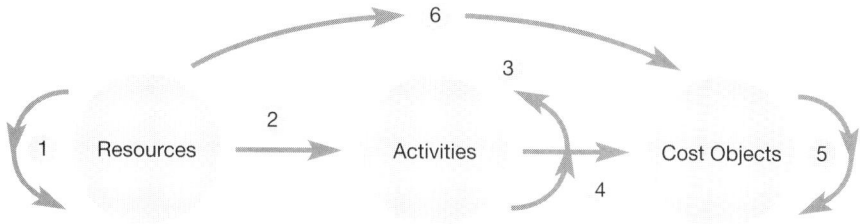

FIG 8.14   The generic ABC process model with re-allocations

The processes are:

1. mapping of ledger balances – the resources – to cost items/pools and possibly re-allocation of support cost items/pools to direct cost items/pools (a cost pool is an aggregation of cost items);

2. resources being allocated to activities;

3. support activities being re-allocated to direct activities;

4. activities being driven to cost objects;

5. 'component' cost objects being re-allocated to 'product' cost objects;

6. business sustaining costs being allocated to cost objects.

In each implementation, the generic ABC business process model as above is delivered in a particular way; this is where the OFA toolkit comes into its own in allowing the designer to meet the precise ABC business process model required for a particular project.

8.3.1 OFA Attributes and ABC

The importance of creating relationships between the structures used in OFA activity-based cost models is considerable. In the generic process model, as in Figure 8.14, there were six processes, all of which could require the set-up and maintenance of relationships, OFA Attributes.

When the OFA Attribute function is used, an object name is set up in the text variable RL.CATALOG to hold the relationship. Whenever the base dimension (e.g.

ACTIVITY) is used, the relationship with the aggregate dimension (e.g. DRIVER) can be referenced through use of the object name. Relationships are commonly used for reporting purposes, but here the issue is their use in calculations, as well as reporting. When we limit, for example, the ACTIVITY base dimension to the particular activity that we wish to allocate, the Attribute will limit the COST DRIVER aggregate dimension to the appropriate driver which should be used to allocate the activity concerned.

When we set up the Attribute in OFA, we give the identifier a description, RL.DESC, e.g. 'Cost centre/account to cost pool', which is helpful during set-up and maintenance; the RL.DESC is meaningful, the actual identifier (which in RL.CATALOG will be something like .RL.IB2648R) is not. It is easy to visualize the Attribute as a two-column table. If we report on an Attribute, it returns the values as below:

ACTIVITY	COST DRIVER
Marketing	Telephone calls
Maintenance	Time sheets
Canteen	Full Time Equivalent
Secretarial	Full Time Equivalent
Depreciation	Machine hours
Insurance	Net Book Value

Note ease of maintenance. If we change 'Full Time Equivalent' in the Maintain Dimension Value menu option, it will be changed in any Attribute dimension wherever it occurs.

The table below shows some of the typical Attribute descriptions which will be generated in OFA ABC implementations:

RL	RL.DESC	What it means
R1	Cost centre/account to cost pool	e.g. relates ledger balance to cost pool
R2	Allocation driver for cost pool	e.g. relates driver 'headcount' to the cost pool 'canteen'
R3	Direct or indirect cost pool type	e.g. a relation to detect whether indirect or direct
R4	Cost driver to activity	e.g. relates driver 'telephone calls' to activity 'Service'
R5	Fixed or variable cost type	e.g. a relation to detect whether fixed or variable
R6	Activity type	e.g. a relation to detect whether value-added or non-value-added, out-sourced or internal, direct or support etc.

We shall look at some of these in detail later.

Let us consider the first two processes, shown in Figure 8.15.

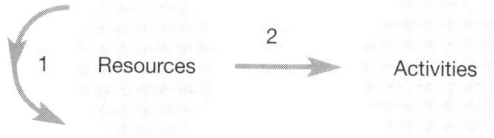

FIG 8.15   **The first two processes**

The requirement, in which P stands for Process, might be:

P1   Load production data:

    P11   Load actuals from GL

P2   Gather data from people

    P21   Gather data for re-allocating direct cost pools to indirect cost pools
    P22   Gather activity allocation driver data to permit allocation of direct cost pools to activities

P3   Perform calculations and aggregations

    P31   Summarize GL costs by cost pool and define as direct or indirect
    P32   Re-allocate indirect cost pools to direct cost pools
    P33   Allocate cost pools to activities

We assume that the ledger balances – the resources to be allocated – are already loaded into OFA, as in Figure 8.16.

FIG 8.16   **The ledger balances are loaded into OFA**

Keep in mind the figure for Marketing, £86,408, which we will trace through all the calculations. The file reader merely loaded the individual account balances, since we may wish to analyze the source data using the Selector, rather than the GL report writer. This figure is the result of aggregating all Marketing cost centre account balances in the ledger. However, as we will see later, since the re-allocation driver information is at the aggregate level of cost pool, the input cost data must then be summarized into cost pools. P31 is the process by which we will summarize the Marketing cost centre account balances to create the Marketing cost pool and define the direct or indirect nature of the cost pool.

P31 Summarize GL costs by cost pool and define direct or indirect nature of cost pool

The OFA Attribute R1 'Cost centre/account to cost pool' is used to link cost centre/account to cost pool:

RL	RL.DESC	What it means
R1	Cost centre/account to cost pool	e.g. relates ledger balance to cost pool

The relationship R1, cost centre/account to cost pool, is set up in the OFA Attribute menu, as in Figure 8.17.

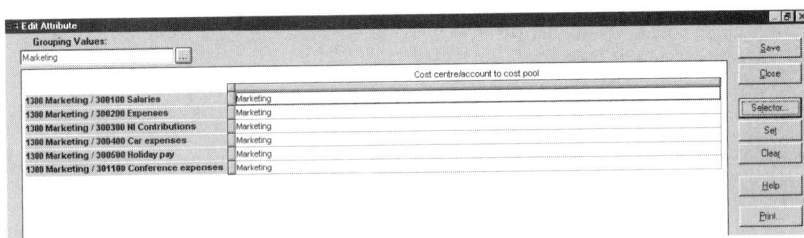

FIG 8.17   The Attribute maintenance screen

The Express SPL routine specification is as below:

Create an attribute to link cost centre/account to cost pool

Create variables to carry source list of cost centre/accounts and target list of cost pools

Using these variables, limit the dimension values to the set required for calculations

For each cost pool, add up the many Cost Centre/Accounts which relate to the cost pool.

The Attribute will be created in Oracle Financial Analyzer front end

The selections for the variables will be created in Oracle Financial Analyzer front end

The limit and calculation process will be an Express SPL program, to be run from Oracle Financial Analyzer as a custom Solve

Let us assume that the Marketing department works directly on generating business and hence would be a direct cost of doing business. In contrast, HR is an indirect cost, as are the Board. There will be a need to allocate indirect costs pools, such as HR, into direct cost pools, before these are allocated to activities. For this, we will need to define a cost pool as either direct or indirect. The OFA Attribute 'Direct or indirect cost pool type' is used to define whether a cost pool is direct or indirect:

RL	RL.DESC	What it means
R3	Direct or indirect cost pool type	e.g. a relation to detect whether indirect or direct

The two attributes used in P31 are shown in the extract from the cube map in Figure 8.18.

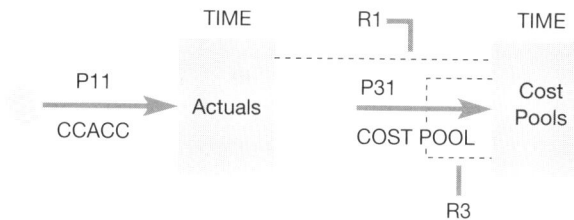

FIG 8.18   Cube map showing actuals aggregated to cost pools and the cost pools attributed as direct/indirect

P32   Re-allocate indirect cost pools to direct cost pools

Consider the logical requirement 'Re-allocate indirect cost pools to direct cost pools', which suggests complexity. Complexity brings risk, and hence this business process must be completely modelled before the build commences. The business process requires that, after aggregation of account balances into cost pools, the cost pools be defined as either direct or indirect. A direct cost pool can be allocated to an activity, while an indirect cost pool must be re-allocated to the direct cost pools, which they support. Cost allocations are then repeated as a number of calculations until all indirect cost pools are re-allocated to direct cost pools. There are many ways of achieving the required result. We now cover one of the many approaches. A simple numeric example may assist in understanding what will be required. The process is:

1. Do individual allocations to cost pools.

2. Calculate running total for each cost pool.

There are three calculations in Table 8.2. The indirect cost pools are first sorted in descending order (0). Then the largest indirect cost pool is allocated first. Each

TABLE 8.2   **Cost allocations**

Running total of cost pools					Individual allocations				
Calculation	0	1	2	3	Calculation	0	1	2	3
Direct CP1	4	7	10	15	Direct CP1	4	3	3	5
Direct CP2	2	4	6	8	Direct CP2	2	2	2	2
Indirect CP3	10	0	1	4	Indirect CP3	10	−10	1	3
Indirect CP4	8	9	0	3	Indirect CP4	8	1	−9	3
Indirect CP5	6	10	13	0	Indirect CP5	6	4	3	−13
Total Indirect CP	24	19	14	7	From CP3–CP5		−5	−5	−7

calculation produces an individual calculation (right table), which increments the running total of cost pools (left table). For each calculation, there are re-allocations back to indirect cost pools, as well as direct cost pools. Total indirect CP is the sum of indirect cost pool balances remaining. For the three calculations, the total of indirect cost pool balances falls and tends towards zero. However, it is possible that re-allocations back to indirect cost pools may result in a rising total indirect cost pool balance. This is divergence, rather than convergence, the desired result. If there is divergence, it may be sensible to stop the iteration process when a threshold level for the total unallocated indirect cost pools is reached, and then:

■ either conduct a second pass to ensure all the indirect cost pools are re-allocated to direct cost pools,

■ or deal with the remaining indirect cost pools in a more pragmatic way.

Conduct a second pass to ensure that all the indirect cost pools are re-allocated to direct cost pools.

The 'second pass' approach is set out in Table 8.3. The program allows the calculations to continue until the sum of indirect costs remaining reaches a given level of indirect costs remaining unallocated. The 'second pass' in calculations 4, 5 and 6 re-allocates the indirect cost pools to direct and indirect cost pools, but excluding the indirect cost pool just allocated. This ensures that possible divergent allocations, rather than convergent allocation as discussed above, are routinely dealt with by the program. We can then simply load and run the data, knowing that whatever the data sets are, the program will deal efficiently with them (a similar approach is required to contain the number of calculations performed).

Deal with the remaining indirect cost pools in a more pragmatic way.

The second pass in our example above allocates all remaining indirect costs to direct costs. However, this may not always be necessary, as a business may want to

TABLE 8.3   Cost allocations – second pass

Running total of cost pools								Individual allocations							
Calculation	0	1	2	3	4	5	6	Calculation	0	1	2	3	4	5	6
Direct CP1	4	7	10	15	16	18	20	Direct CP1	4	3	3	5	1	2	2
Direct CP2	2	4	6	8	8	9	10	Direct CP2	2	2	2	2	0	1	1
Indirect CP3	10	0	1	4	0	0	0	Indirect CP3	10	–10	1	3	–4	0	0
Indirect CP4	8	9	0	3	5	0	0	Indirect CP4	8	1	–9	3	2	–5	0
Indirect CP5	6	10	13	0	1	3	0	Indirect CP5	6	4	3	–13	1	2	–3
Total Ind CP	24	19	14	7	6	3	0	From CP3–CP5		–5	–5	–7	–1	–3	–3
				2nd Pass								2nd Pass			

carry these costs as Business Sustaining Costs directly to cost objects, as discussed earlier. The analyst should seek business decisions on these issues; as they are non-trivial, they should not be left to be clarified in an ad-hoc way during system development, when pressure is on to deliver, not discuss requirements.

The Express SPL routine specification is as below:

Create attribute to relate re-allocation driver to cost pool
Set threshold level for minimum total indirect cost pool before stopping further allocation
Set threshold level for maximum number of calculations before stopping further allocation

----------Main Allocation loop: separate for each time period------

Pass 1

    while   still above the 2 thresholds

    do

        sort costs into descending order with largest indirect cost pool to be allocated first

        find correct allocation driver for that cost pool

        allocate largest indirect cost pool by spreading cost over all other cost pools, based on the appropriate allocation driver selected by attribute

        set negative value to cost pool which has just been allocated, to zero this cost pool.

        calculate running total of calculations

        increment calculation number

    --------------Do allocation to other cost pools-------------

    end

Pass 2

repeat above, except that :

allocate largest indirect cost pool by spreading cost over all other cost pools---EXCEPT THE INDIRECT COST POOL JUST ALLOCATED, based on the appropriate re-allocation driver selected by attribute

Run from Oracle Financial Analyzer as an SPL program, with Oracle Financial Analyzer selections.

The OFA Attribute 'Re-allocation driver for cost pool' is set up to identify, for a particular direct cost pool, which allocation driver should be used:

RL	RL.DESC	What it means
R2	Reallocation driver for cost pool	e.g. relates driver 'headcount' to the cost pool 'canteen'

This time the Attribute will be used to limit, for each value of the base dimension COST POOL, which value on the aggregate dimension REALLOC DRIVER should be referenced when re-allocating indirect cost pools. The OFA Attribute maintenance screen is as shown in Figure 8.19.

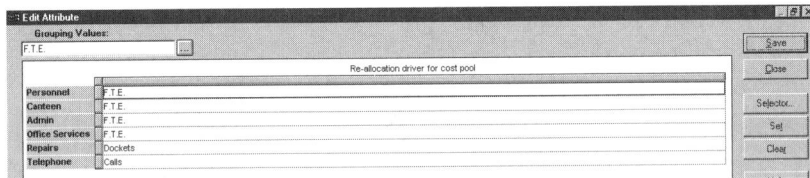

FIG 8.19   **The re-allocation driver is related to the cost pool**

We need to gather re-allocation driver data for the re-allocation of indirect cost pools to direct cost pools. A typical driver for allocation is time spent, often translated into Full Time Equivalents, or FTE, as in Figure 8.20. Here the time spent has been collected at the level of cost pool, using an OFA Worksheet. Note that in Figure 8.20, there is simply a column of numbers which total to 234.70, with the direct cost pools totalling to 165.90. There is 234.70–165.90 = 68.80 of time to be charged to indirect cost pools, providing the basis for an allocation calculation. For example, when we perform a calculation using this data, 7.20/234.70 of the indirect cost pool being allocated will be re-allocated to Indirect Cost Pool 8.

The cube map in Figure 8.21 summarizes the data loading, data gathering and calculations and aggregations to this point. The results are set out in Figures 8.22 and 8.23.

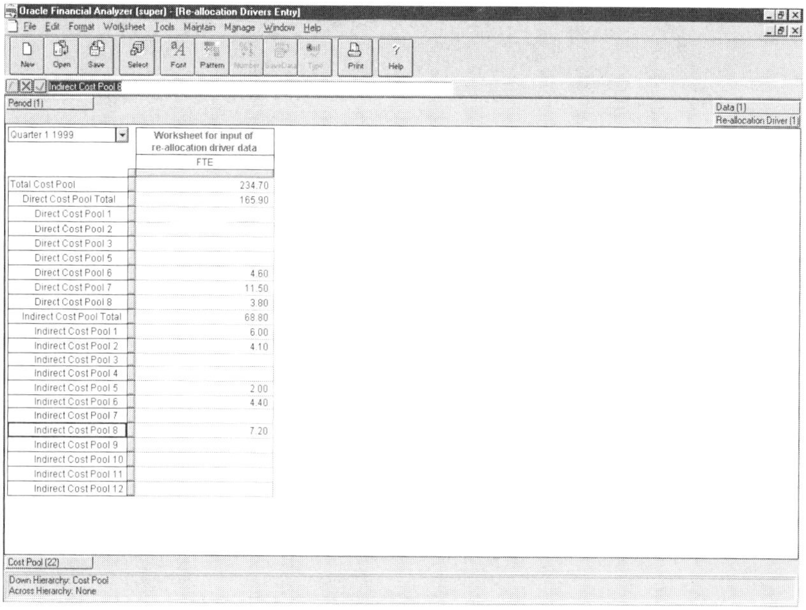

FIG 8.20   The re-allocation driver data capture Worksheet

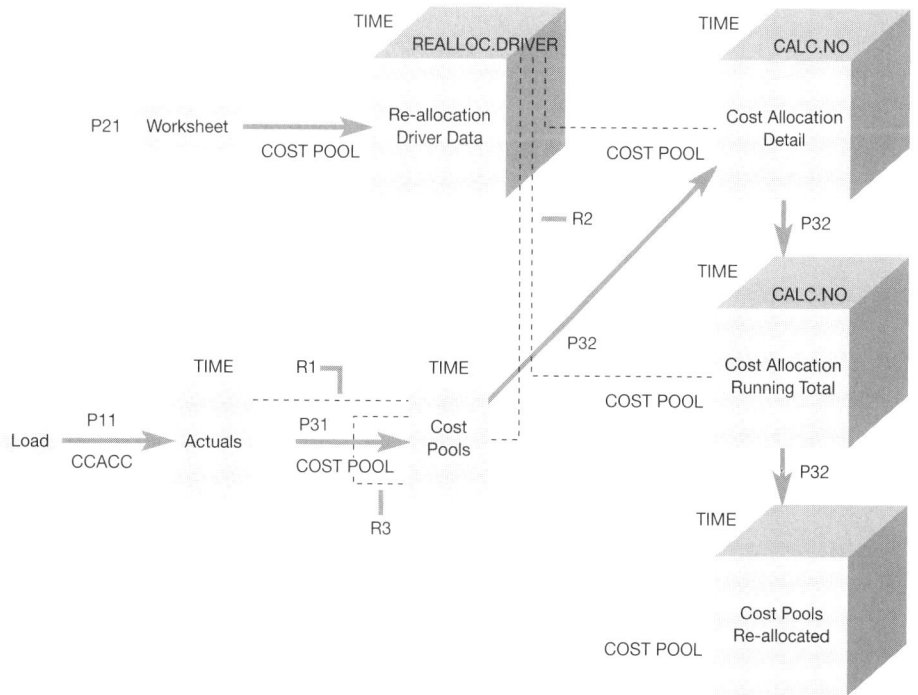

FIG 8.21   From actuals loaded to re-allocated cost pools

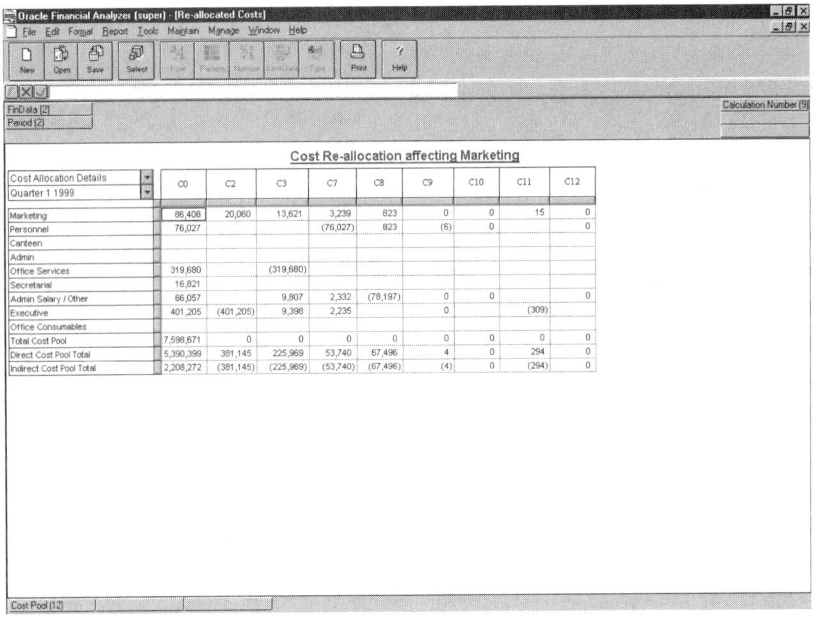

Cost Allocation Details / Quarter 1 1999	C0	C2	C3	C7	C8	C9	C10	C11	C12
Marketing	86,408	20,060	13,621	3,239	823	0	0	15	0
Personnel	76,027			(76,027)	823	(6)	0		0
Canteen									
Admin									
Office Services	319,680		(319,680)						
Secretarial	16,821								
Admin Salary / Other	66,057		9,807	2,332	(78,197)	0	0		0
Executive	401,205	(401,205)	9,398	2,235		0		(309)	
Office Consumables									
Total Cost Pool	7,598,671	0	0	0	0	0	0	0	0
Direct Cost Pool Total	5,390,399	381,145	225,969	53,740	67,496	4	0	294	0
Indirect Cost Pool Total	2,208,272	(381,145)	(225,969)	(53,740)	(67,496)	(4)	0	(294)	0

FIG 8.22 The re-allocation process: calculation details

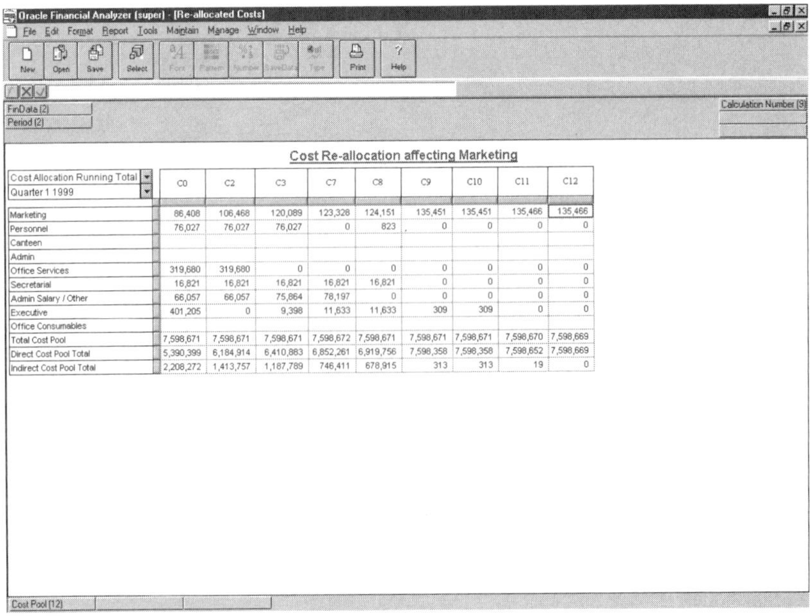

Cost Allocation Running Total / Quarter 1 1999	C0	C2	C3	C7	C8	C9	C10	C11	C12
Marketing	86,408	106,468	120,089	123,328	124,151	135,451	135,451	135,466	135,466
Personnel	76,027	76,027	76,027	0	823	0	0	0	0
Canteen									
Admin									
Office Services	319,680	319,680	0	0	0	0	0	0	0
Secretarial	16,821	16,821	16,821	16,821	16,821	0	0	0	0
Admin Salary / Other	66,057	66,057	75,864	78,197	0	0	0	0	0
Executive	401,205	0	9,398	11,633	11,633	309	309	0	0
Office Consumables									
Total Cost Pool	7,598,671	7,598,671	7,598,671	7,598,672	7,598,671	7,598,671	7,598,671	7,598,670	7,598,669
Direct Cost Pool Total	5,390,399	6,184,914	6,410,883	6,852,261	6,919,756	7,598,358	7,598,358	7,598,652	7,598,669
Indirect Cost Pool Total	2,208,272	1,413,757	1,187,789	746,411	678,915	313	313	19	0

FIG 8.23 The re-allocation process: running total

Recall the original figure for Marketing, £86,408. Most but not every re-allocation results in an amount re-allocated to this cost pool, as each indirect cost pool is re-allocated. After the re-allocation process is complete, using the data gathered by Oracle Financial Analyzer Worksheet, the balance for this cost pool rises to £135,466. The cost allocations have been repeated until all indirect cost pools are re-allocated to direct cost pools, yielding a total for Marketing of £135,466 from the original £86,408.

With all the indirect cost pools re-allocated to direct cost pools, the next step is to allocate these cost pools to activities. For this purpose, we will need to gather activity allocation driver data to permit allocation of direct cost pools to activities. Thereafter we will apply that data to the direct cost pools which have been re-allocated.

The cube map is as shown in Figure 8.24.

P22 Gather activity allocation driver data to permit allocation of cost pools to activities to arrive at activity costs

Typically the basis will be time allocations either in formal systems or collected with informality such as by spreadsheets sent as e-mail attachments. While any formal system driver data should be loaded via file readers written to incorporate validation checks, using an Oracle Financial Analyzer Worksheet or Data Entry Form creates a more robust process for any data that requires review before submission, rather than

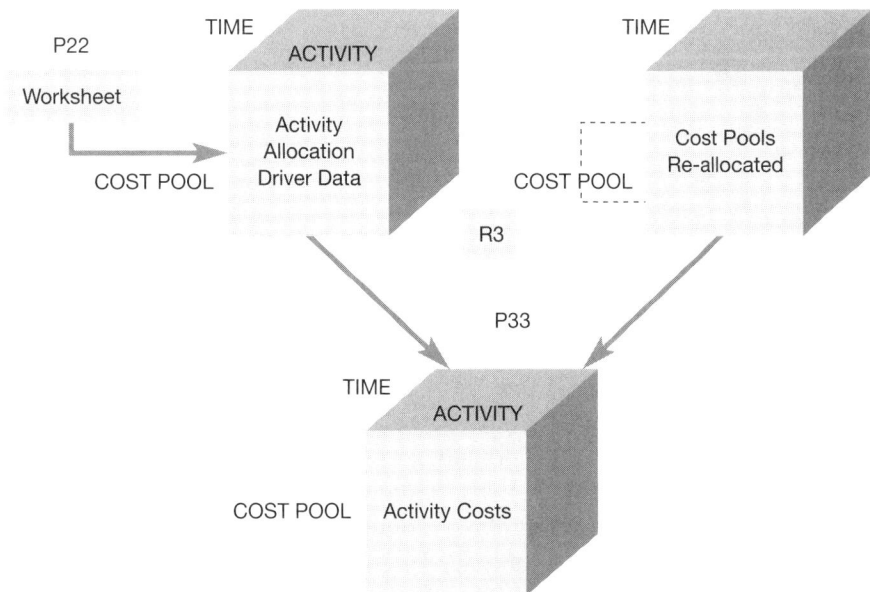

FIG 8.24   Gathering activity allocation data and allocating the cost pools to activities

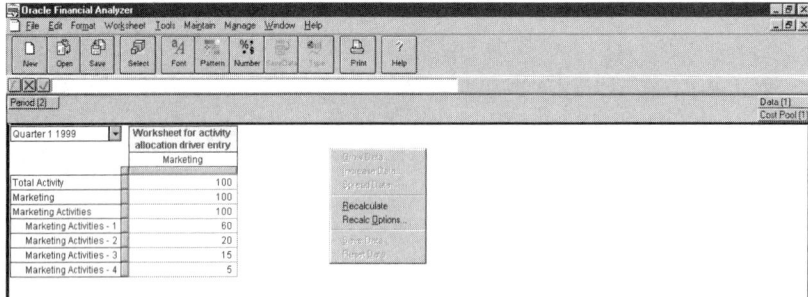

FIG 8.25   **The re-allocation driver data capture Worksheet**

just validation. Figure 8.25 shows capture of the data for Activity Allocations using an Oracle Financial Analyzer Worksheet.

P33   Allocate cost pools to activities

The program performs the allocation of costs from Cost Pools to Activities, using allocation percentage data as collected above, and using an attribute to limit the process to direct cost pools, which has already been created. (Recall that the OFA Attribute 'Direct or indirect Cost pool type' is used to define whether a cost pool is direct or indirect).

RL	RL.DESC	What it means
R3	Direct or indirect cost pool type	e.g. a relation to detect whether indirect or direct

The program logic is:

Determine the cost pools for allocation; only direct cost pools are allocated to activities
Do allocation Activity Cost = Direct Cost Pools * numerator/(denominator = total drivers for each Cost Pool)

The selections for the variables will be created in Oracle Financial Analyzer front end
The limit of dimension values, restriction to direct cost pools, and calculation process will be an Express SPL program, to be run from Oracle Financial Analyzer as a custom Solve

When the calculations are run, the results look like Figure 8.26.

Using Activity Allocation driver data gathered by the Oracle Financial Analyzer Worksheet 'Activity Allocation Drivers', the Marketing cost pool is allocated to Marketing Activities 1, 2, 3 and 4. This results in the £135,466 being split into £81,280, £27,093, £20,320, £6,773. We focus on 'Marketing Activities – 1' cost, £81,280, from now on.

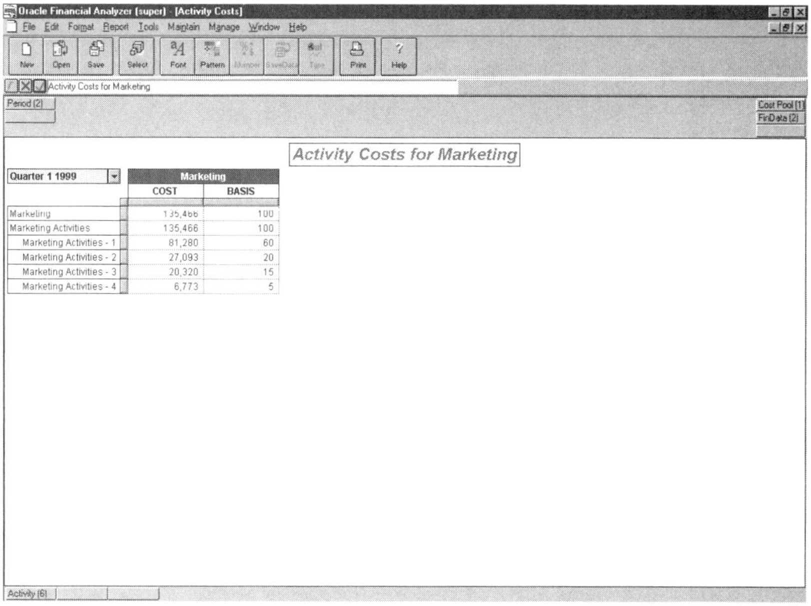

FIG 8.26   The Activity Costs for Marketing Activites 1, 2, 3 and 4

8.3.2 Unit costing

The processes so far have gathered/loaded costs, aggregated certain costs, gathered/ loaded data to re-allocate/allocate these costs and finally allocated them to activities. The next process is focused on calculating the cost of providing one unit of activity, which will be the basis of charging activities to cost objects – or products/outputs. The activity is provided in support of products for a particular time period in a particular region. P12 and P34 are the process requirements, as per the cube map in Figure 8.27: the capture of cost driver data and calculating total driver usage.

P12   Load actual cost driver data from production systems dimensioned by <Cost driver Product Region Time>

We assume that the cost driver data is loaded by a file reader from production systems. Note that the data is highly granular – we need to know for each product, delivered through each region in each time period and for each cost driver, what the volumes are for the cost driver. The next step is to calculate (having due regard for separating productive effort from unproductive effort as discussed earlier), the divisor in the unit costing calculation, thus:

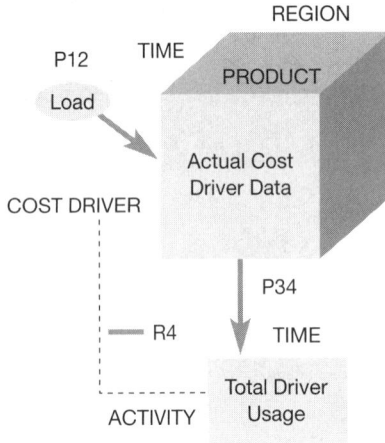

FIG 8.27 **Loading actual cost driver data and calculating total driver usage**

P34 Calculate total driver usage to permit calculation of unit costs
<Activity Time>

The program provides the ability to calculate total driver usage. A cost driver:activity relation is required and the OFA Attribute 'Cost driver to activity' is used to link cost driver to activity:

RL	RL.DESC	What it means
R4	Cost driver to activity	e.g. relates the driver 'telephone calls' to activity 'service'

The Express SPL program will be:

Create an attribute to link cost driver to activity
Create variable to carry list of activities
Using this variable, limit the dimension values to the selection required for calculations
Calculate total driver usage for each ACTIVITY

The attribute will be created In Oracle Financial Analyzer front end
The selections for the variable will be created in Oracle Financial Analyzer front end
The limit and calculation process will be an Express SPL program, to be run from Oracle Financial Analyzer as a custom Solve

We can now calculate unit activity costs, from the aggregate activity costs calculated earlier, the driver data collected and the total driver usage as computed above:

P35   Calculate unit activity costs <Activity Time>

The requirement to calculate unit activity costs is captured in the cube map in Figure 8.28.

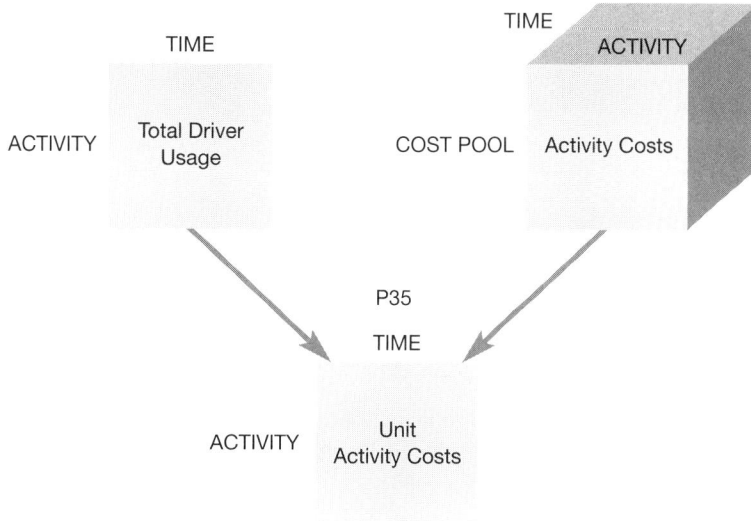

FIG 8.28   **Calculating unit activity cost**

At this point in the process, we have the activity cost in total for an activity, calculated by allocating resource costs based upon the appropriate activity allocation driver. This total activity cost must be divided by the volume of activity performed during the period, the cost (object) driver. Let us assume that the driver is telephone calls. The volume of telephone calls performed by the marketing department in Q2 is 267,485; there are many products requiring marketing and they are distributed through many regions. We divide the total Marketing Activity – 1 cost of £81,280 by 267,485 and produce a unit cost of £0.303867 for that activity.

The program calculates the unit activity costs, using the total driver usage cube as above. This time no attribute will be required, because the target cube shares dimensionality of <Activity Time> with the two cubes used in the arithmetic. By limiting the activity cost cube on the Cost Pool dimension to one value, total cost pools for each activity, we can reduce the dimensionality to, effectively, two dimensions, giving total cost for each activity.

Create variable to carry list of cost pools

Create variable to carry list of activities

Using these variables, limit the dimension values to the selection required for calculations

Select only DIRECT cost pools to allocate

Calculate unit cost = total activity cost for an activity/total driver volume for that activity

The selections for the variable will be created in Oracle Financial Analyzer front end

The limit and calculation process will be an Express SPL program, to be run from Oracle Financial Analyzer as a custom Solve

The results look like Figure 8.29.

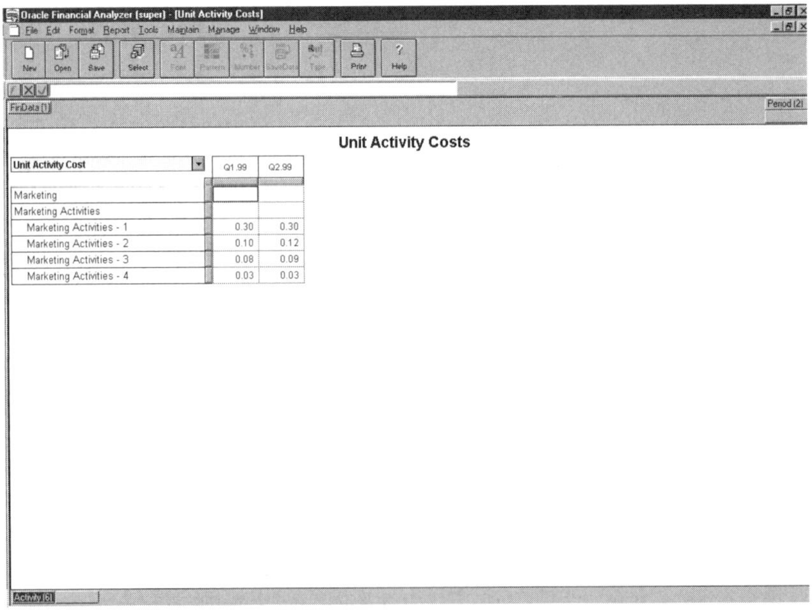

FIG 8.29   **The Unit Costs for Marketing Activities 1, 2, 3 and 4**

P36   **Calculate product activity costs, dimensioned by <Activity Product Region Time>**

The cube map for the calculations is Figure 8.30.

The final step is to apply the data we have already in the Actual Cost Driver cube to unit activity costs to provide Product Cost. The process of costing products ('outputs') is one of multiplying the volume of the cost driver consumed by a cost object by the unit cost of that driver. In our example, the volume of telephone calls done

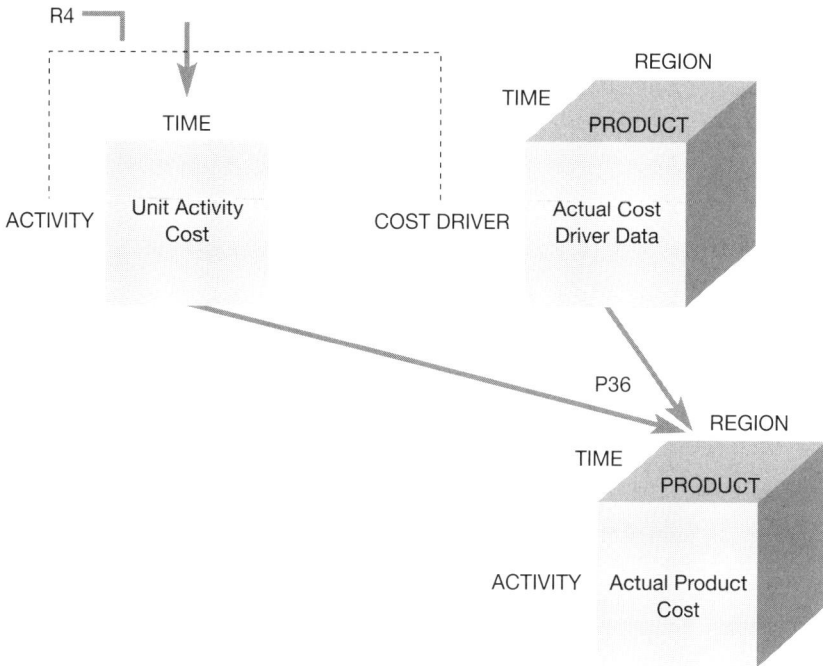

FIG 8.30   **Calculating actual product cost**

for Product 1 basic, distributed in Region C1, is 382 for the period, giving an activity cost of 382 * £0.3038 = £116 for marketing Product 1 basic sold in that region.

(Note: No indication is given that the volume of 382 is high or low and hence utilization high or low. That again might come from a comparison exercise with a peer. The calculation is also silent on whether there were any capacity constraints on marketing, since the unit cost might have been arrived at as in Table 8.4.)

TABLE 8.4   **Calculating activity costs**

	Driver volume	Activity cost	Unit cost
All Products/Regions	267,485	81,280	0.30
Double the volume and cost	534,971	162,560	0.30
Half the volume and cost	133,743	40,640	0.30
Yielding activity cost for P1/R1	382		116.20

The program calculates the final target cube, costs by Activity/Product/Region/ Time. A cost driver:activity relation is required, but has already been created for P34.

Create variables to carry list of activities, products, regions and drivers

Limit the dimension values to the selections required for the calculations

Calculate product costs = unit cost for activity * driver volume, using the appropriate cost driver for that activity

The selections for the variables will be created in Oracle Financial Analyzer front end

The limit and calculation process will be an Express SPL program, to be run from Oracle Financial Analyzer as a custom Solve

The results look like Figure 8.31.

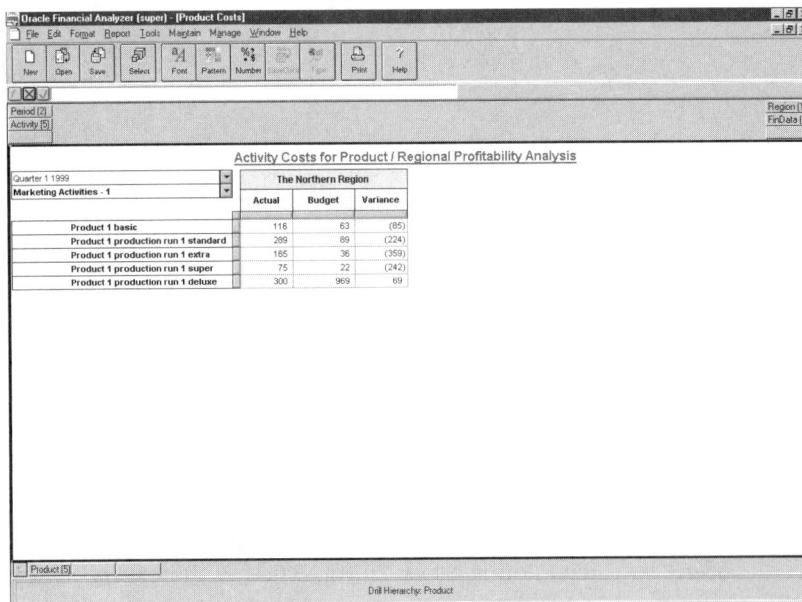

Activity Costs for Product / Regional Profitability Analysis

	The Northern Region		
	Actual	Budget	Variance
Product 1 basic	116	63	(85)
Product 1 production run 1 standard	289	89	(224)
Product 1 production run 1 extra	165	36	(359)
Product 1 production run 1 super	75	22	(242)
Product 1 production run 1 deluxe	300	969	69

FIG 8.31   **The cost of servicing the Northern Region with Marketing Activity 1 for the Products shown in Q1 99**

The data loading, data gathering, calculation and aggregation processes are complete. In the generic OFA process model, reporting and analysis comes next.

P4   Provide reporting and analysis <By all the cubes>

P41   Provide analysis of actual resource, activity cost and product cost cubes

P42   Provide what-if analysis

For P41, the provision of analysis of actual resource (account/cost centre balances, direct and indirect cost pools), activity cost and product cost cubes, the facilities of

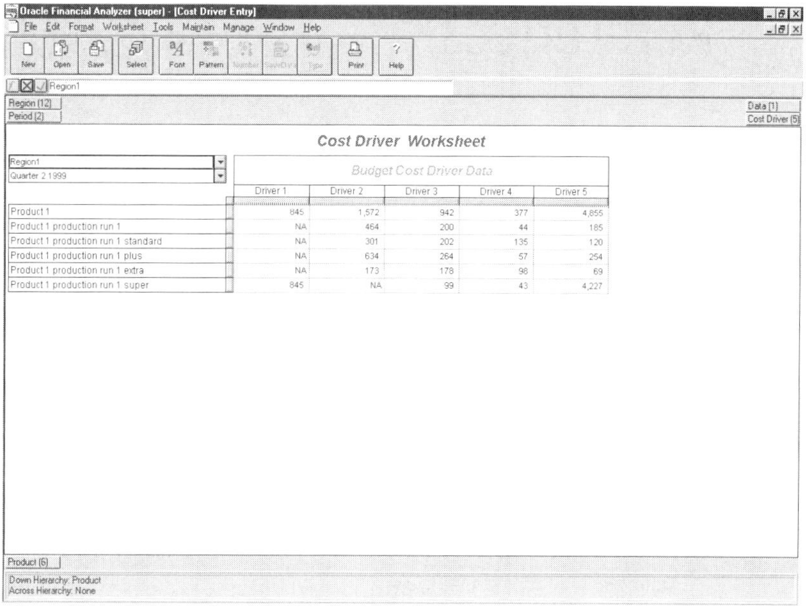

FIG 8.32   Cost driver input Worksheet for what-if modelling

the Selector on those cubes should provide the user with the ability to configure the required report. For P42, a range of what-if analysis facilities can be provided.

For example, having calculated cost of product, by activity, time and region based on actual costs, budgeting could be conducted on the same basis. While many of the actuals will have come from production systems via a file reader, the budget cost drivers can be modelled and input via an Oracle Financial Analyzer Worksheet.

The Worksheet in Figure 8.32 permits, for example, the input of volume for cost drivers 1 to 5 for all products. These may be key capacity constraints. The values can be spread to base products based on the same distribution, before the relevant Model is applied across the Product hierarchy. Saving the data commits new data to the shared view of the truth. The custom program is similar to that which created the actuals costing but uses budget driver data and is run, as before, from Oracle Financial Analyzer as a custom Solve, with Oracle Financial Analyzer selections.

This concludes our review of Oracle Financial Analyzer in ABM at a deeper level of detail.

References

Better Accounting for the Taxpayers' Money, 1994. Her Majesty's Stationery Office, United Kingdom

Gaskin, B., 1998, *Realizing the Strategic Value of Data Warehouses*. Decision Support Technology

Herman, G., 1999, 'Closing the Loop – Using Data Warehousing to Deliver Business Benefits', *Guidelines for IT Management*, no. 240, National Computer Centre, Manchester

Hurren, T., quoted in 'How Do You Score?', Classe, A., *Accountancy*, November 1998. Institute of Chartered Accountants in England and Wales

Kimball, R., 1996, *The Data Warehouse Toolkit, Practical Techniques for Building Dimensional Data Warehouses*. John Wiley

Oracle Documentation:

Application Programming Interface: Structure and Supporting Meta Data Guide
Integrating Oracle Financial Analyzer with Oracle General Ledger
Oracle Financial Analyzer User Guide
Oracle Express Programmer's Guide to the Express Language
Oracle Express Server Installation and Configuration Guide
Oracle Express: Performance and Database Design Guide
Technical Note: 'Optimizing Oracle Financial Analyzer: Performance and Architecture'

A Tuning OFA

The purpose of this appendix is to provide a guide to good practice when setting up the OFA environment, and how to evaluate and improve performance for data processing, and user accessibility. The basis of the discussion will surround two documents provided by Oracle, both available on MetaLink. These are *Oracle Express: Performance and Database Design Guide*, and the Technical Note 'Optimizing Oracle Financial Analyzer: Performance and Architecture'. This appendix should be read in conjunction with these two documents. We try not to repeat advice stated in these documents, but rather to expand and draw out issues from them that are relevant to an OFA installation.

Oracle Express: Performance and Database Design Guide is a generic Express configuration and tuning guide that is not specific to an OFA application. It does make reference to OFA in Chapter 2 in the section 'Plan your dimension order according to your user's application'.

A.1 DIMENSION ORDER

When using an Express application we usually think of the data in the logical sense, i.e. how to interpret the many-dimensioned data, how we can 'slice and dice' the data, and how to aggregate up many hierarchies. This logical interpretation of the data is crucial to designing and building a database that meets user requirements. However, the multidimensional logical data has to be stored physically in a linear fashion on disk. The dimension ordering of the data plays a fundamental part in the storage, and thus the resulting performance, of this data.

A simple example will best illustrate the physical storage of a multidimensioned cube.

Suppose we have a data item, ACTUALS, dimensioned by three dimensions, LINE, PRODUCT and TIME. Each dimension has three values in it, L1 to L3, P1 to P3 and T1 to T3.

Dimension Order: LINE PRODUCT TIME.

TIME is the slowest-varying dimension, and LINE is the fastest-varying. Pictorially it looks like Figure A.1.

FIG A.1

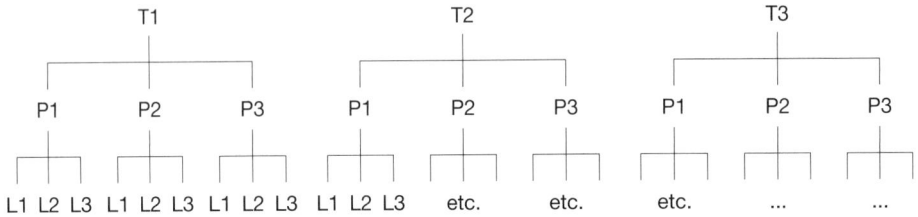

The bottom line represents the physical storage of the data, i.e. for TIME T1 and PRODUCT P1, all the LINE values are stored together, followed by all the LINE values for TIME T1 and PRODUCT P2. The storage moves through the TIME values slower than the other dimensions. The result is that all of the data associated with an individual value of TIME is physically stored together. This will have huge consequences for the database performance, but the effect will depend on the nature of the ACTUALS data. If the data is loaded incrementally, one month at a time, and this single month is subsequently aggregated, then the example above is the optimum order. All of the data for this single month is located on the same area of the disk. The number of pages that must be read is kept to a minimum. Also, all future months that have not yet been loaded are empty. This controlled sparsity is effectively managed because the entire data storage area associated with these time periods is empty and will collapse to nothing, in term of disk space. *No* storage space is required because all of the pages are empty (NA pages).

If TIME becomes the fastest-varying dimension (Figure A2):

FIG A.2

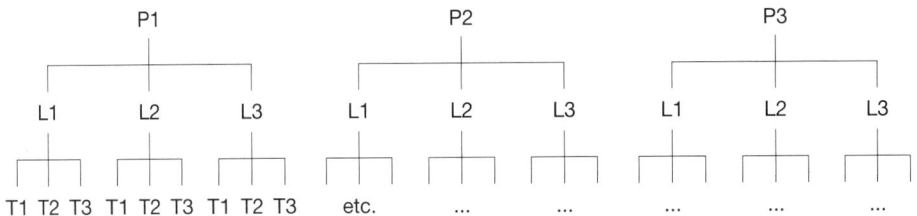

Dimension Order: TIME LINE PRODUCT

we can see that the time periods are spread right across the disk. Any aggregation of a single month here will require access to all the pages associated with the

ACTUALS variable. The performance will be significantly worse. If the TIME values are fully populated and they are all aggregated, such as for forecast or budget data, then this is not a disadvantage. The controlled sparsity management is passed to the PRODUCT dimension.

As an aside, this example also illustrates a basic principle of data readers: that structures should all be loaded in advance of their associated data. If a new LINE dimension value is added to the first example above, the data cannot be inserted into its optimum position as a continuation of the existing trend because there is not space available. Instead the new value is added conceptually at the end of the storage area, or rather, in a different area, creating a new segment (Figure A.3).

This makes data retrieval immediately inefficient. This will happen over time

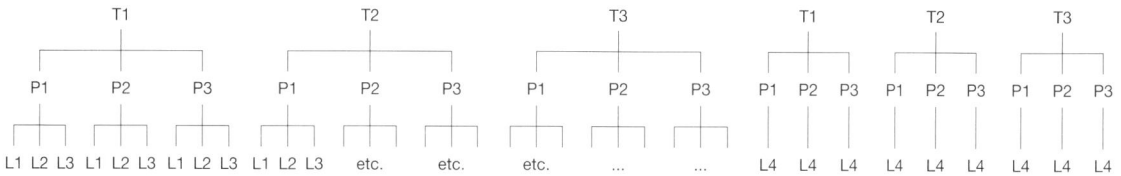

FIG A.3

anyway to a growing database. The only way to tidy up the storage, restoring the neat segmentation, is to export and import the database. See Section 5.9 for more details of these techniques.

The example above is necessarily simplistic, although these basic techniques hold true even when you introduce more dimensions and composites.

A.2   AGGREGATION

The consolidation of data is often the most time-consuming element of data processing in an OFA application. OFA now uses the AGGREGATE command to consolidate hierarchical data, replacing the old slower ROLLUP command in OFA 6.3 (supplied as a patch to the original release). There is not at present any facility in OFA to use the additional functions of the AGGREGATE command to calculate aggregations on the fly when reporting OFA data. In Express terms this means creating an AGGMAP to specify the rules for pre-aggregation and aggregation on the fly. In OFA the Solve Definition creates a temporary AGGMAP for the duration of the Solve, which has no on-the-fly element to it, then deletes it again. This makes customization of this routine difficult, as it means changing part of the OFA program code itself if you want to implement a more sophisticated AGGMAP. This is an important area for future enhancement of OFA, as it is not utilizing the full power of the Express environment to allow flexible aggregation of data.

There are a couple of ways to utilize the AGGREGATE function even though it is not a feature of the OFA front end:

■ The first method is to use the AGGREGATE function to calculate all of the data in any one or more hierarchies on the fly. Create an AGGMAP that will aggregate a hierarchy or hierarchies on the fly. Set the 'NATRIGGER' property to the appropriate AGGMAP for the financial data item. Because we are aggregating the entire hierarchy, this might be slow to run and thus not a very practical solution, unless the hierarchy is very simple. The Oracle advice is to aggregate on the fly only at intermediate levels, i.e. pre-calculate every other level in the hierarchy, in order to achieve adequate performance.

■ The second method is to create two hierarchies on a single dimension, one as the physical aggregation hierarchy, and a second as the reporting hierarchy. The physical aggregation hierarchy is a subset of the reporting hierarchy. The 'NATRIGGER' property for the financial data item will reference an AGGMAP that has the dimension values contained in the aggregation hierarchy identified as physically aggregated, and any remaining levels within the reporting hierarchy as on-the-fly aggregations. This technique implements the skip-level aggregation concept referred to in the Oracle documentation. It does have the overhead of maintaining two hierarchies; the aggregation hierarchy should be a subset of the reporting hierarchy and can, perhaps, be automatically maintained based on an attribute. But it does reduce the amount of pre-aggregation and thus the time taken to physically aggregate the data. The processing is transferred to the user at run time. The levels excluded from the aggregation hierarchy should represent the infrequently used levels within the reporting hierarchy, so the user is not calculating popular reporting levels on the fly.

If your OFA application has been upgraded from an earlier version of OFA, you should review the dimension ordering within any composites used that contain hierarchical dimensions. With the introduction of AGGREGATE, the optimum order of the dimensions to ensure the most efficient aggregation should be based on the number of dimension values of the base dimensions of the composite, ordered from highest to lowest.

A.3   COMPOSITES

OFA will create a new, named composite, each time you create a composite financial data item. If there is a strong relationship between the new financial data item and an existing one, and they both share the dimensions within the composite, then they can share the composite. This will reduce the overhead of maintaining multiple composites. To implement this you will need to create the second financial data item in the front end in the normal way, but then delete it from Express Monitor and redefine it using the named composite of its related financial data item. You must do this before you distribute the new financial data item to the Shared Database or to any users.

A.3.1 Removing redundant composite values

If a dimension value is deleted then the corresponding composite combinations that exist for this dimension value will also be deleted. The composite is automatically tidied up to reflect the reduced number of dimension values because the composite is intrinsically linked to its base dimensions. You may, however, have the case that the dimension value is still required, so cannot be deleted, but a composite value containing this dimension value is no longer required. This situation could arise when historic data is no longer needed by the users; the time dimension values are deleted, but if time is not in the composite, now unused composite combinations may remain. These will be the composite combinations that had data in the older deleted time periods, but not in any later time period. This kind of situation leads to inefficiency in the composite, especially over a long period. The only way to clean the composite and remove this redundancy is at the Express command line. The unwanted combinations must be identified by looking at data stored in the data item dimensioned by the composite. We must identify those values that no longer have any balances. This is complicated by the very nature of composites. The status of a composite dimension cannot be limited in Express in the normal dimension sense. The values in a composite can be limited, however, if the composite is converted to a CONJOINT first. A conjoint can be treated as a dimension in almost every way, specifically limiting the status and dimension maintenance.

As an example of this approach, the code required to identify redundancy in the composite in a financial data item, called BUDGET, dimensioned by LINE CMP.AA1234 <PRODUCT MARKET> TIME, is as follows:

```
Chgdfn CMP.AA1234 dimension
Allstat
Limit CMP.AA1234 remove any(BUDGET ne na CMP.AA1234)
Maintain CMP.AA1234 delete charlist(CMP.AA1234)
Chgdfn CMP.AA1234 composite
Update
```

If the composite is shared by other financial data items. then these variables should be included in the limits to remove valid combinations, i.e. combinations with data. You should exercise great care when performing this maintenance, as deleting a valid combination in error will result in data being lost. Always ensure you have a sufficient backup before embarking on this type of work.

A.4   LARGE NUMBERS OF DIMENSION VAUES

OFA can now deal with much larger numbers of dimension values than in earlier releases. Up to 100,000 values do not cause problems from a user or DBA perspective. After this, the front end becomes very slow to access the dimension.

For the user it is advisable to create saved selections that allow easy selection of groups of values, which can then be subdivided further by the user.

For the DBA, as much maintenance as possible should be automated, such as hierarchy building and attribute maintenance. When running a Solve on a financial data item dimensioned by a very long dimension, make sure you have distributed all values of the dimension to the shared database before running the Solve. If all values of the dimension exist in the shared database when initializing the Solve then the initialization is quick. If some values in the selection do not exist in the shared database, then the initialization of the Solve will limit the shared database dimension to those that exist in the DBA selection. This uses the INLIST Express command to identify values in the shared database that are in the text list of selected values. This will run extremely slowly for a list of over a few thousand. In the case of 100,000 values it may take all day. The Solve will be stuck on the 'initializing Solve' stage in the Task Processor. It will work eventually but it is extremely inefficient.

A.5   DATABASE GROWTH

The control of the database growth that occurs when data is re-solved whilst other users are reading the database is much better from Express 6.3 than in previous releases. The UPDATE command will free unused pages, even if there are users reading the database. This allows temporary disk storage within the Express database to be efficiently reused. In the past this only occurred if there were no other users reading the database when the UPDATE command was issued. If disk space is a constraint you can keep the growth of the database down to a minimum by frequent updates during data processing. You can increase the number of UPDATE commands issued in a Solve Definition and Group Solve by setting 'Model Update' to YES in the Option menu. This updates a Solve Definition at each stage of its progress, i.e. after executing the model and after aggregations. Be aware that this will affect the rollback position if the Solve should fail. It will not roll back to the data position before the Solve started, as is the situation if 'Model Update' is left in the default setting. Instead it will only roll back to the last issued update, which may be halfway through a Solve Definition.

A.6   MEMORY

Oracle Express: Performance and Database Design Guide makes it clear that you cannot have too much memory on your machine. Memory is the primary physical hardware factor influencing database performance. Increasing the memory may conceal a poorly designed database, but it will also enhance a well-designed one. You should make every effort to specify your memory requirements accurately to ensure that this resource is adequate for all your current and future needs.

B Data loading

Data for the OFA application may come from various sources. It can be entered directly into OFA or loaded from an external source. The methods used to load data into the OFA environment will depend on an analysis of the data sources. The considerations that affect the loading method are:

- Frequency of the load. Is the load performed on a regular basis, or is it a one-off exercise?
- Volume of the data to be loaded.
- Reliability of the data. Does the data need to be validated before it is loaded?
- Data source. Is the production of the data file automated?
- Datafile format. ASCII, spreadsheet, external database, or something else?

B.1 FACILITIES WITHIN OFA

OFA provides limited pre-installed functionality for loading data, in addition to the GL link discussed in Chapter 4.

B.1.1 Copy and paste into an OFA Worksheet and Data Entry Form

If data is prepared in off-line spreadsheets and the data volumes involved are easy to manage, then the data can simply be copied from the spreadsheet source and pasted into an OFA worksheet or Data Entry Form. This requires some care from the user to ensure that Dimensions match up to the form of the spreadsheet, but it is quick, easy, and a familiar technique for most users.

B.1.2 Worksheet Data Entry

One note of caution when using the copy and paste method is the treatment of zero balances. In the 'Using Worksheets' chapter of the *OFA User Guide* it states that zero values entered into budget worksheets are stored in the database as NA values. This is not the case. The data is stored as zero. Users will tend to load a large proportion of zero balances from a spreadsheet. For example, you may have pre-prepared OFA worksheets and Excel spreadsheets that have the same definition in terms of rows and columns for all users to aid the cut and paste process. An individual user may be using only a subset of the available rows in Excel, with the rest set to zero in his or her spreadsheet. The user will still, for simplicity's sake, copy and paste the whole spreadsheet into OFA, therefore saving all the unused section of the spreadsheet as zero. This can have two large unwanted side-effects. Firstly, because Express regards zero as a number like any other, these zeros take up disk storage space. The data item becomes bigger. If it is composited, then the composite becomes unnecessarily larger. It is possible that all cells in the cube will become filled, pushing the composite to its theoretical maximum and making its sparsity effect redundant. Secondly, the performance of any data processing on this data item will suffer, directly as a result of its larger physical size and the overhead of managing a larger composite list.

To avoid the problem of unnecessarily saved zeros, they need to be omitted from the save procedure. The method depends on the target document in OFA.

B.1.3 Saving zeros in an OFA Worksheet

A custom hook exists within a worksheet that allows you to run a custom routine before the data is saved. This custom routine can be used to change the selection of the saved data, or change the data itself. We can use this hook to set all zeros to NA values before they are saved to the Shared Database. Express treats these two values completely separately. Zero is a number like any other, as already mentioned above. NA is an empty cell. This is not a number requiring storage. It is simply empty space. The custom routine can be specific to individual worksheets, or we can create a global custom hook that is executed by all worksheets when data is saved. The latter is probably the most appropriate in this case, as the principle needs to be applied to all data that is saved. To create this hook, create an Express program called BW.PRE.SAVE, which resets zeros to NA values. OFA checks to see if a program with this name exists; if it does, it is executed prior to saving the worksheet data.

B.1.4 The Pre-save custom hook

The BW.PRE.SAVE hook is a useful customization in many cases. It can be used in a number of ways to enhance the standard data entry facility:

- amend the saved data, as illustrated above when saving zeros;

- run a validation routine on the data, excluding failures from the save if necessary;

- return a pop-up message to pass information on the saved data to the user;

- record the status of the saved data, for later use. For example, update a saved selection which can be used in reporting or Solves to identify changed data.

All of the above techniques require some Express development, but most of them are not onerous.

B.1.5 Saving zeros in an OFA Web Data Entry Form

Use the Data Option Calculations to specify a Solve Definition with the data item. This Solve must reset zeros to NA values. This can be done either through a front end Model, or a custom program that is hooked to the Solve Definition. The Solve Definition is automatically recalculated when the user chooses to submit data and some of the data has changed. There is currently no custom hook in the same vein as BW.PRE.SAVE available for the Data Entry Form.

B.2   MORE WORKSHEET WARNINGS

Another note of caution regarding data entry through worksheets: the OFA architecture allows multiple user data entry through worksheets because the saved data is simply queued up in the Task Processor queue for sequential updating of the Shared Database. Care is needed when users are updating the same data item simultaneously. Two users changing the same number, saving the data to the queue, will result in one user losing the change he or she has made. The two tasks will be processed by the Task Processor on a first-come, first-served basis. The second change will ultimately replace the first change, and the data saved by the first user is lost. Ideally, user access should be scoped so that users are not amending the same cells of data, i.e. users do not have write access to the same dimension value combinations of a data item. At the very least, users should be made aware of this potential danger.

B.3   EXPRESS SPREADSHEET ADD-IN

The Spreadsheet Add-In primarily provides an alternative interface with the OFA database for reporting purposes. It does provide write-back facilities to the attached Express database using the 'Write' option in Excel Express menu. This is only compatible in the OFA user architecture when using Budget Workstation users. This is the only user type that has stored data that can be immediately manipulated by the user. It is not appropriate for a user to try to write back to any Shared Database. All updates to a Shared Database must be processed through the OFA Task Processor. The controls within OFA should prevent a user writing back to the Shared Database by mistake (or design) using the Spreadsheet Add-In, as only valid DBA user IDs are given write access to the database. These privileges are set in the User Maintenance facilities within the OFA DBA user when assigning user IDs to the DBA user. This does leave the loophole that a valid DBA user ID, accessing the Shared Database through the add-in, has the access rights to save data to the Shared Database. You cannot protect against this by using the operating system access privileges as the DBA users all need to be able to run the Task Processor in the normal way, and hence attach the Shared Database in read/write mode. The only control available is to educate the relevant users.

B.4   DATA COLLECTION TOOLKIT

The Excel VBA macros provided to produce a complex Excel interface with Express was a neat idea to enhance the use of Excel as a front-end client to any Express database. It does, however, suffer from some serious inherent weaknesses with even moderate volumes of data. It is no longer being developed further by Oracle so does not provide a production system solution, unless your data volume requirements are very small.

B.5   OFA DATA LOADER

The data loader facility in the Maintain menu provides the ability to create an Express data reader program using a point and click approach to set the parameters of the reader. The source data file can be a text file of either fixed column width or comma separated. The online help facilities provided with the data loader are comprehensive and should be referenced for explicit details.

The use of the data reader functionality requires the installation of Express Administrator on the user's PC, as it uses a cut-down version of the data loading facilities provided by this maintenance tool. We can summarize the features of the module as follows:

- Mouse point and click to all objects in the OFA database. This allows the DBA to load OFA structures without needing to know the internal object names.

- A two-phase load. This caters for the traditional load technique of two passes of the data file, first reading in all structures (Dimensions, Hierarchies, etc.) before reading the associated data, from the same data file. This technique does not necessarily fit with the usual OFA structural and data flow. Structures are normally loaded into the DBA, then distributed on to the Shared Database and users, whilst data is loaded directly into the Shared Database after the structural distribution. The two cannot therefore be loaded by the same load routine.

- Pre-processor program. A custom Express SPL program can be called in advance of the load.
- Post-processor program. A custom Express SPL program can be called following the load.
- Qualifiers, when creating the link to an FDI, use the 'Qualifiers' button to limit Dimensions that are not referenced in the data file itself.
- Time-series data. A range of dimension values can be specified to read a file with, for example, 12 columns of monthly data.

The loader creates a program in the DBA's Personal Database. Its greatest weakness is the lack of validation that can be performed on the data as it is loaded. The data must first be loaded, then validated, either externally or through the post-processor program hook.

Having created a data reader program, to change its parameters, highlight the program name in the database objects list shown when you are creating a new data loader. Use the right mouse button and choose the 'Modify Settings' option to change the configuration settings of the program (Figure B.1).

You can view and edit the program code in the normal way from the Express command line, but we do not recommend you do this as the code itself is very complicated because of the generic nature of its creation. There are only a few crucial lines in the code reflecting the parameters created by the DBA. The rest is built from a template.

To run multiple data readers, you can run a user-defined program group. This runs all programs that are members of the group. However, you cannot do this for the 'Available Programs' group, which has all the data loader programs as its members. In the example shown in Figure B.2, the 'Weekly Load' group will submit the three programs assigned to the group to the Task Processor (the DBA is operating in Administrator mode). The parameters of each program, i.e. the Data File, Log details, and Start and Stop positions, must all be pre-selected, before the group is submitted. These same three programs also appear in the 'Available Programs' group, but when this group is highlighted the 'Submit' button is greyed out.

Care should be taken to ensure that the loader programs are run from the correct mode. If the DBA is in Administrator mode, the 'Submit' button will submit a task to the Task Processor. If the DBA is in Workstation mode, the 'Run' button replaces 'Submit', and will execute the loaders directly on the Personal Database of the DBA. This toggling of mode is performed through the 'Options' item of the 'Tools' menu. The mode distinction usually reflects the nature of the data file. If it is a structural load, maintaining Dimensions, Attributes and Hierarchies, then the load is performed in Workstation mode, whilst balances are loaded, through the Task Processor, into the Shared Database.

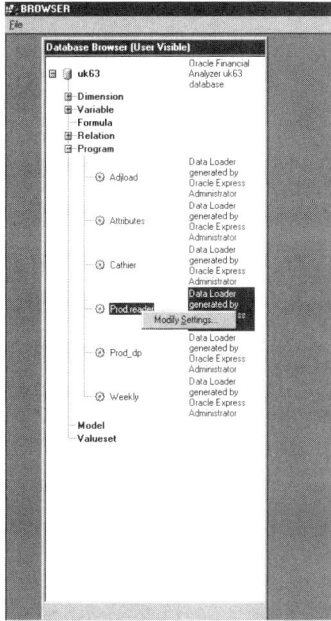

FIG B.1

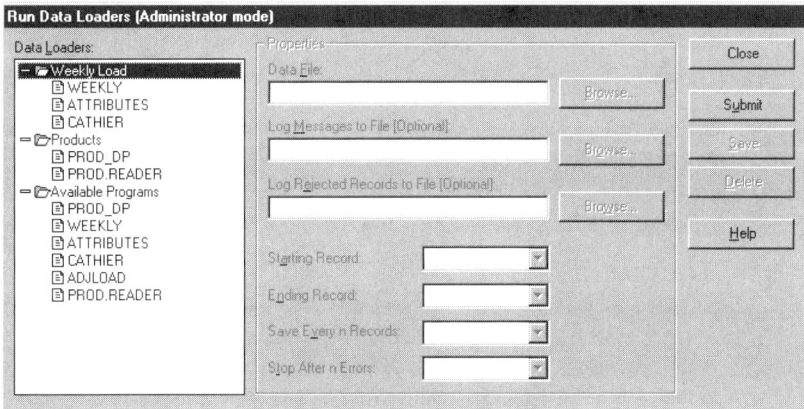

FIG B.2

The data reader option provides a mechanism for running custom programs that are not created using the data reader module. The 'Run Data Loaders' screen allows you to select a data file for use by the custom program. The selected filename at run time will be passed as an argument to the custom program.

The list of available programs generated by the 'Run..' option is driven by the Express properties of the program object. See the Express help facilities for more information on the Express PROPERTY command. The program must have the following properties set in order for it to appear in the 'Run' option:

- DLFILE
- DLSTART
- DLEND
- DLERRORCOUNT
- DLUPDATE
- DLERRFILE
- DLREJECTFILE
- PROGTYPE

These properties normally record the parameters entered through the front end. You can see the properties of an existing data reader by typing the following from Express Monitor:

    Fulldsc program

where program is the program name of the data reader. The easiest way to create your own entry to this list is to define a reader in the front end in the normal way. Then edit the program to remove all the generated code, and replace it with your own custom code.

B.6　CUSTOM-BUILT DATA LOADERS

Data can be loaded into OFA with custom SPL programs using several different techniques.

B.6.1 Loading ASCII files

A good start for those new to the Express SPL and wishing to write their own data loading routines is the *Oracle Express Programmer's Guide to the Express Language* chapter on 'Reading Data from Files'. The main principles to apply when writing your own data loader program are:

- Load dimension values, then their associated data. This will ensure that the database does not become unnecessarily fragmented.
- Use catalogs to define file structure (column position, width, etc.), file locations (data file, error log, etc.). This will allow you to change the structural definition of the source data file quickly without having to trawl through the program code to change hard-coded positional references.
- Process and error logging. Each load should create a detailed log of its operation. Report all failures during the load. Record the total number of records loaded

and read, total of balances, number of dimension values added, etc., i.e. make the operations of the load as visible as possible to allow the DBA to determine its success.

■ Sort data records in the source data file in advance of the load if the data file is a large one. Sort the data records based on the dimension order of the financial data item, and the order of the dimension values within the Dimensions. This will lead to better performance from the data loader.

■ Do not load zeros unless they are really needed. This will keep the database as small as possible and avoid unnecessary creation of composite values.

Initializing data readers can be controlled from the Add-In menus, Solve Definitions, or from the data reader menu option. The option chosen will depend on the arguments required by the reader at the time of initialization, as indicated in Table B.1.

TABLE B.1   Initialization

Initialization method	Arguments available
Tools Menu	One text string. This could be the filename, potentially including the path, although this is not validated on data entry. It must be validated by the data reader itself. If the reader is loading data into the Shared Database, then a task must be submitted. This will require further Express work. See the Oracle document *Hooks in the Oracle Financial Analyzer Application Interface* for your version on how to create custom tasks.
Solve Definition	Any combination of up to 10 Dimensions can be configured to allow the user to use the Selector to choose dimension values that will be in status when the data reader program is called. The submission mechanism to the Task Processor does not require any custom work.
Data Reader Menu	Point and click browse facility to select the data file. Again, the submission mechanism to the Task Processor does not require any custom work. (See Section B.5 for more details on the configuration of this hook.)

B.6.2 Loading spreadsheets

We talked earlier of copying and pasting from spreadsheets into the OFA environment. A more controlled method of loading spreadsheet data is using a data loader program. Collecting data from spreadsheets must be done in a very strict manner. The dynamic nature of spreadsheets means that tight constraints need to be applied to the spreadsheet templates that are used as the data source.

Express can both import and export comma separated data, or WK1 formatted data, using the IMPORT and EXPORT commands. These functions allow us to export OFA data to a spreadsheet as well as load it back in. This may be useful in a budgeting process, for example, where a spreadsheet template can be created from OFA by downloading actual data, the users prepare their budget in the spreadsheet, and then load it back into OFA. Because of the raw format of the export and the tight definition of the data required to load it back in successfully, this process may involve spreadsheet macros, first to present the data in a user-friendly way after the raw OFA export, and second, to convert this user-friendly data back into a rigid format needed for the upload (Figure B.3).

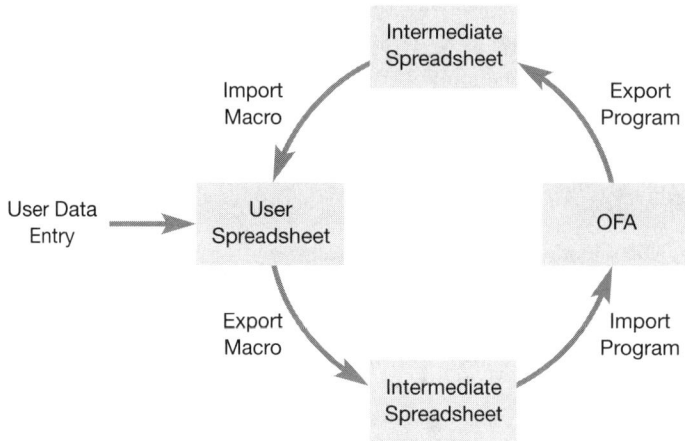

FIG B.3　　　**Spreadsheet loading**

A spreadsheet macro will help the user considerably in creating the required CSV or WK1 format needed to import the spreadsheet into Express. The user spreadsheet can include subtotalling, other formulae, and formatting of data entry areas, to make the screens as easy as possible for the users to use. Print ranges can be set in advance so that hard copies can be produced for review.

The Export program in OFA can produce a spreadsheet for each data entry user, for example every cost centre manager, with data specific to their budget requirements, perhaps the year to date actual data for their respective cost centre. The user will therefore have all of the information that OFA contains in one spreadsheet when preparing his or her return. The data should be written to the template using a series of spreadsheet ranges. A range is defined as a contiguous range of several rows and columns. There can be any number of ranges written into the template. A custom Express catalog is an effective way to specify and manage the down and across selections for each range. A range dimension will store the list of available ranges, to allow for expansion to cover the requirements of different types of user. A different type of template could be created for different user groups. Writing data in separate ranges means that the spreadsheet template can be populated in the cells between the ranges with formulae, e.g. subtotals, or text, e.g. headings or descriptive narrative.

The technique does not require any Express or OFA licences to collect the data. If the data entry users do not require access to OFA after their initial efforts, this can be an effective way of reducing software costs where there is a large user population involved in data gathering.

B.6.3 Embedded SQL

Express has the capability to establish a direct connection to a relational database, such as Oracle RDBMS or another ODBC source. Data can therefore be extracted directly from a source relational database without the need to create a separate extract file. Oracle RDBMS can be on the same machine or on a separate machine if you are running SQL*Net on the Express machine. There is therefore no need to transfer extract files across the network.

Refer to the chapter on 'Using Embedded SQL' in *Oracle Express Programmer's Guide to the Express Language* for details of the techniques to apply. The basic approach is as follows:

1. Use the 'sql connect' command to establish a connection.

2. Declare a cursor using 'sql declare'.

3. Open the cursor and fetch the data into either program local variables or directly into the Express objects.

4. Close the cursor.

5. Disconnect from the connection.

Here is an example program that maintains the COSTCENTRE dimension directly from a Sybase database, and updates the hierarchy.

```
DEFINE FETCH.CC PROGRAM
" Program to update Cost Centre codes and hierarchy

vrb _cc          text
vrb –parent      text
vrb _shortname   text
vrb _sortvalue   integer
trap on HADERROR noprint

pushlevel 'FETCH.CC'
push oknullstatus

oknullstatus = YES
```

```
" Declare ODBC source
" Replace ODBC source, username and password with global variables for flexibility

sql.dbms = 'odbc'
&joinchars('odbc.source = ' sybase.source)
&joinchars('sql connect ' sybase.user ' identified by ' sybase.password)

if sqlcode ne 0
    then do
        show 'Error Accessing Sybase datasource'
        return
        doend

sql declare c1 cursor for –
select CC_ID ,–
        CC_Dept ,–
        shortName ,–
        sortValue –
        from CostCentre_Table

sql open c1

if sqlcode ne 0
    then do
        show 'Error Opening Cursor'
        return
        doend

while sqlcode eq
    do

    sql fetch c1 into–
    :_cc            ,–
    :_parent        ,–
    :_shortname     ,–
    :_sortvalue

    if sqlcode ne 0
        then continue

    "Add to cost centre dimension
```

```
            mnt costcentre merge _cc
            lmt costcentre to _cc
            cc.lbl.col = _cc
            cc.lbl.row = _shortname
            cc.desc = joinchars(cc.lbl.col ' ' cc.lbl.row)
            sort.cc = _sortvalue
            if isvalue(costcentre = _parent)
            then fmshrel.cc = _parent
            doend

    " Establish default sort order

    lmt costcentre to all
    sort costcentre a sort.cc
    mnt costcentre move values(costcentre) first
    " Update OFA hierarchy
    call cm. update.hier('COSTCENTRE' charlist(fmshdim.office))

    ALLDONE:
    if sqlcode eq 0
        then sql close c1
    sql commit
    sql disconnect
    poplevel 'FETCH.CC'
    return

    HADERROR:
    if sqlcode eq 0
        then sql close c1
    sql commit
    sql disconnect
    poplevel 'FETCH.CC'
    return

            END
```

Loading large volumes of data using the direct connection is usually much slower than the extract file approach. If speed is essential it may not be the best solution.

C

The GL Link: hints and tips

LOAD PROCEDURES

The GL extraction process for segments and balances creates temporary files, which OFA must read during the load process. OFA also directly reads and loads data from GL tables using a direct SQL connection. During data extraction, GL automatically places the temporary files it creates for balance and segment values on the machine where the concurrent manager is running. Oracle Financial Analyzer must have access to these temporary files in order to process the segment and balance extracts.

The concurrent manager and OFA must be configured to establish access to the temporary files. The simplest configuration is with the concurrent manager installed on a single machine that is running both Express Server and the GL. Other configurations are described in *Integrating Oracle Financial Analyzer with Oracle General Ledger*.

If OFA and GL are installed in separate environments, the manual offers the following configuration options:

- FTP files from remote GL server to the OFA server;
- run concurrent manager on the OFA machine;
- run concurrent manager on both machines.

One idea not covered in this documentation, when OFA and GL are on different machines, is to map the OFA box to the extract (out) directory on the GL machine, so that the directory appears to the OFA server to be part of the local file system. You can access the remote directory in this way from the OFA server by mapping the OFA box to the extract directory. You will need to enable NFS (Network File System) Server and Client on the respective machines to do this. A common user ID must also exist on both machines. The UID and GID must be identical on both servers. You will need some expert IT knowledge in order to configure this solution for your particular platform.

After OFA has read the balance and segment extract files, it attempts to remove them, in order to tidy up the directory of used extract files. The OFA DBA user ID must therefore have delete privileges to this directory. If the ID does not have this privilege, which is often the case because the GL administrator is reluctant to give it, the load will not fail. However, you should ensure that this directory is tidied up regularly to avoid the disk filling up. This will crash the concurrent manager when it next attempts to write to the directory.

When loading a financial data set into OFA, the routine will delete all existing data for the relevant time periods before performing the load. It uses the Set of Books property in the financial data item catalog (FD.CATALOG) in OFA to identify all data items that should be cleared. This is not quite the same thing as the Financial Data Set, and can be a problem if the Financial Data Set is amended to load a different set of data items. This may happen if you are loading some data items more frequently than others. For example, you may set the Financial Data Set to load some items on a daily basis, then reset it each month to include additional slower-moving data items. In these circumstances the Set of Books property is not changed as a result of the Financial Data Set change, and all of the data items, including the slow-moving ones, will be deleted during the daily load.

In order to work around this problem, you will need to change the FD.CATA-LOG values temporarily to force the selection of only those data items currently included in the Financial Data Set, and then reset them. This will require a custom routine, to be included as part of your load procedures.

C.2   THE LOAD PERFORMANCE

The balance extract file can often be very slow to load, even if data volumes are not large. There are three things you can do to improve its performance:

1. Make the sort order to reflect FDI dimensions. This is set in the Financial Data Set screen in GL. The extract routine will use the sort order to produce the extract data file. If the data is extracted in the same order as the dimensions of the financial data items, the load into OFA will be more efficient and perform quicker. Because GL Time is not mapped to a GL segment, you should ignore it when defining the sort order.

2. Empty balances. The balance extract produces an extract file that contains a row for each balance. Unfortunately, the extract produces a record for each valid segment combination, even if it has no balance. The extract file is therefore unnecessarily large, and subsequently slow to load. See the Oracle document

'Optimizing Oracle Financial Analyzer: Performance and Architecture' for a custom routine that removes empty balances from the balance extract file.

3. Fragmentation. An OFA database linked to GL often becomes disorganized very quickly because of the fractured nature of dimension additions. You should therefore reorganize the database on a regular basis to maintain the general performance of the database. See Section 5.9 on backup and recovery for more information on this area.

C.3 MOVING FROM A TEST GL ENVIRONMENT TO THE LIVE GL

The development of the GL link will usually be done using a test or development version of the GL. To migrate the OFA databases to the live environment without re-creating all of the OFA structures afresh will mean linking OFA to a new GL environment. There are a number of complications with this manoeuvre. Each object must, of course, have exactly the same definition in the live GL as in the original development version. Also, each object linked to the GL, such as dimensions and financial data items, has a unique internal ID which is used to establish the link for these objects. If OFA is linked to a new GL it is essential that these IDs still link to the same objects. Table C.1 indicates the location of the IDs in OFA and GL.

TABLE C.1 Location of IDs in OFA and GL

Object	OFA catalog	OFA catalog property	GL table	GL field
Dimension	DM.CATALOG	DIMENSION.ID	RG_DSS_DIMENSIONS	Dimension_id
Financial Data	FD.CATALOG	VARIABLE.ID SET.OF.BOOKS	RG_DSS_VARIABLES	Variable_id Set_of_books_id
Hierarchy	HI.CATALOG	HIERARCHY.ID	RG_DSS_HIERARCHIES	Hierarchy_id

The IDs in the GL are created sequentially. If the objects are created in the live GL in the same order as they were in the development GL, then the IDs will agree. If they have been created in a different order, then you must change the IDs in the OFA catalogs in the SuperDBA to agree with the new GL IDs. Distribute the objects to the Shared Database before testing the link. If you run a segment extract before aligning the IDs, you may add dimension values to the wrong dimension.

The financial data items also have a Set of Books identifier as well as a unique ID. This is normally set to '1' but you should confirm the alignment with GL.

To identify the variable ID numbers you must start an SQL session onto the Oracle GL database as the RG user. You should then issue the following commands to report the IDs:

SQL>   select object_name, dimension_id, name from rg_dss_dimensions

SQL>   select object_name, variable_id, set_of_books_id from
              rg_dss_variables

SQL>   select object_name, hierarchy_id, name from rg_dss_hierarchies

If there are dimension values in the test system that are not present in the live version of GL, successfully linking to the live GL will not remove these unnecessary values from OFA. You must manually remove them from the dimension in OFA, and also from the OFA metadata dimension. This metadata dimension is called GL_SEG_VALSx, where x is an integer. Each dimension linked to GL will have a different integer value. This system dimension records all values of the dimension possible in the GL, not just the values added to the live dimension in OFA. It provides the picklist for the 'Add GL Dimension Values' option in the 'Oracle General Ledger Interface' menu in the SuperDBA.

| C.4 | **TROUBLESHOOTING THE CONNECTION TO GL** |

Here are some useful techniques to ensure that your connection to the GL is sound before you proceed with the segment and data load.

▪ Test that the connection configuration in the tns.names file is correct by using the following commands available at the operating system prompt of the Express Server machine:

ORACLE_HOME/bin/tnsping xxx

where xxx is the sid for the GL machine.

This will check that the contact to the GL is OK, and give the time taken for the IP packet to return. This confirms that SQL*Net is working properly.

For more information try:

ORACLE_HOME/bin/Trcroute xxx

This will return the following information on the connection for the client and server nodes:

– Address
– Protocol
– Host name
– Port number

Both of these tools are installed as part of the SQL*Net installation.

▩ You can connect to the GL box by creating an OCI connection from the Express command line to ensure that the Express connection to the GL is OK. An OCI (Direct Oracle Call Interface) is an interface that allows Express to issue SQL statements to the GL relational database. OFA will initialize such an interface from the Task Processor at the start of the load task. Type the following in Express Monitor within the OFA DBA:

> Sql.dbms = 'ORACLE'
>
> Sqlmessages = yes
>
> Sql connect oraname identified by 'password@dbname'

where oraname is your Oracle user name, password is the user's password, and dbname is your database alias as set in the SQL*Net configuration.

> Show sqlcode

If this command returns 0 you are connected; if you receive –1 then connection was unsuccessful.

> Show sqlerrm

This will show the text returned by GL because of a connection failure.

Look at the chapter on 'Using Embedded SQL' in *Oracle Express Programmer's Guide to the Express Language* for details of the SQL CONNECT command.

▩ The usual GL user ID required to facilitate the extract load is the APPS account. It is possible to create a new user with access to all the relevant GL tables that can successfully complete the load. This may ease the GL Administrator's worries about releasing the APPS user password. Contact Oracle support, or check out MetaLink for more details about creating this user ID.

▩ Create a log of the load process by setting the Options menu 'Create Balance Request Log' to YES in the OFA DBA. This creates a file called balance.log. This is often a very large file because the data extract file contains zero and empty balances, so the file needs to be cleared regularly. The creation of this file will slow the load down, so do not create it if you don't need it. The file will log the processing of each row in the extract file. The location of balance.log will be the default temporary file location of the Express instance. You can override this by entering a new directory in the TMPFILEPATH parameter of the OFASYSCF.CFG configuration file in the Shared Directory of the SuperDBA.

D History, future developments and their potential impact

HISTORY

The original design decisions on OFA were taken by a US market research company, called Information Resources, Inc. (IRI). Having pioneered the design and implementation of the Express multidimensional database as an aid to market research analysis in the late 1980s, IRI had implemented three Visual Basic front ends to the Express server, one of which was released as the Financial Management System (FMS) in 1994. The other front ends were Sales Analyzer and Express Analyzer, an Executive Information System (EIS)-style front end. A DOS-based product called Financial Consolidation and Reporting System (FCRS) was developed in the UK only. The main development laboratories, as well as all other functions, were based in Waltham, Massachusetts, but separate development teams existed for each of the components, i.e. Express Server and the three 'front ends'.

Originally titled Express FMS Planner, the FMS product had a vision of business solutions being provided which focused on data gathered from people:

- 'FMS allocates goal data downwards through the organization.'
- 'FMS loads and consolidates budget data upwards through the organization.'

File readers had to be written to load production data from production systems of many kinds, but the key design objective was reflected in the 'Manage' menu, where the organization could be modelled to facilitate flow of data downwards and upwards.

By version 4.6, Oracle had bought Express and all the application products except FCRS from IRI. IRI remains an independent company (and a reseller of Express). The deal was completed in September 1995. The decision was a joint decision between Oracle's CFO and the product acquisition division. Oracle's CFO had gone out to market to find an enterprise financial planning tool, had chosen FMS, and the product acquisition people had, in parallel, decided to buy Express from IRI for access to a market-leading multidimensional database. FMS was re-badged as Oracle Financial Analyzer, retaining the version number 4.6.1.

Since Express was already a richly functional SPL product, the functionality delivered in the Visual Basic front end could be supplemented by custom programs written in Express and called by the front end to conceal complexity from the user. The history of development of OFA has been a continuous process of providing more functionality in the front end, so reducing the need for custom programming, while harnessing the increasing power of the underlying Express multidimensional database. The continuous development of Express is a key factor in being able to deliver scalable solutions, while the Visual Basic front end made it progressively more easy for the user to manage larger implementations. The progressive replacement of the Visual Basic front end, in the case of Web clients, by Java applets provides the same benefits but potentially to very large populations of users via the Internet.

D.1.1 Version history

The major releases of OFA have been as follows:

4.6		96
4.8		97
6.0		97
6.2	July	98
6.3	December	99

In line with Oracle's commitment to the Internet delivery model, reflecting the integration with Oracle Applications version 11i and the release of the version 8i of the Oracle relational database, version numbering changed in 2000. OFA 6.3.1, renamed OFA 11i Release 6.3.1 to indicate that it is part of Oracle's completely Web-enabled 11i Applications architecture, is the major release at date of this publication and commenced shipping in November 2000.

D.1.2 Projected releases at date of writing

OFA 11i Release 6.3.2 early 2001

D.2   UPGRADES AND DE-SUPPORT

Oracle provides upgrade paths for all releases, in parallel with publishing de-support dates, to enable customers to plan upgrades. Notice of upcoming de-support for all versions prior to OFA 6.2 was issued in 2000. For OFA 4.8.1.1 and OFA 6.0.1.x, Error

Correction Support ends on 31 March 2001 and Extended Assistance Support ends on 31 March 2004.

D.2.1 Upgrades: an opportunity to be exploited

It is in the interest of the users of installed OFA systems to migrate to the latest versions as versions are de-supported, so that they can continue to get help from Oracle Support with problems. There are two reasons why an upgrade should be treated as an opportunity, rather than as an unwelcome necessity:

1. New functionality offers an opportunity to further smooth the business process for which the original project was designed, or to extend the use of OFA to further business processes that OFA supports, as discussed in Chapter 2. Examples are:

   a) re-implement data gathering with a light footprint Web Data Entry Form, rather than a current client/server Analyst Workstation Worksheet or Budget Workstation;

   b) deliver benefit to the Administrator through better administration functions. OFA's development direction has been towards support for ever-larger distributed user populations. A good example is the Save Distribution function introduced in version 6.3, which offers immediate gains in ease of use over systems delivered in version 6.2.

2. New functionality often provides facilities in the OFA Menu structure which hitherto had been provided by Express SPL programs. By replacing bespoke programs with 'out-of-the-box' functionality, the future upgrade process will be easier and the need for in-house or external Express expertise reduced. The net effect should be to make the cost of ownership lower, while ensuring that the system remains part of the large OFA community using standard functionality. Divergence from this community isolates the system owner from the benefits of packaged software, in particular, the benefit of having many thousands of users collectively pressurizing the OFA product development team for enhancements that benefit all users.

Oracle's own use of OFA followed this path. The initial implementation in version 4.8 was upgraded to version 6.1 and then 6.2, and most recently to 11i. Upgrading to OFA 11i offered Oracle the opportunity to deliver a standard global business process for reporting, budgeting and forecasting from a single instance and over the Web. With OFA 11i, most users access OFA using the Web. Users responsible for reporting create their reports using the Web, while users responsible for entering budgets and forecasts enter that data using the Web. The system is available 24 hours a day and even provides support for the implementation from a self-service Web site.

D.3   USER GROUPS

It is also clearly important that divergence from the core functionality should be contained if membership of user groups is to be effective; debate about the custom code implemented by one user is unlikely to be of interest to all the attendees of a user group. OFA User Groups meet frequently in a number of countries. These are distinct from the Express Special Interest Groups which meet quarterly, and which may feature topics of interest to the OFA user, as well as to the other applications of Express, such as Oracle Sales Analyzer, discussed below. While Oracle Product Management attends both OFA User Groups and the Express Special Interest Groups, it is obviously the Oracle-hosted OFA User Groups that are most influential in providing enhancement requests to the OFA Development people. Membership of the Oracle-hosted OFA User Groups is currently by invitation.

D.4   COMPATIBILITY WITH OTHER EXPRESS CLIENTS

Recall that OFA is only one of the clients to the Express multidimensional database. OFA's compatibility with other Express clients is now reviewed.

As described above, IRI had implemented three Visual Basic front ends to the Express server:

- the Financial Management System (FMS),
- Sales Analyzer, and
- Express Analyzer, an Executive Information System-style front end,

with largely independent development teams. Because of the separate development teams, naturally design decisions were sometimes divergent. For example, in the development path for OFA, it was assumed that the OFA-maintained Express databases, containing financial data, would have smaller data volumes than Oracle Sales Analyzer. Sales Analyzer's origins lay in the need to analyze very large volumes of market research data. We summarize the historic divergence issues before noting how convergence has been a characteristic of more recent developments.

D.4.1 Divergence

Oracle Express Objects

In 1996, a new client called Oracle Express Objects was released. This product was a GUI power developer's tool, which embraced key software engineering principles on maintainability, such as polymorphism, object orientation, etc., while inheriting the 4GL features of the Express multidimensional database. OLE-enabled, it allowed a very attractive client/server interface to Express, mixing text graphics, sound and video. Bespoke functionality could be developed in Oracle Express Objects if the other Express clients did not provide the required functionality. It was definitely a programmer's tool, with huge productivity benefits, rather than a tool intended for the business user such as OFA.

Oracle Sales Analyzer

Oracle Sales Analyzer's development path as a separate product was emphasized in 1996/97 by what was known as RAA/RAM. Fundamentally, this was the ability to create multidimensional structures 'on the fly' in Express, while leaving granular data in the relational database, and being able to store none, some or all of the multidimensional views. RAA/RAM issues were discussed in Section 4.2.

Financial Consolidation and Reporting System

The DOS-based Financial Consolidation and Reporting System was planned to be migrated to the OFA engine, incorporating features to enable true financial consolidation. This plan was eventually abandoned and the product was withdrawn in 1997, in line with Oracle's strategy to make technical financial consolidation a component of the General Ledger, through a product known as the Global Consolidation System. This was discussed in more detail in Chapter 2.

D.4.2 Convergence

The divergent phase was replaced by a strongly convergent phase in July 1998, with the release of OFA 6.2. OFA had maintained its own Express database until version 6.2, with neither Oracle Sales Analyzer nor Oracle Express Objects being able to use an OFA-maintained database. Access was enabled for Oracle Express Objects, Oracle Express Administrator and Oracle Web Agent/Publisher. Web Agent provided a power-user development environment for Web clients on Express, while Web Publisher provided an end-user tool to create Web clients on Express.

In July 1999, Oracle accelerated release plans for a new set of development components code-named Business Intelligence Beans. Integration of Oracle's business intelligence tools across both databases, Oracle relational and Express, and of Oracle Reports, a fixed format SQL-based report writer, had in fact been a major development focus for some time. The BI Beans were intended to continue forward movement along this path by providing a consistent, reusable set of analytical and user interface components. Furthermore, it was expected that using these Beans with a development environment for Java such as Oracle's JDeveloper would offer a powerful solution for customers building analytic applications or adding sophisticated business intelligence capabilities to other enterprise applications. Oracle redirected development resources from a research project known as Express Objects Server – also referred to by the code-name 'Walden' – to enable it to expedite delivery of the

BI Beans. Oracle stated that the long-term needs of customers were best served with a consistent and cross-compatible Internet development environment using standards-based components and an open architecture – benefits that Walden was not intended to deliver.

The Express team in Waltham has continued development projects for Express Objects and Express Analyzer – but focused on usability and productivity enhancements, editing and debugging capabilities, support for multi-project and multi-developer applications, an application packaging and deployment utility, and improved error handling.

Convergence and Express

Allowing just one version of Express to be used by all clients means that the development of Express can potentially be leveraged by all of the applications that use Express. For example, Express developments now support not just Oracle Sales Analyzer's but also OFA's ability to handle very large data volumes, without incurring a performance overhead.

Certification between OFA, Express and the delivery platform

Since there is OFA software with its own versioning and Express with its own versioning, and an implementation will involve both, certification between the products is important. OFA 6.3.0 may have been used to develop a system, but Oracle Express Objects and OEA are used as clients for delivery of some of the end-user functionality. A project will need to understand the certification status of OES 6.3.0.1; 'what is the certified Oracle Express Objects and OEA version for this version of the server?' Furthermore, there are platform issues; if the combination of products is certified to be interoperable, are the platforms for these versions the same, e.g. Windows 95 for clients and HP/UX for the server? The certification matrix is available from Oracle's public Web site.

D.5   TRANSITION TO THE FUTURE

The options for deploying OFA are:

D.5.1 Client/server options

The Windows client/server options with OFA are the Administrator who maintains the structures – the 'metadata' – and controls the flow of structures and data into the Shared Database, to which the Analyst Workstation, the Budget Workstation and the Spreadsheet Add-In, as well as Oracle Express Objects/OEA, have access.

D.5.2 The Web

We have explored the OFA Web clients in detail earlier; they include a read-only Web client, as well as the Data Entry Form, which permits data and text to be written to the Express database in a controlled way. However, any Express database can be accessed by Web Publisher, a Wizard-driven tool that enables non-technical users to publish live, interactive briefings, tables and graphs, or by the Web Agent Developer's Toolkit whereby software developers can create bespoke analytical applications on the Express database maintained by OFA.

The current architecture over which the functionality is delivered is shown in Figure D.1.

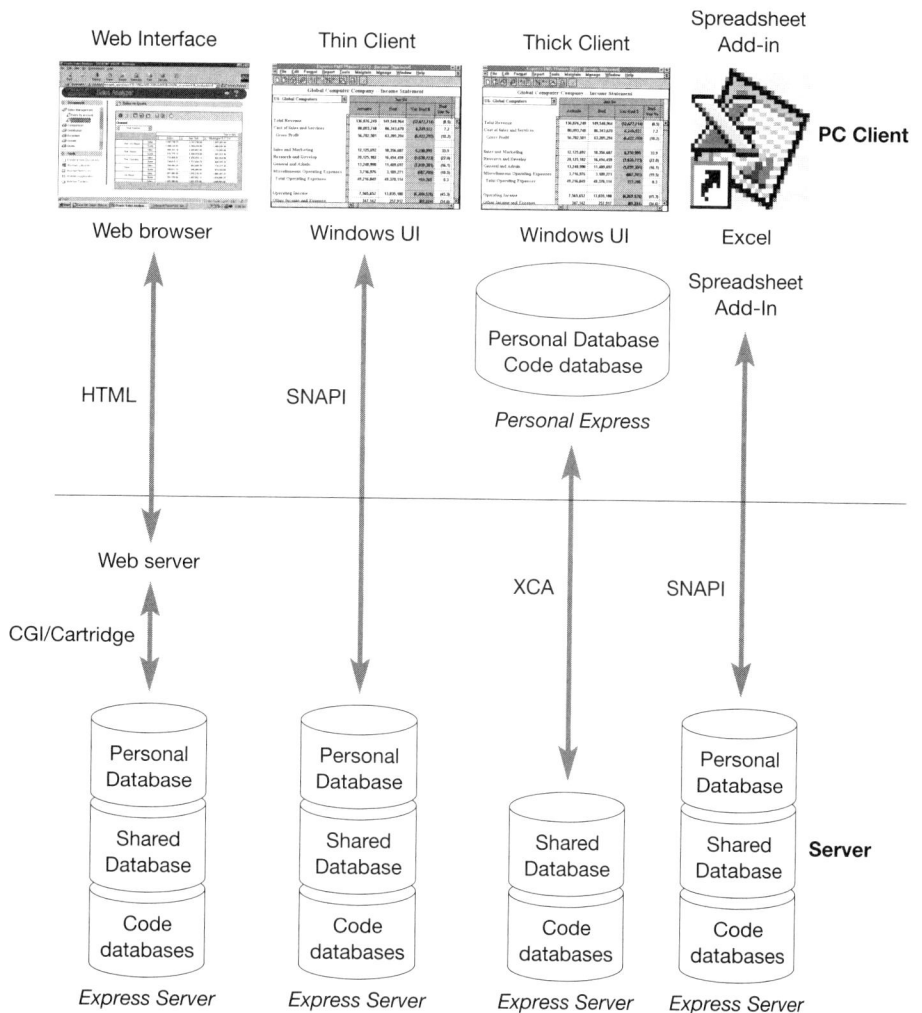

FIG D.1   The current architecture of OFA

THE FUTURE

Forward plans are always subject to change and hence our comments here are based on what was planned at date of writing. One question always arises in considering the future of any Express-based product, such as OFA: will Express continue to be a separate server complementing Oracle RDBMS? In this context, Oracle RDBMS version 8.2 included facilities which have been associated with Express, such as the CUBE and ROLLUP command, and Oracle Discoverer provides analytic functions such as RANKING.

At Oracle Open World in San Francisco in October 2000, Oracle introduced the RDBMS version Oracle 9i. This release is projected to contain new integrated, advanced analytic capabilities (OLAP Services), allowing the RDBMS to perform many of the analytic tasks delivered by Express. In order to take advantage of these new features, Oracle Applications will migrate the existing Express applications onto 9i. OLAP Services within 9i will be available through a new Java-based analytic API. Oracle Tools will provide a presentation layer which works with this API.

D.6.1 What will the migrated applications contain?

Applications hosted on 9i will contain a number of new areas of functionality. For example, there will be a formal process to allocate data. In addition, the applications will be Oracle Workflow enabled, which will make it possible to automate many processes. Oracle Demand Planning, a new Analytic Solutions product introduced in 2000, already used Workflow to control the collection and distribution of data, as well as providing the ability to monitor progress on plan submission and to provide user-defined 'alerts'. Workflow will be used in all analytic applications when they are moved to 9i.

Oracle 9i is projected to be released in the second half of 2001, and the new analytic applications within a year following it.

D.6.2 So what will happen to OFA and OSA?

Oracle's commitment is to create an application on Oracle 9i that delivers everything OFA and OSA do and to which additional features are added. Oracle will support migrating current implementations of OFA and OSA to the next generation of applications. All data, structures, calculation rules and reports, graphs and data entry forms will migrate. However, two issues remain:

1. Most OFA projects have extended the functionality with custom Express SPL programs. Oracle has stated that the new generation will incorporate many of the features which required custom programs as part of the base product and hence the extensions will no longer be needed. This leaves the issue of existing

functionality delivered by custom programs which will not be covered by the new generation software.

2. Within 9i, all data loading will be done through the standard 9i interfaces – not Express. Data loading customizations will have to be rewritten to take advantage of them. Oracle will provide documentation of the new target schemas into which data will be loaded. Of course, this only refers to new data, as existing data in OFA or OSA will migrate to the new application.

D.6.3 Will Express continue to be separate functionality complementing Oracle RDBMS?

Certainly, from the foregoing, in the long run the answer might be no. However, there are four points arising:

1. *Timing.* Oracle 9i is projected to be released in the second half of 2001, and the new analytic applications within a year following it. The older versions will then be 11i and 6.3. Since Oracle normally supports the two previous versions before de-support, it will be some time before Express is de-supported. The de-support process normally takes about three years.

2. *Does it matter?* The benefits to the user of an underlying separate multidimensional database are delivered in terms of ease of use, intuitive end-user manipulation of data, powerful modelling functions etc. The user probably has no awareness that a separate multidimensional database exists to provide such facilities. Hence the existence of Express is irrelevant so long as the new application is as functional as Express and as performant.

3. OFA benefits from a large, stable, high profile and hence influential customer base. As Oracle moves ahead in the next few years in creating applications based on the Oracle 9i OLAP services foundation, the company will still need to ensure the needs of current OFA customers are met.

4. The OFA and Oracle 9i OLAP services development plans give customers a time frame of several years to plan and allocate resources for migrating to future versions while still profiting from the benefits of a robust financial management product now.

Index

Licensing Agreement

This book comes with CD software package. By opening this package, you are agreeing to be bound by the following: